SIOP® support that's right district, only from Pearson

Making Content Comprehensible for English Learners: The SIOP® Model, 5/e
ISBN: 9780134045238 • ©2017 • 360 pp. • $68.80*

**Making Content Comprehensible for Elementary English Learners:
The SIOP® Model, 3/e**
ISBN: 9780134550206 • ©2018 • 368 pp. • $68.80*

**Making Content Comprehensible for Secondary English Learners:
The SIOP® Model, 3/e**
ISBN: 9780134530093 • ©2018 • 368 pp. • $65.80*

The SIOP® Model for Teaching History–Social Studies to English Learners
ISBN: 9780205627615 • ©2011 • 240 pp. • $45.60*

The SIOP® Model for Teaching Science to English Learners
ISBN: 9780205627592 • ©2011 • 240 pp. • $45.60*

The SIOP® Model for Teaching Mathematics to English Learners
ISBN: 9780205627585 • ©2010 • 192 pp. • $45.60*

The SIOP® Model for Teaching English Language-Arts to English Learners
ISBN: 9780205627608 • ©2010 • 216 pp. • $45.60*

Using The SIOP® Model with Pre-K and Kindergarten English Learners
ISBN: 9780137085231 • ©2012 • 144 pp. • $55.60*

Response to Intervention (RTI) and English Learners: Using the SIOP® Model, 2/e
ISBN: 9780133431070 • ©2015 • 176 pp. • $55.60*

99 More Ideas and Activities for Teaching English Learners with the SIOP® Model
ISBN: 9780133431063 • ©2015 • 256 pp. • $51.60*

99 Ideas and Activities for Teaching English Learners with The SIOP® Model
ISBN: 9780205521067 • ©2008 • 208 pp. • $56.60*

**Implementing The SIOP® Model Through Effective Professional Development
and Coaching**
ISBN: 9780205533336 • ©2008 • 208 pp. • $66.80*

The SIOP® Model for Administrators, 2/e
ISBN: 9780134015569 • ©2017 • 120 pp. • $58.60*

Developing Academic Language with the SIOP® Model
ISBN: 9780137085248 • ©2016 • 160 pp. • $45.60*

*Prices and availability are subject to change without notice.

Schools and districts save 25%! (Off of list price.)

To place your order, visit k12oasis.pearson.com or call 1-800-848-9500.

Find your Pearson sales representative: www.pearsonhighered.com/replocator

Full Suite of SIOP® Professional Development Services

SIOP® Services for Teachers

SIOP® Training for Teachers
This training gives educators an in-depth understanding of the components of the SIOP® Model and strategies to implement it in their schools and classrooms. We also offer SIOP® Training for PreK-Kindergarten Teachers, Elementary Teachers, and Secondary Teachers.

Implementation options: 3 days face-to-face, facilitated Virtual Institute, or blended onsite + online.

SIOP® for Mathematics Teachers
This training gives educators an in-depth understanding of the components of the SIOP® Model for use in mathematics classrooms and strategies to implement it in their schools and classrooms. (3 days)

SIOP® and Two-Way Immersion Training for Teachers
This training gives educators an in-depth understanding of the components of the SIOP® Model with a focus on how to implement the features of instruction in two-way immersion or dual language classrooms. (3 days)

SIOP® Component Enrichment (8 Components)
Each one-day session helps educators build a deeper understanding of one of the eight SIOP® components. Prerequisite: SIOP® Training for Teachers;

Implementation options: 1 day face-to-face, or a self-paced Online Workshop.

SIOP® Mathematics Component Enrichment
Each one-day session helps educators build a deeper understanding of three SIOP® components for use in mathematics classrooms. Prerequisite: SIOP® Training for Teachers.

SIOP® English/Language Arts Component Enrichment
Each one-day session helps educators build a deeper understanding of three SIOP® components for use in English/Language Arts classrooms. Prerequisite: SIOP® Training for Teachers. (1 day)

SIOP® Lesson Coaching and Modeling
This job-embedded professional development supports teachers in planning, delivering, and observing lessons using the SIOP® Model. (5 days)

SIOP® Observation and Feedback
This training includes a SIOP® consultant observing 4 teachers per day and completing the SIOP® protocol to provide feedback and coaching. Prerequisite: SIOP® Training for Teachers. (1 day)

SIOP® Services for Leaders and Coaches

SIOP® Training for Administrators

Administrators learn about the SIOP® Model, how to support teachers using the Model, and how SIOP® can have a positive impact on teaching all students, especially English learners.

 Implementation options: 1 day face-to-face, or facilitated Virtual Institute.

SIOP® Coaching and Implementation

This training helps districts develop effective SIOP® coaches and learn to successfully use the SIOP® Model in coaching sessions to improve classroom instruction. (2 days)

SIOP® Coaching and Observation

This training helps SIOP® coaches become effective by developing skills to support their SIOP® delivery and instruction. (2 days) Prerequisite: SIOP® Coaching and Implementation

Response to Intervention for English Learners

Coaches and Leaders will understand specific considerations, interventions, and instruction for English learners (ELs) in the RTI process.

 Implementation options: 2 days face-to-face, or facilitated Virtual Institute.

SIOP® Inter-rater Reliability

Administrators and coaches will learn how to use the observation protocol to establish common standards of effective classroom lessons and rate the quality of instruction and the effectiveness of SIOP® implementation across the school or district. (2 days)

SIOP® Growth Services

SIOP® Component Enrichment Lesson Preparation: Language Acquisition

Participants review the research base for the Lesson Preparation component as well as critical research on language acquisition to deepen their understanding of the processes students go through when acquiring a language. This workshop provides the support needed to plan lessons that incorporate techniques for improving students' language acquisition.

 Implementation options: 1 day face-to-face, or facilitated Virtual Institute.

Developing Academic Language

Participants learn how to examine the language demands of different subject areas, write appropriate language objectives, and incorporate them into SIOP® lessons. This workshop is suitable for teachers who want to extend practice with building academic language and literacy skills and may have already studied the SIOP® Model. (1 day)

Using the SIOP® Model with Newly Arrived Students

This training explains how specific components and features of the SIOP® Model of instruction can be used to make content comprehensible for newcomer students. This workshop is designed for teachers already familiar with the SIOP® Model's components and features.

 Implementation options: 1 day face-to-face, or facilitated Virtual Institute.

Pearson is now an approved IACET provider.

Let's discuss what a SIOP® implementation plan might look like for your school or district.

 siop.pearson.com | 800.848.9500 | K12CustomerService@pearson.com

 Pearson

What's Next? Measure the Impact of SIOP®
Professional Development

Pearson offers districts solutions to support and enhance SIOP® implementation. Take it to the next level by building district capacity and measuring the impact of professional development on teacher practice and student outcomes.

Would you like to have the tools to improve student performance by looking at classroom practices?

Research shows that as educators engage in high-quality professional development, the first observable change is in educator knowledge, then educator practice, and only then in student performance. Waiting to focus on student performance data limits your ability to see if your professional development is having the desired effect on actual classroom practices that lead to improved student performance.

Pearson's Diagnostic & Research Services will help you to measure the critical elements of educators' knowledge and practice, so that you know if you're on a course to positively improve student performance.

Turn over to learn more about SIOP® job-embedded services that combine with professional development workshops to create an implementation path focused on delivering results.

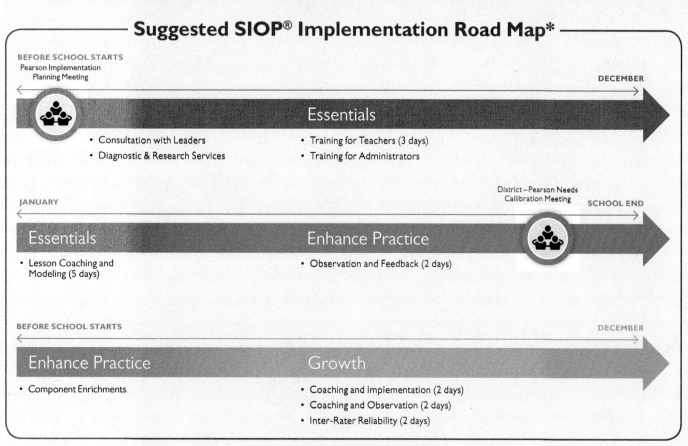

Suggested SIOP® Implementation Road Map*

BEFORE SCHOOL STARTS
Pearson Implementation
Planning Meeting

DECEMBER

Essentials

- Consultation with Leaders
- Diagnostic & Research Services
- Training for Teachers (3 days)
- Training for Administrators

JANUARY

District – Pearson Needs
Calibration Meeting

SCHOOL END

Essentials

- Lesson Coaching and Modeling (5 days)

Enhance Practice

- Observation and Feedback (2 days)

BEFORE SCHOOL STARTS

DECEMBER

Enhance Practice

- Component Enrichments

Growth

- Coaching and Implementation (2 days)
- Coaching and Observation (2 days)
- Inter-Rater Reliability (2 days)

* Road Maps to be refined based on district needs.

Create Your Professional Learning Path with Pearson's Suite of Outcomes-Focused Professional Services†

The individual services within the packages may be exchanged for other Pearson services within this catalog that more appropriately align with your district's needs. Work with your Pearson Account Representative to customize a pathway that is right for you!

SIOP® Services:

- SIOP® Training for Teachers (K–12)
- SIOP® Training for Teachers (Pre-K–K)
- SIOP® Training for Teachers (Elementary)
- SIOP® Training for Teachers (Secondary)
- SIOP® Training for Teachers (Mathematics)
- SIOP® Training for Administrators
- SIOP® and Two-Way Immersion Training for Teachers
- SIOP® Component Enrichment
- SIOP® English Language Arts Component Enrichment
- SIOP® Mathematics Component Enrichment
- SIOP® and Assessment for Learning with English Learners
- SIOP® Lesson Preparation Component Enrichment: Language Acquisition
- Developing Academic Language
- Using the SIOP® Model with Newly Arrived Students

† Services are 1 day in length for cohorts up to 30 unless otherwise indicated.

 siop.pearson.com | 800.848.9500 | K12CustomerService@pearson.com

Making Content Comprehensible for Elementary English Learners: The SIOP® Model

Third edition

JANA ECHEVARRÍA

Professor Emerita, California State University, Long Beach

MARYELLEN VOGT

Professor Emerita, California State University, Long Beach

DEBORAH J. SHORT

Director, Academic Language Research & Training

Pearson

330 Hudson Street, NY NY 10013

Editorial Director: Kevin Davis
Portfolio Manager: Drew Bennett
Content Producer: Yagnesh Jani
Portfolio Management Assistant: Maria Feliberty
Development Editor: Jill Ross
Executive Field Marketing Manager: Krista Clark
Executive Product Marketing Manager: Christopher Barry
Procurement Specialist: Deidra Smith
Cover Designer: Carie Keller, Cenveo
Media Producer: Allison Longley
Media Project Manager: Michael Goncalves
Full-Service Project Management: Michelle Gardner, SPi Global
Composition: SPi Global
Cover Image Credit: Creativa Images/Fotolia; leungchopan/Fotolia; Blend Images/Shutterstock; Zurijeta/Shutterstock; Dzmitry Kliapitski/Shutterstock; Vectorfusionart/Fotolia; Nolte Lourens/ Shutterstock; Nadezda Murmakova/Shutterstock; karelnoppe/Shutterstock; Monkey Business Images/ Shutterstock

Credits and acknowledgments for materials borrowed from other sources and reproduced, with permission, in this textbook appear on the appropriate page within the text.

Every effort has been made to provide accurate and current Internet information in this book. However, the Internet and information posted on it are constantly changing, so it is inevitable that some of the Internet addresses listed in this textbook will change.

Library of Congress Cataloging-in-Publication Data

CIP data is available at the Library of Congress

1 16

ISBN 10: 0-13-455020-X
ISBN 13: 978-0-13-455020-6

In loving memory of my dad, Charles Echevarria,
for his unwavering support and encouragement.
JE

In memory of my dad, Wendell H. Bragonier,
a long-time teacher and master storyteller.
MEV

In memory of my dad, John M. Short,
who taught me to love teaching.
DJS

Contents

3 Building Background   70

4 Comprehensible Input   102

5 Strategies   124

6 Interaction   151

7 Practice & Application   180

8   Lesson Delivery   203

9   Review & Assessment   224

10 Issues of Reading, RTI, and Special Education for English Learners   252

11 Effective Use of the SIOP® Protocol   272

12 Frequently Asked Questions: Getting Started with the SIOP® Model   292

Preface

Even though the Sheltered Instruction Observation Protocol (now known as SIOP) has been used in schools for over 20 years, it has never been more relevant than it is today, with the emphasis on rigorous academic standards for all students such as the Common Core State Standards (CCSS) and Next Generation Science Standards (NGSS). Elementary school teachers—now more than ever—need a proven approach for making instruction understandable for English learners while at the same time developing their academic language skills. The SIOP Model is a mechanism for helping children reach high academic standards, and many of the SIOP features are reflected in these standards, such as the emphasis on speaking and listening skills.

We hope that you will use this book (paper or electronic, depending on the book you've chosen) as a guide for lesson planning and teaching. Elementary SIOP teachers tell us that it is a resource they turn to again and again as they plan and carry out effective lessons, so we encourage you to highlight sections, mark pages with sticky notes, and fill margins with application ideas. We've written the book in a teacher-friendly way, and our hope is that it will become a valuable resource to you as you strive to become a high-implementing SIOP teacher. As you read, you will find lesson plans, teaching ideas, and many effective activities for working with elementary English learners. Our recent research confirms that the SIOP Model makes a positive difference academically for all students, so what works well for English learners will work equally well with the other children in your classroom.

It is hard to believe that so many years have passed since we first began our journey with the SIOP Model. Back then, it would have been difficult to fathom that today, the SIOP Model would be implemented in schools throughout all 50 states in the United States, and in numerous countries. Whether you are already familiar with the SIOP Model or are just now learning about SIOP, we hope that you will find this third edition to be informative, helpful, and, most importantly, beneficial to the young English learners and other children with whom you work. When we began our research, we recognized the need for a comprehensive, well-articulated model of instruction for preparing teachers to work with English learners. From this need, SIOP was created. Now, with the widespread use of the SIOP Model, we have since written more than a dozen additional books on topics related to teaching English learners and SIOP implementation. (See Appendix D.)

Our work on the SIOP Model started in the early1990s when there was a growing population of English learners, but no coherent model for teaching this student population. We began our efforts by reviewing the literature and examining district-produced guidelines for English learners to find agreement on a definition of sheltered instruction, also known as SDAIE (Specially Designed Academic Instruction in English) in some regions. A preliminary observation protocol was drafted and field-tested with sheltered instruction teachers. A research project through the Center for Research on Education, Diversity, & Excellence (CREDE) enabled us to engage in an intensive refinement process and to use the SIOP Model in a sustained professional development effort with teachers on both the East and West Coasts. Through this process of classroom observation, coaching, discussion, and reflection, the instrument was refined and changed, and it evolved into the Sheltered Instruction Observation Protocol, or as it has come to be known, SIOP (pronounced sī-ŏp). SIOP offers teachers a framework for lesson planning and implementation that provides English learners with access to grade-level content standards, including the Common Core and Next Generation Science Standards. By providing this access, we help prepare students for life after high school in colleges or careers as well.

Although a number of approaches to teaching English learners have emerged over the years, at present, SIOP remains the only research-validated model of sheltered instruction. Our studies have appeared in numerous peer-reviewed professional journals. In fact, because of its applicability across content areas, the national Center for Research on the Educational Achievement and Teaching of English Language Learners (CREATE) used the SIOP Model as a framework for comprehensive school-wide intervention in its research aimed at improving the achievement of English learners in middle school. The SIOP Model is now being implemented at all levels of education from pre-K to community colleges and universities.[1] It is used in sheltered content classes (also called integrated ELD in some states), dual language programs, content-based ESL classes, special education instruction, and general education classrooms.

Since the first edition of the core text, *Making Content Comprehensible for English Language Learners: The SIOP® Model* (2000) was published, we have continued to develop and refine the SIOP Model, but we have not changed the eight components and 30 features. They have withstood the test of time. In our work with thousands of teachers and administrators throughout the country, our own understanding of both effective sheltered instruction and the needs of English learners has grown substantially. We believe, and research on SIOP confirms, that when teachers consistently and systematically implement the SIOP Model's 30 features in lessons for English learners and English speakers alike, the result is high-quality, effective instruction and improvement of student achievement.

As the authors of this book, we have approached our teaching, writing, and research from different yet complementary fields. Jana Echevarría's research and publications have focused on issues in the education of English learners, and on English learners with special education needs, as well as on professional development for regular and special education teachers. MaryEllen Vogt's research and publications focus primarily on improving reading instruction, including improving comprehension in the content areas, content literacy for English learners, and teacher change and development. Deborah Short is a researcher and former sheltered instruction teacher with expertise in second language development, academic literacy, methods for integrating language and content instruction, materials development, and teacher change.

The strength of our collaboration is that we approach the issue of educating English learners from different perspectives. In writing this third edition of *Making Content Comprehensible for Elementary English Learners: The SIOP® Model*, we each provided a slightly different lens through which to view and discuss instructional situations. But our varied experiences have led us to the same conclusion: Educators need a resource for planning and implementing high-quality lessons for English learners and other students—lessons that will prepare students eventually for college and careers—and SIOP is fulfilling this need.

---

[1] If you are a pre-K or Kindergarten teacher, you may find this book to be especially helpful: Echevarría, J., Short, D., & Peterson, C. (2012). *Using the SIOP® Model with Pre-K and kindergarten English learners*. Boston: Pearson.

■ What's New in This Edition

In this third edition[2], we have added a number of features based on the feedback we have received from educators who use SIOP. In particular, we have created an enhanced eText version of the book in order to put more resources at your fingertips. The eText includes embedded links to video clips of lessons in elementary classrooms, and interviews, as well as to lesson plan templates. Cognizant of the importance of instructional technology today, we have added sections on "Teaching with Technology" to the chapters describing the SIOP components. Further, we have made the book more interactive with opportunities for you to assess and reflect on what you are learning as you read and apply the ideas in this book.

Specifically, the changes to chapters include the following:

Chapter 1 Introducing the SIOP® Model

- Updated demographics and research throughout
- Updated discussion of English learners' backgrounds and academic performance
- Updated discussion of current educational trends, including the Common Core State Standards, the Next Generation Science Standards, and the Every Student Succeeds Act
- Up-to-date discussion of academic language and literacy
- New video links inserted throughout to illustrate chapter discussion
- New Reflect and Apply eText feature
- Revised discussion questions
- New end of chapter Review & Assessment quiz in eText

Chapter 2 Lesson Preparation

- Updated research throughout
- Enhanced sections discussing content and language objectives and how to write them
- New figures related to Lesson Preparation
- Revised Teaching Scenarios and lesson plan
- New Reflect and Apply eText feature in which readers explain their ratings of teachers' lessons
- New feature: Teaching with Technology
- New video links inserted throughout to illustrate chapter discussion
- Revised discussion questions
- New end of chapter Review & Assessment quiz in eText

---

[2] Three texts that are considered to be the "core" SIOP books: *Making Content Comprehensible for English Learners: The SIOP® Model* (intended for K–12); *Making Content Comprehensible for Elementary English Learners: The SIOP® Model* (K–6); and *Making Content Comprehensible for Secondary English Learners: The SIOP® Model* (6–12), are parallel and can be used together or separately for university classes and professional learning.

Chapter 3 Building Background

- Updated research throughout
- Substantive discussion of three categories of academic vocabulary
- New feature: Teaching with Technology
- New video links inserted throughout the eText to illustrate chapter discussion
- Revised Teaching Scenarios and lessons
- New Reflect and Apply eText feature where readers explain their ratings of teachers' lessons
- Revised discussion questions
- New end of chapter Review & Assessment quiz in eText

Chapter 4 Comprehensible Input

- Updated research throughout
- New feature: Teaching with Technology
- New video links inserted throughout to illustrate chapter discussion
- Revised Teaching Scenarios and lessons
- New Reflect and Apply eText feature where readers explain their ratings of teachers' lessons
- Revised discussion questions
- New end of chapter Review & Assessment quiz in eText

Chapter 5 Strategies

- Updated description of strategic processing
- Reorganized classification of learning strategies
- New feature: Teaching with Technology
- New video links inserted throughout the eText to illustrate chapter discussion
- Revised Teaching Scenarios and lessons
- New Reflect and Apply eText feature where readers explain their ratings of teachers' lessons
- Revised discussion questions
- New end of chapter Review & Assessment quiz in eText

Chapter 6 Interaction

- Updated research throughout
- New feature: Teaching with Technology
- New video links inserted throughout to illustrate chapter discussion
- Revised discussion of the features including examples of the Common Core State Standards

- Revised Teaching Scenarios and lessons
- New Reflect and Apply eText feature where readers explain their ratings of teachers' lessons
- Revised discussion questions
- New end of chapter Review & Assessment quiz in eText

Chapter 7 Practice & Application

- Updated research throughout
- New Reflect and Apply eText feature where readers explain their ratings of teachers' lessons
- New feature: Teaching with Technology
- New video links inserted throughout to illustrate chapter discussion
- Revised Teaching Scenarios and lessons, and a new lesson plan
- Revised discussion questions
- New end of chapter Review & Assessment quiz in eText

Chapter 8 Lesson Delivery

- Revised chapter objectives
- Updated research throughout
- New Reflect and Apply eText feature where readers explain their ratings of teachers' lessons
- Additional ideas for differentiation
- New feature: Teaching with Technology
- New video links inserted throughout to illustrate chapter discussion
- Revised Teaching Scenarios and lessons
- Revised discussion questions
- New end of chapter Review & Assessment quiz in eText

Chapter 9 Review & Assessment

- Updated research throughout
- New discussion exploring the relationship between classroom context and assessment
- New questions to consider during progress monitoring of students' reading development
- Expanded discussion on issues related to the formal and informal assessment of English learners
- New feature: Teaching with Technology
- New video links inserted throughout to illustrate chapter discussion
- Revised Teaching Scenarios and lessons

- New Reflect and Apply eText feature where readers explain their ratings of teachers' lessons
- Revised discussion questions
- New end of chapter Review & Assessment quiz in eText

Chapter 10 Issues of Reading, RTI, and Special Education for English Learners

- Updated discussion of reading and assessment issues for English learners
- New section on the Common Core State Standards or other state English Language Arts Standards
- New Reflect and Apply eText feature
- Revised, comprehensive section on English learners and special education
- Updated research throughout
- New video links inserted throughout to illustrate chapter discussion
- Revised discussion questions
- New end of chapter Review & Assessment quiz in eText

Chapter 11 Effective Use of the SIOP® Protocol

- Updated and revised discussion of best practices in using the SIOP protocol and the use of SIOP scores
- New section: Using Non-Numeric Scores
- New video link to illustrate chapter discussion

Chapter 12 Frequently Asked Questions: Getting Started with the SIOP®
- New video links inserted throughout to illustrate answers to some of the frequently asked questions

Appendix B
- New lesson plan format

Appendix C
- Updated discussion of SIOP research

Appendix D

- Updated list of resources for further information, including books, journal articles, book chapters, and downloadable research briefs: *https://siopblog.wordpress.com/*
- Web site with information about SIOP professional development: *http://siop.pearson.com*
- Web site for accessing SIOP Blogs: *https://siopblog.wordpress.com/*

■ Highlights in the Book

- **Content and language objectives.** One of the most important aspects of SIOP is the inclusion of both content and language objectives for each and every lesson. Many teachers have found writing these objectives to be challenging, even as they acknowledge their importance both for their own planning and for their students' understanding of the lesson's content goals and language focus. Therefore, you will find an expanded section in Chapter 2 (Lesson Preparation) that provides specific guidance for writing a range of language objectives, along with recommendations for how to effectively present them orally and in writing to students.

- **Discussion of the eight components and 30 features of SIOP.** Each chapter begins with discussion of a SIOP component and its various features. For example, the discussion of lesson planning is found in the first half of Chapter 2. As you read about each feature in this section, think about how it would "look" in an actual classroom setting and how teachers might use this information to prepare effective sheltered lessons.

- **Teaching scenarios.** The second half of each component chapter includes teaching scenarios. In these vignettes, teachers, who are teaching the same grade level and content, attempt to include the focal SIOP features, but with varying degrees of success. At the end of each teaching scenario, you will have the opportunity to use that component section of SIOP to rate the effectiveness of the lesson in implementing these particular SIOP features. For example, as you read the teaching scenarios in Chapter 2, think about how well the three teachers included the features of the Lesson Preparation component in their planning and introduction of the lesson to the class. Note that the illustrated lessons throughout the book range from kindergarten to grade 6, and they cover a variety of content areas and student language proficiency levels. The lessons reflect the Common Core State Standards (CCSS: ELA and Math) or Next Generation Science Standards (NGSS) and specific standards are cited in several lessons.

- **Discussion of the three teaching scenarios.** Following the description of the three teachers' lessons, you will be able to see how we have rated the lessons for their inclusion of the SIOP features of effective sheltered instruction. We provide detailed explanations for the ratings and encourage you to discuss these with others in order to develop a degree of inter-rater reliability. In the eText, the Reflect and Apply feature allows you to explain your rating of each teacher's lesson in writing and print a copy for use during discussions in teacher preparation courses, in professional learning sessions, or in learning groups at your school site.

- **Teaching with Technology vignettes.** New to this edition, each chapter has an added vignette that is related to the teaching scenarios. In the vignettes, the school's technology integration specialist, Ms. Palacios, suggests ways to enhance the target lessons by integrating specific technology applications. **Please note**: Due to the evolving nature of the Internet, it is a challenge to ensure that all of the links and Web programs listed in this chapter feature are updated and functional when you read the technology vignettes. While specific tools or services may appear in the narrative, we have also included the general term for each tool. If a specific service does not work or is no longer available, search with the general term for the tool and you should be able to find a comparable Web site.

- **Teaching ideas.** In this section in Chapters 2–10, you will find a variety of ideas and activities for implementing the eight SIOP components. Nearly all of the ideas are appropriate for students in grades K–6, unless identified otherwise. Some activities may be familiar because you use them in your own classroom. We hope you'll be motivated to try the others because they represent best practice—those ideas and activities that are included have been found to be especially effective for English learners and learners still developing academic literacy skills.

- **Differentiating ideas for multi-level classes.** In this section found in Chapters 2–9, we show ways to differentiate instruction for various levels of language proficiency and academic skills.

- **Summary.** Each chapter has easy-to-read bulleted information that highlights the chapter's key points.

- **Discussion questions.** Based upon input from educators who have used this book, we have revised some of the discussion questions found at the end of each chapter to better reflect actual classroom practice with SIOP. We hope these questions will promote thinking about your own practice, conversations during professional development, and opportunities for portfolio reflection for preservice and inservice courses.

- **End of chapter Review & Assessment quiz in eText.** Readers who use an electronic version of the text will be asked to assess their understanding of the chapter through an end-of-chapter quiz.

- **The SIOP protocol.** In Appendix A, you will find both an extended version of the SIOP protocol and a two-page abbreviated protocol. The eight components and 30 features of the SIOP Model are identical in both instruments and they are included as options for your personal use.

- **SIOP lesson plan formats.** We have been asked frequently for assistance with lesson planning for SIOP. In this edition, we have included four different lesson plan formats for lesson plans (see Appendix B); we hope you will find one that is useful for you. In Chapters 2, 5, and 7, you will also find complete plans for three of the lessons featured in the teaching scenarios. These lesson plans are written with different formats, grade levels, and subject areas.

- **Discussion of reading and assessment issues, and special education for English learners.** In our work with the SIOP Institutes and in district trainings, we have heard many educators ask questions about English learners who have reading or learning problems and are struggling academically because of them. Based on the report of the National Literacy Panel on Language-Minority Children and Youth (August & Shanahan, 2006) the Multi-tiered System of Support (MTSS) and Response to Intervention (RTI) approaches, and the Common Core and the Next Generation Science standards, we have updated Chapter 10 with information and recommendations that we hope you will find helpful in SIOP program design and implementation for students with special needs. (More detailed information can be found in Echevarría, Richards-Tutor & Vogt, 2016.)

- **SIOP research.** In Appendix C, you will find an overview of the findings from the original SIOP research as well as a discussion of the findings of several national research studies on the SIOP. If you are involved in a research study in your school, district, state, or university and have findings that contribute to the research literature on SIOP, we would greatly appreciate hearing about them.

■ Overview of the Chapters

The following section briefly describes each of the chapters in this new edition.

- The first chapter in the book introduces you to the pressing educational needs of English learners in grades K–6, and to the SIOP Model of sheltered instruction. Issues related to English learner diversity, school reform accountability, the Common Core State Standards and the Next Generation Science Standards, English learner programming, and academic language are also discussed.

- In Chapters 2 through 9, we explain SIOP in detail, drawing from educational theory, research, and practice to describe each component and feature. Teaching scenarios that are drawn from elementary classroom lessons of sheltered instruction teachers follow. The SIOP features that pertain to each chapter are included for the lesson descriptions in the teaching scenarios. After you read about each of the teachers' lessons, use the SIOP protocol to rate on the 4 to 0 rubric the degree to which the features are present. The eText provides an opportunity to explain your rating in writing and print a copy for use during discussions in teacher preparation courses, in professional learning sessions, or in learning groups at your school site. The classroom scenarios reflect different elementary grade levels and content areas in the chapters and are linked to core curriculum objectives. All the classrooms include English learners, and many also include native English speakers. Some have newly arrived English learners, known as newcomers.

- In Chapter 10, we discuss the special needs of elementary English learners who have reading problems and/or learning disabilities. You may wish to read this chapter before you delve into SIOP, especially if you have had little experience teaching English learners. It will assist you in situating the SIOP in "real" classrooms with English learners who have a wide variety of academic and literacy abilities and needs.

- Chapter 11 provides a discussion of scoring and interpreting the SIOP protocol, explaining how the instrument can be used holistically to measure teacher fidelity to SIOP and strategically to guide the teacher in planning lessons for one or more targeted SIOP components. A full lesson from one research classroom is described and rated, revealing areas of strength and areas for improvement that can guide the teacher in future planning and teaching.

- Chapter 12 provides ideas and recommendations for implementing SIOP in the elementary classroom, and in schools and districts. Frequently asked questions are included to guide you as you begin working with SIOP.

- In the Appendices, you will find the Sheltered Instruction Observation Protocol (SIOP®), both the comprehensive and the abbreviated versions. You will also find four lesson planning formats to guide your lesson design and implementation. Further, we have included an appendix that details SIOP research to date and another that lists a variety of resources including additional SIOP books, research articles, book chapters, research briefs, and SIOP Internet resources. The book concludes with a Glossary of terms related to the instruction of English learners.

■ Acknowledgments

Many educators throughout the United States have contributed to this book through their work as SIOP teachers, bilingual specialists, curriculum coordinators, school and district administrators, and professional developers. We thank them for their insights and critical analyses of SIOP. Further, we appreciate the contributions of those who have participated in the SIOP Institutes and professional development throughout the country (for more information, see *http://siop.pearson.com/*). At each of these Institutes and trainings, we gain new understanding about our work from those who participate in them.

We also thank the many teachers and administrators in whose schools we have conducted research on the SIOP Model, both past and present. Their willingness to let us observe and discuss their teaching of English learners has enhanced our understandings and validated our work. The contributions of these fine educators to the ongoing development of SIOP are many, and we are grateful for their continued interest and encouragement. Our colleagues and fellow researchers on these projects deserve our gratitude as well.

Two talented educators worked with us on the preparation of the manuscript for this book: Daniel Scibienski (ellconsulting.org), a SIOP teacher experienced with technology infusion, who created Ms. Palacios, the technology integration specialist you will meet in the chapters; and Dr. Laurie Weaver (Professor, Bilingual and Multicultural Studies, University of Houston-Clear Lake in Texas), a SIOP expert who created the Checking Your Understanding questions for the eText. We thank them for their contributions, and most especially, for being long-time SIOP supporters. In their respective roles as educators, both have created useful SIOP tools that enhance implementation of the model.

We found the comments and suggestions from Annalee Taylor, Per Diem Education Specialist SIOP Literacy Facilitator, Charlotte Mecklenburg Schools and our two anonymous reviewers to be of great help as we began this revision, and we thank them. We also appreciate the ongoing support, assistance, and patience of our Pearson team.

The original SIOP work was supported under the Education Research and Development Program, PR/Award No. R306A60001, the Center for Research on Education, Diversity & Excellence (CREDE), as administered by the former Office of Educational Research and Improvement, now the Institute of Education Sciences (IES), National Institute on the Education of At-Risk Students (NIEARS), and U.S. Department of Education (ED). The contents, findings, and opinions expressed here are those of the authors and do not necessarily represent the positions or policies of IES, NIEARS, or ED. Additional SIOP research has been supported by the Carnegie Corporation of New York, the Rockefeller Foundation, and the U.S. Department of Education, Institute of Education Sciences, under the CREATE research center.

Finally, we express appreciation to our families, whose ongoing support has enabled us to pursue our professional interests.

About the Authors

Michael Grover, Heinemann, Portsmouth, NH

JANA ECHEVARRÍA, Ph.D., is Professor Emerita at California State University, Long Beach where she was selected as Outstanding Professor. She has taught in general education, special education, ESL, and bilingual programs in US schools, and has lived and worked in Taiwan, Mexico, Spain, and in Macedonia where she was a Fulbright Specialist. Her research and publications focus on effective instruction for English learners, including those with learning disabilities. She has presented her research across the U.S. and internationally including Oxford University (England), Wits University (South Africa), Harvard University (U.S.), Stanford University (U.S.), University of Barcelona (Spain) and South East Europe University (Macedonia). A founding researcher of the *SIOP Model,* her publications include more than 60 books, book chapters and journal articles. Currently she serves as the EL expert for the U.S. Department of Justice on the Lau case. Her blog is found at *www.janaechevarria.com.*

Ron Nabity

MARYELLEN VOGT, Ed.D., is Professor Emerita of Education at California State University, Long Beach. Dr. Vogt, a former classroom teacher, reading specialist, curriculum coordinator, and teacher educator, received her doctorate from the University of California, Berkeley. She is an author of numerous articles and chapters, and is co-author of seventeen books for teachers and administrators, including *Professional Learning in Action: An Inquiry Approach for Teachers of Literacy (Risko & Vogt, 2016).* Her research interests include improving comprehension in the content areas, teacher change and development, and content literacy and language acquisition for English learners. Dr. Vogt has provided professional development in all fifty states and in several countries, including Germany, where she served as a Visiting Scholar at the University of Cologne. She was inducted into the California Reading Hall of Fame, received her university's Distinguished Faculty Teaching Award, and served as President of the International Literacy Association.

DEBORAH J. SHORT, Ph.D., founded and directs Academic Language Research & Training, a consulting company, and provides professional development on sheltered instruction and academic literacy worldwide. Formerly, she was a Division Director at the Center for Applied Linguistics, Washington, DC, where she directed quasi-experimental and experimental studies on English learners funded by the Carnegie Corporation of New York, Rockefeller Foundation, and U.S. Department of Education, among others. Her publications include journal articles, the SIOP® Model book series, and several ESL textbook series for National Geographic/Cengage. She taught English as a second/foreign language in New York, California, Virginia, and the Democratic Republic of the Congo. She has served on the Board of Directors of the TESOL International Association and has presented research in the United States, Canada, New Zealand, Brazil, Europe, and the Middle East.

CHAPTER 1

Introducing the SIOP® Model

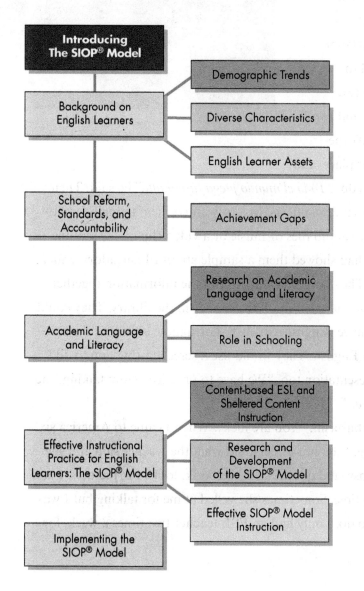

Learning Outcomes

After reading, discussing, and engaging in activities related to this chapter section, you will be able to meet the following **content** and **language objectives**.

Content Objectives

List characteristics of **English learners** that may influence their success in school.

Distinguish between **content-based ESL** and **sheltered instruction**.

Explain the research supporting the **SIOP** Model.

Language Objectives

Discuss the benefits and challenges of school reform and its effects on English learners.

Develop a lexicon related to the SIOP Model.

Compare your typical instruction with SIOP instruction.

Juan looked over at his cousin and asked "*¿Por qué viniste a la casa tarde desde la escuela hoy?*" Ricardo replied "*Estoy tarde porque*...No... I am late because I stay at school for studying. I work on computer with Nicolas and Gabriel. *Este proyecto es tan chévere.*" Ricardo continued to tell Juan about the assignment he found fun. He was researching a country with two classmates and would present a PowerPoint slideshow about it. They decided to study Brazil. They needed to tell two facts about the country's history and two facts about the geography, identify the language and a famous person or place, and explain what kids like themselves do. "*Todo el mundo juega fútbol alli*," he said. Their third-grade co-teachers, Mr. Hernandez and Ms. Myers, wanted them to include photographs or other images, and add audio files of music or a video clip of the famous person or place. Mr. Hernandez had showed them a sample about El Salvador. "*¿Sabía que El Salvador tiene volcanes?*" They had three days to put the information together and they could use books and computers in the classroom or in the library. They could find the information in any language (English, Spanish, Portuguese even) but the text on the slides should mostly be in English. They would use a screencasting app to add their own commentary to the presentation too. "We have to practice before talking," he explained. "Ms. Myers will help us."

© Rob Marmion/Shutterstock

Juan smiled at Ricardo's enthusiasm. "You are lucky. When I came to America six years ago, my classes were boring. I did not understand what the teacher said and she talked a lot. We copied words, answered questions in the book, looked at pictures. I had to ask my friends for help all the time. Sometimes she yelled at me for talking but I was trying to find out what we had to do. I only had an ESL teacher two times a week, for like only 30 minutes." ●

Ricardo and Juan had different experiences when learning English in their elementary classrooms. Juan's teacher used a more traditional approach six years ago. She dominated the class discussions and had the students work frequently in textbooks. She provided little language development or **scaffolding** for her English learners—indeed, little scaffolding for any of her students. When Juan tried to figure out assignments, she assumed he was off-task and was disrupting the lesson. With only one hour per week for **ESL** lessons, he had limited opportunity to develop academic English.

Ricardo, in contrast, experienced a more positive learning environment. Ms. Myers, the ESL teacher, worked side by side with Mr. Hernandez, the third-grade teacher. The children were assigned projects that promoted collaboration and taught research skills. They learned academic language in context. The teachers presented models of the assignments, clearly explained what to do and what the expectations for performance were, and supported the student groups. The children could use their **native language** as a resource, as well as trade books and Web sites. Technology was integrated seamlessly. The lessons were well prepared, which would lead to the success of all the students.

Ricardo is luckier than a number of English learners. He has co-teachers who provide effective instruction as he learns content through English, a new language. If more teachers learn the techniques that Mr. Hernandez and Ms. Myers use, then many more English learners will have a chance to develop academic literacy in English and be successful in elementary school. But it will take significant effort on the part of schools, districts, and universities to make this happen for Ricardo and other students like him.

■ Background on English Learners

Demographic Trends

Ricardo is one of many English learners in our schools. In fact, he represents the fastest growing group of students. In the 10 years from 2002–03 to 2012–13, the population of students participating in English learner programs in pre-K–12 public schools increased 7%, while the total pre-K–12 public school population (including these students) grew only 3% (U.S. Department of Education [USED] National Center for Education Statistics [NCES], 2016). Recent data report that in 2013–14, more than 10% of the students in U.S. schools were English learners, equaling more than 4.9 million students out of a total enrollment of close to 50 million (NCES, 2016, tables/dt15_204.27.asp).

However, it is important to recognize that the reported number refers to the *identified* English learners in language support programs. In some situations, students are no longer in English learner programs because they have completed the available course levels, yet they have not met the criteria to be redesignated as a former English learner (Parish et al., 2006). The number would be much higher, perhaps doubled, if we also add in the students who have passed their proficiency tests but are still struggling with *academic* English, the language used to read, write, listen, and speak in content classes to perform academic tasks and demonstrate knowledge of the subject standards. The increases in English learner enrollment will continue over the next several decades, so all educators need to be prepared to address these students' language and academic needs.

The results of the 2014 American Community Survey estimated that 13% of the U.S. population was foreign born. Immigrants and their children who have been born in the United States represent about 26% of the total U.S. population. In 2014, one in four children under the age of 18 lived with at least one immigrant parent (Zong & Batalova, 2016). The states with the highest numbers of **limited English proficient** individuals in 2013 were California, Texas, New York, Florida, Illinois, and New Jersey. These six states accounted for 67% of the limited English population in the United States (Zong & Batalova, 2015).

Within the U.S. population of all people age 5 or older, 21% spoke a language other than English at home. Children ages 5–17 make up about 17% of the U.S. population, and within this group, 22% are reported as speaking a language other than English at home and 5% are reported as not speaking English very well (the U.S. Census Bureau's classification of limited English proficiency).[1] Furthermore, about 85% of English learners in our elementary schools (pre-K–grade 5) were born in the United States, as were 62% of English learners in secondary schools (grades 6–12). Combined, about three-fourths of our English learners are second- or third-generation immigrants (Zong & Batalova, 2015).

In 2013–14, the states with the highest percentages of English learner students (more than 10% of the enrollment) in our public elementary and secondary schools were Alaska, California, Colorado, Nevada, New Mexico, and Texas, plus the District of Columbia. The top six states that have experienced the greatest percentage growth in public school English learner enrollment from 2002–03 to 2013–14 were Arkansas, Delaware, Kansas, Maryland, South Carolina, and Washington (NCES, 2016).

Changes in the geographic distribution of English learners may challenge the numerous districts that have not served large numbers of these students before. Academic programs are typically not well established; sheltered curricula and appropriate resources are not readily available; and, most important, many teachers are not trained to meet the needs of these second language learners.

Diverse Characteristics

In order to develop the best educational programs for English learners, we need to understand their diverse backgrounds. These learners bring a wide variety of educational and cultural experiences to the classroom as well as considerable linguistic differences, and these characteristics have implications for instruction, **assessment**, and program design. Further, they bring linguistic assets and other funds of knowledge that we ought to acknowledge. When we know students' backgrounds and abilities in their native language, we can incorporate effective techniques and materials in our instructional practices.

All English learners in elementary schools are not alike. They enter U.S. schools with a wide range of language proficiencies (both in English and in their native languages) and much divergence in their subject matter knowledge. In addition to the limited English proficiency and the approximately 180 native languages among the

---

[1]Calculations for children ages 5–17 not speaking English very well are based on data found at *http://factfinder. census.gov/faces/tableservices/jsf/pages/productview.xhtml?pid=ACS_14_5YR_B16007&prodType=table* (retrieved July 9, 2016).

students, we also find diversity in their educational backgrounds, literacy levels in the native language, expectations of schooling, socioeconomic status, age of arrival, personal experiences while coming to and living in the United States, and parents' education levels and proficiency in English. Some English learners are newcomers (i.e., new arrivals to the United States), some have lived in the United States for several years, and many are native born. Foreign-born English learners may be immigrants, refugees, asylees, permanent residents, or naturalized citizens.

Figure 1.1 shows some background factors that should be considered when planning programs and instruction so English learners can succeed in school. Some important points to keep in mind follow:

- Some immigrant English learners had strong academic backgrounds before coming to the United States. Some are at or above equivalent grade levels in certain subjects—math and science, for example. They are literate in their native language and may have started studying a second language. Much of what these learners need is **English language development (ELD)** so that as they become more proficient in English, they can transfer the knowledge they learned in their native country's schools to the courses they are taking in the United States. A few subjects not previously studied, such as social studies, may require special attention. These students have a strong likelihood of achieving educational success if they receive appropriate English language and content instruction in their U.S. schools.

- Other immigrant students had very limited formal schooling—perhaps due to war in their native countries or the remote, rural location of their homes. These students have little or no literacy in their native language, and they may not have had such schooling experiences as sitting at desks all day, changing classrooms for different subjects, or taking high-stakes tests. They have significant gaps in their educational backgrounds, lack knowledge in specific subject areas, and need time to become accustomed to school routines and expectations. These English learners with limited formal schooling and below-grade-level literacy are most at risk for educational failure.

- There are also English learners who have grown up in the United States but who speak a language other than English at home. Some students in this group are literate in their home language, such as Mandarin, Arabic, or Spanish, and will add English to their knowledge base in school. If they receive appropriate English language and content instruction, they, too, are likely to be academically successful.

Watch this video to hear Mark Poulterer and Dr. Robert Jimenez talk about the variety in the educational and cultural backgrounds of their students. Note the ways they work to reduce student anxiety in classroom settings. How do you reduce anxiety for your students?

- Some other native-born English learners who do not speak English at home have not mastered either English or their native language. There is a growing number of English learners in this group who continue to lack proficiency in English even after five, six, or more years in U.S. schools. These students are referred to as **long-term English learners** (Menken & Kleyn, 2010). They typically have oral proficiency in English, but lack English reading and writing skills in the content areas. They struggle academically (Flores, Batalova, & Fix, 2012; Olsen, 2010) and often are unable to pass state tests required for reclassifying as fully English proficient (Saunders & Marcelletti, 2013).

FIGURE 1.1 Diverse Characteristics of English Learners

Knowledge of the English Language

- Exposure to English (social and academic)
- Familiarity with Roman alphabet and numbers
- Proficiency in oral English (speaking and listening)
- Proficiency in written English (reading and writing)
- English being learned as a third or fourth language

Knowledge of the First Language (L1)

- Proficiency in oral L1 (speaking and listening)
- Proficiency in written L1 (reading and writing)

Educational Background

- On-grade level schooling in home country
- On-grade level schooling in U.S. schools (in L1 or English)
- Partial/interrupted schooling in L1
- No schooling in L1
- Entrance age in U.S. schools
- Partial/interrupted schooling in English
- No schooling in English
- Receiving language support services for five years or less
- Receiving language support services for six years or more (= long-term English learner status)
- Expectations for schooling
- Degree of absenteeism

Sociocultural, Emotional, and Economic Factors

- Age of arrival in the United States
- Poverty level
- Mobility
- Living situation
- Exposure to trauma, violence, abuse, and other serious stressors
- Refugee or asylee status
- Unaccompanied minor status
- Cultural norms for communication
- Parents' educational background
- Parents' level of English proficiency

Other Educational Categories

- Special education status
- Tier 2 or Tier 3 (Response to Intervention)
- Migrant status
- Former/Reclassified English learner
- Gifted and talented status

Sociocultural, emotional, and economic factors also influence English learners' educational attainment (Dianda, 2008).

- Poorer students, in general, are less academically successful (Lacour & Tissington, 2011; Palardy, 2008) than all others.
- Undocumented status affects socioeconomic opportunities for some students and sometimes affects their well-being.

- Mobility and absenteeism can impinge on school success: Students who had moved were twice as likely not to complete high school as those who had not faced such transitions (Glick & White, 2004). Students who are chronically absent are more likely to demonstrate poor academic performance (Balfanz & Byrnes, 2012).

- Post-traumatic stress, violence, abuse, family reunification, and experiences as a refugee or an asylee are all issues that may lead an English learner to struggle in school.

- Although they comprise a small percentage of English learners, the rapid influx of **unaccompanied minors** that began in 2014 has called attention to the educational and basic human needs of these students, such as serving older learners and ensuring the minors have shelter.

- The parents' level of education also influences their children's success. Parents with more schooling are typically more literate and have more knowledge to share with their children, whether through informal conversations or while helping with homework.

Some students are dually identified, which has implications for educational services. For example, besides being English learners, some children have learning disabilities or are gifted and talented.

- English learners tend to be over- or underrepresented in special education because a number of districts struggle to distinguish between a delay in developing second **language proficiency** and a learning disability. Even when students are appropriately identified, some districts have difficulty providing effective services to bilingual special education students. Federal regulations require students to receive instructional hours for language development as well as for identified special education needs (U.S. Department of Justice, Civil Rights Division, & U.S. Department of Education, Office of Civil Rights, 2015).

- Some English learners and former English learners who score poorly on reading assessments may need additional services to improve their reading achievement, such as Tier 2 or Tier 3 in a **Response to Intervention (RTI)** or **Multi-tiered System of Support (MTSS)** program. While we believe that the SIOP Model we present in this book is the best option for Tier 1 instruction and may help avoid Tier 2 and 3 placements (see Echevarría, Richards-Tutor, & Vogt, 2015), not all schools utilize SIOP instruction.

- Some children are migrant English learners who move from school to school in the same year, jeopardizing their learning with absences and potentially incompatible curricula and assessments across districts or states.

- Some students have abilities that fit the criteria for gifted and talented services, but schools struggle to identify (and then instruct) them, particularly if they have low or no proficiency in English and speak a language other than Spanish.

English Learner Assets

When planning programs and instruction for English learners, we sometimes focus solely on what they are not yet proficient in and fail to consider the assets they bring to school. These assets are related to language and cultural practices in the home and schooling in other countries. For example, children learn to make guesses and predictions at home that act as precursors to **academic language** development in school, where they learn to call these notions *estimates, hypotheses,* or *theories* depending on the subject area. In some **cultures** older children mentor younger siblings in performing chores and other tasks. Teachers can build on these relationship roles to construct collaborative learning environments in the classroom.

Teachers need to be aware of the language and literacy skills their students have and use outside of school. Figure 1.2 identifies some that are particularly relevant.

- **Oral language skills in the native language**—Many aspects of the native language learned at home through oral interaction can apply or transfer to learning academic English (August & Shanahan, 2006; Genesee et al., 2006; Guglielmi, 2008). These include phonemic awareness and phonics, grasp of vocabulary cognates, knowledge of affixes and roots, and listening comprehension strategies.

- **Literacy (reading and writing) skills in the native language**—Knowing how to read and write in the native language facilitates learning those skills in a second or new language (August & Shanahan, 2006; Genesee et al., 2006). Consider someone who can read and find the main idea in a native language text. That learner has mastered the cognitive reading strategy already. She or he may need to learn the words and syntax of English, but not how to find the main idea.

- **Out-of-school literacy skills**—Students use literacy outside of school, sometimes for family purposes (e.g., making a shopping list, reading a utility bill) and sometimes for personal reasons (e.g., using social media). These practices help them understand that literacy is used for different purposes and is found in different formats (Alvermann & Moore, 2011; Skerrett & Bomer, 2011).

- **Strong educational backgrounds**—Through schooling in their home country, some children may be at or above grade level relative to the curricula in their U.S. school. These students need to learn English but have few gaps in their academics.

- **Language brokering roles**—School-age English learners often assume the role of language broker in families where the adults do not speak English well (Cline, Crafter, O'Dell, & de Abreu, 2011). Students learn to engage with others using English, experiencing different interaction patterns, and being responsive to others' utterances. They learn to turn-take, ask for clarification, paraphrase, interpret, and translate.

FIGURE 1.2 Linguistic and Sociocultural Assets of English Learners

- Oral language skills in the native language
- Literacy (reading and writing) skills in the native language
- Out-of-school literacy skills
- Strong educational backgrounds
- Language brokering roles
- Cultural funds of knowledge
- Life experiences

- **Cultural funds of knowledge**—In their homes, children participate in language and cultural practices and activities that can be shared in the classroom. Teachers may learn about these funds through home visits and interviews. They may plan authentic classroom tasks around these funds that connect with the curriculum and invite parents as guest speakers (Gonzalez, Moll, & Amanti, 2005).

- **Life experiences**—Our students do not enter schools as blank slates. Many have had life experiences that are pertinent to the curricula. Some students farmed in their native countries and know about plant growth, animal reproduction, and more. Some students' families had market stalls, and the children learned about supply and demand, revenue and debt. They have lived in different climatic zones and biomes or have traveled across countries and continents. These children have much to offer the instructional process.

■ School Reform, Standards, and Accountability

Our English learners are entering U.S. schools at a time when the academic rigor of instruction that increased under the **No Child Left Behind (NCLB) Act** of 2001 is continuing under the **Every Student Succeeds Act (ESSA),** which will be fully implemented in the 2017–18 school year. Except for those in bilingual programs, English learners do not have time to learn academic English before they study the different subject areas in English. NCLB and now ESSA hold schools accountable for the success of all of their students, and each state has standards for mathematics, reading, language arts, English language development, and science, at a minimum. Further, all states are required to administer high-stakes tests based on these standards, although more of the accountability is in the hands of the states under ESSA. Notably, the accountability for English learners' performance is no longer under Title III; it is placed under Title I.

As a result of changes in policy since 2001, the education of English learners is part of school improvement conversations, with attention being given to providing better educational opportunities for the learners and monitoring their language proficiency growth and academic progress. More schools regularly analyze assessment data to determine the progress of their efforts and to adjust programs, instruction, and resources as indicated. Some funding is available under ESSA to help practicing teachers strengthen their instruction so students develop academic literacy skills and can access core content. Schools can tap federal and state funds to provide sustained professional development opportunities, including job-embedded coaching. Some states have also allocated additional resources for English learner programs, such as grants for specialized services for newcomers and students with interrupted educational backgrounds (Short & Boyson, 2012).

Unfortunately, the number of English learners has increased without a comparable increase in ESL or bilingual certified teachers. Despite the demographic trends, only six states require specific coursework for *all* teacher candidates on topics like ESL methods and second language acquisition: Alaska, Arizona, California, Florida, Pennsylvania, and New York (National Comprehensive Center on Teacher Quality, 2009). As a result, most mainstream teachers are underprepared to serve English learners when they exit their preservice institutions (McGraner & Saenz, 2009). In addition, ESSA has removed the requirement for highly qualified teachers in the subject areas.

A concern still remains when English learners do not attain testing achievement targets set for **native English speakers** on tests that have not been designed or normed for English learners (Abedi, 2002). This is especially problematic because most students are tested in English before they are proficient in the language. Teachers report pressure to "teach to the test," which reduces their implementation of creative lessons, project-based learning, and interdisciplinary units (Short & Boyson, 2012).

Additional reforms have taken place in terms of **standards-based** instruction and **assessment**, with the goal of preparing all students for colleges and careers. As of the 2015–16 school year, 37 states and the District of Columbia, and several U.S. territories have adopted in full or with modifications a common set of K–12 English language arts/literacy and mathematics standards called the **Common Core State Standards** (National Governors Association, Center for Best Practices, and Council of Chief School Officers [NGA & CCSSO], 2010a, 2010b). One state (MN) adopted only the language arts/literacy standards. Educators in these states have modified their curriculum frameworks to ensure the required standards are included. If the standards are implemented as envisioned, high school graduates will be autonomous learners who effectively seek out and use resources to assist them in daily life, in academic pursuits, and in their jobs. The standards have been problematic for some English learners, however, because the developers did not address English learners' second language development needs. For instance, although there are standards related to foundations of literacy in grades K–5 (e.g., standards related to phonics), there are none in grades 6–12. This oversight ignores the needs of newly arrived adolescent English learners who are not literate when they enter secondary school.

A set of K–12 science standards has also been written and adopted by 17 states and the District of Columbia (as of the 2015–16 school year). In contrast to the CCSS, the authors of these **Next Generation Science Standards** (NGSS Lead States, 2013) did consider the second language acquisition process in their guiding principles and proposed practices for science and engineering.

The states that have adopted the Common Core language arts and mathematics standards also revised their state assessments for these areas.[2] Many of these states decided to use one of two new national assessments that were initially developed with federal funding, **SBAC** (Smarter Balanced Assessment Consortium) or **PARCC** (Partnership for Assessment of Readiness for College and Careers). Both are computerized, which has implications for newly arrived English learners who may not yet have the technical skills to perform the online tasks. Yet, these computerized assessments also have some features that may assist English learners such as a translated pop-up glossary, a highlighter tool, and a digital notepad. The language arts tests are planned to measure all four language domains (reading, writing, listening, and speaking) so students will have opportunities to demonstrate their knowledge in several ways. The assessments include multiple-choice items but also have short constructed responses and essays.

---

[2]At the time of this writing, no national assessment has been developed for the Next Generation Science Standards, although some states are revising their state tests to align to these standards.

The testing situation across the United States is still in flux. The results from the first administration of the SBAC and PARCC tests in spring 2014 (the latest year for which data were available) showed that all students performed poorly, including English learners, when compared to results from prior years on other state tests. Some states have dropped these assessments. Further, some states have adopted either the SAT or the ACT test as their high school accountability test under new ESSA options. A report from the Council of the Great City Schools questions the quality of tests and the number of hours spent on mandated and local assessments (Hart et al., 2015); it recommends streamlining tests to reduce redundancies and to ensure tests are aligned to standards and used for intended purposes. The U.S. Department of Education responded with a new set of principles for assessment (USED, 2015), but only time will tell if the changes make a substantial difference in schools.

Achievement Gaps

These challenging academic standards and assessments have not resulted in closing the achievement gap between English learners and non-English learners. While the number of students with limited proficiency in English has grown exponentially across the United States, their level of academic achievement continues to lag significantly behind that of their language-majority peers. Consider the following statistics:

- On the National Assessment for Educational Progress (NAEP) exam for reading in 2015, English learners performed significantly worse at fourth grade than non-English learners. Scores for all students remained stagnant compared to 2013 (USED, n.d.).

  - The achievement gap between the average scores of English learners and non-English learners was 37 points. Sixty-eight percent of the fourth-grade English learners performed Below Basic, but only 27% of the non-English learners did. Only 8% of English learners scored as Proficient or Advanced in Reading, whereas 39% of non-English learners reached those higher levels.

- The pattern of achievement on the 2015 fourth-grade NAEP mathematics assessment was similar to the results for reading. English learners had significant gaps in performance compared to non-English learners; moreover, the scores for all students declined compared to 2013 (USED, n.d.).

  - The achievement gap between the average scores of English learners and non-English learners was 25 points. Forty-three percent of the fourth-grade English learners performed Below Basic, but only 15% of the non-English learners did. Further, only 14% of English learners performed at Proficient or Advanced levels, while 43% of non-English learners were Proficient or Advanced.

- Spanish-speaking students enter kindergarten with a gap in language and math skills compared to **English-only** students. In some states, this gap widens as students progress to fifth grade (Rumberger, 2007); in others, it narrows, but non-English speakers do not come close to catching up (Reardon & Galindo, 2009).

- English learners are more likely to drop out than members of other student groups (Dianda, 2008; New York City Department of Education, 2011; Rumberger, 2011).

Watch this video to hear Dr. Jim Cummins discuss second language development and explain BICS and CALP. Where are your students on the continuum between social language and academic language development?

It is suspected that some language policies play a role in the achievement gap as well by limiting language support services. In some cases, services are offered for only one year before moving students into regular classrooms. Research demonstrates that students need more time with specialized language support (Saunders & Goldenberg, 2010).

We know that conversational fluency (also known as **social language** or **basic interpersonal communicative skills [BICS]**) develops inside and outside of the classroom and can be attained in one to three years (Thomas & Collier, 2002). However, the language that is critical for educational success—academic language (or **cognitive/ academic language proficiency [CALP]**) (Cummins, 2000)—is more complex and develops more slowly and systematically in academic settings. It may take students from four to seven years of study, depending on individual and sociocultural factors, before they are proficient in academic English (Collier, 1987; Cook, Boals, & Lundberg, 2011; Hakuta, Butler, & Witt, 2000; Lindholm-Leary & Borsato, 2006; Thomas & Collier, 2002). So programs that do not accommodate the time needed for acquisition of academic language do the students a disservice.

In contrast, when policies and programs that complement the research on second language acquisition are in place, we see more positive outcomes. For example, analyses from New York City and the states of New Jersey, Washington, and California reveal that former English learners outperformed students as a whole on state tests, exit exams, and graduation rates (DeLeeuw, 2008; New York City Department of Education, 2015; State of New Jersey Department of Education, 2006; Sullivan et al., 2005). Longitudinal studies of 18,000 English learners in the San Francisco school system found that students instructed through two languages outperformed those who studied only in English on academic and English language proficiency measures, including the state tests. Although they performed less well in second grade, by late elementary or middle school they had caught up or surpassed their peers (Umansky & Reardon, 2104; Valentino & Reardon, 2015). The results of these studies indicate that when English learners are given time to develop academic English proficiency in their programs and are exited (and redesignated) with criteria that measure their ability to be successful in mainstream classes, they perform, on average, as well as or better than the state average on achievement measures.

Academic Language and Literacy

One area where we know that English learners need support is in developing academic language and literacy skills in English. These skills serve as the foundation for school success because we learn primarily through language and use language to express our understanding. Age-appropriate knowledge of the English language is a prerequisite in the attainment of **content standards** because as the grade levels rise, language use becomes more complex and more content area-specific. The skills students need to be college and career ready are more extensive than knowledge of vocabulary words and paragraph formation. They include analytical reading and writing, effective communication and interaction, critical thinking, and creativity. These are the goals of the Common Core State Standards for English language arts/literacy and for Mathematics, and of the Next Generation Science Standards. We also find these skills in the standards of states like Texas and Virginia that did not adopt the Common Core.

We argue that academic language is a second language for *all* students. Even native-English speaking students do not enter kindergarten or first grade classrooms using embedded clauses and long, modified noun phrases in their conversations, nor do they analyze text for an author's use of imagery or write problem-solution essays about local issues. They learn these ways of using language for specific purposes over time in school. And school is where children and young adults mostly use academic language.

In *Developing Academic Language with the SIOP® Model* (Short & Echevarría, 2016, p. 2), we explain that

> Academic language involves the use of higher-level vocabulary, more complex sentence structures, and more sophisticated forms of expression than is generally found in everyday conversation. It is the type of language students need to discuss complex ideas, articulate a position, summarize material, and contrast points of view. . . . [W]hile there is no singular definition, there is consensus that academic language includes the application of reading, writing, listening, and speaking skills to knowledge of vocabulary, language structures, language functions, genres, discourse patterns, and strategic competencies that students need to be successful in school with spoken and written academic text. There is also agreement that academic language demands and linguistic elements vary, at least partially, by subject area.

Research on Academic Language and Literacy

Findings from two major syntheses of the research on academic literacy and the education of English learners are useful to keep in mind as we plan instruction and programs for English learners. The National Literacy Panel on **Language-Minority** Children and Youth (August & Shanahan, 2006) analyzed and synthesized the research on these learners with regard to English literacy attainment. The review conducted by researchers from the former National Center for Research on Education, Diversity & Excellence (CREDE) focused on oral language development, literacy development (from instructional and cross-linguistic perspectives), and academic achievement (Genesee et al., 2006). Both syntheses led to similar findings:

- Processes of second language literacy development are influenced by a number of variables that interact with each other in complex ways (e.g., first language [L1] literacy, second language [L2] oralcy, socioeconomic status, and more).

- Certain L1 skills and abilities transfer to English literacy: phonemic awareness, comprehension and language **learning strategies**, and L1 and L2 oral knowledge.

- Teaching the five major components of reading (National Institute of Child Health and Human Development [NICHD], 2000) to English learners is necessary but not sufficient for developing academic literacy. English learners need to develop oral language proficiency as well.

- Oralcy and literacy can develop simultaneously.
- Academic literacy in the native language facilitates the development of academic literacy in English.
- High-quality instruction for English learners is similar to high-quality instruction for other, English-speaking students, but English learners need instructional accommodations and support to fully develop their English skills.
- English learners need enhanced, explicit vocabulary development.

(More information on these findings and their implications for developing academic literacy can be found in California Department of Education, 2010; Cloud, Genesee, and Hamayan, 2009; Freeman and Freeman, 2009; Goldenberg, 2006; and Short and Fitzsimmons, 2007.)

Role in Schooling

Academic language is used in school settings by all students—both native English speakers and English learners alike. However, this type of language use is particularly challenging for English learners who are beginning to acquire English at the same time that school tasks require a high level of English usage. English learners must develop literacy skills for each content area *in* their second language as they simultaneously learn, comprehend, and apply content area concepts *through* their second language (Short & Fitzsimmons, 2007).

Specifically, English learners must master academic English, which includes semantic and syntactic knowledge along with functional language use. Using English, students, for example, must be able to

- read and understand the expository prose in textbooks and reference materials,
- write persuasively,
- argue points of view,
- take notes from teacher lectures or Internet sites, and
- articulate their thinking processes—make hypotheses and predictions, express analyses, draw conclusions, and so forth.

In content classes, English learners must integrate their emerging knowledge of the English language with the content information they are studying in order to complete the academic tasks. They must also learn *how* to do these tasks—generate the format of an outline, negotiate roles in cooperative learning groups, interpret charts and maps, and such. These three knowledge bases—knowledge of English, knowledge of the content topic, and knowledge of how the tasks are to be accomplished—constitute the major components of academic literacy (Short & Echevarría, 2016).

There is some general agreement about how best to teach academic language to English learners, including some targeted focus on the lexical, semantic, and discourse levels of the language as they are applied in school settings (Saunders & Goldenberg, 2010). Brown and Ryoo (2008) found that elementary students who learn science content through everyday vernacular before learning the scientific language assimilate the content better. Researchers such as Bailey and Butler (2007) found that there is content-specific language (e.g., technical terms like *latitude* and *longitude*, phrases like "We hypothesize that . . .") and general academic language (e.g., cross-curricular words like *effect, compare, except*) that are used across subject areas. Similarly, there are general academic tasks that one needs to know how to do to be academically proficient (e.g., create a timeline, cite evidence from a text) and more specific subject assignments (e.g., explain steps to the solution of a math word problem). Teachers and curriculum developers should pay attention to this full range of academic language. As a result, the enhancement of English learners' academic language skills should enable them to perform better on assessments. This conclusion is bolstered by an older study: Snow et al. (1991) found that performance on highly decontextualized (i.e., school-like) tasks, such as providing a formal definition of words, predicted academic performance, whereas performance on highly contextualized tasks, such as face-to-face communication, did not.

The emphasis on teaching academic language is also reflected in the national ESL standards (Teachers of English to Speakers of Other Languages, 2006). Four of the five *Pre-K–12 English Language Proficiency Standards* specifically address the academic language of the core subject areas. Standards 2, 3, 4, and 5 state: "English language learners communicate information, ideas, and concepts necessary for academic success in the area of _____ [language arts (#2), mathematics (#3), science (#4), and social studies (#5)]." As of 2016, 35 states, plus the District of Columbia, the U.S. Virgin Islands, and the Northern Mariana Islands had adopted **English language proficiency (ELP) standards** similar to TESOL's, known as the WIDA standards (WIDA, 2012). Almost all of these entities use the companion English language proficiency test, *ACCESS for ELLs* (ACCESS: Assessing Comprehension and Communication in English State to State for English Language Learners) or *ACCESS for ELLs 2.0* (a newer computer-based version), to guide and measure annual gains in English language proficiency. As of 2016, 10 states are participating in a similar English language proficiency standards and assessment system known as ELPA21[3].

? Reflect and Apply

Click here to reflect on out-of-school factors that affect language acquisition and developing academic literacy for all learners.

Effective Instructional Practice for English Learners: The SIOP® Model

One positive outcome of the student performance measures put into place in response to the federal legislation is that schools have focused on the development of academic language and literacy skills in students who struggle academically, including English learners. Schools have sought to improve the educational programs, instructional practices, and the curricula and materials being offered to these students. Opportunities for ongoing professional development are moving teachers in

---

[3]More information about the ACCESS assessments can be found at www.wida.us and about the ELPA21 assessments at www.elpa21.org.

the right direction. However, we have a long way to go, as the data and research findings about the poor performance of English learners on accountability measures presented in this chapter reveal.[4]

Content-based ESL and Sheltered Content Instruction

Currently, in the United States, content-based English as a second language (ESL) and sheltered instruction are acknowledged methods for developing academic English and providing English learners access to core content coursework in grades K–12. Ideally, these two approaches work in tandem: one focuses on academic (and where needed, social) language development while addressing content topics; the other focuses on making content standards and topics accessible while teaching the academic language of the particular subject area. In the content-based ESL classes (also known as **Designated ELD** in CA), the curricula are tied to the state standards for English language proficiency, the students are all English learners, and the teacher is ESL or bilingual certified. In sheltered content instruction classes (also known as **Integrated ELD** in CA), the curricula are tied to the state subject area standards, such as the Common Core and NGSS, and the students may be all English learners or mixed with native English speakers. The teachers have elementary or secondary content certification and typically an endorsement or certification in ESL or **bilingual education** (see Figure 1.3).

In content-based ESL and designated ELD, material from multiple subject areas is often presented through thematic or interdisciplinary units. For example, in an upper elementary classroom, one theme might be "The Marketplace," and lessons could include objectives drawn from economics, science, geography, social studies, and mathematics. Students might create maps showing how goods move from farms and manufacturing plants to city markets; design a brochure to sell a good or service; use online reference materials to learn about the supply and demand of certain goods; or develop a business plan for a good or service they would like to sell. They might study persuasive language to advertise their good or service. English learners may contribute valuable insights to this topic because some have lived in places where their parents or neighbors moved goods to market. Some may have experienced the effects of adverse weather on the production of foodstuffs or the effects of poor infrastructure on the transportation of goods.

In general, content-based ESL/ELD teachers seek to develop the students' English language proficiency by incorporating information from the subject areas that students are likely to study or from courses they may have missed if they are new immigrants. Whatever subject matter is included, for effective content-based ESL instruction to occur, teachers need to provide practice in academic skills and tasks common to regular, grade-level classes.

In sheltered content and integrated ELD classes, teachers deliver grade-level objectives for the different subject areas to English learners through modified instruction that makes the information comprehensible to the students while

---

[4]Recent policy reports and federal guidance accentuate the need for better programming and attention to academic language and literacy development. See, for example, Baker et al., 2014; Council of Great City Schools, 2009; U.S. Department of Education, Office of English Language Acquisition, 2015; and U.S. Department of Justice, Civil Rights Division, & U.S. Department of Education, Office of Civil Rights, 2015.

FIGURE 1.3 Integrated Content and Language Courses

	Integrated Content and Language Courses	
Type of Class	Content-based ESL, also known as Designated ELD	Sheltered instruction in a content area, also known as Integrated ELD, SDAIE, or structured English immersion
Language Goals	Academic English proficiency	Academic English proficiency
Academic Content Goals	May emphasize English language arts in some states; often introduces content topics from the other core areas (math, science, social studies) too; may help fill in gaps in educational backgrounds	Typically focuses on the curriculum and standards from a content area (e.g., sheltered Algebra); the language is modified and scaffolding techniques used but the grade-level concepts are addressed
Standards	English language proficiency and/or English language arts standards	Content standards (any or all subjects)
Language of Instruction	English, some native language for clarification or support	English, some native language for clarification or support
Student Characteristics	Variety of language/cultural backgrounds	Variety of language/cultural backgrounds
	All English proficiency levels, although some districts target the newcomer through intermediate levels	All English proficiency levels
		Some programs mix native English speakers and English learners and former English learners in certain courses, particularly as English learners reach intermediate and advanced proficiency levels
Grades Served	All grades (until students exit ESL/ELD program)	All grades (until students no longer need language support, usually decided on a case-by-case basis by content area)
Teachers	ESL/ELD/Designated ELD teachers; typically ESL- or bilingual-certified or endorsed, sometimes English language arts certified with specialized training	Typically content-certified teachers with ESL or bilingual certification or endorsement, sometimes content-certified with specialized training
Role of the SIOP Model	For lesson planning and delivery	For lesson planning and delivery
Additional Information	The number of hours of instruction per week may be reduced as proficiency levels rise	These courses are often the bridge to general education content courses while students are developing academic English skills. May be used in any class where students need to develop academic literacy.

promoting their academic English development. In elementary schools, sheltered instruction is generally taught by classroom teachers rather than ESL specialists and can be offered to students with any level of English proficiency. A goal is to teach content to students learning English through a developmental language approach.

Effective sheltered instruction is *not* simply a set of additional or replacement instructional techniques that teachers implement in their classrooms. Instead, it draws from and complements methods advocated for both second language and mainstream classrooms. For example, some techniques include cooperative learning, connections to student experiences, **culturally responsive** activities, targeted vocabulary development, slower speech and fewer idiomatic expressions for less proficient students, use of visuals and demonstrations, and use of adapted text and supplementary materials.

In the 1990s, there was a great deal of variability in the design of sheltered instruction courses and the delivery of sheltered lessons, even among trained teachers and within the same schools (August & Hakuta, 1997; Echevarría & Short, 2010). Some schools, for instance, offered sheltered courses in only one subject area, but not in other core areas. It was our experience as well that one sheltered classroom did not look like the next in terms of each teacher's instructional language; the tasks the students were to accomplish; the degree of interaction that occurred between teacher and student, student and student, and student and text; the amount of class time devoted to language development versus content knowledge; the learning strategies taught to and used by the students; the availability of appropriate materials; and more. In sum, there was no model for teachers to follow and few systematic and sustained forms of professional development.

This situation, along with the underachievement of English learners, was the impetus for our research: to develop a valid, reliable, and effective model of sheltered instruction that would improve the academic performance of the students.

Research and Development of the Sheltered Instruction Observation Protocol (SIOP®) Model

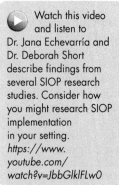

Watch this video and listen to Dr. Jana Echevarría and Dr. Deborah Short describe findings from several SIOP research studies. Consider how you might research SIOP implementation in your setting. https://www.youtube.com/watch?v=JbbGlklFLw0

We developed the Sheltered Instruction Observation Protocol (SIOP) Model as an approach for teachers to integrate content and language instruction for students learning through a new language. Teachers would employ techniques that make the content concepts accessible and also develop the students' skills in the new language. We have been fortunate in securing funding and the participation of many schools and teachers since 1996 to research, develop, and refine the SIOP Model. Details of the SIOP Model research studies can be found in Appendix C of this book and in Short, Echevarría, and Richards-Tutor (2011). We present a brief overview here.

The first version of the Sheltered Instruction Observation Protocol (SIOP) was drafted in the early 1990s. We used it exclusively as a research and supervisory tool to determine if observed teachers incorporated key sheltered techniques consistently in their lessons. This early draft, like subsequent ones, integrated findings and recommendations from the research literature with our professional experiences and those of our collaborating teachers on effective classroom-based practices.

The protocol evolved into a lesson planning and delivery approach, known as the SIOP Model (Echevarría, Vogt, & Short, 2000), through a seven-year research study, "The Effects of Sheltered Instruction on the Achievement of Limited English Proficient Students," sponsored by the Center for Research on Education, Diversity & Excellence (CREDE) and funded by the U.S. Department of Education. The study began in 1996 and involved collaborating middle school teachers who worked with the researchers to refine the features of the original protocol: distinguishing among effective strategies for beginner, intermediate, and advanced English learners; determining "critical" and "unique" sheltered teaching strategies; and making the SIOP more user friendly. A substudy confirmed the SIOP to be a valid and reliable measure of sheltered instruction (Guarino et al., 2001).

The SIOP is composed of 30 features grouped into eight main components. (See the overview in Figure 1.4.) You will read about each component and its features in subsequent chapters of this book. We are gratified that the original model has stood the test of time; it has not needed to be revised. The model also has been shown to be effective in numerous districts and schools across the United States.

During four years of field testing, we analyzed teacher implementation and student effects. This CREDE research showed that English learners whose teachers were trained in implementing the SIOP Model performed statistically significantly better on an academic writing assessment than a comparison group of English learners whose teachers had no exposure to the model (Echevarría, Short, & Powers, 2006).

From 1999 to 2002, we field tested and refined the SIOP Model's professional development program, which includes professional development institutes, videotapes of exemplary SIOP teachers (Hudec & Short, 2002a, 2002b), facilitator's guides, and other training materials.

We continued to test and refine the SIOP Model in several later studies. From 2004–07, we replicated and scaled up the SIOP research in a quasi-experimental study in two districts at the middle and high school levels. The treatment teachers participated in the professional development program with summer institutes, follow-up workshops, and on-site coaching. Students with SIOP-trained teachers made statistically significant gains in their average mean scores for oral language, writing, and total proficiency on the state assessment of English language proficiency (the IPT [Idea Proficiency Tests]), compared to the comparison group of English learners (Short, Fidelman, & Louguit, 2012).

From 2005–12, we participated in the Center for Research on the Educational Achievement and Teaching of English Language Learners (CREATE), looking at the SIOP Model first in middle school science classrooms (Himmel, Short, Richards, & Echevarría, 2009) and later as the professional development framework for a

FIGURE 1.4 Overview of the SIOP®'s Eight Components

- The features under *Lesson Preparation* initiate the lesson planning process, so teachers include content and language objectives, use supplementary materials, and create meaningful activities.
- *Building Background* focuses on making connections with students' background experiences and prior learning, and developing their academic vocabulary.
- *Comprehensible Input* considers how teachers should adjust their speech, model academic tasks, and use multimodal techniques to enhance comprehension.
- The *Strategies* component emphasizes teaching learning strategies to students, scaffolding instruction, and promoting higher-order thinking skills.
- *Interaction* prompts teachers to encourage students to elaborate their speech and to group students appropriately for language and content development.
- *Practice & Application* provides activities to practice and extend language and content learning.
- *Lesson Delivery* ensures that teachers present a lesson that meets the planned objectives and promotes student engagement.
- The *Review & Assessment* component reminds teachers to review the key language and content concepts, assess student learning, and provide specific academic feedback to students on their output.

school-wide intervention (Echevarría & Short, 2011). In this set of studies, we used an experimental-control design and English learners, former English learners, and native English speakers were part of the student population. The results from the studies showed that students who had teachers who implemented the SIOP Model with greater fidelity performed better on criterion-referenced assessments than those who did not implement the SIOP Model to a high degree (Echevarría, Richards-Tutor, Chinn, & Ratleff, 2011). So, the level of implementation mattered. Further, students in SIOP curriculum groups outperformed control students on criterion-referenced vocabulary, science, and social studies measures (Echevarría, Richards-Tutor, Canges, & Francis, 2011; Short & Himmel, 2013). These findings indicate that English-speaking students are not disadvantaged when they are in SIOP classes with English learners and that they also benefit from SIOP practices.

During the past decade, a number of school districts have also conducted program evaluations on their implementation of the model. A number of these can be reviewed in *Implementing the SIOP® Model Through Effective Professional Development and Coaching* (Echevarría, Short, & Vogt, 2008). In addition, other researchers have studied SIOP Model professional development programs (Batt, 2010; Friend, Most, & McCrary, 2009; Honigsfeld & Cohan, 2008; McIntyre et al., 2010; Song, 2016).

A note about terminology is helpful before you read further. SIOP is the term for this empirically validated model of sheltered instruction designed to make grade-level academic content understandable for English learners while at the same time developing their academic English language proficiency. Formerly spelled out as the Sheltered Instruction Observation Protocol, the authors have decided to stop using the full acronym definition because the acronym SIOP is more commonly used in schools and in the professional literature. SIOP refers to the observation instrument for rating the fidelity of lessons to the model (as shown in Appendix A) and the instructional model for lesson planning and delivery that we explain in detail in the following chapters. It is often used as an adjective too, as in SIOP teachers, SIOP lessons, and SIOP classrooms.

Effective SIOP® Model Instruction

This book, *Making Content Comprehensible for Elementary English Learners: The SIOP® Model*, introduces the research-based model of sheltered instruction (that is also used for content-based ESL), provides teaching ideas for each of the model's eight components, suggests ways to **differentiate instruction** in multi-level classrooms, and demonstrates through lesson scenarios how the model can be implemented across grades and subject areas. The model provides guidance for the best practices for English learners, grounded in more than two decades of classroom-based research, the experiences of competent teachers, and findings from the professional literature. It has been used successfully in both language and content classrooms, and with this approach, teachers can help English learners attain the skills and knowledge associated with college and career readiness.

In effective SIOP lessons, language and content objectives are systematically woven into the curriculum of one particular subject area, such as kindergarten math,

Watch this video to see Dr. MaryEllen Vogt explain the value of sheltered instruction for English learners. Look at Appendix A. Which SIOP features do you already include in your lessons?

fourth-grade language arts, or sixth grade social studies, or in one ESL level, such as beginner, intermediate, or advanced. Teachers develop the students' academic language proficiency consistently and regularly as part of the lessons and units they plan and deliver.

In subsequent chapters, you will explore the components and features of the SIOP Model in detail and have the opportunity to try out numerous techniques for SIOP lessons. You will see that the SIOP Model shares many features recommended for high-quality instruction for all students, such as collaborative discussion groups, strategies for reading comprehension, writers' workshop, and differentiated instruction. However, the SIOP Model adds key features for the academic success of these learners, such as the inclusion of language objectives in every content lesson, the development of background knowledge, the acquisition of content-related vocabulary, and the emphasis on academic literacy practice.

Here we briefly describe the instructional practices that effective SIOP teachers use. You can compare your typical instruction with that of SIOP teachers, and you might find that you are already on the path to becoming a skillful SIOP teacher!

Watch this video and listen to teacher Arpan Chickshi describe his professional learning about teaching the academic language in his subject area after attending a SIOP Institute. What can you do to promote more academic language learning among your students?

- Classroom teachers generally present the regular, grade-level subject curriculum to the students through modified instruction in English, although some special curricula may be designed for children who have significant gaps in their educational backgrounds or very low literacy skills.
- Classroom teachers identify how language is used in the different subjects and give students explicit instruction and practice with it.
- ESL teachers advance students' English language development with curricula addressing language proficiency standards, but also incorporating the types of texts, vocabulary, and tasks used in core subjects to prepare the students for success in the regular, English-medium classroom.

Accomplished SIOP teachers determine students' baseline understandings in their subject area and move them forward, both in their content knowledge and in their language skills through a variety of techniques.

- SIOP teachers provide rigorous instruction aligned with state content and language standards, such as the Common Core, NGSS, WIDA, and ELPA21.
- SIOP teachers make specific connections between the content being taught and students' experiences and prior knowledge, and they focus on expanding the children's vocabulary base.
- SIOP teachers modulate the level of English they use and the texts and other materials used with and among students.
- SIOP teachers make the content comprehensible through techniques such as the use of visual aids, modeling, demonstrations, graphic organizers, vocabulary previews, adapted texts, cooperative learning, peer tutoring, and native language support.
- SIOP teachers help English learners articulate their emerging understandings of the content both orally and in writing, often with sentence starters and language frame scaffolds.

- Besides increasing students' declarative knowledge (i.e., factual information), SIOP teachers highlight and model procedural knowledge (e.g., how to accomplish an academic task like solving a two-step math problem) along with study skills and learning strategies (e.g., note-taking and self-monitoring comprehension when reading).

In effective SIOP lessons, there is a high level of student **engagement** and interaction with the teacher, with other students, and with text, which leads to elaborated discourse and critical thinking.

- Student language learning is promoted through social interaction and contextualized communication as teachers guide students to construct meaning and understand complex concepts from texts and classroom discourse (Vygotsky, 1978).
- Students are explicitly taught functional language skills, such as how to negotiate meaning, confirm information, describe, compare, and persuade.
- Teachers introduce English learners to the classroom discourse community and demonstrate skills such as taking turns in a conversation and interrupting politely to ask for clarification.
- Through instructional conversations (Goldenberg, 1992–93) and meaningful activities, children practice and apply their new language and content knowledge.

Not all teaching is about the techniques in a lesson. SIOP teachers also consider their students' affective needs, cultural backgrounds, and learning styles. They strive to create a nonthreatening environment where students feel comfortable taking risks with language.

- SIOP teachers engage in culturally responsive teaching and build on the children's potentially different ways of learning, behaving, and using language (Gay, 2010).
- They socialize English learners to the implicit classroom culture, including appropriate behaviors and communication patterns.
- They plan activities that tap into the auditory, visual, and kinesthetic preferences of the students and consider their multiple intelligences as well.
- SIOP teachers reach out to the families of English learners and orient them to the expectations of schooling in the United States; they also seek to determine the funds of knowledge in the children's households (Gonzalez, Moll, & Amanti, 2005).

The SIOP Model is also distinguished by use of supplementary materials that support the academic text. The purpose of these materials is to enhance student understanding of key topics, issues, and details in the content concepts being taught through means other than teacher lecture or dense textbook prose.

- To present key topics or reinforce information, SIOP teachers find related texts (e.g., trade books, leveled readers), graphics and illustrations, models, multimedia and computer-based resources, adapted text, and the like.

- SIOP teachers use supplementary materials to make information accessible to learners with mixed proficiency levels of English. For example, some students in a mixed class may use the textbook, while others may need an adapted text.

When advances in technology are used effectively in the classroom, English learners can reap many benefits. Digital content is motivating for students, allows for a personalized learning experience, is multimodal, and can give children experience with meaningful and authentic tasks (Lemke & Coughlin, 2009).

- Technology such as interactive whiteboards with links to the Internet, visual images, podcasts, educational apps, and more offer a wealth of resources to support English learners' acquisition of new information and of academic English.
- SIOP teachers give students opportunities to use the technology for multiple purposes, such as access to information presented in the students' native language, cyber-group learning interactions such as simulations and virtual field trips, speaking practice through audio recordings on cellphones, self-paced research, and writing and editing tools.

Depending on the students' proficiency levels, SIOP teachers offer multiple pathways for children to demonstrate their understanding of the content. In this way, teachers can receive a more accurate picture of most English learners' content knowledge and skills through an assortment of assessment measures than they could through one standardized test. Otherwise, a student may be perceived as lacking mastery of content when actually he or she is following the normal pace of the second language acquisition process (Abedi & Lord, 2001; Solano-Flores & Trumbull, 2003).

- SIOP teachers plan pictorial, hands-on, or performance-based assessments for individual students; group tasks or projects; oral reports; written assignments; and portfolios, along with more traditional measures such as tests and quizzes to check student comprehension and language growth.
- Teachers use rubrics to measure student performance on a scale leading to mastery, and they share those rubrics with students in advance.
- Teachers dedicate some time to teaching students how to read and understand standardized test questions, pointing out the use of specific verbs or synonyms in the question stems and possible responses (Bailey & Butler, 2007).

It is important to recognize that the SIOP Model does not require teachers to discard their favored techniques or to add copious new elements to a lesson. Rather, this model of sheltered instruction brings together *what* to teach by providing a framework for *how* to teach it. It acts as an umbrella, allowing teachers the flexibility to choose techniques they know work well with their particular group of students (see Figure 1.5 on the next page). It reminds teachers to pay attention to the language development needs of their children and to select and organize techniques that facilitate the integration of district- or state-level standards for ESL and for specific content areas.

FIGURE 1.5 The SIOP® Model Framework for Organizing Best Practices

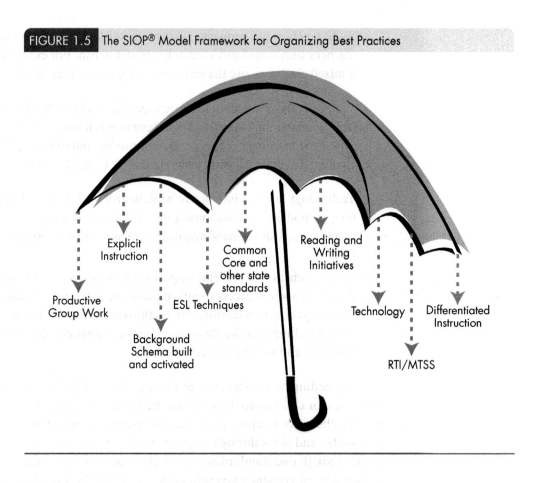

Implementing the SIOP® Model

The goal of this book is to prepare teachers to teach content and academic language and literacy skills effectively to English learners. The SIOP Model may be used as part of a program for preservice and inservice professional development, as a lesson planner for sheltered content and content-based ESL lessons, and as a training resource for university faculty. Research shows that professional development approaches that improve teaching include the following: sustained, intensive development with modeling, coaching, and problem solving; collaborative endeavors for educators to share knowledge; experiential opportunities that engage teachers in actual teaching, assessment, and observation; and development grounded in research but also drawing from teacher experience and inquiry, connected to the teachers' classes, students, and subjects taught (Darling-Hammond & Richardson, 2009; Short, 2013).

In our research studies, we found that SIOP implementation does not happen quickly. Teachers may take one to two years before they implement the model consistently to a high degree, and coaching helps get them to that level (Short, Fidelman, & Louguit, 2012). McIntyre and colleagues (2010) suggest that teachers' proficiency in implementing the model may depend on their background teaching experiences and the design of their professional development.

Effective implementation of the SIOP Model is one key to improving the academic success of English learners. Preservice teachers need to learn the model to develop a strong foundation in best practice for integrating language and content in classes with English learners. Practicing teachers need the model to strengthen their lesson planning and delivery and to provide students with more consistent instruction that meets language and content standards. Site-based supervisors and administrators use the model to train and coach teachers and systematize classroom observations. Teacher education faculty also present the SIOP Model in their methods courses and use it in student teacher supervision.

Any program in which students are learning content through a nonnative language could use the SIOP Model effectively. It may be an ESL program (with **pull-out** or **self-contained** classes), a late-exit **bilingual** program, a **dual language/ two-way bilingual** program, a **newcomer program**, a sheltered program, or even a foreign language immersion program. The model has been designed for flexibility and tested in a wide range of classroom situations: with children who have strong academic backgrounds and those who have had limited formal schooling; with students who are recent arrivals and those who have been in U.S. schools for several years; and with learners at beginning levels of English proficiency and those at advanced levels. For students studying in content-based ESL or bilingual courses, SIOP instruction often provides the bridge to the general education program. More discussion of getting started with the SIOP Model is found in Chapter 12.

? **Reflect and Apply**
Click here to reflect on general concepts of the SIOP® Model.

✔ **Check Your Understanding**
Click here to check your understanding of Chapter 1, Introducing the SIOP® Model.

Summary

As you reflect on this chapter and the impact of the SIOP Model on English learners' content and academic language learning, consider the following main points:

- Students who are learning English as an additional language are the fastest-growing segment of the school-age population in the United States, and almost all candidates in teacher education programs will have linguistically and culturally diverse students in their classes during their teaching careers. However, many of these future teachers—as well as most practicing teachers—are not well prepared to instruct these learners.

- School reform efforts, standards, and increased state accountability measures put pressure on schools and districts to improve their educational opportunities and practices with English learners. This pressure has had both positive and negative outcomes. Teachers can use the SIOP Model to help students meet

Common Core, NGSS, and other state standards and to prepare English learners for college and careers.

- The SIOP Model has a strong, empirical research base. It has been tested across multiple subject areas and grade levels. The research evidence shows that the SIOP Model can improve the academic literacy of English learners.

- The SIOP Model does not mandate cookie-cutter instruction; instead, it provides a framework for well-prepared and well-delivered lessons in any subject area. As SIOP teachers design their lessons, they have room for creativity. Nonetheless, critical instructional features must be attended to in order for teachers to respond appropriately to the unique academic and language development needs of English learners.

- The model is operationalized in the SIOP protocol, which can be used to rate lessons and measure the level of SIOP implementation.

- Our research shows that both language and content teachers can implement the SIOP Model fully to good effect. The model is best suited for content-based ESL and sheltered content classes that are part of a program of studies for English learners, and for English-medium classrooms with English learners and struggling readers. Together, these classes can be a promising combination when implemented school-wide.

- We need children like Ricardo to be successful in school and beyond. In the long run, such success will benefit the communities in which these students live and the national economy as a whole.

■ Discussion Questions

1. In reflecting on the content and language objectives at the beginning of the chapter, are you able to:
   a. List characteristics of English learners that may influence their success in school?
   b. Distinguish between content-based ESL and sheltered instruction?
   c. Explain the research supporting the SIOP Model?
   d. Discuss the benefits and challenges of school reform and their effects on English learners?
   e. Develop a lexicon related to the SIOP Model?
   f. Compare your typical instruction with SIOP instruction?

2. Consider one class of English learners. Identify the individual and sociocultural factors that might influence the educational success of these students. In what ways might instruction using the SIOP Model help them?

3. How would you characterize the type(s) of instruction offered to English learners in your school or in schools you know: traditional ESL, content-based ESL, sheltered content, bilingual content, traditional content, dual language? Provide evidence of your characterization in terms of curricula and instruction. Are the

English learners successful when they exit English language support programs and are placed in regular classrooms without support? Explain.

4. Many sheltered content teachers fail to take advantage of the language learning opportunities for students in their classes. Why do you think this is so? Offer two concrete suggestions for these teachers to enhance their students' academic language development.

5. Look at one of your own lesson plans. Which characteristics of the SIOP Model do you already incorporate? Consider the components and features of the model as found in Appendix A.

CHAPTER 2

Lesson Preparation

Learning Outcomes

After reading, discussing, and engaging in activities related to this chapter, you will be able to meet the following **content** and **language objectives**:

Content Objectives

Identify content objectives for **English learners** that are aligned to state, local, or national standards.

Incorporate supplementary materials suitable for English learners into a lesson plan.

Select from a variety of techniques for adapting content to the students' proficiency and cognitive levels.

Language Objectives

Write language and content objectives.

Discuss advantages for writing both language and content objectives for a lesson and sharing the objectives with students.

Explain the importance of meaningful academic activities for English learners.

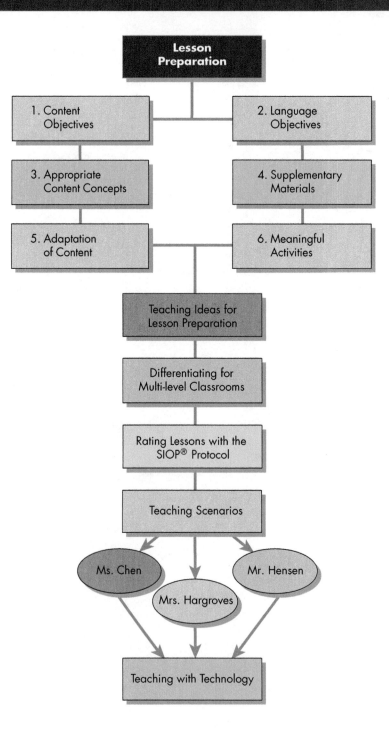

In this chapter, and in subsequent chapters, we explain each **SIOP** Model component and its features. Each chapter begins with an explanation of the component, offers classroom activities, and then describes how three teachers approach the same lesson. The lesson scenarios throughout the book are about varied topics and represent different grade levels.

This chapter introduces the first component of the SIOP Model, Lesson Preparation. We present background information and the rationale for each of the six features in this component, list some teaching ideas for this component and for differentiating instruction in multi-level classrooms, demonstrate through the teaching scenarios how the model can be implemented, and offer technology enhancements. As you read the scenarios, we encourage you to check your understanding of the SIOP features that have been explained in the chapter by rating the scenario lessons according to best practice. Reflect on how effectively each teacher is meeting the needs of English learners in relation to each feature. At the conclusion of the teaching scenarios, we discuss our assessment of the teachers' efforts to provide SIOP instruction, and we invite you to compare your appraisal to ours. ●

ZUMA Press, Inc./Alamy Stock Photo

■ Background

As we all know, lesson planning is critical to both a student's and a teacher's success. For maximum learning to occur, planning must produce lessons that target specific learning goals, enable students to make connections between their own knowledge and experiences and the new information being taught, give children practice using and applying the new information, and assess student learning to determine whether to move on or reteach the material. With careful planning, we make learning meaningful and relevant by including appropriate motivating materials and activities that foster real-life application of concepts studied.

We have learned that if children's exposure to content concepts is limited by vocabulary-controlled materials or watered-down curricula, the amount of information they learn over time is considerably less than that of their peers who use grade-level texts and curricula. The result is that the learning gap between **native English speakers** and English learners widens instead of closes, and eventually it becomes nearly impossible for English learners to catch up (Gándara & Rumberger, 2008). Therefore, it is imperative that we plan lessons that promote the acquisition of academic English and include age-appropriate content and materials. Our lessons, however, must provide appropriate scaffolds so our students can meet the rigor of state standards, such as the **Common Core** and **Next Generation Science**, over time and be prepared for college and careers.

This component, Lesson Preparation, is therefore very important to the SIOP Model. If properly prepared, a lesson will include most of the SIOP features in advance. It is then up to the teachers and class to accomplish them as the lesson unfolds. However, when planning, teachers have asked how they can meet all 30 features in a given period. We explain that one SIOP lesson may be completed in a single day or it may require multiple days. Over the course of several days, all 30 features should be met.

SIOP Lesson Planning.   As you first learn the model, we strongly encourage you to write out lessons in detail. We suggest you use the short form of the SIOP protocol (Appendix A) as a checklist to ensure all of the features are incorporated. You may want to try one or more of the lesson plan templates that we have included in Appendix B or the templates in Chapter 7 of *Implementing the SIOP® Model Through Effective Professional Development and Coaching* (Echevarría, Short, & Vogt, 2008). These templates have been used successfully in a variety of classrooms and across grade levels. In addition, sample lesson plans and units can be found in the SIOP content books for English language arts, mathematics, science, and history and social studies (Echevarría, Vogt, & Short, 2010; Short, Vogt, & Echevarría, 2011a, 2011b; Vogt, Echevarría, & Short, 2010).

Another option is to *SIOPize* a lesson you have already written. Using the checklist, see which features are already present and then enhance your lesson with the missing features. You may need to add explicit instruction for a language objective or more activities for oral interaction, for instance.

"How do I start implementing SIOP lessons?" is a frequent question from elementary school teachers new to the SIOP Model. We suggest that you start with one subject area. It is better to begin on a small scale so you do not have to write multiple SIOP lessons each day while you are learning the model. In some cases, teachers learn the SIOP Model over time, component by component in a cumulative manner, and they build their lesson planning skills in the same way. Once you have internalized the model, you may write less detailed lesson plans, and you will probably find that writing SIOP lessons for different subjects is easier.

To guide your SIOP lesson planning, let's now explore each feature in the SIOP component of Lesson Preparation.

SIOP® FEATURE 1:

Content Objectives Clearly Defined, Displayed, and Reviewed with Students

In effective instruction, concrete content objectives that identify what students should know and be able to do must guide teaching and learning. They are often easier for teachers to write because they typically come directly from the curricular frameworks of the subject areas. When planning content objectives, keep the following guidelines in mind:

- Plan objectives that support **content standards** and learning outcomes. The Common Core State Standards for English language arts and mathematics (NGA 2010a, 2010b), the Next Generation Science Standards (NGSS Lead States, 2013), and individual state standards are sources of content objectives, and well-implemented SIOP instruction can help students meet them.

- Write lesson-level objectives (something that can be taught and learned in one lesson or two) and use student-friendly language that suits the age and proficiency levels in the class. For example, some kindergarten and first grade teachers post key words for the objectives rather than complete sentences. Content objectives and state standards are frequently complex and not written in a manner that is accessible to English learners. Often standards are too generic or broad, or in the case of young learners, confusing—such as "Order three objects by length; compare the lengths of two objects indirectly by using a third object" (NGA, 2010b, p. 16). So standards are not useful as a single lesson's learning goal.

- Write objectives in terms of student learning, not as an agenda item or an activity. See Figure 2.1 for several ways that teachers in our research studies have started their objectives. You will note that all focus on the student.

- Limit the number of content objectives to only one or two per lesson to reduce the complexity of the learning task and to ensure that instruction can meet the objectives.

Watch this video to learn how Magali Williams, a bilingual resource teacher, introduces the lesson objectives to her students. What techniques does she use to ensure the students understand what they will be learning in this lesson?

| FIGURE 2.1 | How to Start an Objective |

Students will be able to (SWBAT) _____

Students will (SW) _____

We will _____

Today I will _____

I can _____

Our job is to _____

- Share objectives with children, orally and in writing. In many classes teachers do not consistently present objectives to children. As a result, students do not know what they are supposed to learn each day. SIOP teachers tell children the objectives for every lesson, and in this way students share the responsibility for learning.

- Plan lessons so you provide some explicit instruction and practice opportunities related to each objective.

- Review the objectives at the end of the lesson to determine if children have mastered them. Use that assessment when deciding whether to move to the next topic or spend some time reteaching.

We know from our research studies and professional development experiences that presenting objectives each day can be challenging for teachers. But the effort is worth it. Teachers consistently report the value of displaying and clearly stating content objectives for English learners. As one teacher said, "I just wanted to say that defining the objectives each day definitely brings more focus to my planning and thinking, and it helps bring order to my classroom procedures." Another teacher remarked, "It's our GPS for the lesson."

Content-based ESL teachers sometimes need assistance in identifying appropriate content objectives to add to their lessons. They may feel unprepared for in-depth instruction on a content topic, they may not know the key concepts that should be taught, and they may not know what types of activities usually support the topic. In some elementary schools these teachers serve students from different grade levels at the same time. For these reasons, we strongly advocate that content and language teachers collaborate closely as they prepare lessons and help their students meet language and content goals.

By writing content objectives related to the lessons English learners receive in subject-area classes, content-based ESL teachers address the children's academic needs better. Some teachers might draw from one content area, focus on one subject per quarter, or concentrate on academic tasks needed to work in those subjects (e.g., extracting information from text to create a timeline, writing a descriptive essay, explaining steps in an experiment).

The bottom line for English learners is that content objectives need to be written in terms of what students will learn or do; they should be stated simply, orally and in writing, use active verbs, and be tied to specific grade-level content standards.

Examples of content objectives and language objectives, discussed below, can be found throughout each chapter in this book, in *99 Ideas and Activities for Teaching English Learners with the SIOP® Model* (Vogt & Echevarría, 2008), in *99 MORE Ideas and Activities for Teaching English Learners with the SIOP® Model* (Vogt, Echevarría, & Washam, 2015), in *Helping English Language Learners Succeed in Pre-K–Elementary Schools* (Lacina, Levine, & Sowa, 2006), in lesson plans presented in *Science for English Language Learners* (Fathman & Crowther, 2006), and in the SIOP content books mentioned above.

SIOP® FEATURE 2:
Language Objectives Clearly Defined, Displayed, and Reviewed with Students

While carefully planning and delivering content objectives, SIOP teachers must also incorporate into their lesson plans objectives that support children's **academic language** development, and **ESL** teachers may have to build social and classroom-related language skills too (Gersten et al., 2007; Saunders & Goldenberg, 2010). The same guidelines we discussed above for content objectives also should apply to planning language objectives:

- Language objectives should be written clearly and simply with active verbs, and children should be informed of them in each lesson, both orally and in writing.
- The objectives should be limited in number for a given lesson and reviewed at the end.
- They should be drawn from the state **English language proficiency standards** and English language arts standards.
- Most importantly, the objectives should represent an aspect of academic language that students need to learn or master.

Both types of objectives are equally essential in SIOP lessons. When planning, remember the following:

- Content objectives are the *what*—what children need to learn about the content topic
- Language objectives are the *what* too—what children need to learn about English in order to
  - learn, express, practice, and apply new information
  - demonstrate knowledge
  - perform academic tasks

> Watch this video to hear Professor Cynthia Lundgren explain why teachers need to include language objectives in their lessons and how objectives help students meet standards. What role does language play in your content area? https://www.youtube.com/watch?v=del47uaZMJs

Although incorporating language objectives in all content lessons is a hallmark of the SIOP Model, we recognize that some classroom teachers are not used to thinking about the language demands of the subjects they teach, apart from language arts. What we propose in the SIOP Model calls for a new perspective on the subject areas.

If you are a classroom or content area teacher, it is not sufficient to only have deep knowledge of topics in your subject area. Rather, to be effective, you also need to know how language is used in the subject area in order to convey information (whether orally or in text) and to use and apply that information (through class reading, writing, and discussion activities). You also need to know your students' proficiency levels so the language objectives can be targeted to what students need to learn about the academic language of history, science, mathematics, or other subjects, yet not be at a level too high for their current understanding.

Because it may be a new way of thinking for you, here are guidelines to keep in mind from research on second language acquisition:

- *Remember that acquiring a second language is a process* (Ellis, 2008; Gass, 2013). When considering which language objectives to include in a lesson and how to write them, be sure to reflect a range from process-oriented to performance-oriented statements over time so that children have a chance to explore and then practice before demonstrating mastery of an objective. The following objectives from a SIOP language arts class show the progression of objectives that might be taught over several days:

  Students will be able to

  1. Recognize figurative language in text (Day 1)
  2. Discuss the functions of figurative language such as similes and metaphors (Days 1–2)
  3. Write examples for types of figurative language (Day 2)
  4. Write a character description that incorporates figurative language (Days 3–4)

  For the first lesson (Day 1), children learn to recognize figurative language in text, focusing on descriptive terms and key words *like* and *as*. The class discusses the purpose of figurative language and how similes and metaphors differ. After that (Day 2), they might discuss reasons why authors use figurative language and then generate their own examples in decontextualized sentences. On Day 3 they write for an authentic purpose, like a book or movie review, and draft a paragraph describing a character using figurative language. On Day 4 the teacher might have students edit their paragraphs and then share some aloud.

  Figure 2.2 displays possible verbs for objective statements that reflect this process-to-performance continuum.

- *Teach both receptive and productive language skills from the start.* English learners tend to develop receptive skills (listening and reading) faster than productive skills (speaking and writing), but all the skills should be worked on in a symbiotic manner. Children don't have to learn to speak, for instance, before they learn to read and write (August & Shanahan, 2006; Saunders & Goldenberg, 2010).

FIGURE 2.2 Process-to-Performance Verbs

Process-Oriented -------➤------➤------➤ *Performance-Oriented*

Explore	Define	
Listen to		Draft
Recognize		Write
Discuss in small groups		Give an oral presentation
		Edit

- *Recognize the importance of oral language practice; be sure you do not focus your objectives solely on reading and writing.* We know from research (Cloud, Genesee, & Hamayan, 2009; Goldenberg, 2008) that the absence of planned speaking practice—be it formal or informal—by English learners in content classrooms is detrimental to their development of academic English. Gibbons (2015) argues that skillful teachers should take advantage of oral interaction to move learners from informal, everyday explanations of a content topic (e.g., a scientific process) to the more specialized academic register of the formal written and spoken code.

- *Focus on function* and *form to move students to advanced levels of academic English and full proficiency, and consequently to set them up to be college and career ready.* ESL and English language arts teachers play important roles in making this happen, but teachers should not let children coast in class during the other subjects. If some English learners are ready to produce more sophisticated language (e.g., during an oral presentation, in a science fair project), they should be challenged to do so. SIOP teachers might make the development of specialized grammar and lexical forms related to their subject area part of their scope and sequence of language objectives (Dutro & Kinsella, 2010; Ellis, 2006; Hinkel, 2006; Schleppegrell, 2004; Schleppegrell, Achugar, & Orteíza, 2004; Turkan, de Oliveira, Lee, & Phelps, 2014).

- *Recognize that the more exposure students have to academic language and the more time they spend using it, the faster they will develop* **language proficiency** (Echevarría & Graves, 2010; Gass, 2013; Saunders & Goldenberg, 2010). If the ESL teacher is the only educator who works on language development with English learners during the school day, less progress will be made than if the grade-level classroom teachers also attend to language development and practice (Snow & Katz, 2010).

- *Assess the language objectives to determine if students are making progress toward mastery.* You can plan for multi-level responses from the children according to their proficiency in English. For example, use group response techniques (e.g., thumbs-up/thumbs-down), gestures, sketches, or labeling for children who are in the early stages of **English language development**. For students who are more proficient, incorporate activities that involve partner work and small-group assignments so that English learners can practice their English in a less threatening setting. Accept approximations and multiple-word responses rather than complete sentences from children at early stages of English development, but expect English learners with greater proficiency to give answers in one or two complete sentences. This practice develops language skills because it requires children to move beyond what may be their comfort zone in using English. You will find this topic discussed in more detail in Chapter 9.

Sources of Language Objectives. As you plan, it is helpful to know about sources of language objectives.

Watch this video to learn how the WIDA standards can be used as a source for planning language objectives across subject areas. What other sources do you have access to?

- *State English language proficiency (ELP) standards.* This is the place to start so that your objectives will be aligned to the language goals your state has set for English learners.
  - ◆ Additional sources are the WIDA and ELPA standards mentioned in Chapter 1 (if you are in a state that does not use them).
  - ◆ The WIDA consortium has compiled a list of "Can Do" descriptors that can help teachers identify the kind of language tasks students should be able to perform according to five differing levels of English proficiency and different grade-level clusters. (To view these descriptors, navigate to the "Can Do" page at www.wida.us.)
- *State and **Common Core English language arts standards.*** Ideas for objectives will be found in all of these official documents as well as in local district curricula and instructional materials. Some states also have content area standards that include a strand focused on communication.
- *Colleagues.* One critically important source for successful content and language integration is your colleagues.
  - ◆ If you are a grade-level classroom teacher, pair up with an ESL or bilingual teacher. Tap his or her expertise for language topics and knowledge of the English learners' academic language needs.
  - ◆ If you are an ESL or reading teacher, you have a plethora of language objectives at your disposal. Partner with one or more classroom teachers to identify content objectives and lesson tasks that the English learners need assistance with and align those content goals to your language objectives. You may want to focus on thematic units to cover a variety of content topics or focus on one subject area per quarter. (See Lacina, Levine, and Sowa 2006, and TESOL 2013 for examples of collaboration.)
- *The course textbook and other materials.* By reviewing instructional materials to be used in class, you can see if there are language skills and academic vocabulary that the children need to develop in order to comprehend the information.

Identifying and Writing Content and Language Objectives

Lesson objectives derive from state standards, but transforming standards into objectives is not an easy process. A teacher has to break down the standards into learning chunks and also consider the proficiency levels of the children. Then the objectives must be written as learning targets for students using language that they understand.[1]

Every content and language objective should evolve from the lesson topic and be part of the instructional plan. After you write content and language objectives, post

---

[1] See *Developing Academic Language with the SIOP® Model* (Short & Echevarría, 2016) for detailed information on selecting and writing language objectives for SIOP lessons and for activities to help you apply the guidelines to your own classes.

them, and discuss them with the children at the start of class, you must, at some point in the lesson, provide explicit instruction on these objectives. We know from research that explicit instruction speeds up language development (Gass, 2013). Children then need practice opportunities aligned to the objectives and later should be assessed on their progress toward meeting the objectives at the close of the lesson. In sum, each objective is what we want the students to learn, and each needs explicit attention.

Consider this science standard about life processes: "The student will investigate and understand the life processes of plants, including photosynthesis and dormancy." Posting it as an objective word for word in an upper elementary science classroom would not be helpful for your students, and you would need several lessons to address this standard well.

Suppose you have newcomers or children with interrupted educational backgrounds. You might have to begin with the basics and write a content objective like "Identify parts of a plant and their functions." When you explain it, you might elaborate, *"Today you will learn about parts of a plant* (showing a picture or real plant). *You will be able to identify the parts* (point to the different parts) *and tell what the parts do* (e.g., *Leaves make food for the plant.*)."

After you write an appropriate content objective for the newcomers based on that standard, you will need to plan the lesson and determine a language objective. One teacher we worked with decided the language objective would be "Students will represent a plant part visually and write a sentence about its function." She augmented the science lesson with a walking field trip. In a park near the school, she and her newcomer students each found one living plant and sketched it.

Then they collected plants and plant parts, such as fallen leaves, twigs, stems, roots, and so forth. Back in the classroom, triads were given one part to become familiar with. They were to prepare a poster including a close-up illustration of the plant part and a caption telling what function the part plays for the plant. The teacher had bookmarked some Web sites for the groups on the class computer and also had some photographic picture books on plants in her classroom library. She then taught them the definition of "function." To support the language objective, she provided a sentence stem for children to use in writing their caption: "This _____ helps the plant because it _____."

When children practice objectives that are explicit learning targets, they advance their knowledge base. Objectives, it is critical to understand, are not activities; they are not the agenda on the board nor the tasks the students do during the lesson. Objectives are the learning targets related to the content and language knowledge students must acquire, and they are necessary for children to be able to accomplish the activities and master the curriculum.

> **Remember:** Writing an agenda or list of activities on the board is not the same as writing the content and language objectives!

Categories of Language Objectives.   Language objectives should be planned to meet learning goals and prepare children for the type of academic language they need to understand the content and perform the activities in the lesson. But the activities alone are not language objectives, although they often provide language practice. For example, completing a Venn diagram is not an objective. Reading a text to find and record similarities and differences between two things, or using comparative language to discuss similarities and differences would be language objectives. The Venn diagram might be a tool used to capture or talk about information but it is not the learning target.

In some lessons, language objectives may focus on developing students' vocabulary, introducing new words and concepts, or teaching word structure to help English learners discern the meaning of new words. Other lessons may lend themselves to practice with reading comprehension skills or the writing process. Sometimes objectives will highlight functional language use, such as how to request information, justify opinions, negotiate meaning, provide detailed explanations, and so forth. Higher-order thinking skills, such as articulating predictions or hypotheses, stating conclusions, summarizing information, and analyzing an author's purpose can be tied to language objectives, too. Sometimes specific grammar points can be taught as well; for example, learning about capitalization when studying famous historical events and persons.

We suggest you draw from the following four categories when generating language objectives.

- **Academic Vocabulary.** Key words needed to discuss, read, or write about the topic of the lesson (e.g., names of important people, places, and events; scientific and mathematical terms; social studies or health concepts) can be the focus of language objectives. Vocabulary for a lesson can be drawn from three subcategories, which are described in detail in Chapter 3:

  - *Content vocabulary:* These key words and technical terms are subject specific. They are often the highlighted words in textbooks. Children need them to understand lesson concepts, but they are generally low-frequency words (i.e., not regularly used outside of the classroom). (Ask yourself: When was the last time you used *magma* or *phloem* in conversation?)

  - *General academic vocabulary:* These words include cross-curricular academic terms (e.g., *circumstances, impact, observe*), transition words and logical connectors (e.g., *however, because, next*), and language function words (e.g., *compare, persuade*). This category includes medium- and high-frequency words that are used in academic and social conversations.

  - *Word parts:* This category refers to roots, prefixes, suffixes, and base words. Attention to the structure of words can help expand a student's vocabulary knowledge considerably. For example, if a child knows that *re* is the prefix meaning "to repeat," she can begin to guess the meaning of words like *reread, rewrite,* and *recycle.*

- **Language Skills and Functions.** This category reflects the ways children use language in the lesson.

  - Students are expected to read, write, listen, and speak, but how well they do so varies. English learners need some direct instruction in these language skills, along with opportunities to practice. The skills taught need to link to the topic of the lesson. In a language arts class, for example, will students need to read and find key details in the text to cite as evidence? In social studies, will they need to listen to an audio recording of a speech by an historical figure? In science class, will they have to record their observations during an experiment?

- ◆ Any lesson may also call for children to use language for a specific purpose—to *describe*, *compare*, or *predict*, for example. English learners need instruction here as well, particularly in ways to articulate their descriptions or comparisons or predictions.

- **Language Structures or Grammar.** Teachers can pay attention to the language structures in the written or spoken discourse of their subjects and teach children the structures that are widely used. For example, students might be struggling with a text that includes the passive voice, imperatives, or if-then sentences. If so, the teacher may teach students how to interpret these sentences. If you are an ESL teacher, this category might offer the opportunity to teach grammatical forms that will really advance your students' language proficiency.

- **Language Learning Strategies.** This category provides a way for teachers to give children resources to learn on their own. **Learning strategies** to be taught may include
  - ◆ corrective strategies (e.g., reread confusing text),
  - ◆ self-monitoring strategies (e.g., make and confirm predictions),
  - ◆ prereading strategies (e.g., preview headings, relate to personal experience),
  - ◆ language practice strategies (e.g., repeat or rehearse phrases, imitate a native speaker), or
  - ◆ cognate strategies (e.g., teach students with Latin-based or Greek-based **native languages** to consider cognates when they see new academic terms). More discussion on strategies is found in Chapter 5.

Selecting Potential Language Objectives. One of the difficulties teachers face is narrowing down the wide range of possible language objectives. English learners need lots of academic language development, so how should a teacher select one or two language targets for a lesson? We suggest that you think about how language will be used in your lesson: in texts (reading passages and instructions), in talk (your speech and student discussions), in tasks (activities and assignments), and in tests. While doing this, also consider the four categories of language objectives. Where might your students need assistance? Given the content topic and your knowledge of the students' level of academic language acquisition, what objective(s) might be written that complements the topic and that you will explicitly address in the lesson?

A colleague of ours, Amy Washam (personal communication), who is a very experienced SIOP professional developer, uses some effective techniques to help teachers conceptualize academic language in their lesson planning process:

First, I ask teachers what they would need in order to learn another language fluently enough to attend a graduate course in a country where that language is spoken. Teachers brainstorm ideas, which often include a tutor, a specialized glossary of key terms in the course, extra time spent in the country before the class starts practicing the language, and language learning programs on tape that they can listen to over and over.

I tell them that what they listed—modeling, repetition, feedback, practice speaking the language—are all good language activities for their English learners. But they also need to have a language target for each activity.

So next I ask teachers to think of an English learner they have worked with recently and write down all of the reasons this student is not considered English proficient in their class. Common reasons cited are poor reading comprehension, technical difficulties in writing, problems with English pronunciation, and limited background knowledge which results in limited academic vocabulary.

My response at this point is, "The reasons you listed for your student not being classified as English proficient are your language objectives. You can have language objectives for reading comprehension, academic vocabulary development, grammar, and even pronunciation." I then push them to think about their planning and ask, "Is it more important for this student to work on the content standards in their classes or the list of skills that you say this student does not possess yet in English?"

Now they typically say both are important. So we move to the next step: I ask them to respond to these questions:

1. What language will children need to know and use to accomplish this lesson's content objectives?

2. How can I move my students' English language knowledge forward in this lesson?

Writing Language Objectives.   In Figure 2.3, we show how language objectives might be written for these four categories. One column shows language objectives for a first-grade social studies class. The next column shows language objectives for a third-grade math lesson on geometric shapes. The third column shows language objectives for a fifth-grade language arts class. These objectives are illustrative and would not all be addressed in one lesson; instead, they could be used over a series of lessons.

Remember that it is important to include a variety of language objectives over the course of each week. Many teachers feel comfortable teaching vocabulary as their language objective. This is a good first step, but it is not the complete picture of the language development our English learners need to be successful in school and beyond.

As you write your objectives, keep the verbs in Figure 2.4 on page 42 in mind. You'll see that they are all active verbs. In SIOP lessons, you should avoid using verbs like *learn*, *know*, and *understand* because the processes are not observable. Although the verbs in the chart are not exclusive to one category or another, they are more common to the category presented. Over time, add to this list to further distinguish between the content and language goals of your lesson.

For those of you who are new to writing language objectives, we want to offer the following language frames as scaffolds (Short & Echevarría, 2016). To complete them, follow the suggestions we made earlier: Think about which category of academic language your students need to learn and where in the lesson (e.g., the text, talk) the language will be needed or practiced. Use this analysis to determine a

FIGURE 2.3 Categories and Examples for Developing Language Objectives

Type of Language Objective	Grade 1 Social Studies Example	Grade 3 Math Example	Grade 5 Language Arts Example
Academic Vocabulary →	We will use key words (e.g., *park, library, school, apartment building, house*) and prepositions (e.g., *next to, beside, across*) to describe locations in the neighborhood.	Students will be able to define the terms *square, rectangle, rhombus, trapezoid,* and *parallelogram* orally and in writing.	Students will be able to contrast figurative and literal expressions.
What it means instructionally	Teacher teaches students key terms and prepositions and models how to use them to describe the locations of different buildings in the neighborhood.	Teacher teaches (or reminds) students how to define a term: state attributes, give an example, draw a picture, or use it in a sentence.	Using examples (e.g., "My shirt is blue" and "My shirt is like the summer sky"), the teacher explains the difference between figurative and literal language. Students evaluate sample statements as figurative or literal and explain why.
Language Skills and Functions →	We will compare features of neighborhood locations using comparative phrases.	Students will be able to listen to the teacher's descriptions in order to draw different types of parallelograms.	Students will be able to express an author's purpose and cite text evidence.
What it means instructionally	Teacher teaches comparative language frames, such as "Both ___ and ___ have ___," and "___ and ___ are alike/different because ___."	Teacher teaches a listening comprehension skill—paying attention to key words—and asks students to draw the shapes or construct them on a geoboard.	Teacher expresses an author's purpose for a particular text. She cites evidence in the text and teaches frames like "The author's purpose is to ___. We know this because ___," and "On page ___, the author wants to tell us about ___." Students apply the frames to other texts.
Language Structures or Grammar →	We will use singular and plural nouns with past tense irregular verbs.	Students will be able to use comparative phrases, such as *greater than, larger than, smaller than, less than,* and *equal to* orally and in writing to compare geometric figures and angles.	Students will be able to use conjunctions to join ideas in compound sentences.
What it means instructionally	Teacher introduces (or reviews) the difference between singular and plural nouns (using neighborhood examples) and models sentences with past tense irregular verb forms (e.g., "I went to two stores on Ash Street.").	Teacher introduces (or reviews) these comparative phrases and also shows the corresponding mathematical symbols (i.e., $>$, $<$, and $=$).	Teacher introduces (or reviews) conjunctions and their use to create sentences with two related ideas. Students practice writing such sentences.
Language Learning Strategies →	We will listen for key words to mark a journey on a map and monitor our result.	Students will be able to visualize and relate the geometric shapes to their lives.	Students will be able to rehearse an oral presentation with a peer.
What it means instructionally	Teacher models a jigsaw activity where one student gives directions orally and a partner records the route on a map. The pairs check for accuracy.	Teacher explains how to visualize and make a personal connection and how to articulate the mental image, using a think-aloud technique.	Teacher teaches class how to listen and give feedback to an oral presentation based on certain criteria (e.g., word choice, intonation) and provides class time for rehearsing.

Identifying and Writing Content and Language Objectives

| FIGURE 2.4 | Sample Verbs for Writing Content and Language Objectives |

Verbs for Content Objectives	Verbs for Language Objectives
Identify	Listen for
Solve	Retell
Investigate	Define
Distinguish	Find the main idea
Hypothesize	Compare
Create	Summarize
Select	Rehearse
Draw conclusions about	Persuade
Determine	Write
Find	Draft
Calculate	Defend a position on
Observe	Describe

language target. Then include the language target with a language function in a statement like one of the following:

A: **Students will <u>(function: active verb phrase)</u> using/with (*<u>language target</u>*).**

B: **Students will [use] (*<u>language target</u>*) to <u>(function: active verb phrase)</u>.**

C: **Students will (*<u>language target as active verb</u>*) [with/to___].**

Here are some examples of these objectives from the frames above:

A: Students will explain a science experiment using if-then statements.

B: Students will use cognates to determine word meaning.

C: Students will read to find the main idea.

Note that even if you have students with mixed levels of English proficiency in class, do not write different language objectives for each proficiency level. Instead, write an objective that all children should attain based on the content concepts in the lesson, but adjust the intended outcome or performance to match the students' ability levels. Some children may master the objective by the end of the lesson; others will be at some point on a path toward mastery.

Connecting Content and Language Objectives.   Sometimes the language and content objectives may be closely linked as in the following upper elementary math lesson:

- Students will solve word problems using a two-step process.
- Students will write a word problem requiring a two-step process for a classmate to solve.

The first statement is the content objective. It focuses on a mathematical procedure. The second is the language objective, wherein children practice mathematical writing skills.

At other times, the language objective might extend the content knowledge, as in this social studies lesson:

- Students will explain the results of the American Revolution.
- Students will use if-then statements to suggest alternative results to the American Revolution.

In this lesson, students may review their notes and textbook to determine the result of the American Revolution and explain it orally or in writing. The teacher may then ask children to imagine a different result and describe the situation in the colonies with phrases like "If the British won the war, then…" and "If the colonists did not write the Declaration of Independence, then…."

For language arts and reading teachers, distinguishing language and content objectives can be tricky. Certain curriculum concepts like *plot* and *setting* are clearly candidates for content objectives because they are specific to the language arts subject, but other possibilities like "produce writing that conveys a clear point of view" could be either a language or a content objective. It could even be a language objective in a history class.

Despite possible overlap, we advise language arts and reading teachers to consistently identify both a content and a language objective for each lesson, even if some might be placed in either category. You may decide, for instance, that reading and writing-related objectives will be content objectives and speaking and listening targets will be language objectives. Because we are aiming for whole-school implementation of the SIOP Model, having students recognize and expect both types of objectives in all their classes is a valuable goal.

Checking Your Objectives.   After you have written your content and language objectives, we suggest you refer to this checklist to evaluate them:

_____ The objectives are aligned to state or district standards.

_____ The objectives are observable.

_____ The objectives are written and will be stated simply in language children can understand.

_____ The objectives are written in terms of student learning.

_____ The content objective is related to the key concept of the lesson.

_____ The language objective promotes student academic language growth (i.e., it is not something most students already do well).

_____ The language objective connects clearly with the lesson topic or lesson activities.

_____ The objectives are measurable. I have a plan for assessing student progress on meeting these objectives during the lesson.

SIOP® FEATURE 3:

Content Concepts Appropriate for Age and Educational Background Level of Students

SIOP teachers must carefully consider the content concepts they wish to teach, and use district curriculum guidelines and grade-level content standards as guides. In SIOP classrooms, this entails ensuring that although materials may be adapted to meet the needs of English learners, the content is not diminished. When planning lessons around content concepts, consider the following:

- the children' first language literacy,
- their English language proficiency,
- their schooling backgrounds and academic preparation for grade-level work,
- their background knowledge of the topic,
- the cultural and age appropriateness of instructional materials, and
- the difficulty level of any text or other material to be read.

Our goal as SIOP teachers is to provide the grade-level curriculum to our English learners. By employing the type of techniques we propose in the SIOP Model, teachers skillfully make that content comprehensible to them. Sometimes we adapt the materials being read or the materials used to accomplish a task. The following considerations are worth keeping in mind.

- In general, it is inappropriate to use the curriculum materials and books from much earlier grades. Students also deserve books with age-appropriate illustrations. As necessary, the teacher should provide the **scaffolding** that English learners need to understand the content concepts and complex text of the materials used in the lesson.
- In some cases, children with major gaps in their educational backgrounds may be placed in newcomer programs or specialized classes that pull objectives and content concepts from earlier grades in order to provide the foundational knowledge the students need to perform grade-level work successfully and catch up to their classmates (Short & Boyson, 2012). Ideally, specialized courses would be developed to accelerate the learning of children with limited formal schooling; for example, FAST Math was developed by Fairfax County (VA) Public Schools (Helman & Buchanan, 1993) to help students gain several years' worth of mathematics instruction in six months or one year.
- We should also be mindful of concepts our English learners may have already acquired through their life experiences or prior schooling. Sometimes, an illustration or demonstration can help children recall a concept and then the teacher can help them learn new English words to describe the concept and add to their understanding of it. As Torgesen and colleagues (2007) point out, "ELLs who already know and understand a concept in their first language have a far simpler task to develop language for the concept in English than do students who lack knowledge of the concept in either language" (p. 92).

- To help children make connections to the content topics, reflect on the amount of background knowledge needed to learn and apply the concepts, and plan ways to build or activate students' prior knowledge related to them. For example, fourth-grade students typically learn about magnetism, yet some newly arrived children may not have studied this concept. Rather than diminish the content, use what prior knowledge students do have, perhaps about attraction, and then explicitly build background on magnetism as a foundation for the lesson.

- Another way to build background for a small group of learners is through a minilesson that precedes the regular whole-class lesson (Rance-Roney, 2010; Vogt, 2000). This minilesson provides a "jump-start" by reviewing key background concepts and introducing vocabulary. It develops context and gives access to children who may lack appropriate background knowledge or experience with the grade-level content concepts. It can be accomplished in a number of ways:

  - leading a picture or text "walk" through the reading material,
  - watching a video clip online,
  - engaging students in simulations or role-plays,
  - having learners participate in hands-on experiential activities,
  - asking peer tutors to teach some of the requisite background information, and
  - teaching the minilesson in the students' native language.

- In schools where an ESL teacher and a classroom teacher work collaboratively with the same group of children, the ESL teacher can offer lessons that build background and vocabulary before the English learners study the topic in their regular class.

SIOP® FEATURE 4:

Supplementary Materials Used to a High Degree, Making the Lesson Clear and Meaningful

Information that is embedded in context allows English learners to understand and complete more cognitively demanding tasks. Effective SIOP instruction involves the use of many supplementary materials that support the core curriculum and contextualize learning. This is especially important for students who do not have grade-level academic backgrounds and/or who have language and learning difficulties. Because lectures and pencil-and-paper activities centered on a text are often difficult for these children, remember to plan for supplementary materials that will enhance meaning and clarify confusing concepts, making lessons more relevant.

A variety of supplementary materials also support different learning styles and multiple intelligences because information and concepts are presented in a multifaceted manner. Children can see, hear, feel, perform, create, and participate in order to make connections and construct relevant meanings. The use of technology (e.g., interactive whiteboards, pre-loaded apps on tablets) and multimedia can enhance

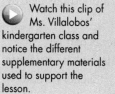

Watch this clip of Ms. Villalobos' kindergarten class and notice the different supplementary materials used to support the lesson.

student understanding and engagement with the content topics and related language practice opportunities.

Supplementary materials can help create a **culturally responsive** classroom as well (Nieto & Bode, 2008). They can provide a real-life context and enable students to bridge prior experiences from their own backgrounds with new learning.

Examples of supplementary materials and resources that can be used to create context and support content concepts include the following:

- **Hands-on Manipulatives:** These can include anything from counter chips for math to microscopes for science to interactive maps for social studies. Manipulating objects physically can reduce the language load of an activity; beginning-level students in particular can still participate and demonstrate their understanding.

- **Realia:** These are real-life objects that enable children to make connections to their own lives. Examples include play money (coins and bills) for a unit on money; **realia** such as photos, recordings, and artifacts for a social studies unit; or nutrition labels on food products for a health unit.

- **Pictures and Visuals:** Photographs and illustrations are available that depict nearly any object, process, or setting. Web sites, magazines, commercial photos, and hand drawings can provide visual support for a wide variety of content and vocabulary concepts and can build background knowledge. Models, graphs, charts, timelines, maps, and bulletin board displays also convey information. Many teachers now have electronic document viewers that they use to display book pages, photos, and more to the class. They also use PowerPoint slides and interactive whiteboards. Children with diverse abilities often have difficulty processing an inordinate amount of auditory information, and so instruction that is supported with visual clues is more beneficial to them.

- **Multimedia:** A wide variety of multimedia materials are available to enhance teaching and learning. These range from simple audio recordings to DVDs, interactive CD-ROMs, podcasts, and an increasing number of resources available on the Internet. Brief video clips at sites like www.discoveryeducation.com, www.pbs.com, and www.nationalgeographic.com are effective tools. For some children and tasks, media in the students' native language may be a valuable source of information, with audio links as well as written text. It is important to preview Web sites for appropriateness and readability, especially when using them with beginning and intermediate-level students or young learners.

- **Demonstrations:** Demonstrations provide visual support and modeling for English learners. If you have a lesson task that includes supplementary materials, then you can scaffold information by carefully planning demonstrations that model how to use the materials and follow directions. Children can then practice these steps in groups or alone, with you or other experienced individuals nearby to assist as needed.

- **Related Literature:** A wide variety of fiction and nonfiction texts can be included to support content teaching, including material written in the students' native languages or with accompanying audio versions. Many teachers create class libraries with trade books and leveled readers on key topics. Some teachers ask librarians to set aside books on related topics as well.[2] Children can read them as supplements to the textbook. They offer a motivating way to look at a topic in more depth. Class libraries can promote more independent reading among students, which is valuable for vocabulary development and reading comprehension practice.

- **Hi-lo Readers and Thematic Sets:** Some publishers offer classic literature as well as fiction and nonfiction selections in a hi-lo format. The stories are of high interest but have lower readability levels and tend to include many visuals and a glossary. Some books are grouped into thematic sets (e.g., Civil Rights Leaders Around the World) and can accompany different content area courses. The books in each set cover unique but related topics and are written at different reading levels (e.g., one below-level book, two on-level books, one above-level book). Other book sets may have several versions of the same book available, each written at a different reading level. These resources are useful for classes that have children with multiple proficiency levels in English.

- **Chapter Summaries:** Some textbook publishers provide one-page summaries of each chapter, which present the key ideas. The summaries are often available in Spanish and sometimes in other languages as well. They can be used to preview the topic or to review it afterward.

- **Adapted Text:** A type of supplementary reading material that can be very effective for English learners as well as struggling readers is adapted text. Without significantly diminishing the content concepts, a piece of text is adapted to reduce the reading level demands.[3] Complicated, lengthy sentences with specialized terminology may be rewritten in smaller chunks. Definitions are given for difficult vocabulary in context. Please note that we are not advocating "dumbing down" the textbook, an approach that in the past yielded easy-to-read materials with few content concepts left intact. Rather, we suggest that the major concepts be retained, but the reading level demands of the text be aligned to the learners' abilities.

SIOP® FEATURE 5:

Adaptation of Content to All Levels of Student Proficiency

In many schools, teachers are required to use textbooks that are too difficult for English learners to read. Earlier we discussed the problem of "watering down" text to the point where all students can read it; namely that content concepts are frequently lost when the text is adapted in this way. However, we also know English learners cannot be expected to learn all content information by listening to lectures.

Therefore, we must find ways to make the text and other resource materials accessible for all children, adapting them so that the content concepts are left intact.

---

[2]See Short, Cloud, Morris, and Motta (2012) to learn about a project organizing library books by lesson topic and English proficiency level and creating bookmarks for book sets.
[3]Some Web sites like *www.newsela.com* offer articles on a wide variety of topics that have already been adapted.

Several ways of doing this have been recommended for students who have reading difficulties (Readence, Bean, & Baldwin, 2012; Ruddell, 2007; Vacca, Vacca, & Mraz, 2010), and they work equally well for English learners. These approaches can be used throughout a lesson, as a prereading instructional strategy, as an aid during reading, and as a postreading method for organizing newly learned information.

Native language supports can help with adapting written content, too. If some children are literate in their native language, texts written in that language may be used to supplement a textbook or clarify key concepts. Students may conduct research using native language materials and share the information with classmates in English. Increasingly, the Internet offers native language Web sites, especially for the more commonly taught languages, and authentic materials such as newspapers can be found online. For students who are not literate in their native language but have oral skills, native language broadcasts, podcasts, and audio books, along with access to knowledgeable adults who speak their language may be additional sources of information.

Suggestions for adapting text to make it more accessible include the following:

- **Summarizing the text to focus on the key points of information:** This approach can help focus the learning on key historical events, steps for solving a math problem, or understanding the plot in a story. The new text might be written as an outline, a list of bulleted points, or a graphic organizer like a flow chart.
- **Elaborating the text to add information:** This approach may make a text longer, but the adapter can embed definitions of difficult words or provide more background information.

Although it is time consuming, rewriting text is an effective modification of curricular materials because information can be organized either in small sequential steps or in other logical chunks of information. Ideally, rewritten paragraphs should include a topic sentence with several sentences providing supporting details. Maintaining a consistent format promotes easier reading for information-seeking purposes. All sentences included in the rewritten text should be direct and relevant to the subject. In the following example, a paragraph of original text is taken from an anthology theme in a reading series. This passage was excerpted from a piece of nonfiction literature, *Into the Mummy's Tomb*, written by Nicholas Reeves.

Original text: "Tutankhamen's mummy bore a magnificent mask of burnished gold, which covered its face and shoulders. Its head cloth was inlaid with blue glass. The vulture and cobra on its forehead, ready to spit fire at the pharaoh's enemies, were of solid gold" (Reeves, N., & Froman, N., 1992).

We have rewritten the original text as follows:

Adapted text: "King Tutankhamen's mummy wore a magnificent mask, made of very shiny gold. It covered the face and shoulders of the body. The part of the mask over the forehead looked like a gold head cloth. Blue glass was sewn into the head cloth. Shapes of a vulture (a type of bird) and a cobra (a type of snake) were above the eyes on the mask. They were made of solid gold. They looked like they could attack King Tut's enemies."

As you compare the texts, you will see some thought was involved in the rewrite. Some words, like "magnificent," are Latin cognates and should be retained if you have students who speak a language such as Spanish, French, or Portuguese. Some patterns and expressions are repeated, such as "made of," because once children figure them out, they can read more fluently the next time they encounter them. Here are some guiding principles to keep in mind when rewriting text:

- Decide what students need to learn from the text.
- Focus on concrete concepts first, then abstract.
- Reduce nonessential details.
- Relate new information to children's experiences (e.g., include a familiar analogy).
- Use visual representations—maps, charts, timelines, outlines.
- Simplify vocabulary, but keep key concepts and technical terms.
- Elaborate to explain concepts if necessary.
- Check word choice and sentence order (e.g., for a question, begin with the question word; for an *if-then* statement, begin with the *if* clause).

Obviously, adapting text like this takes time, and it is not easy to do. Note here that the adapted version is slightly longer than the original, which often happens when definitions are embedded. If you have a large number of English learners in your classroom, adapted text can be very beneficial, and it is worth the time and effort to be able to provide children with more accessible material. Be sure to have a colleague read the adapted text to make sure it clarifies rather than confuses the content.

So far, we have discussed adapting the text used to deliver content information. Other types of adaptations in class may involve the worksheets and other instructional supports that students use to complete a task. Some children might benefit from having a word bank available while they are writing a summary or paragraph about a topic while others will not need that support. If the students are to take notes in a T-chart format (e.g., main ideas in left column and key details in right), some students might use a blank chart and others might have a version that is partially completed. In other words, by differentiating the materials you can adapt the content to student proficiency levels.

SIOP® FEATURE 6:

Meaningful Activities That Integrate Lesson Concepts with Language Practice Opportunities for Reading, Writing, Listening, and/or Speaking

To the extent possible, lesson activities should be planned to promote language development in all skills while English learners are mastering content objectives. We want to provide oral and written language practice that is relevant to the lesson concepts, but remember: Activities that generate language practice are not language objectives.

Language objectives require explicit instruction, for example, about a language skill or structure needed to accomplish the activities.

English learners are more successful when they are able to make connections between what they know and what they are learning by relating classroom experiences to their own lives. These meaningful experiences are often described as "authentic," because they represent a reality for students. That is, classroom experiences mirror what actually occurs in the learner's world. Authentic, meaningful experiences are especially important for English learners because they are learning to attach labels and terms to things already familiar to them. Their learning becomes situated rather than abstract when they are provided with the opportunity to actually experience what they are being taught.

Too often, however, English learners have been assigned activities that are not meaningful and are unrelated to the content and activities pursued by the other English proficient students in their classes. It is essential that content standards that apply to children with English proficiency also apply to English learners, and that the planned activities reflect and support these standards.

Consider a class of third-grade children studying insects—butterflies in particular. While the rest of the class learns the scientific names and habitats of various kinds of butterflies, the teacher has the beginning-level English learners color and cut out pictures of butterflies to make a mobile. This activity is neither authentic nor relevant for these students. In this instance, the teacher obviously has not provided meaningful activities that support the grade-level science content standards.

As you continue to read this chapter and the remaining ones, you will find a host of teaching ideas for meaningful activities that integrate the concepts with language practice. The resources listed in Appendix D provide many more as well.

Teaching Ideas for Lesson Preparation

Watch this video to see Amy Collinge, a first-grade teacher, discuss the value of presenting objectives to the students. How do the posted objectives help her, and how do they help her students? *https://www. youtube.com/ watch?v=TMgeoXkOViw*

- **Presenting Objectives to the Class.** Effective SIOP teachers do more than just go through the motions by writing the objectives on the board and reading them quickly to the class. Getting the children involved in thinking about the objectives provides a teaching opportunity that should not be squandered. Here are some ways to make the presentation of objectives more productive. Other ideas can be found in Echevarría, Vogt, and Short (2010, p. 21).

  ◆ Ask students to pick out important words from the objective and highlight them—for example, the verbs and nouns.

  ◆ Ask students to paraphrase the objectives with a partner, each taking a turn, using the frame: "We will _____."

  ◆ Present the objective and then do a Think-Pair-Share, asking students to predict some of the things they think they will be doing for the lesson that day.

- **Number 1, 2, 3 for Self-Assessment of Objectives** (Short, Vogt, & Echevarría, 2011a, p. 71; Vogt & Echevarría, 2008, p. 179). In this activity, children are asked to diagnose their knowledge about a topic and then take some responsibility for learning new information during the lesson. At the beginning of the lesson, display the objectives and ask students to rate themselves on how well they understand each one. You may read each aloud and have children show with their fingers which of the following ratings fit:

1. I understand this concept.

2. It looks familiar, or I have studied something like this before.

3. I don't know this.

At the end of the lesson, return to the objectives and ask students to rate again, "How well did you meet the objective today?"

1. I can teach the concept to someone else.

2. I understand most of it, but not everything.

3. I don't understand completely. I need more time/practice/examples.

- **Jigsaw Text Reading** (Aronson et al., 1977). Originally designed as a cooperative learning activity for all students, Jigsaw works well with English learners when there is a difficult-to-read text.

  1. Form cooperative learning "home" groups and then have one or two members from each group come together to form a new group of "experts."

  2. Assign each new "expert" group a different section of the text to read. This group can take turns reading the text aloud, have partners read to each other, or have group members read the text silently.

  3. Following the reading, each "expert" group reviews and discusses what was read, determining the essential information and key vocabulary. You may have a worksheet for them to complete to record key information.

  4. Check carefully with each "expert" group to make sure all members understand the material they have read.

  5. After you are confident that the "experts" know their assigned information, they return to their "home" groups and teach fellow group members what they learned. You may have another worksheet for the group to complete.

  This process scaffolds the learning of English learners because in both groups they are working with others to understand the text. Some classmates may have more background information on the topic. Text can be read with other students, reducing the demands of tackling lengthy sections alone. Depending on English proficiency, English learners may join an "expert" group individually or with a partner. It is important that you form the "expert" groups rather than letting the students choose their own group members.

- **Graphic Organizers.** These schematic diagrams are ubiquitous in today's classrooms, but that does not reduce their value. When preparing a lesson, teachers should think about possible graphic organizers that can provide conceptual clarity for information that is difficult to grasp. Graphic organizers help children identify key content concepts and make relationships among them (McLaughlin & Allen, 2009). They also provide children with visual clues they can use to supplement written or spoken words that may be hard to understand.

  ◆ When used *before reading*, graphic organizers can build background for complex or dense text.

◆ When used *concurrently with reading*, they focus students' attention and act as a guide to the information. They help students make connections (e.g., a Venn diagram can elicit comparisons), take notes, and understand the text structure (e.g., a timeline informs students the text will be organized chronologically).

◆ When used *after reading*, graphic organizers can be employed to record key content information or personal understandings and responses (Buehl, 2009). It can also be used as a prewriting tool when students have to "draw evidence from literary or information texts to support" written analysis or reflection, as noted in the writing standard from the Common Core.

Graphic organizers include story or text structure charts, Venn diagrams, story or text maps, timelines, discussion webs, word webs, thinking maps, and flow charts. Vogt and Echevarría (2008) include a number of templates for these graphic organizers.

● **Outlines.** Teacher-prepared outlines equip students with a form they can use for note-taking while reading dense portions of text, thus providing scaffolded support. These are especially helpful if major concepts, such as the Roman numeral level of the outline, are already filled in. The students can then add other information to the outline as they read. For some children, an outline that is entirely completed may be helpful to use as a guide to reading and understanding the text. Figure 2.5 shows an example of a scaffolded outline for a reading on the circulatory system.

FIGURE 2.5	Scaffolded Outline

The Circulatory System

I. Major Organs

  A. Heart
    1. Pumps blood throughout the body
    2. _____
  B. _____
    1. _____
    2. _____

II. Major Vessels

  A. Artery
    1. Takes blood away from heart
    2. _____
  B. Vein
    1. _____
    2. _____
  C. _____
    1. Connects arteries and veins
    2. _____

III. Types of Blood Cells

  A. Red blood cells
    1. _____
  B. _____
    1. Fights disease
  C. Platelets
    1. _____

● **Audio Supported Text.** Technology tools have the promise of making teaching more meaningful and rewarding. Through audio supports, teachers can help convey new information to students, scaffolding their understanding of the main concepts. Translation and interpretation tools have improved considerably in the past decade. Teachers can now type a sentence or paragraph about a concept to be studied into a Web site that provides translation services and have the concept rewritten in a student's native language. Many sites offer an audio version children can listen to. Several textbook publishers provide their texts on CDs or a Web site, too, and some have audio options in English or Spanish. Students are encouraged to listen to the audio text while they follow along in the book. For some children, multiple exposures to the audio version of the text may result in a more thorough understanding. Ideally, audio support should be available for both home and school use.

Our goal is to help students understand text and information presented orally in English, and our job is to teach the vocabulary, sentence structure, connections between sentences and paragraphs, and other necessary information to the children so they can increase their independence. If we can give them the gist of what they will be learning beforehand through their native language, we can then build on that new knowledge, and, with careful lesson planning, advance their English language skills and strengthen their content knowledge.

■ Differentiating Ideas for Multi-level Classes

The Lesson Preparation component offers teachers multiple opportunities to meet the needs of children with different abilities or language proficiency levels in their classrooms. Although it takes time to prepare a lesson for different groups of students, the investment pays off when all of your students learn the material and you do not have to reteach.

- The first step is knowing your students: their literacy skills both in English and in their native language, their schooling backgrounds (including the number of years they have completed in school), their learning styles, and their multiple intelligences. With this knowledge you can have realistic expectations about what they can accomplish and plan activities accordingly.

- The second step is to consider where in your lesson students will need some **differentiated instruction**.

  ◆ Is it when you introduce new content? If so, should you use different texts or a different presentation style? Should you modulate your speech? Preteach vocabulary?

  ◆ Is it when the learners must perform a task to practice or apply the new information or language target? If so, you may have to consider how you will group the children. Or you may assign different tasks to different groups (based on language proficiency or learning style, for example). You may prepare different handouts or other materials.

  ◆ Is it when you are checking for comprehension? Then you might plan leveled questions so you can address students in ways that they will be able to comprehend the question and have a chance to respond. Or you may pro-rate the assignment students complete (e.g., a one-page report versus a three-page report).

A few specific examples of differentiated activities follow.

- **Differentiated Sentence Starters** (Short, Vogt, & Echevarría, 2011a, pp. 30–31). This technique converts teacher-developed leveled questions into sentence starters that the students might use orally or in writing.

  1. Begin with the essential question of a lesson.
     For example: How do animals change as they grow?

  2. Write questions at a variety of levels of difficulty.
     For example: (a) How does a caterpillar change as it grows up?
     (b) Do all animals look different when they grow up? Explain.
     (c) Why do animals change as they grow?

  3. Convert the questions into sentence starters.
     For example: (a) When a caterpillar grows up, it . . . .
     (b) Yes, all animals look different because . . . . [or] No, not all animals look different. For example, ...
     (c) Animals change as they grow for several reasons. For one, ...

  4. Post the questions and have the children respond, either by self-selecting a sentence starter or by being assigned one.

- **Leveled Study Guides.**   Study guides to accompany assigned text or a unit's topics can be specifically written for diverse students' needs and their stages of language and literacy development. All students are expected to master the key concepts in the text or unit; however, some need support for comprehension while others can delve more deeply into the material on their own.

  - For students who can easily read the text material, write a study guide so they can extend and enrich their knowledge of the topic, and be sure to include challenging questions or tasks.

  - For those who need a little support, write a study guide with definitions and "hints" for unlocking the meaning to lead them through the text. Include fewer challenging questions and tasks.

  - For some English learners and struggling readers, create a study guide with brief summaries of the text or topic along with more manageable questions and tasks.

    Questions and tasks in the leveled study guides can be marked with asterisks as follows (from most manageable to most challenging):

  *   All children are to respond to these questions/tasks.
  **   Group 1 students are required to complete these questions/tasks.
  *** Group 2 students are required to complete these questions/tasks.

    Of course, the option to try the more challenging questions or statements should be open to all students.

- **Highlighted Text.**   Mark up a few reading anthologies or content textbooks in advance and reserve them for children acquiring English and/or those struggling with academic literacy[4]. Highlight major ideas, key concepts, topic sentences, important vocabulary, and summary statements using a highlight pen or highlight tape. Encourage students to first read only the highlighted sections. As confidence and reading ability improve, suggest they read more of the unmarked text. The purpose of highlighted text is to reduce the reading demands of the text while still maintaining key concepts and information.

Rating Lessons with the SIOP® Protocol

As we mentioned at the start of this chapter, we want to give you the opportunity to check your understanding of the SIOP features and learn to use the SIOP protocol, both for your own teaching and for coaching other teachers. So, we present scenarios of three teachers who teach the same concepts at the same grade level. After we describe each teacher's lesson, we will ask you to score the SIOP features for this component on a scale of 4–0, with 4 meaning the feature was well implemented in the lesson and 0 meaning it was not present. You will probably notice that some ratings for the features will seem quite obvious to you (usually those that merit 0, 1, or 4 on the scale), while others will be more challenging.

You must rate each feature as reliably as possible. That is, you need to develop consistency in your rating by having a clear understanding of each feature and how it "looks" during a SIOP lesson. Therefore, it is very important that you discuss with other teachers, coaches, or supervisors how you determined your ratings on the various SIOP features for the lessons depicted in this book. Some teachers work with a partner to establish **inter-rater reliability**. A number of schools have SIOP teacher groups that meet to read the scenarios and discuss the ratings. After these groups deepen their understanding of how the features should be implemented, they may watch video clips of teachers delivering instruction and rate those lessons, too. With practice in multiple classes and subject areas and discussion about the ratings you give, you will develop consistency in your ratings. Chapter 11 provides more explanation on scoring and interpreting the SIOP protocol.

Although we organized this book so that you can score the lessons as you read, in real life, you may not want to give numerical scores on each feature, especially as teachers are learning to implement the model. You can record comments and note if a feature is present or absent, and then use the protocol to offer targeted feedback. You will also notice that five of the 30 features have an NA option (see Appendix A). After years of research, we determined that those five (such as Adaptation of Content, in Lesson Preparation) might not be needed in every SIOP lesson. Adaptation of Content, for example, may not be necessary in a class with advanced English learners.

The Lesson

The lesson described below is intended to teach fourth-grade children about the Gold Rush, in particular, about the trails taken by the pioneers to get from the eastern and midwestern parts of the United States to California.

---

[4]Some teachers have asked parents who volunteer in the classroom to help them with the highlighting task.

The Gold Rush (Fourth Grade)

The classrooms described in the teaching scenarios in this chapter are in a suburban elementary school with heterogeneously mixed students. English learners represent approximately 30% of the student population, and the children speak a variety of languages. In the fourth-grade classrooms of teachers Ms. Chen, Mrs. Hargroves, and Mr. Hensen, the majority of the English learners are at the intermediate stage of English fluency.

As part of the state's fourth-grade social studies curriculum, Ms. Chen, Mrs. Hargroves, and Mr. Hensen have planned a unit on the California Gold Rush. The school district requires the use of the adopted social studies series, although teachers are encouraged to supplement the text with primary source materials, literature, illustrations, and realia. The content topics for the Gold Rush unit include westward expansion, routes and trails to the West, the people who sought their fortunes, hardships, settlements, the discovery of gold, the life of miners, methods for extracting gold, and the impact of the Gold Rush.

Each of the teachers has created several lessons for this unit. The first is presented here, a 55–60 minute lesson on routes and trails to the West. Specifically, the content of this lesson covers the Oregon Trail, the Overland Trail, and the route around Cape Horn. To address the Common Core standards for literacy in history, the teachers plan various ways to help children access the textbook.

■ Teaching Scenarios

To demonstrate how Ms. Chen, Mrs. Hargroves, and Mr. Hensen prepared their first lesson on the trails west, we visit them in their fourth-grade classrooms. As you read, consider the SIOP Model features for Lesson Preparation: content objectives, language objectives, appropriate content concepts, supplementary materials, adaptation of content, and meaningful activities.

Ms. Chen

As Ms. Chen began the first lesson on the Gold Rush, which would take two days to complete, she referred students to the content objectives written on the board: (1) Students will use map skills to find and label the three main routes to the West; (2) Students will identify one or two facts about each of the three trails. After reading the content objectives aloud, Ms. Chen then explained the language objectives: (1) Students will take notes to distinguish among the trails; (2) Students will categorize vocabulary terms.

Next, Ms. Chen asked the children to brainstorm why people would leave their homes and travel great distances to seek their fortunes. She listed students' responses on the board and then asked them to categorize the words or phrases, using a List-Group-Label activity. The students determined the following categories: For Adventure, To Get Rich, For a Better Life. Examples of phrases they placed under the first category included *riding in a wagon train, seeing new places,* and *climbing mountains.*

Ms. Chen then assigned her students a quick-write about the Gold Rush. She distributed two picture books on the topic for each of the table groups (four or five children per group) and directed students to use their background knowledge, the List-Group-Label categories and phrases, and the books to generate a few sentences or a brief paragraph on the Gold Rush. Children were encouraged to work quietly with a partner, and each pair was expected to have a written text for later whole-class discussion.

While the rest of the class were preparing their quick-writes, Ms. Chen asked the five English learners with very limited English proficiency to meet with her. For six minutes, she provided the small group of children with a jump-start for the Gold Rush unit they were about to begin. She introduced key vocabulary with illustrations and simple definitions, led the students through a picture walk of a picture book and the textbook chapter, showed them the trails on the U.S. map, and talked about where the pioneers began their journey and where they headed in California. She showed the children some samples of fool's gold (iron pyrite) and asked them how they thought the gold miners were able to get the gold from the earth.

After the jump-start minilesson, Ms. Chen convened the entire class for a brief discussion of the quick-writes and a whole-class introduction to the unit. Several of the pairs volunteered to share their quick-writes with the entire class.

Ms. Chen then referred to the key vocabulary she had previously written on the board: Oregon Trail, Overland Trail, Route around Cape Horn. She asked students to think about the names of the trails they were going to be reading about. She explained that often we learn about places and surrounding areas by examining their names.

Ms. Chen asked the children to examine maps of the United States and the Western Hemisphere on the interactive whiteboard and try to determine where the three main trails were located, given their names. The students volunteered appropriate ideas for the first one, the Oregon Trail. Ms. Chen drew it on the whiteboard. She then wrote "Over + land = Overland." One child said, "I get it! They went over the land!" The teacher reinforced this by highlighting the "over the land" route on the whiteboard map too. She then wrote "Route around Cape Horn" and asked students to think about the name's meaning while directing them to look at the map. One child said, "See, the land looks like a horn. And they had to sail around it!" That student came up to the board and drew the route on the interactive map.

Next, Ms. Chen distributed paper copies of a map of the Western Hemisphere and directed the children to work together as a team to complete their groups' maps. To check understanding, Ms. Chen asked each student to tell a partner a fact or two about one of three western routes.

Ms. Chen distributed and explained a scaffolded outline of the chapter that students would complete individually. The outline had subheadings labeled for each of the trails: "Location," "Characteristics," "Challenges," and "Advantages." Following a shared reading of the Oregon Trail section of the social studies text, she elicited ideas from the students to write as notes on the outline for the first trail. She told the children they would have about 10 minutes to keep working on the outline, using their maps and their text chapter and that they would finish the next day. Ms. Chen completed the lesson by reviewing the content and language objectives and by having student partners share a number of facts about each of the trails using complete sentences and then report out to the class.

Check your understanding: On the SIOP form in Figure 2.6, rate Ms. Chen's lesson on each of the Lesson Preparation features.

FIGURE 2.6 Lesson Preparation Component of the SIOP® Model: Ms. Chen's Lesson

4	3	2	1	0
1. **Content objectives** clearly defined, displayed and reviewed with students		**Content objectives** for students implied		No clearly defined **content objectives** for students

4	3	2	1	0
2. **Language objectives** clearly defined, displayed and reviewed with students		**Language objectives** for students implied		No clearly defined **language objectives** for students

4	3	2	1	0
3. **Content concepts** appropriate for age and educational background level of students		**Content concepts** somewhat appropriate for age and educational background level of students		**Content concepts** inappropriate for age and educational background level of students

4	3	2	1	0
4. **Supplementary materials** used to a high degree, making the lesson clear and meaningful (e.g., computer programs, graphs, models, visuals)		Some use of **supplementary materials**		No use of **supplementary materials**

4	3	2	1	0	N/A
5. **Adaptation of content** (e.g., text, assignment) to all levels of student proficiency		Some **adaptation of content** to all levels of student proficiency		No significant **adaptation of content** to all levels of student proficiency	

4	3	2	1	0
6. **Meaningful activities** that integrate lesson concepts (e.g., interviews, letter writing, simulations, models) with language practice opportunities for reading, writing, listening, and/or speaking		**Meaningful activities** that integrate lesson concepts but provide few language practice opportunities for reading, writing, listening, and/or speaking		No **meaningful activities** that integrate lesson concepts with language practice

? **Reflect and Apply**
Click here to explain your ratings for Ms. Chen's lesson on each of the Lesson Preparation features.

Mrs. Hargroves

Mrs. Hargroves began her lesson on the trails west by stating, "Today you'll learn about the Oregon Trail, the Overland Trail, and the Route around Cape Horn. We'll also be working on maps, and I want you to color the Overland Trail a different color from the color you use for the Cape Horn route. When you learn about the Oregon Trail, you'll complete the map with a third color. By the time you're finished, you should have all three routes drawn on the map using different colors." She held up a completed map for the students to see as an example.

Mrs. Hargroves then presented a brief lecture on the trails west. Using an electronic document reader, she pointed out where the pioneers traveled on the map in the textbook. She referred students to pictures in the book and answered questions. She read the chapter title and the first few paragraphs about the trails west and then assigned the remainder of the chapter as independent reading. She suggested that if students had difficulty with any words, they should hold up their hands and she would circulate to give assistance.

About half the class (mostly the native English speakers) finished reading in 10 to 15 minutes. Some chatted quietly. After about 20 minutes, Mrs. Hargroves asked the class to stop reading. She distributed the U.S. maps and colored pencils and asked the children to work with a partner to complete their maps by locating and coloring in the three trails. When most were finished, Mrs. Hargroves asked three of the students to show and explain their maps to the other students. All maps were then submitted for a grade. At the conclusion of the lesson, students were given the following writing assignment for homework: "If you had been a pioneer, which trail would you have chosen? Why?"

Check your understanding: On the SIOP form in Figure 2.7 on the following page, rate Mrs. Hargroves's lesson on each of the Lesson Preparation features.

Mr. Hensen

Mr. Hensen began his lesson on westward expansion by introducing the topic and asking how many children had been to California. He then asked, "How did you get to California? Did you go by car? By plane? By boat? Or did you go by wagon train? Today you're going to learn how the pioneers made their voyages to California." Mr. Hensen then showed a brief video on the westward expansion. At the end of the video, he introduced the terms Oregon Trail, Overland Trail, and Route around Cape Horn, and then read aloud two paragraphs from the textbook that described the routes.

Next he numbered off the students to form six new groups and quickly moved children into the groups. With their team members, students did a Jigsaw activity for the remainder of the chapter, and when they had finished reading, everyone returned to their original home groups to report on what they had read. The English learners with limited English proficiency were partnered with other students during the Jigsaw reading activity.

Mr. Hensen then wrote the names of the three trails on the board, and on his wall map he pointed out where the pioneers had traveled along the three routes. He directed the groups to divide the three trails, with one or two students in each group drawing the Oregon Trail and the other children drawing either the Overland or

FIGURE 2.7 Lesson Preparation Component of the SIOP® Model: Mrs. Hargroves's Lesson

4	3	2	1	0
1. **Content objectives** clearly defined, displayed and reviewed with students		**Content objectives** for students implied		No clearly defined **content objectives** for students

4	3	2	1	0
2. **Language objectives** clearly defined, displayed and reviewed with students		**Language objectives** for students implied		No clearly defined **language objectives** for students

4	3	2	1	0
3. **Content concepts** appropriate for age and educational background level of students		**Content concepts** somewhat appropriate for age and educational background level of students		**Content concepts** inappropriate for age and educational background level of students

4	3	2	1	0
4. **Supplementary materials** used to a high degree, making the lesson clear and meaningful (e.g., computer programs, graphs, models, visuals)		Some use of **supplementary materials**		No use of **supplementary materials**

4	3	2	1	0	N/A
5. **Adaptation of content** (e.g., text, assignment) to all levels of student proficiency		Some **adaptation of content** to all levels of student proficiency		No significant **adaptation of content** to all levels of student proficiency	

4	3	2	1	0
6. **Meaningful activities** that integrate lesson concepts (e.g., interviews, letter writing, simulations, models) with language practice opportunities for reading, writing, listening, and/or speaking		**Meaningful activities** that integrate lesson concepts but provide few language practice opportunities for reading, writing, listening, and/or speaking		No **meaningful activities** that integrate lesson concepts with language practice

? **Reflect and Apply**
Click here to explain your ratings for Mrs. Hargroves's lesson on each of the Lesson Preparation features.

Cape Horn trails. Their next task was to tell the other students in their group how to draw and color their maps, using the map in the text and the language on the board as a guide. Mr. Hensen circulated through the room while the students completed the mapping activity, assisting as necessary. At the lesson's conclusion, children were directed to pass in their maps. If they had not finished, their maps were assigned as homework.

Check your understanding: On the SIOP form in Figure 2.8, rate Mr. Hensen's lesson on each of the Lesson Preparation features.

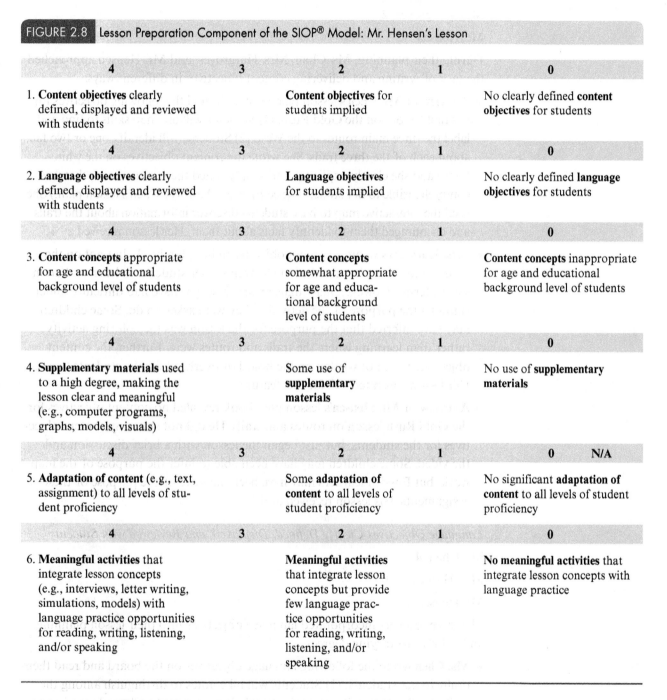

FIGURE 2.8 Lesson Preparation Component of the SIOP® Model: Mr. Hensen's Lesson

4	3	2	1	0
1. **Content objectives** clearly defined, displayed and reviewed with students		**Content objectives** for students implied		No clearly defined **content objectives** for students
2. **Language objectives** clearly defined, displayed and reviewed with students		**Language objectives** for students implied		No clearly defined **language objectives** for students
3. **Content concepts** appropriate for age and educational background level of students		**Content concepts** somewhat appropriate for age and educational background level of students		**Content concepts** inappropriate for age and educational background level of students
4. **Supplementary materials** used to a high degree, making the lesson clear and meaningful (e.g., computer programs, graphs, models, visuals)		Some use of **supplementary materials**		No use of **supplementary materials**

4	3	2	1	0	N/A
5. **Adaptation of content** (e.g., text, assignment) to all levels of student proficiency		Some **adaptation of content** to all levels of student proficiency		No significant **adaptation of content** to all levels of student proficiency	

4	3	2	1	0
6. **Meaningful activities** that integrate lesson concepts (e.g., interviews, letter writing, simulations, models) with language practice opportunities for reading, writing, listening, and/or speaking		**Meaningful activities** that integrate lesson concepts but provide few language practice opportunities for reading, writing, listening, and/or speaking		**No meaningful activities** that integrate lesson concepts with language practice

Reflect and Apply

Click here to explain your ratings for Mr. Hensen's lesson on each of the Lesson Preparation features.

■ Discussion of Lessons

1. *Content Objectives Clearly Defined, Displayed, and Reviewed with Students*

   Ms. Chen: 4

   Mrs. Hargroves: 2

   Mr. Hensen: 1

   During their planning, Ms. Chen, Mrs. Hargroves, and Mr. Hensen approached the task of writing and delivering content objectives in different ways.

   - A review of **Ms. Chen's** lesson plan book indicated the following objectives for her first lessons on the Gold Rush: (1) Students will use map skills to find and label the three main routes to the West; (2) Students will identify one or two facts about each of the three trails. She wrote the content objectives on the whiteboard and she clearly, explicitly, and simply stated them in a manner that was comprehensible to her students. (See Figure 2.9 for Ms. Chen's lesson plan.) She used the interactive map to have students discover information about the trails and encouraged them to identify facts about them. Her lesson received a "4."

   - **Mrs. Hargroves** wrote a content objective in her plan book, but not on the board, and she orally stated what she wanted her students to learn and do in simple terms. However, her English learners might have had difficulty understanding the purpose of the activities they were asked to do. Some children may have inferred that the purpose for the lesson was the coloring activity rather than learning where the trails and routes were. Further, the content objectives were not written on the board or overhead for the students to see. Her lesson was rated "2" for this feature.

   - A review of **Mr. Hensen's** lesson plan book revealed no content objectives for the Gold Rush lesson on routes and trails. He did not state any content objectives for the students, but just began the lesson with a brief discussion and the video. Some children may have been able to infer the purpose of the map work, but English learners may have been unaware of the purpose of these assignments. His lesson received a "1."

2. *Language Objectives Clearly Defined, Displayed, and Reviewed with Students*

   Ms. Chen: 4

   Mrs. Hargroves: 0

   Mr. Hensen: 2

   The three teachers incorporated language objectives into their lesson planning and delivery to varying degrees.

   - **Ms. Chen** wrote the following language objectives on the board and read them orally to her students: (1) Students will take notes to distinguish among the trails; (2) Students will categorize vocabulary terms. Ms. Chen planned opportunities for students to meet the objectives by helping them generate and categorize key terms, encouraging class and small-group discussion, and providing an outline for taking notes. She scaffolded students' understanding of the

FIGURE 2.9 Ms. Chen's SIOP® Lesson Plan

Date: Feb. 10–11   Grade/Class/Subject: 4 – Social Studies

Unit/Theme: Gold Rush   Standards: History—Social Studies 4.3, CCSS L.4a, L.4b

Content Objective(s): Students will use map skills to find and label the three main routes to the West; Students will identify one or two facts about each of the three trails

Language Objective(s): Students will take notes to distinguish among the trails; Students will categorize vocabulary terms

Key Vocabulary	Supplementary Materials
Oregon Trail Overland Trail Route around Cape Horn	Picture books Outlines Iron Pyrite U.S. map (PowerPoint slide)

SIOP Features

Skel. Outline
Jumpstart

Preparation	Scaffolding	Grouping Options
✓ Adaptation of Content	✓ Modeling	✓ Whole class
✓ Links to Background	✓ Guided practice	✓ Small groups
✓ Links to Past Learning	___ Independent practice	___ Partners
✓ Strategies incorporated	✓ Comprehensible input	✓ Independent
List / Group / Label		
Integration of Processes	**Application**	**Assessment**
✓ Reading	✓ Hands-on maps	✓ Individual
✓ Writing	✓ Meaningful	✓ Group
✓ Speaking	✓ Linked to objectives	✓ Written
✓ Listening	✓ Promotes engagement	___ Oral

Min.	Lesson Sequence
2	1. Content/language objectives
5	2. Brainstorm — Why would people leave their homes to seek fortunes?
	3. List-Group-Label brainstormed words and phrases
10	4a. Quick-write on Gold Rush
	4b. Jump-start minilesson — vocabulary, pictures, text, pyrite
	5. Quick-write share out
10	6. Map skills — interactive whiteboard, names of trails, group maps, check comprehension
20	7. Note-taking — scaffolded outline, shared reading (pp. 214–15), modeling
	8. Group/individual note-taking
5	9. Wrap-up — review objs., state facts

Reflections:
Busy lesson, perhaps a bit rushed for English learners. They loved the fool's gold! Review tomorrow and do a jump-start on notetaking.

names of the trails and modeled how to take notes based on the shared reading of the textbook. At the end of the lesson, she orally reviewed the language objectives for the students. Her lesson was rated a "4."

- **Mrs. Hargroves** did not include any language objectives in her lesson plan and she did not suggest any to the students. She did not discuss the meanings of the names or terms used in her demonstration and explanations, nor did she encourage her students to use the terminology and concepts during discussion. Further, Mrs. Hargroves expected students to read the textbook with very little support. She mostly conveyed information orally, and she expected students to complete the writing assignment as homework with no modeling or assistance. Her lesson received a "0."

- Although **Mr. Hensen** had no stated language objectives, he did write key vocabulary on the board. He scaffolded the mapping activity and the text reading by having the children work in groups and by having each group member explain the map and key words to the others. This activity was appropriate for beginning English learners because they were supported by peers, and their oral explanations were not "public" for the entire class. The lesson would have been more effective had Mr. Hensen explained his language objectives to the students, emphasizing the importance of listening carefully and of giving clear directions. Although one purpose of the lesson was to build listening and speaking skills, the class was not informed of these objectives either orally or in writing. His lesson was rated a "2."

3. *Content Concepts Appropriate for Age and Educational Background Level of Students*

   Ms. Chen: 4

   Mrs. Hargroves: 4

   Mr. Hensen: 4

   Each of the teaching scenarios indicates that the three fourth-grade teachers, **Ms. Chen, Mrs. Hargroves,** and **Mr. Hensen,** were teaching a unit on the Gold Rush. The content concepts were appropriate because they are congruent with the fourth-grade state and district standards for the social studies curriculum. Each lesson was rated a "4."

4. *Supplementary Materials Used to a High Degree, Making the Lesson Clear and Meaningful*

   Ms. Chen: 4

   Mrs. Hargroves: 1

   Mr. Hensen: 3

   - **Ms. Chen** used a number of supplementary materials to make the content more accessible to the learners: picture books on the Gold Rush, a sample rock of fool's gold, and the maps of the United States and the Western Hemisphere, as well as technology (interactive whiteboard) to model how students might label the trails on their maps. Her lesson received a "4" on this feature.

- **Mrs. Hargroves** used only the electronic document reader and the textbook during her lecture and when the children were coloring their maps. She did not demonstrate, model, or show visuals or other resources to support student learning other than the illustrations in the textbooks. Because Mrs. Hargroves delivered the content orally, some English learners may have had difficulty making connections between the lecture and the text illustrations and maps. Her lesson received a "1."

- **Mr. Hensen's** video enabled his English learners and other students to connect with the pioneers in the Gold Rush, and his use of the wall map enhanced student learning about the location of the three trails. His lesson was rated "3."

5. *Adaptation of Content to All Levels of Student Proficiency*

Ms. Chen: 4

Mrs. Hargroves: 0

Mr. Hensen: 3

- **Ms. Chen** adapted the grade-level content for her English learners and struggling readers in a number of ways. First, she had students brainstorm, categorize, and then quick-write information about the Gold Rush. She then differentiated instruction by providing a "jump-start" for her lowest level English learners by preteaching the lesson concepts and key vocabulary. She also had a variety of picture books that were easier to read and more comprehensible than the textbook. In addition, she used a scaffolded outline that included some key information. The students used this outline to organize their understanding of the content concepts. Her lesson was rated "4."

- **Mrs. Hargroves** did not adapt the content for her English learners, other than by lecturing on the topic. Without any supplementary support except the pictures in the textbook and her oral reading of the first few paragraphs, the English learners may have had difficulty learning key concepts just by listening and reading independently. Further, Mrs. Hargroves did not paraphrase or clarify important points during her lecture, nor did she explain or define key language or vocabulary before or during reading. Her lesson plans made no mention of other ways to adapt the content or text. Her lesson received a "0."

- **Mr. Hensen** provided access to the textbook content through the Jigsaw activity and the video. He grouped the children for their reading so that they read with the support of others and then later conveyed what they had learned to another group of students. However, he did not preteach vocabulary they might need to know in order to fully understand the reading. He also had the students complete their work on the maps in small groups, and he encouraged them to help each other with the assignment. His lesson was rated "3."

6. *Meaningful Activities That Integrate Lesson Concepts with Language Practice Opportunities for Reading, Writing, Listening, and/or Speaking*

Ms. Chen: 4

Mrs. Hargroves: 2

Mr. Hensen: 4

- Recall that **Ms. Chen** asked students to brainstorm what they knew about the Gold Rush in order to activate and build background. They then worked on a vocabulary categorization activity. Her jump-start minilesson for the English learners included picture walks and discussion of key vocabulary, and the children were able to see and hold iron pyrite, which simulated the feel and look of gold. The picture books supported their learning, and the scaffolded outline provided a meaningful way to take notes on the key concepts. Students practiced map skills to locate and label the trails after Ms. Chen's modeling on the interactive whiteboard. Her lesson received a "4."

- **Mrs. Hargroves's** lesson plan included her lecture, the mapping activity, and the independent reading. Locating the trails by coloring the map was meaningful for children if they understood what they were doing; however, if they were unable to access the text or the lecture, the mapping activity may have been irrelevant. Mrs. Hargroves's lesson received a "2." It was teacher centered, with lecture and independent seatwork as the predominant activities. She expected students to complete the homework assignment based only on the information they could gather from the lecture and text. If students did not understand the lecture or comprehend the chapter, it is unlikely that they would be able to write a meaningful essay on what they learned.

- **Mr. Hensen** activated prior knowledge and background when he asked which students had traveled to California. He also showed the video on the westward expansion, incorporated a Jigsaw reading activity, and had the children complete and explain their maps in triads. All of these activities helped make the content concepts more comprehensible for his English learners, and were considered to be meaningful and appropriate. His lesson was rated a "4."

(For more examples of lesson and unit plans in social studies and history for grades K–12, see Short, Vogt, and Echevarría, 2011a.)

> Watch this video, in which two teachers co-plan a joint first-grade lesson for English speakers and English learners. Listen for the ways they address the six features of Lesson Preparation in the lesson. How do they prepare the students for the content and ensure language practice will occur?

Teaching with Technology

After talking with the teachers and discussing the lessons you read about in the Scenarios earlier in the chapter, our tech integrator, Ms. Palacios, offered some technology suggestions to enhance the teachers' lessons.

Differentiated Reading: One of the most challenging parts of teaching units such as the Gold Rush is finding diverse materials at various reading levels. For the first part of the unit, Ms. Chen, Mrs. Hargroves, and Mr. Hensen spent hours searching the Internet for such differentiated texts. When their searches ended in frustration, they resorted to rewriting articles and stories themselves, simplifying the vocabulary, shortening sentences, and adding images to better support students with different **levels of language proficiency**. While it was time consuming, this was one way that the teachers were able to guarantee access to the material and help students engage in class discussions and complete assignments.

Feeling overwhelmed by the searching and simplifying, Ms. Chen, Mrs. Hargroves, and Mr. Hensen reached out to Ms. Palacios to try to find adapted resources more efficiently. They wondered, "Is there a tool that can simplify text easily and appropriately?" "Can a Web site do this task for us?" In her e-mail back to the team, Ms. Palacios explained that there are some online tools that will convert text, but they have limits. Like translation tools, the text converters provide accurate output only to a certain degree. The programs do not pick up on some nuances of language as a human would. In turn, these issues could further complicate the text.

As an alternative, Ms. Palacios shared a number of Web sites that offer multiple versions of the same article at different reading levels. While preparing for an upcoming lesson in the Gold Rush unit, Mr. Hensen used the Web site *Newsela* to find an article about migrant farm workers at two different Lexile levels. Ms. Chen used *News in Levels* to find a short article with three different levels and a video about migrants from North Africa attempting travel to Malta. Mrs. Hargroves found a number of books on both gold and migration on the site *Reading A–Z*. The teachers then shared these articles with each other and used them to help the children explore the motivations of those who were part of the Gold Rush. By incorporating relevant texts at varied reading levels, the teachers facilitated collaborative discussions among students who were able to connect the Gold Rushers' experiences with their own, particularly for the students who were born abroad or who had family in other countries.

Other terms for this type of tool: differentiated articles, same text—different levels

Related products: *News in Levels, For the Teachers, CommonLit, Books that Grow, Reading A–Z, Newsela*

Videos: In hopes of adding more supplementary resources beyond print, Ms. Chen, Mrs. Hargroves, and Mr. Hensen checked in with Ms. Palacios again. Ms. Palacios quickly recommended two sites for quality videos and animations: *BrainPOP* and *TED-Ed*. The teachers visited the sites during a grade-level team meeting and found that both sites had a large collection of videos related to a variety of topics. *BrainPOP* offers a wide range of material for students in grades K–12. Additionally, there are lesson ideas, quizzes, and searchable standards, among other features.

TED-Ed, a platform created by the TED organization known for its popular talks, offers a wealth of options for teachers interested in integrating video into their lessons. The site offers hundreds of lessons that educators can use or adapt. The site also enables teachers to develop original lessons by linking videos from *YouTube* with its lesson template. Using another online service named *Amara*, the teachers were able to find many of the *TED-Ed* videos with subtitles and transcripts in numerous languages.

Other terms for this type of tool: Video sites for the classroom, best video sites for educators/students

Related products: *TeacherTube, LearnZillion, WatchKnowLearn, PBS*

Worth Visiting: Sites for Videos to Support Teacher Development: *Edutopia* and *The Teaching Channel*

Note: Due to the constantly evolving nature of the Internet, it is a challenge to ensure that all of the links and Web services listed here are updated and functional when you read the technology sections. While specific tools or services may appear in the narrative, we have also included the general search term for each tool. If a specific service does not work or is no longer available, search with the general term for the tool and you should be able to find a comparable Web site.

Check Your Understanding
Click here to check your understanding of Chapter 2, Lesson Preparation.

◼ Summary

As you reflect on this chapter and the benefits of lesson planning with clear content and language objectives in mind, consider the following main points:

- Lesson Preparation is a critical foundation for delivering a high-quality SIOP lesson. Thoughtful planning leads to effective teaching—but a great plan does not always guarantee a great lesson for English learners. Teachers must plan lessons that are aligned to the grade-level curriculum and based on content standards and learning outcomes, but they must also be **culturally responsive** to student needs and acutely aware of how well students are learning during a lesson in case adjustments to the plan is needed.

- All SIOP lessons need attention to language with at least one objective devoted to furthering the English learners' academic English development. This should be a learning objective—an achievement target, not an activity—and teachers must teach to it during the lesson.

- If children lack background knowledge and experience with content concepts, effective sheltered teachers provide it through explicit instruction, and they enhance student learning with appropriate supplementary materials. They provide scaffolded support by adapting dense and difficult text.

- SIOP teachers situate lessons in meaningful, real-life activities and experiences that involve the children in reading, writing, and discussing important concepts and ideas.

- The principles of effective **sheltered instruction** and content-based ESL instruction should be reflected in teachers' lesson plans. As we explore the other features of the SIOP Model and see how teachers apply other important principles in their classrooms, remember that the first step in the instructional process is comprehensive lesson design.

In sum, teachers must learn to identify and then teach the academic language of their subject explicitly in their lessons and use a variety of techniques to build background, convey new information to English learners in accessible ways, plan for meaningful tasks that practice and apply the content and language knowledge, and then review what has been learned.

◼ Discussion Questions

1. In reflecting on the learning outcomes in the content and language objectives at the beginning of the chapter, are you able to:
   a. Identify content objectives for English learners that are aligned to state, local, or national standards?
   b. Incorporate supplementary materials suitable for English learners into a lesson plan?
   c. Select from a variety of techniques for adapting content to the students' proficiency and cognitive levels?

    d. Write language and content objectives?

    e. Discuss advantages for writing both language and content objectives for a lesson and sharing the objectives with children?

    f. Explain the importance of meaningful academic activities for English learners?

2. What are some advantages to writing both content objectives and language objectives for students to hear and see? How might written objectives affect teacher and student performance in the classroom?

3. Think of a lesson you have recently taught or one you might teach. What would be an appropriate content objective and language objective for that lesson?

4. In many elementary schools, one ESL teacher supports English learners from several classrooms, sometimes across different grade levels. How can the ESL and grade-level classroom teachers collaborate to share the responsibility for teaching both language and content objectives to these students? Try this: Co-plan a mini-unit in which some lessons will be taught by the ESL teacher and others by the grade-level classroom teacher.

5. Many teachers rely on mini-lectures or textbook chapters for teaching key concepts. Think of a curricular area (e.g., science, language arts, math, social studies) and discuss some meaningful activities that could be used to teach a concept in that area. What makes each of these activities "meaningful," and how would they provide language practice?

6. Begin writing a SIOP lesson. Identify the topic and your content and language objectives. Find or create supplementary materials and adapt content as needed. Determine at least one meaningful activity the children can engage in during the lesson. Decide how many class periods will be needed to complete the lesson. When you finish, share your initial lesson plan with a colleague and garner feedback. Revise your lesson.

CHAPTER 3

Building Background

Learning Outcomes

After reading, discussing, and engaging in activities related to this chapter, you will be able to meet the following **content** and **language objectives**.

Content Objectives

Identify techniques for connecting children's personal experiences and past learning to lesson concepts.

Determine ways to develop background knowledge for children for whom there is a mismatch between what they know and have experienced and what is being taught.

Language Objectives

Select key vocabulary for a **SIOP** lesson using words from these three groups: content vocabulary, general academic vocabulary, and word parts—roots and affixes.

Write a lesson plan incorporating activities that build background and provide explicit links to children's backgrounds, experiences, and past learning.

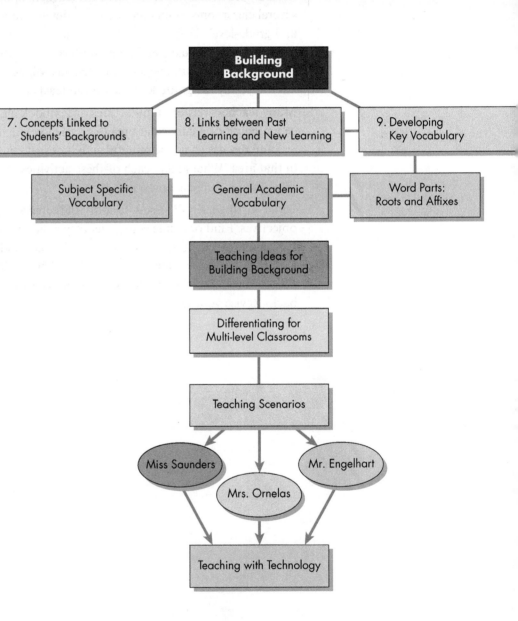

Reflect on two instances when you attended workshops for professional development. During one workshop, you were highly engaged, and you came away from the training renewed and eager to try a new idea or activity. What aspects of this particular workshop clicked for you? Now, recall a workshop during which you were disengaged, bored, and basically unconnected to what the facilitator was talking about. Why was this particular workshop such an unsatisfying experience?

Jani Bryson/Getty Images

There might be several reasons why there were such differences in your reactions, including the effectiveness of the trainer, the time of day, your physical comfort, and so forth. But consider another possibility: There was a mismatch between what you know and have experienced with your own students and the concepts and information that were being presented. Because of your background knowledge and personal experiences, (1) you didn't understand what was being presented; or (2) you didn't care about what was being presented because of the mismatch; and/or (3) you couldn't connect with what was being taught, so you turned off and became disengaged. Now ponder what these two workshops would be like if the facilitator were speaking in a language that you do not understand. ●

■ Background

English learners, particularly recent immigrants, are frequently disadvantaged because their schooling experiences (whether they have had little schooling or excellent schooling) may be considerably different from U.S. educational contexts. For example, the K–6 curriculums can be quite different from country to country, and depending on circumstances, some children may have experienced interrupted schooling, especially if they have been refugees or lived in remote areas. Further, English learners, including both immigrants and children born in the United States, may lack the **academic language** and key vocabulary necessary to understand content

Watch this video to hear Dr. MaryEllen Vogt's explanation of the Building Background component. Think of two or three students in your own classroom who are struggling, and reflect on lessons that you're currently teaching. What might you do to better develop background knowledge for these students and others?

information (August & Shanahan, 2010; Donnelly & Roe, 2010). However, not all English learners lack background experiences and academic language; some children may have rich experiential backgrounds and sufficient academic language in their **native language**, but they do not know the equivalent English terms and thus are unable to connect with the concepts being taught.

Effective teaching takes students from where they are and leads them to a higher level of understanding (Vygotsky, 1978). Effective SIOP teachers present information in a way that children can understand, bearing in mind their language development needs and possible gaps in their educational experiences. In SIOP lessons, new information is explicitly linked to students' backgrounds and experiences, and instructional **scaffolding** provides students with access to grade-level content concepts. This chapter focuses on Building Background, which is closely tied to Lesson Preparation and the teacher's **assessment** of students' knowledge of and experience with the topic at hand.

SIOP® FEATURE 7:

Concepts Explicitly Linked to Students' Background Experiences

During the past four decades, researchers have investigated how highly proficient readers and writers process new information (Baumann, 2005; Carrell, 1987; Dole, Duffy, Roehler, & Pearson, 1991). It is a widely accepted notion among experts that a learner's "schemata"—knowledge of the world—provides a basis for understanding, learning, and remembering facts and ideas found in texts. Individuals with knowledge of a topic have better recall and are better able to elaborate on aspects of that topic than those who have limited knowledge of the subject (Chiesi, Spilich, & Voss, 1979).

Connecting children's experiences to a text, developing background knowledge, and teaching key vocabulary are all effective ways to increase comprehension and achievement (Biemiller, 2005; Neuman, Kaefer, & Pinkham, 2014; Vogt, 2014). Teachers can assist children in developing background knowledge by:

- Including techniques in lessons such as chapter previews or anticipation guides. As children begin to develop a conceptual framework for their own learning and understanding, they build a repertoire of background experiences from which to draw.

- Recognizing that children from culturally diverse backgrounds may struggle with comprehending a text or concept presented in class because their schemata do not match those of the culture for which the text was written (Anderson, 1984; Zwiers, O'Hara, & Pritchard, 2014). In the United States, most school reading materials, such as content area texts, rely on assumptions about students' prior knowledge, especially related to curriculum. When introducing a new concept, SIOP teachers often use visuals (pictures, photos, and so forth) to provide context and a reference point for English learners. It's interesting to have students occasionally share in their home languages the name for what a picture represents. Then, the English word can be introduced and explained.

Watch the video
and listen to
SIOP author, Dr. Jana
Echevarría, describe
another classroom
incident where a cultural
mismatch in schemata
caused confusion. Think
of a time in your own
classroom when a
misunderstanding may
have been caused
by students' varied
background experiences.
What could you have
done in advance to
better situate the lesson
topic so confusion could
have been avoided?

- Acknowledging that many English learners emigrate from other countries and bring an array of experiences that are quite different from those of the majority culture in the United States. Even for those students born in the United States, culture may have an impact on reading comprehension. Therefore, **culturally responsive teaching** is especially important. Consider this example: As a teacher reads, "The barking dog ran toward the boy on the bike," do all students perceive a sense of fear or danger? Anderson (1994), a pioneer in schema theory research, questioned whether we can assume that students from every subculture will have the same experience with, or emotional reaction to a story or article, or whether we should expect the same outcomes from them. For an actual example of cultural mismatch of schemata that occurred in a diverse second grade classroom, see Figure 3.1.

Teachers of English learners need to be aware that what may appear to be poor comprehension and weak memory skills may in fact be children's lack of experience or background knowledge associated with or assumed by a message or a text. Further, what might look like a lack of prior knowledge actually may be a lack of accessibility in prior lessons that were taught. Background material may have been "covered," but it was not learned meaningfully. Through SIOP, we urge teachers to activate children's background knowledge explicitly and provide links from their experiences to the key concepts. The interactive emphasis of the SIOP Model (see Chapter 6 for specific features) enables teachers to elicit children's prior

FIGURE 3.1 An Example of a Mismatched Schema

A second-grade teacher in a large urban district began teaching map skills, a state history-social studies standard for second grade, by having students identify on a grid some familiar locations and features of their school. The next step of the teacher's lesson plan was to focus on the children's local community and the location and features of the police and fire departments, city hall, post office, community hospital, and so forth. Then, she planned to work on another social studies standard by talking with the children about those individuals in the community who "make a difference." She intended to connect the individuals' contributions with those of some of the historical figures students had learned about previously.

The teacher thought that focusing on the features and location of the local community would be a relatively simple task for her students. She soon realized, however, that the task was quite difficult for many children, especially her immigrant English learners and others who had scarcely ventured from their own city blocks during their lifetimes. Although the ocean was just a few blocks away, the teacher discovered that some of her younger students had never seen it. Also, while many children frequently heard and saw ambulances and fire trucks race by their apartment buildings, they had not seen a fire department or a hospital. These children were unable to engage in a class discussion of the community beyond the school. They lacked the knowledge and experience needed to sketch a map of the community or to describe some of the people who worked within it, except for the small market that was down the street from the school.

This teacher quickly realized that she needed to rethink her lesson plans for this unit, begin again, and determine what her students knew about the concept of *community*, including the one in which they lived. Not surprisingly, her students' backgrounds and experiences varied widely. For some who had a large extended family, this defined their "community." For others, they described their community as their home, church, and school. For still others, who had attended the ballet and theater, who regularly shopped with their family at large local shopping centers, and who had siblings who participated in competitive sports programs, their understanding of community was quite different.

knowledge and discuss ideas, issues, concepts, or vocabulary that are unfamiliar to them, in order to develop necessary background information.

Something to Think About

As you begin to write SIOP lessons with techniques to develop children's background knowledge, reflect on the following questions:

- What is meant by activating prior knowledge?
- What is meant by building background?
- How do they differ instructionally?

In the past, we have used the terms "activating prior knowledge" and "building background" somewhat synonymously. However, we now know there are some instructional differences that need to be considered when teaching English learners. All children have prior knowledge gained from schooling and life experiences, and teachers can informally assess what they know and can do, as well as determine any mismatches in schemata through brainstorming, structured discussion, quick-writes, and techniques such as the familiar KWL (Ogle, 1986).

However, if some English learners have little or no prior knowledge about a content topic (e.g., "Our Community"), brainstorming about it may not be helpful because the brainstormed terms, names, and places may be unfamiliar to these children. Therefore, it is of critical importance that teachers build background using techniques that fill in the gaps and help children connect what they do know with what is being taught. And when teachers' explanations are made more concrete with supplementary materials (e.g., photos, models, illustrations, websites, etc.), children are more likely to make the appropriate connections. Essential questions, found in many textbooks and required in some districts, can be developed from a lesson's content and language objectives. They may assist children in making connections to a lesson's topic and also thinking about the wider range of background knowledge and experiences they have.

SIOP

SHELTERED INSTRUCTION
OBSERVATION PROTOCOL

SIOP® FEATURE 8:

Links Explicitly Made between Past Learning and New Concepts

In addition to building background for students, it is also important for teachers to make explicit connections between new learning and the material, vocabulary, and concepts previously covered in class. Decades of research clearly shows that in order for learning to occur, new information must be integrated with knowledge students have previously acquired (Rumelhart, 1980). The teacher must build a bridge between previous lessons and concepts, and the material in the current lesson. Many children do not automatically make such connections, and they benefit from having the teacher explicitly point out how past learning is related to the information at hand.

Explicit links between past learning and new learning can be encouraged through questioning, such as, "Let's look again at the graphic organizer we used yesterday to help us compare and contrast the fire department with the police department. Who can remember and share one way that they are alike? What is an example of one way they are different? Do you all agree? Share with your partner two more differences. You may look at your graphic organizer if you need some help remembering." Teachers can also refer to a previous lesson's PowerPoint slides, a text that was read, or other visuals that are related to the topic. By preserving and referring to photos, word banks, illustrations, charts, maps, and graphic organizers, teachers have tools for helping children make critical connections. This is particularly important for English learners who receive so much input through the new language. An explicit, if brief, review of prior lessons focuses on the key information that students should remember and connect with today's lesson.

SIOP

SIOP® FEATURE 9:

Key Vocabulary Emphasized (e.g., introduced, written, repeated, and highlighted for students to see)

Vocabulary development, critical for English learners, is strongly related to academic achievement (August & Shanahan, 2006; Hart & Risley, 2003; Lesaux, Kieffer, Faller, & Kelley, 2010; Zwiers, 2008). In addition, for over 80 years, we have known of the powerful relationship between vocabulary knowledge and comprehension (Baumann, 2005; Fisher & Frey, 2014; Gillis, 2014; Stahl & Nagy, 2006). Therefore, it may not be surprising that the word *vocabulary* is found more than 150 times in the **Common Core State Standards** document (Manyak et al., 2014).

Systematic and comprehensive vocabulary instruction is particularly necessary for English learners (Graves & Fitzgerald, 2006). The Common Core and other rigorous state standards require that children be able to read texts of increasing complexity that include very sophisticated vocabulary. Accompanying content and literacy assessments rely on wide-ranging vocabulary knowledge, so English learners' vocabulary instruction must be accelerated in order to meet the high **standards**. Yet, achieving deep understandings of word meanings is very challenging, especially for English learners.

Vocabulary experts recommend a combination of plentiful and wide-ranging language experiences that include learning individual words, employing word-learning **strategies**, and developing word consciousness, loosely defined as an appreciation for and interest in words. All are needed in a comprehensive vocabulary program (Graves, 2011). Students must learn tens of thousands of words, so they also need meaningful language practice opportunities, a variety of instructional approaches, motivation, and encouragement.

Some studies suggest that a limited number of words should be taught per lesson or per week, and those words should be key words in the text (Beck, Perfetti, & McKeown, 1982). Others recommend teaching English learners the meanings of basic words, such as those that **native English speakers** know already

(Diamond & Gutlohn, 2006; Stahl & Nagy, 2006). Beck, McKeown, Kucan, 2002 Beck, McKeown, and Kucan (2002), have developed a three-tier scheme for teaching vocabulary words that is widely used in U.S. schools. It is clear that students must know many more words than teachers can possibly teach. Therefore, in SIOP lessons, teachers purposefully select words that are critical for understanding texts and content concepts, and provide a variety of ways for children to learn, remember, and use those words. In that way, students develop a core vocabulary over time (Blachowicz & Fisher, 2000; Graves & Fitzgerald, 2006).

Academic Vocabulary

Academic language (as described in Chapter 1), involves the use of more sophisticated sentence structures and forms of expression than are found in everyday conversation. An important aspect of academic language is academic vocabulary, words and phrases that are used widely in the academic disciplines. Deep knowledge of the academic vocabulary of the content subjects taught in schools is necessary for students' overall academic success (Nagy &Townsend, 2012; Townsend, 2015).

The Common Core State Standards for vocabulary development suggest that children must develop proficiency with subject-specific vocabulary, as well as other types of academic vocabulary:

Grades K–5: Acquire and use accurately grade-appropriate general academic and domain-specific words and phrases, including those that signal contrast, addition, and other logical relationships (e.g., however, although, nevertheless, similarly, moreover, in addition). (© Copyright 2010. National Governors Association Center for Best Practices and Council of Chief State School Officers. All rights reserved.)

For better understanding of the varied types of academic vocabulary that teachers need to focus on, especially for English learners, we have classified them into three groups. Each should be considered when planning SIOP lessons—when deciding on academic vocabulary to teach, and when writing language objectives.

1. **Content Vocabulary—Subject-Specific and Technical Terms:** These are the key words and terms associated with a particular topic being taught (e.g., for a social studies lesson on the American Revolutionary War: *Redcoats, democracy, Patriots, freedom of religion, Shot Heard 'Round the World, Paul Revere*; for a language arts lesson on parts of speech: *nouns, verbs, adjectives, adverbs*). These words and phrases are found primarily in the informational and expository texts that children read, and frequently they are highlighted or in bold in textbooks. In English language arts, they may be terms like *characterization, setting, plot, imagery*; and while they are not usually in the fiction passages themselves, they are used to talk about the passages, author's craft, and so on. More important than listing words for children to learn is conveying the importance of knowing particular words related to a given topic, and determining whether a certain word represents a key concept that is being taught (Graves, 2011).

2. **General Academic Vocabulary—Cross-Curricular Terms/Process & Function:** These are academic words and phrases children must learn because they are used in all academic disciplines. Often, these words are not explicitly taught; yet, they are the ones that frequently trip up English learners and struggling readers. This category also includes words with multiple meanings. These words may have both a **social language** and an academic language use, such as *table* and *chair* versus *data table* and *chair of a committee*. Or the word's meanings may differ according to academic subject, such as the distinctions among legislative *power*, electrical *power*, and logarithmic *power*.

   a. Cross-curricular terms: Most of the general academic vocabulary terms can be used across the curriculum. They describe relationships (*friendship, conflict, encounter*) and actions (*describe, argue, measure*). They help illustrate information (*chart, model, structure, symbol*), and are used to speculate (*predict, infer*) and conclude (*effect, result, conclusion, drawback*). They are expressions we usually only see in academic text (*In addition to . . . , Moreover . . . , Subsequently . . .*), and terms we might use in casual conversation as well as academic discussions (*situation, circumstances, source, evidence, modify*).

   b. Language processes and functions: Another subset of the general academic terms indicates what we want to do with language—the kind of information we convey or receive and the tasks we engage in that require language to accomplish. Some English learners may know the terms in their **home languages**, but they may not know the English equivalents. Examples of some of these language process and function words and phrases that are common in classroom discourse are *discuss, skim, scan, question, argue, describe, compare, explain, list, debate, classify, support your answer, provide examples, summarize, outline, give an opinion*, and so forth. Additional examples are words and phrases that indicate transitions and connections between thoughts, such as *therefore, in conclusion, whereas, moreover*, and *furthermore*, and words that indicate sequence such as *first, then, next, finally*, and *at last*. This category also includes the verbs that students encounter in state tests and during other assessments, such as *determine, identify, select, critique, define, match, estimate*, and *contrast*.

3. **Word Parts: Roots and Affixes:** These include word parts that enable children to learn new vocabulary, primarily based on English morphology. By grade 6, students have acquired thousands of words that include roots and affixes. There is no way that English learners can realistically learn all these words through instruction and memorization. Therefore, all teachers must help children understand that many English words are formed with roots, which have prefixes and suffixes (affixes) attached to them.

   For example, during science when teaching photosynthesis, a teacher can help students learn the meaning of *photosynthesis* by introducing the meaning of the root, *photo* (light). By comparing the words *photosynthesis, photocopy, photograph, photography, photoelectron*, and *photogenic*, students can see how these English words are related by both structure (prefix + root + suffix), and meaning. The root *photo* means "light," thus providing a clue to a word's

In this video, you will hear language expert Dr. Jim Cummins explain how teachers can help English learners acquire knowledge using morphology (word structure: roots, prefixes, suffixes). Review the list of Common Word Roots (Figure 3.2). How can you use this list to increase your own understanding of morphology, as well as that of your students?

meaning if it has this root. In fact, in English, words that are related by *structure* are usually also related by *meaning* (Bear, Invernizzi, Templeton, & Johnston, 2016; Helman, Bear, Templeton, Invernizzi, & Johnston, 2012).

To assist with teaching English word structure, we include in Figure 3.2 some of the most common Latin roots that are found in thousands of English words. The 14 roots with asterisks provide the meaning of over 100,000 words! By adding prefixes and suffixes to many of the words that are included with each root (e.g., *dis*respect*ful*, *extrac*tion, *inform*ed), you can increase further the number of words on this list.

We urge caution about sharing the Common Word Roots list, or others like it, with children. It is not included here as a list for students to memorize the roots, words, and their meanings. Instead, use what children already know about words. For example, if they know how the words *import, export, portable, transport*, and *port-a-potty* are all related (they all have to do with carrying something), they can transfer that knowledge to learning the meanings of *important* (carrying value) and *unimport-ant* (not carrying value). These roots and words should be used for your reference and for helping students understand how roots and affixes work in the English language. (For more information about word parts (morphemes) and English structure, see Bear, et al., 2016; Helman et al., 2012).

FIGURE 3.2 Word Root List

There are hundreds of Latin word roots that are used frequently with prefixes and suffixes. This is only a partial list of the most frequently used roots; you can find many more with a search of "words with (root)." The roots with asterisks (*) are the 14 roots that provide clues to the meaning of over 100,000 words!

Aud: to hear
Auditory, audible, inaudible, audience, audiobook, audiotape, audiovisual, audition, auditorium, audacity, audacious, applaud, audit, auditor, unaudited, laudatory

Capit or capt: head, chief, leader
Capital, decapitate, capitol, capitalize, capitalist, overcapitalize, capitalism, anticapitalism, captivate, captain, capitulate, recapitulate

*Cept, cap, ciev, or ceit: to take, seize, receive
Capable, capsule, captive, captivity, captor, capture, accept, deception, exception, intercept, conception, susceptible, perceptive, precept, receive, receipt, deceive, deceit

Cred: to believe
Credit, credential, credence, credible, incredible, credibility, creditable, creditor, accredit, credulity, incredulity

Dic or dict: to say, tell
Dictate, dictator, dictatorial, diction, dictation, dictum, didactic, contradict, contradictory, edict, indicate, indict, indictment, predict

*Duc, duce, or duct: to lead
Conduct, deduct, educate, induce, introduction, reduce, reduction, reducible, production, abduction, aqueduct

*Fac, fact, fic, or fect: to make
Fact, manufacture, faculty, facilitate, satisfaction, factor, beneficiary, benefactor, amplification, certificate, confection, affect, defective, disinfect, efficacy, proficient, sufficient, facade

*Fer: to bring, bear, yield
Refer, reference, confer, conference, inference, suffer, transfer, defer, difference, fertilize, fertility, circumference, odoriferous, aquifer, confer, conference

Flect or flex: to bend
Flex, flexible, flexibility, inflexible, deflect, inflection, reflect, reflexive, reflective, reflector, circumflexion

Form: to shape
Reform, deform, deformity, inform, information, transform, conform, conformable, conformist, cuneiform, formula, formal, informal, formality, informative

(continued)

FIGURE 3.2 *Continued*

Jac or jec or ject: to throw, lie

Abject, dejected, rejection, adjective, conjecture, eject, ejection, inject, injection, interjection, object, objective, objectify, objectionable, project, rejection, adjacent

*Mit or miss: to send

Mission, missile, missive, admit, admission, commit, dismissed, emissary, intermission, intermittent, remiss, remit, remittance, submit, submission, transmit, transmission, permit, permission, permissive

Ped or pod: foot (*ped* is Latin; *pod* is Greek)

Pedestrian, pedestal, podium, pedometer, centipede, pedal, expedition, impede, podiatry, podiatrist, peddler, centipede

Pel or puls: to drive, push, throw

Impulse, compel, compulsion, expel, expelled, propel, dispel, dispelling, impulsive, pulsate, compulsive, repel, repellent, pelleted

Pend or pens: to hang

Pendant, suspend, suspense, pendulum, pending, dependent, perpendicular, appendix, appendage, appendix, dependents, impending, interdependent

*Plic or ply: to fold

Implicit, implicitness, explicit, explicate, implication, replicate, complicated, application, ply, apply, imply, reply

Port: to carry

Import, export, portable, transport, porter, deport, report, support, portal, important, importantly, unimportant

*Pos, pon, or pose: to put, place, set

Compose, composite, dispose, disposable, oppose, component, postpone, proponent, deposit, compound, depose, proposal, preposition, disposal, exposition, exponent, expose, impose, suppose, opponent, proposition, position

Rupt: to break

Rupture, disrupt, disruptive, disruption, abrupt, abruptly, bankrupt, bankruptcy, corrupt, corruptors, corruption, erupted, eruption, interrupt; erupt, incorruptible

*Scrib or script: to write

Scribble, ascribe, describe, description, conscript, inscribe, inscription, superscription, prescribe, prescriptive, scripture, transcribe, transcript, transcription, manuscript, nondescript, script, scripted, unscripted

*Sist, sta, or stat: to stand, endure

Persist, persistence, persistent, consist, consistent, desist, assist, assistant, insist, stamina, constant, circumstance, distant, obstacle, standard, substance, adversity, resist, resistance

*Spec or spect: to see, watch, observe

Spectator, spectacular, spectacle, respect, disrespect, spectrum, specter, inspect, inspector, retrospective, species, special, specimen, bespectacled, respectable, disrespectfulness

Stru or struct: to build

Structure, structural, construct, construction, destruction, destructive, reconstruct, instruct, instructor, obstruct, instrument, construe, infrastructure, instructive, macrostructure

*Ten, tent, or tain: to have, hold

Tenant, tenable, tenacity, tenacious, contents, contented, discontented, contentment, intent, maintain, retain, retentive, attention, attentiveness, contentious, détente, competent, incompetent

*Tend or tens or tent: to stretch, strain

Intend, intention, intently, extended, tense, intense, pretense, tension, intensity, attention, inattention, unintentionally, distend, detention, détente

Tract: to draw or pull

Tractor, attract, abstract, contract, retract, contractual, detract, distract, distracted, extract, subtract, tractable, intractable, traction, protract, protractor, attractive, contract

Vis: to see

Visual, visa, visor, vision, visible, visitor, visitation, visualize, invisible, visibility, improvise, improvisation, supervise, supervision, televise, television, visionary

Vet or vers: to turn

Convert, convertible, converter, revert, reversible, extrovert, introvert, divert, avert, aversion, aversive, vertigo, advertise, advertisement, overt, overtly, subvert

Greek Combining Forms:

Beginning: *auto, phono, photo, biblio, hydro, hyper, hypo, tele, chrom, arch, phys, psych, micro, peri, bi, semi, hemi, mono, metro, demo*
Examples: *automobile, phonograph, bibliography, hydroelectric, hyperactive, telephone, telegraphy, chromosome, physical, periodontal, semicircle, demonstration*
Ending: **graph, gram, meter, *ology, sphere, scope, crat, cracy, polis*
Examples: *photograph, microscope, hemisphere, telegram, chronometer, physiology, metropolis, perimeter, archeology, bibliography, democracy, autocrat*

Word Consciousness

In many classrooms, word study is interesting, active, and fun, and teachers in these classrooms create environments in which words are discovered, examined, and appreciated (Kucan, 2012). Stahl and Nagy (2006) suggest the importance of developing children's *word consciousness*, a phrase used to describe the interest in and awareness of words, which should be a goal of vocabulary instruction. As with any type of learning, word consciousness is developed, in part, by the tone set by the teacher when it's time for word study. Activities in which children manipulate words, sort words, laugh and giggle about funny words, and choose words they want to know about can be important for vocabulary growth as the more academic aspects of vocabulary teaching and word learning.

Teaching Academic Vocabulary

From 20 years of research on vocabulary instruction, we have learned the characteristics that make vocabulary lessons effective (Blachowicz & Fisher, 2000; Fisher & Frey, 2014). When you are planning vocabulary lessons, regardless of the grade level you teach, remember to:

1. *Involve children in actively developing their understanding of words and ways to learn them.* Such ways include use of semantic mapping, word sorts (see Figure 3.3 and Figure 3.4), Four Corners Vocabulary Charts (see Figure 3.5), and Concept Definition Maps (see Figure 3.6), and also developing strategies

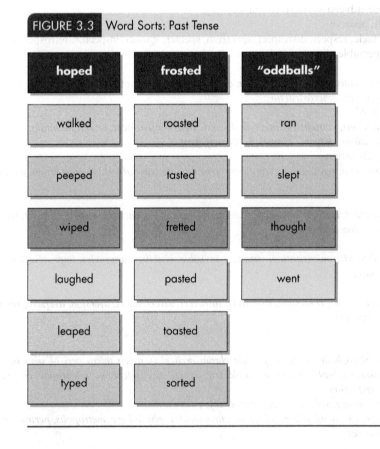

FIGURE 3.3 Word Sorts: Past Tense

hoped	frosted	"oddballs"
walked	roasted	ran
peeped	tasted	slept
wiped	fretted	thought
laughed	pasted	went
leaped	toasted	
typed	sorted	

FIGURE 3.4 Word Sorts: Content Vocabulary

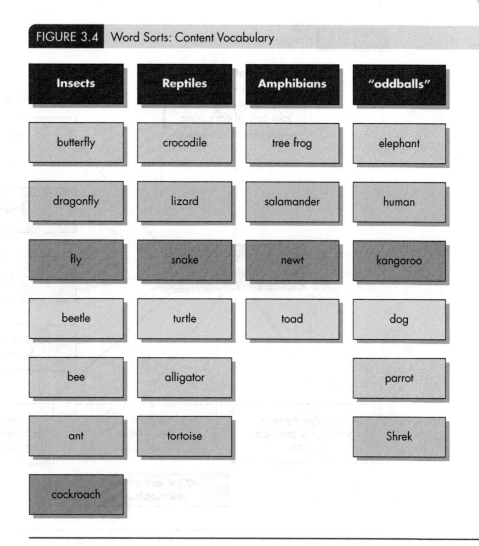

Insects	**Reptiles**	**Amphibians**	**"oddballs"**
butterfly	crocodile	tree frog	elephant
dragonfly	lizard	salamander	human
fly	snake	newt	kangaroo
beetle	turtle	toad	dog
bee	alligator		parrot
ant	tortoise		Shrek
cockroach			

FIGURE 3.5 Four Corners Vocabulary Chart

Illustration (1)	Sentence (2)
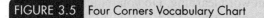	The fluffiest clouds, that look like cotton, are called *cumulus* clouds.
Definition (3)	**Word (4)**
A white billowy cloud type with dark, flat base (from the Latin *cumulus*, meaning a "heap.")	cumulus

FIGURE 3.6 Concept Definition Map

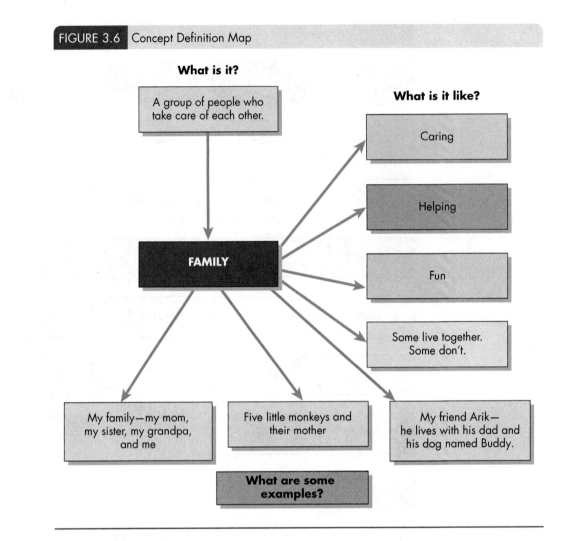

for independent word learning. Do you remember the earlier examples with the root "photo" (p. 77)? After children have learned the meaning of "photo" they can generalize the meaning of "light" to other words that include the same root. That's an example of developing a strategy for word learning.

2. *Encourage children to personalize their word learning* through such practices as Vocabulary Self-Collection Strategy (VSS) (Ruddell, 2007) (see Teaching Ideas section, p. 87), mnemonic strategies, and personal dictionaries.

3. *Immerse children in rich language environments that draw their attention to learning words.* Word Walls, and comparing/contrasting words with the same morphemic element (e.g., *import, export, portable, transport*), aid children in recognizing and using the words around them.

4. *Provide children with multiple sources of information to learn words through repeated exposures.* Letting children see and hear new words more than once and drawing on multiple sources of meaning are important for vocabulary development. Children also should be encouraged to use the words in speech and writing.

Following a three-year research study with English learners and native English speakers in high-poverty schools, Manyak (2010) recommended vocabulary instruction that provides rich and varied language experiences that develop word consciousness and focuses on the teaching of individual words and word-**learning strategies**. For example, depending on the age of your students, provide them with:

1. Student-friendly definitions: "*Disruptive* means to disturb others. Another meaning is *unruly*."

2. Examples of use: "Alex was *disruptive* when he made three trips to the waste can while the teacher was reading the story."

3. Opportunities to create their own examples using the word: "What is an example of something that is *disruptive* to you?"

Clearly, there is little benefit in selecting 10 to 20 isolated vocabulary terms and asking English learners (and other students) to copy them from the board and look up their definitions in the dictionary (Allen, 2007; Fisher & Frey, 2008). Many of the words in the definitions are unfamiliar to these students, which renders the activity meaningless. Although using the dictionary is an important school skill to learn, the task must fit the students' learning and language needs. The number of terms should be tailored to the students' English and literacy levels, and the terms should be presented in context, not in isolation. Picture dictionaries (definitions enhanced with pictorial representations) are excellent resources for contextualizing terms. For children with minimal literacy skills, using the dictionary to find words can serve to reinforce the concept of alphabetizing, and it familiarizes them with the parts of a dictionary; however, defining words should not be the only activity used. Many SIOP teachers introduce dictionary skills to English learners by using words that are already familiar to them.

Short and Echevarría (2016) offer the following guidelines for teaching academic vocabulary. These suggestions are drawn from research and represent a common-sense approach to teaching the words that students need to know. First, carefully select words that are connected to an essential question, topic, or theme. Second, teach the words with visual supports, easily understood examples, personal connections, and bilingual support, as needed. Third, provide extensive practice with the new words, while teaching and reinforcing word-learning strategies. And finally, as mentioned previously, develop students' word consciousness.

Teaching Ideas for Building Background

Additional activities that activate prior knowledge, build students' background knowledge, and develop academic vocabulary include the following:

- **Read aloud.** Teachers regularly read aloud a Big Book, story, article, play, or picture book about a particular topic to build children's background knowledge, or view a DVD or Internet video on the topic.

- **Pair-Share-Chart** (Vogt, Echevarría, & Washam, 2015). This activity begins with a structured partner-share about a familiar topic. After 2–3 minutes, children share their conversation with the whole class. As children share what they know or think they know about the topic, the teacher records their thoughts on chart paper. Using the information that is charted, the teacher introduces a new concept and helps students make connections between what they already know and the new topic. The charted information is saved and added to during the lesson or unit, and the teacher continues to help forge connections with new information.

- **Digital Jump-starts (DJs)** (Rance-Roney, 2010). Jump-starting (also referred to as "front-loading"), is a technique in which teachers preteach a small group of children the concepts, vocabulary, and processes prior to beginning a lesson for the whole class. The purpose is to build background and vocabulary knowledge for children who need extra time and support. Rance-Roney (2010) points out that as effective as jump-starting is, it can cause some management issues for those children who are not working with the teacher in the jump-start group. Therefore, she created "digital jump-starts" that allow children who need the extra time and support to work on a computer, playing and replaying a reading preview, practicing new vocabulary words, and so forth. The DJs can be put on DVDs for home viewing or they can be uploaded to free-access Web sites, such as YouTube.

- **The Insert Method** (Vogt & Echevarría, 2008). This activity is appropriate for grades 2–6 and all subject areas. The teacher provides a copy of a nonfiction article on the topic being taught. In partners, children read the article. During their reading, they insert the following codes directly into the text:

  ✓ A check mark indicates a concept or fact that is already known.

  ? A question mark indicates a concept or fact that is confusing or not understood.

  ! An exclamation mark indicates something that is unusual or a surprise.

  + A plus sign indicates an idea or concept that is new to the reader.

  When the partners finish reading and marking the text, they share their markings with another pair of students. If any misconceptions or misunderstandings are cleared up, then the question mark is replaced with an asterisk (*). When groups finish working, the whole class discusses with the teacher what they have learned and read.

- **Plot Chart** (Vogt & Echevarría, 2008). Many (if not most) young English learners are unfamiliar with the fairy tales that are referred to and practiced (for reading fluency and comprehension) in U.S. schools. For children in pre-K to third grade, the Plot Chart provides an opportunity for English learners to become familiar with common fairy tales, and to learn about the elements of short stories, such as character and plot development. For pre-K–2, use four simple boxes on a graphic organizer with the headings *Somebody, Wanted, But, So*. For older children, use a more complex graphic organizer with five boxes: *Somebody, Wanted, So But, So, In the end*. The Plot Chart is also great for children who may have learned a similar fairy tale in their home language but don't know the English version. Older students who are literate in their first language can write and compare both versions on two Plot Charts. (Did you know that the Cinderella story is found in many versions and languages throughout the world, and was shared with children long before Walt Disney's version—in fact, for hundreds of years?)

Example:

Somebody:	Goldilocks
Wanted:	Some food and a place to rest.
So:	She stopped at the bears' house.
But:	The bears were not home.
So:	Goldilocks found some food that was too hot or too cold, and beds that were too hard or too soft.
In the end:	Goldilocks found porridge (or food) and a bed that was just right! Then the bears came home and found her and she ran away.

● **Pretest with a Partner.** This activity is helpful for children in grades 2–6 and is appropriate for any subject area. The purpose of Pretest with a Partner is to allow students the opportunity at the beginning of a lesson or unit to preview the concepts and vocabulary that will be assessed at the conclusion of that lesson or unit. One pretest and pencil is distributed to each pair of students. The pretest should be similar or identical to the posttest that will be administered later. The partners pass the pretest and pencil back and forth to one another. They read a question aloud, discuss possible answers, come to consensus, and write an answer on the pretest. This activity provides an opportunity for children to activate prior knowledge and share background information, while the teacher circulates to assess what children know, noting gaps and misinformation.

● **Word Clouds.** A word cloud is created based on the frequency of words in a text. There are numerous Web sites that children can use to make word clouds, and some provide support in several different languages, which, depending on the languages, might be especially helpful for English learners. The teacher selects some interesting text that students have read, and copies and pastes it into the text box on the word cloud Web site. The display can be manipulated by selecting a background color, layout, and font. Word clouds enable students to see key words and headings, and they provide prompts for discussion and writing. When children create their own designs, they integrate visual and verbal information, while practicing important digital skills (Dalton & Grisham, 2011). Note that on the word cloud, the larger the word, the more frequently it appears in the text selected for the cloud. To see an example of a word cloud, see Figure 3.8, p. 95 in Mrs. Ornelas's lesson.

● **Word Sorts** (Bear et al., 2016; Helman et al., 2012). During a Word Sort, children categorize previously introduced words or phrases into groups predetermined by the teacher. Words or phrases can be typed on a sheet of paper (46-point type on the computer works well), they can be duplicated from blackline masters in the books by Bear et al. (2016) and Helman et al. (2012), or they can be downloaded from several Web sites by doing a search for "words for word sorts." The teacher or students cut the paper into word strips and then sort the words according to meaning or similarities in structure.

For example, a variety of words in the past tense are listed in mixed order on a sheet of paper (see Figure 3.3, p. 80). After you orally read and then have children chorally read the words, ask them to cut out each of the words and sort them according to spelling pattern and ending sound. You might wish to differentiate here by having your fluent speakers and capable readers determine for themselves several possibilities for sorting, such as by ending sound, by words that end in "*e*" before the "*-ed*" ending is added, and so forth. Depending on their age, children can also do a "word hunt" (Bear et al., 2016), to search for additional words that fit the varied patterns they have identified.

For English learners and struggling readers, you may wish to engage in a small-group lesson with word sorts to teach and reinforce how the past tense is formed in English words. Contextualize the sorts by providing sentences in which the words are used. For very young students, provide the word cards to eliminate the inordinate amount of time and frustration required for children to cut the words themselves.

Other examples of Word Sorts involve words and phrases related to the content concepts being taught (see Figure 3.4, p. 81). Consider the ways this activity could be differentiated: (1) children who may be unfamiliar or shaky with English words for concepts being reviewed can be given labels to use; (2) children for whom this content sort is quick and easy can be directed to a free online encyclopedia to investigate other topics that could be added to the topic of insects, reptiles, and amphibians; (3) children can add more columns to the sort and fill them in with appropriate information, using books or other resources. Adding the "oddball" column in sorts encourages children to think about both examples and non-examples during the classification activity.

- **Contextualizing Key Vocabulary.** SIOP teachers peruse the material to be learned and select several key terms that are critical to understanding the lesson's most important concepts. The teacher introduces the terms at the outset of the lesson, systematically defining or demonstrating each one and showing how that term is used within the context of the lesson. Experienced SIOP teachers know that having children understand completely the meaning of a few key terms is more effective than helping them gain a cursory understanding of a dozen terms. One way of contextualizing words is to read with children in small groups and, as they come across a term they do not understand, pause and explain it to them, using as many examples, synonyms, or cognates as necessary to convey the meaning. Another way is to embed a definition within a sentence when introducing and reviewing a new word or concept, such as:

  ◆ *Amphibians, like frogs and salamanders that have smooth, scale-less skin that must stay wet, are most active at night when there is less evaporation of water.*

  ◆ *The migratory birds, those that flew in a group from one place to another in autumn, stayed near our lake for several days before flying on.*

  ◆ *Discussion, a conversation that focuses on a particular topic, gives everyone a chance to talk.*

  ◆ *Sara, an athletic girl who is healthy, strong, and active, won the race.*

- **Vocabulary Self-Collection Strategy (VSS)** (Ruddell, 2007). Following the reading of a content text, children self-select several words that are essential to understanding content concepts. Words may be selected by individuals, partners, or small groups, and they are eventually shared and discussed by the entire class. The teacher and students mutually agree on a class list of vocabulary self-collection words to study, and these words are reviewed and studied throughout a particular lesson or unit. They also may be entered into a word study notebook, and students may be asked to demonstrate their knowledge of these words through written or oral activities. Ruddell (2007) has found that when students are shown how to identify key content vocabulary, they become adept at selecting and learning words they need to know, and, when given opportunities to practice VSS, their comprehension of the text improves (Ruddell & Shearer, 2002; Shearer, Ruddell, & Vogt, 2001; Stahl & Nagy, 2006). The VSS is an effective method for teaching and reviewing content vocabulary because children learn to trust their own judgments about which content words are the most important to learn. This approach is most appropriate for English learners with high-intermediate and advanced English proficiency and for all students in the upper elementary grades.

- **Word Wall.** During a lesson, key vocabulary is reviewed with a word wall where relevant content vocabulary words are listed alphabetically, usually on a large poster, sheet of butcher paper, or pocket chart (Cunningham, 2004). Originally designed as a method for teaching and reinforcing sight words for emergent readers, word walls are also effective for displaying content words related to a particular unit or theme. The words are revisited frequently throughout the lesson or unit, and children are encouraged to use them in their writing and discussions. Cunningham (2004) recommends that teachers judiciously select words for a word wall and that the number be limited to those of greatest importance. We would add that teachers should resist the temptation to have multiple word walls in one classroom because the walls quickly become cluttered with words that are difficult to sort through, especially for English learners. One word wall, carefully maintained and changed as needed, is what we recommend.

- **Personal Dictionaries.** Similar to VSS, personal dictionaries are created as an individual vocabulary and spelling resource for children at all levels of English proficiency. Students can read together in pairs or small groups and write unknown words they encounter in their personal dictionaries. The teacher can work with each group and discuss the words students have written in their dictionaries, providing correction or clarity as needed. Have children draw a picture to help them remember key words.

- **Four Corners Vocabulary Charts** (Vogt & Echevarría, 2008). These charts provide more context and "clues" than typical word walls, because they include an illustration, a definition, and a sentence for each vocabulary word (see Figure 3.5, p. 81). For academic words that are challenging to illustrate (e.g., *discuss or summarize*), simply take a photo of your students during a discussion or when summarizing, and insert the photo on the chart as a reminder of the word's meaning.

- **Concept Definition Map.** The Concept Definition Map is a great way to learn and remember content vocabulary and concepts (Buehl, 2014). For example, in one first-grade classroom, the children were learning about families as their teacher read aloud and discussed several picture books about different kinds of families, including *My Family* by Debbie Bailey and Susan Huszar (1998, Annick Press); *The Family Book* by Todd Parr (2003, Little, Brown Books for Young Readers); and *Five Little Monkeys Jumping on the Bed* by Eileen Christelow (1989, Clarion). At the beginning of the day's lesson, the teacher introduced a partially completed Concept Definition Map (see Figure 3.6, p. 82), with the word *Family* in the center box. As the children discussed the different kinds of families they had read about, the teacher began filling in some of the boxes in a large Concept Definition Map drawn on chart paper. The next day, after another story, the children completed their own maps and used them to write sentences about their own family and other families. The teacher honored the fact that English learners, including those who were recent immigrants, knew about families and could contribute what they knew during the class discussions, even if they didn't know some of the English words for the familiar concepts. For upper-elementary teachers, even though the Concept Definition Map is a simple graphic organizer, it can be used to discuss complex concepts such as *freedom, democracy*, or *revolution*, and literary terminology, such as *symbolism* or *irony*. The Concept Definition Map is also an excellent prewriting activity for teaching summarizing. Children begin the summarizing process by organizing content concepts in the graphic organizer. Then sentences can be created from the information in the Concept Definition Map and subsequently written into paragraph form.

- **Cloze Sentences.** Cloze sentences can be used to teach and review content vocabulary. Children read a sentence that has strong contextual support for the vocabulary word that has been omitted from the sentence. Once the meaning of the word is determined and possible replacement words are brainstormed, the teacher (or a student) provides the correct word. For example, *During an_____, the ground moves and shakes, and sometimes, buildings fall down (earthquake)*.

- **Word Generation.** This activity helps English learners and others learn and/or review new content vocabulary through analogy. For example, the teacher writes *port* on the board and invites children to brainstorm all the words they can think of that contain *port*. Examples might include *report, import, export, important, portfolio, port-a-potty, Portland, deport, transport, transportation, support, airport*, and so on. The meaning of each brainstormed word is discussed and children are asked what they think the root *port* means ("to carry"). Each brainstormed word is revisited to see if the definition "to carry" has something to do with the word's meaning. Note that the teacher does not define *port* first; rather, we recommend that children generalize meanings of content words from words that they already know that contain the same syllable or word part. Many of the roots found in Figure 3.2, pp. 78–79, can be used for Word Generation.

- **Word Study Books.** A Word Study Book is a student-made personal notebook containing frequently used words and concepts. The Word Study Book can be organized by English language structure, such as listing together all the words studied so far that end in *-tion, -sion,* and *-tation.* Word Study Books can also be used for content study where words are grouped by topic.

- **Vocabulary Games.** Playing games like *Pictionary* and *Scrabble* can help children recall vocabulary terms. Word searches for beginning English speakers and crossword puzzles for students with more English proficiency are additional vocabulary development tools. Word searches and templates for crossword puzzles are readily available online.

- **Self-Assessment of Levels of Word Knowledge** (Diamond & Gutlohn, 2006). As English learners are acquiring vocabulary, it may be helpful for them to self-assess their knowledge of new words. Four levels of word knowledge that can be used to describe the extent of a person's understanding of words are:

  1. I've never heard or seen the word before.

  2. I've seen or heard the word before, but I don't know what it means.

  3. I vaguely know the meaning of the word, and I can associate it with a concept or context.

  4. I know the word well.

  With effective vocabulary instruction and repeated exposures to unfamiliar vocabulary, students' knowledge of the words increases and they move up the levels from 1 to 4. When teachers introduce the four Levels of Word Knowledge, children can self-assess their knowledge as words are introduced and studied.

■ Differentiating Ideas for Multi-level Classes

Nearly all of the teaching ideas in the previous section provide ways to **differentiate instruction** while developing children's background and vocabulary knowledge. The following idea is geared specifically to differentiating according to English learners' levels of English proficiency. (If you need to refresh your memory of these stages, please see the Glossary, p. 323, where they are described.)

- **Differentiated Signal Words.** Signal Words (see Vogt and Echevarría, 2008) are an effective way to provide English learners (and other students) with words related to particular language functions, such as comparing/contrasting, determining cause/effect, sequencing events, summarizing, drawing conclusions, making generalizations, etc. Rothenberg and Fisher (2007) suggest that signal words can be differentiated for varied **levels of language proficiency**. For example, for sequencing events, beginning speakers are encouraged to use in their writing and speaking words such as *first, second, next, later, then.* In addition to these signal words, intermediate speakers are encouraged to use words and phrases such as *while, before, now, after, finally, in the past. . . .* Advanced speakers and older elementary students add the following to their repertoire while writing and speaking about sequential events: *prior to, previously, since, eventually, subsequently.*

■ The Lesson

Short Story: *Two Were Left* by Hugh B. Cave (Sixth Grade)

Three teachers in an urban K-6 school with a large population of English learners are teaching a well-known and suspenseful short story by the author Hugh B. Cave. Although it was written in 1942, it remains an exciting, suspenseful, and intriguing story for upper elementary children (grades 4-6). Each of the teachers' self-contained classes includes English learners with a variety of levels of English proficiency. The classes are heterogeneously mixed with native English speakers and English learners, and all children are reading at a variety of reading levels. This story is part of a larger literature unit focusing on stories and poetry, with the theme of "Decisions and Their Consequences."

The short story, *Two Were Left*, begins with a description of a boy named Noni and his devoted husky, Nimuk, stranded on a floating ice island in the sea. It is not evident from the text exactly how they got there, but it is implied that the boy and dog had been with village hunters, and the ice they were on had broken away from the others. Noni and Nimuk had been there for an undetermined time, and both were exhausted, hungry, and increasingly wary of each other. Noni's leg had been hurt at a previous time, and he was wearing a simple brace made of a harness and iron strips. The boy decided to make a weapon in case the starving Nimuk decided to attack him. In Noni's village, it was not uncommon to use dogs for food in times of hunger. The story continues as Noni works on making a knife, and boy and dog become increasingly weak. The suspense builds as Noni considers the consequences of attacking his dog. Eventually, he decides he can't possibly kill his beloved dog, and he flings the crude knife away from both of them. It lands point first in the ice some distance away. Nimuk growls in a frightening way, but eventually licks Noni's face and falls, exhausted, by his owner. Sadly, boy and dog cuddle together, unable to save themselves any longer. Not much later, an airplane pilot sees two figures on the ice island and swoops in for a closer look. He settles his plane on the ice and saves an unconscious Noni and his dog, Nimuk. What had caught the pilot's attention was the reflection of a quivering knife stuck in the ice.

In their state, the language arts teachers in grade 6 are expected to address the Common Core State Standards (CCSS, 2010). The following standards guided the development of the following lessons.

Key Ideas and Details

1. Read closely to determine what the text says explicitly and to make logical inferences from it; cite specific textual evidence when writing or speaking to support conclusions drawn from the text.

2. Determine central ideas or themes of a text and analyze their development; summarize the key supporting details and ideas.

3. Analyze how and why individuals, events, and ideas develop and interact over the course of a text.

Note: The story, *Two Were Left*, can be found on the Internet by searching the title and author.

■ Teaching Scenarios

The teachers have prepared their own lesson plans for teaching the short story, *Two Were Left* by Hugh B. Cave. Their individual instructional approaches and SIOP ratings follow.

Miss Saunders

Miss Saunders began her lesson by reviewing with her students the lesson's content objectives (connecting the day's story to the theme of "Decisions and Consequences") and language objectives (reading a story; locating and defining vocabulary words) that were written on chart paper. Next, she asked the table groups to turn over the four photos that were face down on their tables. Each was a photo of Alaska: One was of a glacier, another was of the tundra, the third was of the sea with large, broken pieces of ice floating in it, and the fourth was of an Inuit village. Miss Saunders asked her students to do a Think-Pair-Share and consider what they observed in the photos, what they had questions about, and what they thought life must be like for the people living in the village. She then described her experiences on a vacation to Alaska and showed some of her photos.

Miss Saunders next introduced several vocabulary words that were taken from the story. She mentioned that understanding these words would help children better understand the story. She wrote the following on the board: *Noni, Nimuk, ice island, momentarily, intentions, suspiciously, unconscious.* She explained the first two words were the characters' names in the story. Miss Saunders then distributed copies of the two-page story and asked students to find the remaining vocabulary words in the story. Once they found the words, children were asked to highlight them, and, with a partner, try to define the words using contextual clues. Then, the students, in pairs, were expected to match their informal definitions with those found in the dictionary and make corrections, as needed.

When everyone was finished with the vocabulary assignment, Miss Saunders and the class went over the vocabulary words' definitions. She then asked the children to read the story silently. The evening's homework assignment was to create a "storyboard" of *Two Were Left*. Miss Saunders reminded the class of what the word *sequence* means and noted that events in a story generally follow in particular order or sequence. She said, "You remember when we talked about this, right?" Her students nodded affirmatively. She then asked the students what the first event was in *Two Were Left*. A student responded that Noni and Nimuk were on a piece of ice that broke off

FIGURE 3.7	Building Background Component of the SIOP® Model: Miss Saunders's Lesson

4	3	2	1	0	N/A
7. **Concepts explicitly linked** to students' background experiences		**Concepts loosely linked** to students' background experiences		**Concepts not explicitly linked** to students' background experiences	

4	3	2	1	0
8. **Links explicitly made** between past learning and new concepts		**Few links made** between past learning and new concepts		**No links made** between past learning and new concepts

	4	3	2	1	0
9. **Key vocabulary emphasized** (e.g., introduced, written, repeated, and highlighted for students to see)		**Key vocabulary** introduced, but not emphasized		**Key vocabulary** not introduced or emphasized	

? **Reflect and Apply**

Click here to explain your ratings for Miss Saunders's lesson on each of the Building Background features.

from a larger piece. "That's right, Louis!" She then distributed a large piece of white construction paper to each student with the instructions to fold it into eighths, and draw the first event in the first box in the upper left hand corner. After a few moments, Miss Saunders asked the class to take the construction paper home and to continue making the storyboard sequence by drawing pictures that depicted seven other important events in the story. She quickly went over the day's objectives, with mixed feelings about her students' progress toward meeting them, and the bell rang shortly thereafter.

Check Your Understanding: On the SIOP form in Figure 3.7, rate Miss Saunders's lesson for each of the Building Background features.

Mrs. Ornelas

Mrs. Ornelas began the story, *Two Were Left*, by asking her students to close their eyes for a moment and put their heads down on their desks. She then turned down the lights and turned on a recording of heavy winds blowing. Then, she said in a slow and careful cadence: "Imagine for a moment . . . you are in the Arctic, farther north than Alaska, where the winds blow almost continuously. You live here with your family in a small village. During the winter, it snows every day until there are so many feet of snow piled high that all walking paths are solid ice. The only time there is any natural light is around lunch time and it's only a glimmer; then it becomes black as night once again. In the summer, the sun never sets so you have to put heavy cloth or tarps on window openings so you can sleep. This is your home, and you share it with your parents and best friend, your dog. You are happy that you have family, good friends, and enough food. However, one day, everything changes. You and your dog become separated from the other hunters in your village and you end up alone on a chunk of ice, floating with only your dog. Think about what you might do in this situation to save yourself."

Mrs. Ornelas then turned off the recording and raised the lights. She turned on the document reader so the students could see the brief paragraph that she had just read to them. She read aloud the directions that followed the paragraph: "With your group members, jot down the ways that your lives are different from this boy's life. Think of as many different things as you can. Now, how are your lives like this boy's life?" Mrs. Ornelas asked each student to draw a Venn diagram graphic organizer (this was familiar to them) on a piece of paper, and as they talked among themselves, they filled out the organizer. The class then briefly reported out what they had discussed.

Mrs. Ornelas then explained the lesson's content objectives (comparing and contrasting their lives with the main character's life; predicting events in the story) and language objectives (finding examples of foreshadowing in the story; reading the story while confirming or disconfirming predictions). Next, she displayed on the interactive whiteboard a map of the Arctic region, so all children had an idea of the setting for the story they were going to read. Mrs. Ornelas pointed to Alaska and northern Canada, and asked students if they had ever read, seen, or heard anything (other than what she had just read) about this part of the world. One girl said, "I remember when we were studying climate change in Science and we looked at photos of melting glaciers. That's what I thought of when you started telling us your story." Mrs. Ornelas displayed on the white board several large photos of glaciers and said, "You mean these pictures, Esmeralda? You're right. The setting for today's story is very much like what we talked about in science, so think about these photos as you begin reading about the setting in today's story."

Mrs. Ornelas next displayed on the whiteboard the following academic vocabulary words: *predicting* and *foreshadowing*, because these words are critical to understanding the story deeply. She reviewed the meaning of *predicting* because this was a familiar process while reading stories. She then introduced *foreshadowing* by pointing to the word on the board and asking what *fore* made them think of. Someone said "Before?" Another said, "Doesn't it have something to do with golf?" She wrote on the board *foreground* and *forethought*, and asked students to try to figure out the words' meanings, with *fore* meaning "before or in front of"; then she asked them to have a partner conversation about whether the three words might be related because of the prefix *fore*. Mrs. Ornelas walked around the room listening while her students grappled with their task. She then asked the children to share with their partner what *shadowing* might mean. Nearly everyone knew what a shadow was, but they were struggling with the term *foreshadowing*. Mrs. Ornelas asked the students if, when she was reading the brief vignette at the beginning of class, they had formed any ideas of what today's story might be about. Many students' hands flew into the air. After taking a few responses, Mrs. Ornelas told the class, "I used foreshadowing to help you think about the story we're going to read before we actually read it. You're now already making some predictions based on the hints I provided, right? What are they?"

After taking some responses, Mrs. Ornelas told the students that in the story, *Two Were Left*, the author would also give some hints about what was going to happen later in the story. She said, "These hints are called *foreshadowing*. Throughout our reading, we will make predictions and as we continue, we will either confirm or disconfirm our predictions, sometimes based on the foreshadowing the author provides." Mrs. Ornelas reminded students that they had worked with confirming and disconfirming predictions before in other stories, and she reminded them about how to use the strategy. She also told them that the author's use of foreshadowing would help them predict what would happen in the story. She encouraged them to see if they could find examples of *foreshadowing* and to underline them while they read the story together. Mrs. Ornelas then distributed copies of *Two Were Left* and the class engaged in a familiar group reading activity called the Directed Reading-Thinking Activity (DR-TA) (see Chapter 5, p. 132 for more details).

Mrs. Ornelas began by asking the children to cover with another piece of paper everything but the title, *Two Were Left*. She then asked, "With a title like *Two Were Left*, what do you think this story is going to be about?" The children laughed and said, "About a boy and a dog!" Mrs. Ornelas directed the students to uncover and read the next brief paragraph that provided more information. She then said, "Okay . . . now you have new information. What do you think is going to happen next? Why do you think so?" And off they went, uncovering more and more of the story while reading, predicting, discussing, confirming, and disconfirming their ideas, until Noni and Nimuk were finally rescued. Most students could find some foreshadowing, starting with the title, and one even identified the quivering knife that eventually signaled the pilot. The story concluded with a brief discussion of the unit's theme (Decisions and Consequences) and Noni's decision to throw away the knife. After reviewing their objectives, students and teacher alike agreed that their content and language objectives had been met.

The next day, for a follow-up vocabulary activity, the students in pairs or triads selected their favorite part of *Two Were Left*, and typed it into a word cloud box on the classroom computers. The most frequent words from the story were emphasized on the word clouds. Later, the students discussed how important these words were to the story (see Figure 3.8 on the following page).

Check Your Understanding: On the SIOP form in Figure 3.9, rate Mrs. Ornelas's lesson for each of the Building Background features.

Mr. Engelhart

Mr. Engelhart began his lesson by telling his students the objectives: *You will learn some new words from the story we are going to read and complete a story plot graphic organizer*. He then distributed a worksheet that had vocabulary word definitions and sentences from the day's story, *Two Were Left*. He gave each student eight index cards so that they could copy the information from the worksheet, one vocabulary word per card so that students would have eight flash cards for practice. The words on the worksheet included the following: *marooned, warily, labored, inventions, thrust, aroused, feebly, quivering*.

The following are examples of four of the vocabulary words, definitions, and sentences that the students copied onto their index cards from the words on the worksheet.

Marooned: to place or leave alone without hope of escape; "And, now, the two, completely alone, *marooned* on the ice, eyed each other warily."

Warily: careful and watchful for danger; "And, now, the two, completely alone, marooned on the ice, eyed each other *warily.*"

FIGURE 3.8 Word Cloud from Two Were Left

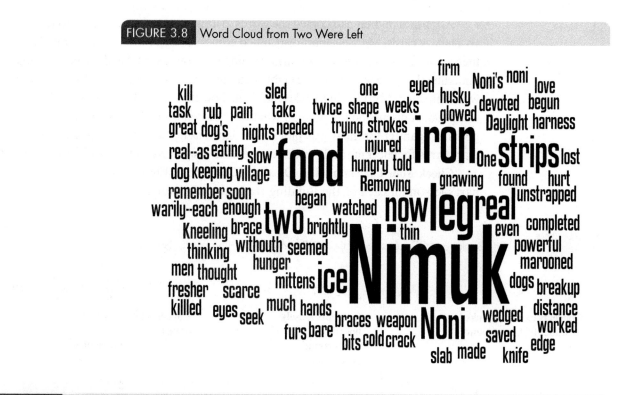

FIGURE 3.9 Building Background Component of the SIOP® Model: Mrs. Ornelas's Lesson

4	3	2	1	0	N/A
7. **Concepts explicitly linked** to students' background experiences		**Concepts loosely linked** to students' background experiences		**Concepts not explicitly linked** to students' background experiences	

4	3	2	1	0
8. **Links explicitly made** between past learning and new concepts		**Few links made** between past learning and new concepts		**No links made** between past learning and new concepts

4	3	2	1	0
9. **Key vocabulary emphasized** (e.g., introduced, written, repeated, and highlighted for students to see)		**Key vocabulary** introduced, but not emphasized		**Key vocabulary** not introduced or emphasized

---

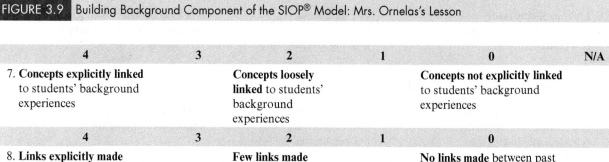

Reflect and Apply

Click here to explain your ratings for Mrs. Ornelas's lesson on each of the Building Background features.

Labored: to move with great effort; "He could see hunger and suffering in the dog's *labored* breathing and awkward movements."

Intentions: a planned way of acting; "Closer Nimuk came, aware of Noni's *intentions.*"

After the children had copied the words, definitions, and sentences onto their eight vocabulary cards, Mr. Engelhart distributed copies of the *Two Were Left* story. He then asked for volunteers to take turns reading the story aloud. He directed students to underline the sentences where the eight vocabulary words were found. When the story was completed, Mr. Engelhart asked students how they liked the story, and all said it was good. A discussion followed on what the children liked about the story, and why. A graphic organizer for the story's plot was assigned as homework. He collected the vocabulary cards for checking and concluded the lesson, satisfied that his goals had been met.

Check Your Understanding: On the SIOP form in Figure 3.10, rate Mr. Engelhart's lesson for each of the Building Background features.

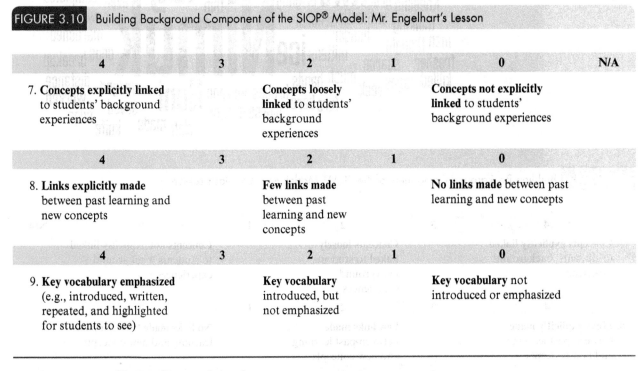

FIGURE 3.10 Building Background Component of the SIOP® Model: Mr. Engelhart's Lesson

4	3	2	1	0	N/A
7. **Concepts explicitly linked** to students' background experiences		**Concepts loosely linked** to students' background experiences		**Concepts not explicitly linked** to students' background experiences	

4	3	2	1	0
8. **Links explicitly made** between past learning and new concepts		**Few links made** between past learning and new concepts		**No links made** between past learning and new concepts

4	3	2	1	0
9. **Key vocabulary emphasized** (e.g., introduced, written, repeated, and highlighted for students to see)		**Key vocabulary** introduced, but not emphasized		**Key vocabulary** not introduced or emphasized

? Reflect and Apply

Click here to explain your ratings for Mr. Engelhart's lesson on each of the Building Background features.

Discussion of Lessons

7. *Concepts Explicitly Linked to Students' Background Experiences*

Miss Saunders: 3

Mrs. Ornelas: 4

Mr. Engelhart: 0

- **Miss Saunders's** lesson received a "3" for this feature. She chose to develop students' background knowledge for the story, *Two Were Left*, by showing them photographs of Alaska that were similar to the setting of the story. The Think-Pair-Share activity was a good one to choose so that students could share their impressions of the photos with each other and the class. While Miss Saunders's vacation photos and stories were interesting, they didn't directly relate to the setting of the story the children were going to read. Perhaps a video clip from the Internet could have been shown, and, depending on the location of Miss Saunders's school, having the students contrast their living conditions (such as southern California or Florida) with the story's setting would have been meaningful. Also, since the main characters are a boy and a dog, bringing children's feelings about their pets (or others' pets they know) could have prepared them for the emotional aspect of this story.

- **Mrs. Ornelas's** lesson received a "4" for this feature. She spent about 15 minutes activating her students' prior knowledge and building their background about the setting of the story, *Two Were Left*. Because the setting and the situation were so very different from the students' experiences, the time was well spent. It's not just the actual setting that is so different (the Arctic area), but it's also the culture of the people in the story, where dogs aren't pets, but rather commodities that can mean the difference between life and death. In the lesson, the students' predictions and ability to grapple with a challenging literary device like foreshadowing were enhanced by the visualization exercise (with students' eyes closed and the wind blowing) and the comparison/contrast of their lives to Noni's via the Venn diagram. Also, the DR-TA is a powerful activity that enables teachers to really understand where children's predictions and ideas are coming from while they're reading. Children use their background experiences and knowledge throughout a DR-TA to make and then confirm/disconfirm their predictions while developing comprehension of the story. (Note that confirming predictions requires citing text evidence, which is a Common Core State Standard.)

- **Mr. Engelhart's** lesson received a "0" for this feature. He didn't attempt to activate students' background knowledge or build background information related to the story's content concepts or vocabulary. He did state his goals, but these were not written as content and language objectives. The verbs used in objectives should be measurable and observable; the verb "learn" is neither. Also, "completing a graphic organizer" is an activity, rather than a learning goal. When objectives are well written, they provide information that begins to activate students' prior knowledge and build background knowledge.

8. *Links Explicitly Made between Past Learning and New Concepts*

Miss Saunders: 1

Mrs. Ornelas: 3

Mr. Engelhart: 0

- **Miss Saunders's** lesson received a "1" for this feature. She made only one reference to the students' past learning and it was toward the end of the lesson. When she asked her students if they recalled talking about the story sequence, the children gamely replied with a unison nod. Because understanding story sequence was critically important for the homework assignment, explicitly reviewing (and if necessary, re-teaching) the steps taught previously (e.g., introduction, rising action, falling action, climax, conclusion; or beginning, event 1, event 2, . . . conclusion) was very important. English learners would have benefitted from working together with the teacher and/or a small group to identify the story sequence prior to creating the storyboard. There will also most likely be confusion when doing the homework if the number of boxes (8) doesn't match the number of story events they identify at home.

- **Mrs. Ornelas's** lesson received a "3" for this feature. She was prepared to make an explicit link between the students' previous learning about the Arctic area and the story they were going to read in this lesson. She had the photos from the Science lesson ready to display on the interactive whiteboard so students could make the connections. It would have been a good idea to be more explicit in reminding students of how readers make predictions, and more importantly, how they could confirm and disconfirm predictions while reading. This was especially important because Mrs. Ornelas was connecting making predictions to the author's use of foreshadowing in the story. This might have been confusing to some English learners and struggling readers who still needed more practice in understanding making predictions as a metacognitive strategy (see Chapter 5 for more information).

- **Mr. Engelhart's** lesson received a "0" for this feature because it included nothing to connect past learning to today's lesson in terms of content concepts, vocabulary, or language. Although students may have completed vocabulary cards previously, there was no attempt to connect former vocabulary to today's new words.

9. *Key Vocabulary Emphasized*

Miss Saunders: 2

Mrs. Ornelas: 4

Mr. Engelhart: 1

- **Miss Saunders's** lesson received a "2" for this feature. She selected some interesting and perhaps tricky words from the story for her students to work with. However, the time that was spent on finding informal and formal definitions of these words was not necessarily going to enable the English learners (and other students) to better understand this story. That is, they were not critical to the story's outcome, especially character names, which are easily learned. It would have been more relevant to this particular story and the objectives (sequencing the events in the story) if she had spent the time reviewing the academic vocabulary related to sequencing, perhaps with signal words the students could have used on their storyboards (*first, next, then, finally, in the end,* and so forth). She then could have identified and talked about some of the more interesting and challenging words in the story, working with the children to use the context clues for the informal definitions.

- **Mrs. Ornelas's** lesson received a "4" for this feature. She chose to teach explicitly two academic vocabulary words that she felt were essential to fully comprehending the story. One is an important literary term related to author's craft (*foreshadowing*), and the other is a critical strategy for reading (*predicting*). Notice how she introduced these concepts with the visualizing activity. She then divided the word *foreshadowing* into two parts (*fore + shadowing*) before writing *foreground* and *forethought* on the board, leading students to generalize the meanings of the three words. There are many other very interesting words in this story, and on the following day, the children worked with them when creating their word cloud designs. Because the word clouds emphasized the most frequent words in the passages the children chose, they could readily compare them with the interesting, but less frequently used words.

- **Mr. Engelhart's** lesson received a "1" for this feature. He provided his students with a list of vocabulary words, definitions, and sentences from the story they read, but the students' assignment to copy them onto the flash cards didn't have a clear purpose and it's unlikely the words carried much meaning for them. Making connections to the words would have been difficult to do since several were somewhat unique to this story, and thus challenging for grade 6 students. One exposure to these words would not ensure retention of either the words or their meanings. Mr. Engelhart's students may have enjoyed listening to and reading the story, but his lesson missed many opportunities to develop their content and language knowledge.

(For more ideas of lessons and units in English-language arts in grades K–6, please see Vogt, Echevarría, Short, 2010 Vogt, M.E., Echevarría, J., and Short, D. (2010). *The SIOP® Model for Teaching English-Language Arts to English Learners.* Boston: Allyn & Bacon.)

Watch this video to hear Dr. Jana Echevarría review the Building Background Component and see a grade 3 language arts lesson on fact and opinion. To what extent are each of the three features of Building Background present in this lesson?

Teaching with Technology

After talking with the teachers and discussing the lessons you read about in the Scenarios earlier in the chapter, our tech integrator, Ms. Palacios, offered some technology suggestions to enhance the teachers' lessons.

Digital Flashcards: The three teachers featured in the scenarios for this chapter all agreed that their students could benefit from an engaging way to reinforce vocabulary. Ms. Palacios suggested that the teachers build sets of digital flashcards on the Web site *Quizlet*. During a technology workshop, Ms. Palacios worked with Mr. Englehart, Miss Saunders, and Mrs. Ornelas to create lists on *Quizlet* using vocabulary from the short story *Two Were Left*. The teachers made various sets of flashcards, some with words and definitions and others with words and images. The three teachers then posted links to the vocabulary sets on their class Web pages. After a

(continued on the next page)

few days of use, the teachers saw positive results. A quick survey in class showed that children were practicing words at home on computers, various types of tablets, and smartphones. Many students reported preferring the online study versus traditional index cards or notes. In the weeks following, the teachers explored the application further. They were happy to discover a number of other valuable features such as support for over a dozen languages, audio with a realistic voice, options to record your own voice, and multiple ways to practice the words including spelling and games.

Other terms for this type of tool: online vocabulary review/practice

Related products: *StudyBlue*, *Brainscape*, and *Spelling City*

Surveys for Vocabulary Self-Collection: Many schools around the world have adopted Google Apps for Education, a free suite of apps that includes *Docs*, *Sheets*, and *Forms*, and others. For an introduction to the suite, Ms. Palacios focused on the app named *Forms*, which provides an easy way to create surveys and collect information from students. This tool connects well with the Vocabulary Self-Collection Strategy (VSS) (p. 87). The activity gives students the opportunity to select vocabulary that they consider essential to understanding a particular text. While VSS has proven to be consistently valuable, teachers have found that compiling students' word lists can be time consuming. Ms. Palacios thought using *Forms* could expedite that process. To test out the new tool, Mr. Englehart, Miss Saunders, and Mrs. Ornelas created a Google Form to collect the students' vocabulary selection for the short story that followed *Two Were Left*. They shared the Form with the children via their class Web sites. For homework, the students read the new story and entered their essential vocabulary into the form. One feature of *Forms* that the teachers found convenient was the response sheet. All of the data that entered into a Form gets automatically sent to a spreadsheet, where it's sorted into columns corresponding to each question on the survey. It took much less time than collecting and compiling paper word lists from all of the students. Also, for teachers interested in using word clouds, it is simple to copy all of the student vocabulary submissions from the form response sheet and then paste them into a word cloud generator.

Related products: *Survey Monkey*

Note: Due to the constantly evolving nature of the Internet, it is a challenge to ensure that all of the links and Web services listed here are updated and functional when you read the technology sections. While specific tools or services may appear in the narrative, we have also included the general search term for each tool. If a specific service does not work or is no longer available, search with the general term for the tool and you should be able to find a comparable Web site.

Check Your Understanding
Click here to check your understanding of Chapter 3, Building Background.

▪ Summary

As you reflect on this chapter and the impact of connecting children's background knowledge and learning experiences to the content being taught, and the importance of explicitly teaching academic vocabulary, consider the following main points:

- Explicitly linking a lesson's key content and language concepts to children's background knowledge and experiences enables them to forge connections between what they know and what they are learning.

- In addition, explicitly connecting past content and language learning to a new lesson's content and language concepts assists children in understanding that their previous learning connects to the lesson they will have today.

- English learners may have a difficult time with the academic vocabulary of various disciplines. Three types of academic vocabulary discussed in this chapter are: (1) subject-specific and technical vocabulary; (2) general academic: cross-curricular/process/function vocabulary; and (3) word parts: roots and affixes.

- Teaching ideas, such as using visuals to provide concrete meanings, Four Corners Vocabulary charts, differentiated signal words, and word clouds, engage children in interactive practice with words that promotes academic vocabulary development for English learners.

Discussion Questions

1. In reflecting on the content and language objectives at the beginning of the chapter, are you able to:
   a. Identify techniques for connecting children's personal experiences and past learning to lesson concepts?
   b. Determine ways to develop background knowledge for children for whom there is a mismatch between what they know and have experienced and what is being taught?
   c. Select key vocabulary for a SIOP lesson using words from these three groups: content vocabulary, general academic vocabulary, word parts: roots and affixes?
   d. Write a lesson plan incorporating attention to building background, links to students' past learning, and key vocabulary?

2. Some educators assert the importance of connecting new information to English learners' own cultural backgrounds in order to make content concepts meaningful. Others disagree, stating that children relate more to popular American influences than they do to their parents' traditional cultural practices. What are some merits and problems with both positions? What about English learners born in the United States who have never lived in their native cultural setting?

3. Think about a joke or cartoon that you didn't understand, such as from a late-show monologue or a political cartoon. Why was it confusing or not amusing? What information would you have needed for it to make sense? What are the implications for teaching content to all students, including English learners?

4. Add to the SIOP lesson you have started. Think about how you will activate children's prior knowledge and build background. What explicit connections to past learning can you make? What are your key academic vocabulary words, and how will you teach them? Choose some techniques or activities for the lesson.

CHAPTER 4

Comprehensible Input

Learning Outcomes

After reading, discussing, and engaging in activities related to this chapter, you will be able to meet the following **content** and **language objectives**:

Content Objectives

Identify techniques for presenting content information in ways that students comprehend.

Review various ways to provide directions for completing academic tasks.

Language Objectives

Discuss modifications to teacher speech that can increase student comprehension.

Write the steps needed for students to perform an academic task and have a partner perform each step.

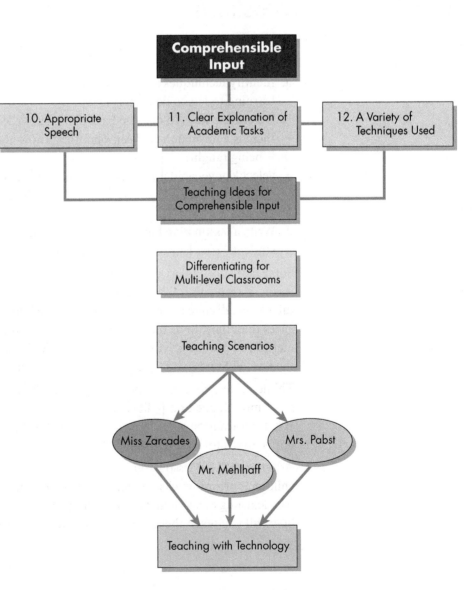

As you look through the features of **SIOP**, you will see that they reflect what we know about effective instruction for all students—English speakers and **English learners** alike. However, implementation of particular features is critical for making content understandable for English learners. The features of the Comprehensible Input component make SIOP instruction different from "just good teaching." While English learners benefit from many of the teaching practices that are effective for all students, these students also require modifications to make instruction meaningful (August & Shanahan, 2006, 2010). Making a message understandable for students is referred to as *comprehensible input* (Krashen, 1985). A **culturally responsive** SIOP teacher takes into account the unique linguistic needs of English learners and modifies teaching accordingly. Whether instruction is for a designated **English language development** or **ESL** lesson or for a content area lesson that makes subject matter accessible while also developing **English language proficiency**, comprehensible input techniques are essential. ●

© Juice Images/Alamy

Have you ever tried to water ski without a boat? Impossible, right? No matter how much you want to ski, it can't happen without a boat. A teacher using the features of Comprehensible Input functions as the boat because English learners, no matter how motivated, can't be successful academically if they don't understand what the teacher is saying, what they are expected to do, or how to accomplish a task. Humans don't "pick up" language solely from exposure. For example, many of us have been around speakers of Spanish, Vietnamese, or Farsi, but we understand little, if anything of what is being said. Comprehensible input techniques are necessary for students to understand the essence of what is being said or presented. A SIOP teacher makes verbal communication more understandable by consciously using supports that are matched to students' levels of English proficiency.

In this chapter, we present ways to support English learners' comprehension so that lessons are understandable for them.

■ Background

Watch this video to see teachers demonstrate what comprehensible input is all about. Can you identify several techniques that are shown? How might you increase comprehensibility using some of the ideas mentioned by Dr. Vogt? https://www.youtube .com/watch?v= mTnHonxao70

Specialized teaching techniques are needed when working with English learners who are expected to master rigorous content material to meet high academic standards in a language they do not speak or comprehend completely. Acquiring a new language takes time and is facilitated by many "clues"—by speech that is geared to individual proficiency levels and by techniques that are used consistently in daily teaching routines.

Comprehensible input entails much more than simply showing pictures as visual clues during a lesson. It involves a conscious effort to make the lesson accessible through a variety of means. Communication is made more understandable with speech that is appropriate to students' proficiency levels. The teacher enunciates and speaks more slowly, but in a natural way, chunking text into meaningful phrases, for students who are beginning English speakers. More repetition may be needed for beginners and, as students gain more proficiency in English, the teacher adjusts her speech to the students' levels. Teachers will increase children's understanding by using appropriate speech coupled with a variety of techniques that will make the content clear.

These techniques are particularly important as students aim to meet the **Common Core State Standards (CCSS)** and other state standards in each grade level. Across grade levels, the standards ask students to comprehend information presented orally and to express their understanding in a variety of ways, such as recounting key ideas and details, and paraphrasing or summarizing the information presented. The way information is presented orally will have a significant impact on the degree to which English learners will be able to achieve these standards.

We will discuss a number of ways to make teacher talk comprehensible to students in the next sections. In the scenarios that follow later in the chapter, you will see examples of teachers who use comprehensible input techniques with varying degrees of effectiveness.

SIOP® FEATURE 10:

Speech Appropriate for Students' Proficiency Levels

For this feature, speech refers to (1) rate and enunciation and (2) complexity of language. The first aspect addresses *how* the teacher speaks and the second aspect refers to *what* is said, such as level of vocabulary used, complexity of sentence structure, and use of idioms.

Students who are at the beginning **levels of language proficiency** benefit from teachers who slow down their rate of speech, use pauses, and enunciate clearly while speaking. As children become more comfortable with the language and acquire higher levels of proficiency, a slower rate isn't as necessary. In fact, for advanced and transitional students, teachers should use a rate of speech that is normal for a regular classroom. Effective SIOP teachers adjust their rate of speech and enunciation to their students' levels of English proficiency.

Likewise, students will respond according to their proficiency level. The following example illustrates the variation in responses that may be expected when elementary students at six different levels of English proficiency are asked to describe the setting in a story. The levels reflect the WIDA performance definitions (*http://www.wida.us/standards/elp.aspx*).

Watch this video and notice how the teacher makes a multiple-meaning words lesson more comprehensible for English learners. Note her slower, well-articulated speech and how she effectively uses gestures. What are some other ways she makes the lesson comprehensible?

- Entering: "Cold day."
- Beginning: "Day is cold and there snow."
- Developing: "The day is cold and there is lots of snow."
- Expanding: "The day is very cold and heavy snow is falling."
- Bridging: "It is a cold, winter day and it is snowing more heavily than usual."
- Reaching: "The unusually heavy snow on the day the story takes place causes a number of problems for the characters."

While still providing English learners with exposure to grade-level language, SIOP teachers carefully monitor the vocabulary and sentence structure they use with English learners in order to match the students' proficiency levels, especially with students at beginning levels of English proficiency. The following are ways to monitor classroom speech:

- Enunciate clearly. Sometimes it is easy to rush through information or instructions because of the time pressure of a class period or because you want the pace to move along so that children don't lose interest. For English learners, a brisk speaking pace is difficult to follow, especially if care isn't taken to enunciate clearly. When each syllable of each word isn't pronounced properly but naturally, the words get slurred together. Students have difficulty understanding, especially if there is other noise around the room.

- Ask students for elaboration. Especially with students at intermediate and advanced levels, teachers should frequently ask students to: explain their answers; provide evidence for their answers; say it another way; answer *why*, *how*, or *what if* questions; and show where they found something in the text. Teachers should also ask students to connect words, phrases, and short sentences into compound sentences that represent their ideas and thoughts, teaching them conjunctions and logical connectors (Short & Echevarría, 2016). In this way, students not only use the language but also think about *how* to use it as well.

- Model what you want children to say before having them produce language. For example, in science the teacher might say, "We've been studying that there are many changes that occur in the earth's crust. Some come quickly and others take millions of years. Ask your partner, 'What is one change that comes quickly?'" In this way, students know what to say when they turn to their partners because they have heard correct sentence or question formation. Providing students with a model of what to say increases the likelihood that on-point discussion will occur.

- Reduce use of synonyms, unless they have been taught. We use synonyms to vary our language and make it interesting. We encourage students to write with synonyms (and pronouns and other referents) to improve their texts. But for beginners, synonyms can be confusing if they have not been explicitly taught. A math teacher may not realize that we have more than ten ways to indicate addition (add 4 and 5, add 4 to 5, the sum of 4 and 5, increase 4 by 5, 4 plus 5, 4 and 5 more, 4 more than 5, the total of 4 and 5, and so on). It's best to teach the process of addition using only one or two of these terms and then introducing the rest over time as the addition procedure is being practiced.

- Avoid idioms, particularly with beginners. These common sayings that do not have exact translations create difficulty for students who are trying to make sense of a new language. Some common idioms include "below the belt" for unfair; "put one's foot down" meaning to be firm; "see eye to eye" for being in agreement; "get the hang of" meaning to become familiar with; and "get a person's back up" indicating to make someone annoyed. English learners are better served when teachers use language that is straightforward, clear, and accompanied by a visual representation.

- Employ paraphrasing and repetition to enhance understanding. English learners may require repeated exposures to a word in order to hear it accurately since they often lack the auditory acuity to decipher sounds of English words. Then they need to see and hear the words used repeatedly, preferably in a variety of ways. Brain research tells us that repetition strengthens connections in the brain (Jensen, 2005).

- Point out cognates to promote comprehension for children whose **native language** has a Latin or Greek base. For example, using "calculate the mass/volume ratio" (*calcular* in Spanish) may be easier for some students to understand than "figure out the mass/volume ratio." (See Vogt and Echevarría, 2008, for more examples of cognates.)

- Simplify sentence structures to reduce the complexity that some English learners find confusing. Use subject–verb–object with beginning students and reduce or eliminate embedded clauses and passive voice. For example, in a social studies lesson, the teacher may use the following complex sentence structure that is difficult to understand: "English colonists brought free enterprise, the idea of owning and controlling their own businesses, from England but because England's leaders wanted the colonies' financial support, laws were passed by Parliament to limit the free enterprise system in the colonies." It might be better stated as, "English colonists brought the idea of owning and controlling their own businesses from England to America. This idea is called free enterprise. But England's leaders wanted the colonies' financial support. So Parliament passed laws to limit the free enterprise system in the colonies."

  Reducing the complexity of language is effective for beginners but should be used judiciously. Oversimplification of spoken or written language eliminates exposure to a variety of sentence constructions and language forms (Crossley et al., 2007), especially complex text called for in the Common Core State Standards. The best way for English learners to acquire the language of complex texts is through exposure to those texts and explicit instruction in ways to make sense of embedded clauses such as those seen above. However, a text that is one proficiency level up *is* complex; beginners and low intermediates need scaffolding/support to build up to the complex texts given to **native English speakers**. Too often English learners are regarded as incapable of interacting with more rigorous text and are not given the opportunity to learn the very language they need.

Using appropriate speech patterns and vocabulary for English learners contributes to comprehensible input and provides a basis for students to be successful. It is difficult for students to learn if a teacher's way of delivering information is too fast, too complex, or inarticulate.

SIOP® FEATURE 11:

Clear Explanation of Academic Tasks

English learners at all levels (and native English speakers) perform better in academic situations when the teacher gives clear instructions for assignments and activities. In their discussion of working memory, which is central to learning, Baily & Pransky (2014) point out that when students are confused about the lesson's topic or the activity's purpose, they either disengage or frantically try to make connections with what they already know. In this manner, they are wasting valuable working memory processing space. So, when the teacher isn't clear, there is more at stake than just taking up time repeating unclear instructions.

Effective teachers present instructions in a step-by-step manner, preferably using modeling or demonstrating the task for students. Ideally, the teacher shows a finished product such as a business letter, a research report, or a graphic organizer to students so that they know what the task entails. Oral directions should always be accompanied by written ones so English learners can refer back to them at a later point in time as they complete the assignment or task. Children with auditory processing difficulties also require clear, straightforward instructions written for them to see.

According to case study data collected from English learners in **sheltered instruction** classes (Echevarría, 1998), students were asked what their teachers do that makes learning easier or more difficult. The following are some student comments:

- "She doesn't explain it too good. I don't understand the words she's saying because I don't even know what they mean."
- "She talks too fast. I don't understand the directions."
- "He talks too fast. Not patient."
- "It helps when he comes close to my desk and explains stuff in the order that I have to do it."

These students' comments illustrate the importance of providing a clear explanation of teachers' expectations for lessons, including delineating the steps of academic tasks. This point cannot be overstated. In our observations of classes, many "behavior problems" are often the result of students not being sure about what they are supposed to do. A cursory oral explanation of an assignment can leave many children unsure about how to get started. The teacher, frustrated with all the chatter, scolds students, urging them to get to work. However, students do not know *how* to get to work and oftentimes do not know how to articulate that fact to the teacher. Bottom line: Making expectations clear to students contributes to an effective and efficient classroom.

SIOP teachers go over every aspect of the lesson, showing visuals with each step, if needed. For example, in a language arts class, the teacher wants students to complete a graphic organizer with information about the characters, setting, problem, resolution of the problem, and theme of a piece of literature the class has been reading. Using this information, students will write a summary. Figure 4.1 on the next page contrasts clear directions and step-by-step instruction with unclear directions and unguided instruction. Which column more closely applies to the way you present directions to your students?

Watch this video and listen to the teacher describe how she prepares students to do academic tasks. How does she set them up for success?

FIGURE 4.1 Clear Explanation Contrasted with Unclear Explanation

Clear Explanation	Unclear Explanation
The teacher writes on the board: 1. Review your notes from yesterday. 2. Use your notes to answer the 5 questions on the board. 3. Write your answers on your whiteboard. 4. Complete the graphic organizer. 5. Write a summary of the information contained in the graphic organizer. After giving students a few minutes to review their notes with a partner (more fluent speaker paired with a less-proficient one; additional information is added as needed), the teacher gives them a set amount of time to answer the first of five questions. She gives them a 30-second signal and then asks the class to "show me" their whiteboards where they have written their answers. She can see from a glance at their boards who got it right and who needs assistance or clarification. This process continues until all five questions are answered. The teacher shows a copy of the graphic organizer on the document reader and completes the first part with the class. Then students use the information from the five questions to complete the graphic organizer. Students are allowed to work with a partner on completing the graphic organizer, but the teacher circulates and observes to make sure that both partners have mastered the content. She asks questions to ensure understanding. Finally, the teacher models how to use the information in the graphic organizer to write a brief summary. Students then write a summary using their information.	The teacher gives an oral review of what was discussed in the story the previous day. Then she asks a series of questions about the characters, the story's problem, and how the problem in the story was resolved. Several students raised their hands to answer the questions. The teacher talks about the theme and the importance of recognizing a story's theme. Then the teacher hands out a graphic organizer and tells the students that they have the remainder of the period to complete it using the story and the information they have talked about. For homework, the students are to write a summary of the story based on the information.

The teacher described in the left column uses a written agenda so if students don't understand, weren't paying attention, or simply forgot, they have the written steps to guide them and keep them on task. Depending on the age and proficiency levels of the group, the teacher may need to model one or more of the steps. By the time students complete the graphic organizer, they will have received feedback on the accuracy of the information they will use and will have seen a model of a partially completed graphic organizer. Likewise, using information in the graphic organizer to write a summary is modeled for them. This type of teaching facilitates writing an accurate, complete summary.

In contrast, the teacher in the right column gives information and instructions orally, and only a handful of students participate in the whole-class, teacher-dominated Q&A. When it is time to complete the graphic organizer, most likely many students will be unsure about where to begin or what information is pertinent.

A critical academic task, writing a summary, is left to be done as homework and undoubtedly few students will be able to complete the assignment because the teacher gave no model or guidance.

As a check of how clear your task explanations are, write out the directions you would give your students for completing an academic task and ask a colleague to follow them. It can be eye opening!

In the area of writing, students need to be shown very specifically—and have opportunities to practice what has been clearly explained—the essential elements of good writing. Showing students what constitutes good writing, explaining it clearly, and providing opportunities to practice will result in improved writing (Echevarría & Vogt, 2011; Graham et al., 2012; Short & Echevarría, 2016). For intermediate and advanced speakers, focused lessons on "voice" or "word choice" may be appropriate, while beginning speakers benefit from using models of complete sentences (with adjectives, adverbs, and prepositional phrases) to write their own.

SIOP®
SHELTERED INSTRUCTION
OBSERVATION PROTOCOL

SIOP® FEATURE 12:

A Variety of Techniques Used to Make Content Concepts Clear

Effective SIOP teachers make content concepts clear and understandable for English learners through the use of a variety of techniques. We have observed some teachers who teach the same way for English learners as they do for native English speakers, except that they use pictures to illustrate ideas or words for English learners. English learners benefit from a wider range of supports to make the material understandable. The actual techniques a teacher uses should match the task. For example, when explicitly teaching academic vocabulary words in depth, the teacher might use examples and non-examples, video clips, and other concrete representations of the words (Baker et al., 2014). High-quality SIOP lessons offer students a variety of ways for making the content accessible to them. Some techniques include:

- Use gestures, body language, pictures, and objects to accompany speech. For example, in a lesson on informational text the teacher points to a poster that illustrates text features and says, "There are a number of features used in informational text that help the reader. One is (holds up 1 finger) headings (points to the heading). Headings tell us what the text will be about. What is the heading for this text? (Class reads together.) Another feature is captions (holds up 2 fingers and points to the caption below an illustration). Captions give information about a photo or illustration. There are also bold words (holds up 3 fingers points to bold words). These words are important for understanding the text." Gestures and visual aids assist students in organizing and making sense of information that is presented verbally.

- Provide a model of a process, task, or assignment. For example, as the teacher discusses the process of water changing to ice, she shows or draws a model of the process as it is being described. When students are later instructed to record conditions under which the change in ice from a solid to a liquid is accelerated or slowed, the teacher shows an observation sheet that is divided into three columns on a document reader, interactive whiteboard, or chart paper. The teacher has a number of pictures (e.g., lamp, sun, and refrigerator) that depict various conditions such as heat and cold. She demonstrates the first condition, heat, with a picture of the sun. She models how students will describe the condition in the first column (e.g., heats). Then she asks the children what effect the sun, or heat, has on ice. They answer and in the second column she records how the ice changed (e.g., melted), and in the third column she indicates if the process was accelerated or slowed by the condition (e.g., accelerated). Providing a model as the students are taken through the task verbally eliminates ambiguity and gives the message in more than one way. Students are then able to complete the rest of the worksheet. Furthermore, in this case, there is a written example students can consult if they have questions later.

- Preview material for optimal learning. When children's attention is focused on the specific material they will be responsible for learning in the lesson, they are able to prepare themselves for the information that is coming, making it more comprehensible for them. Further, they have an opportunity to access prior knowledge and make the connections that they will need to understand the lesson. Previews can occur through book walks, anticipation guides, brief video clips, and the like.

- Allow students alternative forms for expressing their understanding of information and concepts. Often English learners have learned the lesson's information but have difficulty expressing their understanding in English, either orally or in writing. Hands-on and kinesthetic activities can be used to reinforce the concepts and information presented, with a reduced linguistic demand on these students. In a kindergarten class, children might mime the stages of plant growth: squatting with arms around knees for a seed, extending one arm for the sprout, standing with arm extended and foot extended for seedling and root, standing with both arms up and feet apart for plant.

- Use multimedia and other technologies in lessons. Teachers may use PowerPoint slides, interactive whiteboards, a document projector, or relevant Web sites and apps as supplements to a presentation. In so doing, they not only provide more visual support but also model the use of the technology.

- Provide repeated exposures to words, concepts, and skills. English learners are learning through a new language, and in order for the input to be comprehensible, they need repetition. However, excessive practice of a single word or skill can become monotonous and defeat the purpose. Jensen (2005) discusses a process for introducing material repeatedly in a variety of ways. He suggests introducing terms and skills well in advance of learning the material (pre-exposure); explicitly previewing the topic at the start of the lesson; exposing students to the target information (priming); reviewing the material minutes after students have learned it; and allowing students to revise or reconstruct information hours, days, or weeks after the lesson to revisit the learning. Research indicates that teachers ought to provide students with the specifics of what they need to learn—the key details of the unit—and then find ways to expose students to the details multiple times (Marzano, Pickering, & Pollock, 2001).

- Use graphic organizers effectively. New ideas and concepts presented in a new language can be overwhelming for English learners. Graphic organizers take the information, vocabulary, or concept and make it more understandable by showing the key points graphically. To paraphrase the saying "a picture is worth a thousand words," a graphic organizer can capture and simplify a teacher's many potentially confusing words. While graphic organizers are used commonly in school, they are most effective when they match the task and lead students to attaining the lesson's objectives.

  Some graphic organizers may be simple, such as a problem/solution chart or a web with vocabulary definitions. For upper elementary students, graphic organizers may be more elaborate. For example, the CCSS and other state standards call for students to have an understanding of the argumentation process. Prior to giving a presentation that requires argumentation or an argumentative writing assignment, a **scaffold** might be to have students complete the following Argumentation Map:

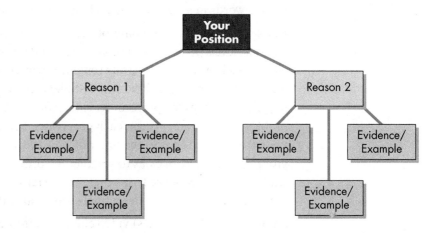

- Offer audiotape texts for greater comprehension. There are a variety of commercially available resources that provide an audio version of a story or book. Publishers often include access to audio versions of a text, accessible on class computers. Also, software exists for creating MP3 files by scanning text and reading it aloud. Children can listen to the file on a smartphone or tablet. An audio version of the text not only allows for multiple opportunities to hear the text, but also enables adjustments for different proficiency levels. When the teacher (or someone else) records the text himself or herself, the same passage may be read more slowly with clear enunciation for beginning speakers, or synonyms may be substituted for difficult words.

The Comprehensible Input techniques we present in this chapter assist English learners in understanding the lesson's information. Whether the teacher is giving directions, conveying content information, or teaching a skill or concept—any time a message is delivered verbally or in writing—it must be made understandable for all students. Many English learners adapt to the classroom environment by pretending they understand, when, in fact, they may not. SIOP teachers use frequent checks to gauge how well students comprehend material and to discern how speech or text may need to be differentiated based on proficiency.

Watch this video of Dr. Jana Echevarría conducting two lessons in Mandarin. Which lesson would you rather be in and why? Did you learn any Mandarin? If so, how?

Teaching Ideas for Comprehensible Input

In the section that follows, you will find some teaching ideas to help you with preparing SIOP lessons.

- Record step-by-step instructions for completing a task or project, using an electronic tablet application. English learners, individually or in pairs, listen to the instructions as many times as needed, using the speech speed feature to slow the output to their level of understanding. You may also generate questions for partners to ask each other, such as "Which pages do we read before completing the graphic organizer?" or "Are the words we use in the graphic organizer found in the reading passage or somewhere else?" In this way, children listen to the instructions again with a focus on specific questions whose answers will help them complete the task. English learners may be unaware that the headings or bolded words in a text are those often used to complete a graphic organizer.

- Use sentence strips. This common technique can be used in a variety of ways at all grade levels. In reading/language arts, students can review events in a story by writing each event on a separate sentence strip, scrambling the strips, and then sequencing them to retell the story. Students in math might work in groups to sequence the steps for problem solving. After the group has put the strips for its problem in the correct order, each group member takes a strip and everyone lines up in front of the class in the order of how the math problem is solved. Other groups provide feedback as to whether the order is correct. Similarly in science, students might sequence strips that reflect steps of an experiment they conducted, but each pair or group writes a final strip to state the result of the experiment.

- Show a brief (2–4 minutes) video clip that reinforces the content objective and complements the reading assignment prior to reading a passage of informational text. Have children work in pairs to discuss specific questions about the video clip so that they have a grasp of the big ideas before participating in reading (Reutebuch, 2010).

- Spell difficult words or math formulas to the tune of B-I-N-G-O or another song while clapping out each letter, number, or symbol.

- Make lectures or presentations easier to remember by using objects, photographs, slides, graphs, bulletin board displays, and color. Visuals are important for remembering information. Change things up: Use vivid posters, drawings, videos, and other ways to grab attention (Jensen, 2008).

Differentiating Ideas for Multi-level Classes

We know that most classes with English learners have students with multiple proficiency levels. Even those designated **ESL** 2, for example, may have some students who have stronger listening skills than writing skills or stronger reading skills than speaking skills. Teachers have at their disposal a variety of ways to differentiate spoken English to make it comprehensible for our diverse English learners. Almost every utterance can be modified in some way to address the variety of proficiency levels of students in your classrooms. Several considerations include the following.

- Use a slower rate, clear enunciation, and simple sentence structure for beginning speakers; use a more native-like rate and sentence complexity for intermediate and advanced speakers of English.

- Remember that you make a huge contribution to your students' attitude toward school. Particularly in the early grades, students' experiences form their impressions about school and learning. At any age, learners in a positive environment are more likely to experience enhanced learning, memory, and self-esteem (Jensen, 2008, 2013). Differentiating how information is delivered so that it is comprehensible helps students with lower levels of proficiency feel accepted, understood, and as much a part of the class as native speakers of English.

- Allow students to provide differentiated responses to questions and assignments. For oral responses, provide sentence frames for those students who need them. With written assignments, beginning speakers may require partially completed information (e.g., Cloze procedure), while advanced speakers may only need a word bank, or other support, to complete the assignment. Level of support should be differentiated so that students at each level of proficiency are able to understand expectations and be successful in lessons.

- Offer options when students explore content information on their own. Bookmark a variety of Web sites with a range of text and visual options, and if possible include some in the native languages of your students. Work with the school librarian to create a temporary classroom library with books at different reading levels on the topic being studied. Provide a picture glossary for key terms that the children are likely to encounter when exploring the topic.

The Lesson

Economics: Natural Resources and Products (Third Grade)

The following lessons take place in an urban elementary school where English learners make up approximately 30% of the school population. In the classrooms described, a mix of language proficiency levels are represented, ranging from beginning speakers to advanced English speakers. Students have varying levels of literacy in their native languages.

Teachers in this school have a weekly grade-level planning meeting, where they co-plan lessons. During this time, teachers develop content and language objectives and share ideas for the week's lessons, thus ensuring that they follow similar pacing as they address Common Core State Standards. As you will see, although the objectives are the same, the teachers have their own ways of teaching the lessons.

(continued)

Economics: Natural Resources and Products (Third Grade) *(continued)*

Third-grade teachers Miss Zarcades, Mr. Mehlhaff, and Mrs. Pabst are all teaching a unit on Economics. The lessons described focus on distinguishing the difference between a natural resource and a product, and address Common Core State Standard, RI.3.4: *Determine the meaning of general academic and domain-specific words and phrases in a text relevant to a grade 3 topic or subject area.* The classes have been studying natural resources, learning about which ones are renewable and nonrenewable, and examining the problems associated with scarce resources.

The current lesson takes place over two days. On the first day, the three teachers introduced the lesson by pointing out that we use products every day and that most come from natural resources. They used the example of paper (product) being made from trees (natural resource) and the classes read a text about the production of paper. Then the children were told that they would select a product they wanted to research. The vignettes that follow describe Day 2 of the lesson.

The lesson's objectives are:

Content: Students will

- investigate how a product is made and the natural resources used to produce it.
- distinguish between a finished product and a natural resource.

Language: Students will

- write a summary of the production process using key vocabulary.
- orally present their research findings.

■ Teaching Scenarios

Miss Zarcades

As was her practice, Miss Zarcades reviewed the content and language objectives she had posted for students. She asked students to read along with her, pointing to each word as she read aloud so that all students, including English learners, could follow along. She began this second day of the lesson by asking each group to quickly say what product they had researched the previous day from texts and Internet sources. Since she had distributed a worksheet to guide—or scaffold—their information gathering, she reviewed on the document reader a sample completed worksheet about the production of a pencil. She went through each section, being careful to enunciate clearly and repeat the specific academic vocabulary words that were key terms in the lesson, such as *renewable resource*, *product*, and *production*. She paused periodically to make sure that all group members were following along on their own worksheets and checking that they had filled in the section correctly. She told the groups that they had 10 minutes to review their worksheets and add any additional information. She set an online timer on her interactive whiteboard. During this time, Miss Zarcades circulated around the classroom, assisting groups or individuals who needed support.

Next, she distributed poster board and pointed to the samples displayed on the wall. She instructed groups to draw a similar poster to reflect the production process outlined on their worksheet. Each member of the group was assigned one section of the worksheet to illustrate—that is, the product, the natural resource used in the product, the source of the natural resource, and whether it was a renewable or non-renewable resource. The groups were given 15 minutes to complete a simple illustration of the process as a visual to accompany their oral presentations. Again, Miss Zarcades set the online timer.

After the posters were completed, the groups gave oral presentations of their projects. Each member of the group told about his or her part of the poster using complete sentences and academic terms. Miss Zarcades had sentence frames written on the whiteboard for those students who needed language support: "The product we researched was _____." and "Production of _____ uses _____ resources" (renewable or nonrenewable). After the oral presentations were made, Miss Zarcades played a quick game of Stand Up/Sit Down. She named an item and asked students to stand if it was a finished product or sit if it was a natural resource. Throughout the lesson, Miss Zarcades used language structures and vocabulary that she believed the students could understand at their level of proficiency. For beginning learners, she spoke slowly, often contextualizing vocabulary words, and enunciated clearly. Also, she avoided the use of idioms, and when she sensed that children did not understand, she paraphrased to convey the meaning more clearly. At the conclusion of the lesson, she reviewed the content and language objectives with her students.

Check your understanding: On the SIOP form in Figure 4.2, rate Miss Zarcades's lesson on each of the Comprehensible Input features.

FIGURE 4.2 Comprehensible Input Component of the SIOP® Model: Miss Zarcades's Lesson

4	3	2	1	0
10. **Speech appropriate** for students' proficiency levels (e.g., slower rate, enunciation, and simple sentence structure for beginners)		**Speech** sometimes inappropriate for students' proficiency levels		**Speech** inappropriate for students' proficiency levels

4	3	2	1	0
11. **Clear explanation** of academic tasks		**Unclear** explanation of academic tasks		**No** explanation of academic tasks

4	3	2	1	0
12. **A variety of techniques** used to make content concepts clear (e.g., modeling, visuals, hands-on activities, demonstrations, gestures, body language)		**Some techniques** used to make content concepts clear		No **techniques** used to make concepts clear

---

? **Reflect and Apply**
Click here to explain your ratings for Miss Zarcades's lesson on each of the Comprehensible Input features.

Mr. Mehlhaff

Mr. Mehlhaff began the lesson by reading the content and language objectives. Then he told students to continue researching the products they had started investigating the day before. He had asked each student to select a product and work independently to gather information. Some students seemed lost about how to extract pertinent information from text and Internet sources. Quite a few sat quietly, while others began talking among themselves. Mr. Mehlhaff sensed that some children were off task so he stood and repeated the directions orally, speaking rather quickly and curtly. He wrote on the board: *Product, Natural Resources Used*, to help guide students in completing the task. He pointed to the words and repeated that they were supposed to be looking for information about their product (pointed to word) and writing down which natural resources (pointed to word) were used. He gave students more time to "get to work."

After a while, Mr. Mehlhaff paired students and told the class that the partners were going to share information about their products with one another. He reminded them that they needed to use academic language, including the specific terms that were the focus of the lesson. He referred them back to the language objective and read it to them, stressing that he wanted to hear students using key academic terms and phrases. He called on two of the top students in class and asked them to come up and demonstrate what partners were supposed to do. The students faced each other and Mr. Mehlhaff told one, "Ask him the name of his product" and the student asked his partner, who then answered. Next Mr. Mehlhaff prompted, "Now, what about natural resources?" and the student asked his partner which natural resources were used to make the product. After this demonstration, Mr. Mehlhaff told the class that partners were going to follow the same questioning format, asking one another about their products. Students began talking with their partners, asking and answering questions with varying levels of success.

Check your understanding: On the SIOP form in Figure 4.3, rate Mr. Mehlhaff's lesson on each of the Comprehensible Input features.

Mrs. Pabst

Mrs. Pabst asked the class to chorally read the lesson's content and language objectives, which were written on the board. She was sure to read slowly so that all students, including English learners, were able to follow along. She asked if there were any questions from the previous day's assignment and requested a show of hands of children who knew what their product was. All children raised hands. The previous day Mrs. Pabst had let students pick a partner and then work in pairs to select a product and gather information about its associated natural resources.

Mrs. Pabst told the students that today they would identify where the natural resources in their products came from. She pointed to the large map on the wall. Children were told that they would create a symbol that represented each resource used in their product. As Mrs. Pabst explained this process, she used her normal,

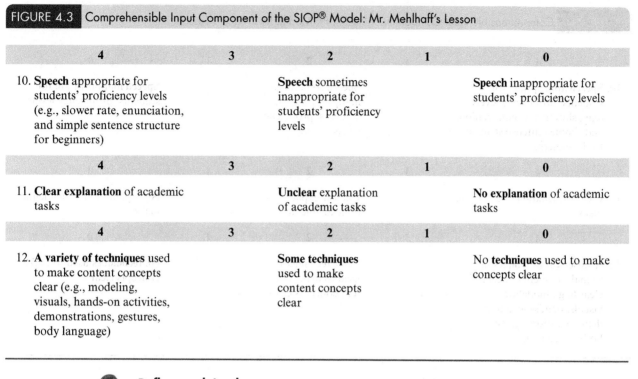

FIGURE 4.3   Comprehensible Input Component of the SIOP® Model: Mr. Mehlhaff's Lesson

4	3	2	1	0
10. **Speech** appropriate for students' proficiency levels (e.g., slower rate, enunciation, and simple sentence structure for beginners)		**Speech** sometimes inappropriate for students' proficiency levels		**Speech** inappropriate for students' proficiency levels

4	3	2	1	0
11. **Clear explanation** of academic tasks		**Unclear** explanation of academic tasks		**No explanation** of academic tasks

4	3	2	1	0
12. **A variety of techniques** used to make content concepts clear (e.g., modeling, visuals, hands-on activities, demonstrations, gestures, body language)		**Some techniques** used to make content concepts clear		No **techniques** used to make concepts clear

Reflect and Apply

Click here to explain your ratings for Mr. Mehlhaff's lesson on each of the Comprehensible Input features.

somewhat rapid speaking style that she used with her English-speaking students. Then she passed out paper for making two copies of each symbol—one to put on the large world map and the other for the map key, or legend. She pointed out that a *map legend* is a key to the symbols used on a map. "It is like a dictionary so you can understand the meaning of what the map represents." She modeled what the children would complete by showing a symbol for trees (paper products) and placed one on the map where logging takes place and another on the map legend, writing "trees for paper production" next to the symbol. Mrs. Pabst then told students to get started working with their partners to create a symbol and find the location of their product's natural resources. Most pairs could design a symbol, but several struggled locating the sources. After all students had completed this task, Mrs. Pabst had each pair come to the map and tell the name of the product, the natural resource used, and where the natural resource came from. They then put one symbol on the map and the other on the map key. When all students had completed their oral report, Mrs. Pabst reviewed the content and language objectives and asked if they were met.

Check your understanding: On the SIOP form in Figure 4.4, rate Mrs. Pabst's lesson on each of the Comprehensible Input features.

FIGURE 4.4   Comprehensible Input Component of the SIOP® Model: Mrs. Pabst's Lesson

4	3	2	1	0
10. **Speech** appropriate for students' proficiency levels (e.g., slower rate, enunciation, and simple sentence structure for beginners)		**Speech** sometimes inappropriate for students' proficiency levels		**Speech** inappropriate for students' proficiency levels

4	3	2	1	0
11. **Clear explanation** of academic tasks		**Unclear** explanation of academic tasks		**No** explanation of academic tasks

4	3	2	1	0
12. **A variety of techniques** used to make content concepts clear (e.g., modeling, visuals, hands-on activities, demonstrations, gestures, body language)		**Some techniques** used to make content concepts clear		**No techniques** used to make concepts clear

? **Reflect and Apply**
Click here to explain your ratings for Mrs. Pabst's lesson on each of the Comprehensible Input features.

■ Discussion of Lessons

10. *Speech Appropriate for Students' Proficiency Level (Rate and Complexity)*

Miss Zarcades: 4

Mr. Mehlhaff: 0

Mrs. Pabst: 1

- **Miss Zarcades** was attuned to the benefit of modulating her speech to make herself understood by the children. She slowed her rate of speech and enunciated clearly to accommodate beginning learners, and she adjusted her speech for the other, more proficient speakers of English. She used a natural speaking voice, but paid attention to her rate of speech and enunciation. Further, Miss Zarcades repeated key academic vocabulary terms, which helps all students, but especially English learners. Finally, she adjusted the level of vocabulary and complexity of the sentences when speaking and also used sentence frames so that all students could participate at their level of proficiency. For this reason, Miss Zarcades's lesson received a "4" for this feature.

- **Mr. Mehlhaff** seemed unaware that his students would understand more if he adjusted his oral presentation to accommodate the proficiency levels of English learners in his class. He gave few instructions to assist students in completing the task, and those instructions he gave did not take into consideration his rate of speech or complexity of speech, variables that impact English learners' ability to comprehend information in class. Also, making sense of written information independently and creating original sentences are inordinately difficult tasks for English learners. Unwittingly, Mr. Mehlhaff set the students up for failure, and then he was frustrated when they were off task. He spoke quickly and curtly, which did not enhance comprehension. Mr. Mehlhaff's lesson was given a "0" for this feature.

- Generally, **Mrs. Pabst's** rate of speech and enunciation was similar to that used with native English speakers. She didn't consciously adjust her speech (rate or complexity) to the variety of proficiency levels in the class, although she did have students chorally read the objectives slowly so all could follow along. Mrs. Pabst could have paraphrased some of her instructions and questions, using simpler sentence structure, when some children struggled to understand. Because Mrs. Pabst made minimal adjustments while speaking to English learners, her lesson received a "1" for this feature.

11. *Clear Explanation of Academic Tasks*

    Miss Zarcades: 4

    Mr. Mehlhaff: 2

    Mrs. Pabst: 3

Making your expectations crystal clear to students is one of the most important aspects of teaching, and when working with English learners, explicit, step-by-step directions can be critical to a lesson's success. It is difficult for almost any student to remember directions given only orally, and oral directions may be incomprehensible to many English learners. A lesson is sure to get off to a rocky start if students don't understand what they are expected to do. Written procedures provide students with a guide.

- **Miss Zarcades's** lesson received a "4" for this feature because she used a teaching style that supported student success by making her expectations for completing academic tasks clear and understandable. She modeled almost every task students were expected to complete. During the lesson she first checked for understanding by using a "popcorn" approach, quickly asking each group the name of their product. Then she modeled for the class a completed worksheet and gave each student a chance to check his or her own work from the previous day. If an individual student or group was confused or had done the worksheet incorrectly, it was important for Miss Zarcades to make sure they all understood what to do and were doing it correctly before the children spent more time on the task. She then provided time to make additions or corrections, and was careful to oversee their work. Throughout the lesson, tasks were modeled so that students at all levels of English proficiency knew the expectations and, with the scaffolding she offered, were more likely to be successful in completing the work. She took into account the linguistic differences in her class and differentiated accordingly. The sentence frames let the students know exactly the kinds of complete sentences that were expected during their oral presentations.

    Using the online timer for time management, Miss Zarcades provided students with boundaries for the tasks—letting them know how much time she expected them to spend—and helped them learn to manage their time.

Overall, she understood the value of being explicit in what she wanted the students to do and walked them through each step of the lesson.

- Although **Mr. Mehlhaff** was a veteran teacher, he did not provide the kind of guidance that all students benefit from and that is critical for English learners. He expected young children to work independently, gathering information from text and Internet sources. Exposing students at all levels of English proficiency to complex text is important, but scaffolding is essential to help students access the information. Many students, and especially English learners, were unsure of the expectations or process for completing the assignment. When students were off task, Mr. Mehlhaff attempted to explain further by rereading the objectives, but that probably did little to make the task clearer. He did assist students by having two children model how to work in pairs asking questions about the assignment. This gave students an idea about how to conduct their pair work. Thus, Mr. Mehlhaff's lesson was given a "2" for this feature.

- **Mrs. Pabst** first got students focused on the task by reading the objectives and asking them to remember the product they had chosen the previous day. She told them explicitly what they were going to do first: Identify where the natural resources came from that were used to make the products. This kind of clarity helps English learners to know precisely what is expected. In addition, she modeled part of the task that children were to work on. She showed the symbol she had created to represent paper products and put it on the map, just as they would do when they finished. Even without words, the students, including English learners, could see what the process was: Find out where your natural resource comes from, draw a symbol, and prepare to place it on the map and legend with a brief explanation. The lesson would have received a higher rating had Mrs. Pabst actually modeled or explained how students were to extract information about where the natural resources come from. She said that they would create a symbol to represent it, but didn't sufficiently explain how children would go about finding the information that their symbol would represent. A worksheet to guide them, as Miss Zarcades provided, would have scaffolded the task better for students. Mrs. Pabst's lesson received a "3" for this feature.

12. *A Variety of Techniques Used to Make Content Concepts Clear*

Miss Zarcades: 4

Mr. Mehlhaff: 1

Mrs. Pabst: 2

Concepts become understandable when teachers use a variety of techniques, including modeling, demonstrations, visuals, and body language.

- Throughout the lesson, **Miss Zarcades** used a number of techniques that supported students' learning and helped them be successful in completing the assignment. She provided a worksheet to scaffold children's organization of information and she showed the sample completed worksheet, carefully going through each section. All of the visuals she showed and pointed to increased students' comprehension. By giving students a worksheet and poster board for their illustrations, she made the lesson more hands-on and provided more than one way to express the information they had gathered. One can imagine that the atmosphere in Miss Zarcades's class is positive, encouraging, and nonthreatening

Watch this video to see how the teacher uses the classroom smartboard to review vocabulary. What techniques does she use to ensure her students understand the key vocabulary she's reviewing? https://www.youtube.com/watch?v=VrF6yvFNMFc

for English learners. This kind of environment instills confidence in children about their ability to learn and be successful in school. Because of the variety of effective techniques used, Miss Zarcades's lesson received a "4" for this feature.

- **Mr. Mehlhaff** is a kind and friendly teacher, but he did not use many teaching techniques that increased children's comprehension of the lesson. His teaching style was one of teacher lecture and student performance without scaffolding. He expected young learners to work independently, which is difficult for all children, especially English learners who may not even understand the words in the text. Thus, completing a summary of the natural resources used to produce a product was a nearly impossible task. He modeled how to discuss the information in pairs, but one might expect that few English learners had actually independently gathered sufficient information for the oral exchange. Think about the difference between Miss Zarcades's scaffolded lesson and Mr. Mehlhaff's reliance on independent work. This lesson received a "1" for use of comprehensible input techniques.

- **Mrs. Pabst** used teaching techniques in the lesson, but some her choices were not useful, especially for English learners. First, she asked if there were any questions. Few English learners typically ask for clarification or assistance in front of the class. Then she provided them with the hands-on activity of creating a symbol to place on the map. However, there was no technique used to check for understanding as to whether the children investigated how a product was made and learned about the natural resources used to produce it (the objective). Although she modeled how to create a symbol and place it on the map, she depended on the map symbol activity to guide students' understanding of the content. Instead, she might have used a technique for checking understanding of the production process, or provided an outline or graphic organizer for students to make sense of the information they were expected to gather. Gestures, modeling, hands-on activities, and the like are important for increasing English learners' understanding of the lesson, but these techniques must lead to meeting the lesson's objectives. For these reasons, Mrs. Pabst's lesson received a "2" for this feature.

Watch this video of a science lesson on earthquakes. To what extent is each of the three SIOP features for Comprehensible Input present in the lesson? Do you think the students understood the key concepts by the end?

(For more examples of lesson and unit plans in history and social studies for grades K–6, see Short, Vogt, and Echevarría, 2011.)

Teaching with Technology

After talking with the teachers and discussing the lessons you read about in the Scenarios earlier in the chapter, our tech integrator, Ms. Palacios, offered some technology suggestions to enhance the teachers' lessons.

Student Response System: When Mrs. Pabst reflected on her lesson, she wasn't sure the students understood the production process, and she realized several pairs could not easily find the location of the natural resources used in their products. She wondered if a technology component that might enhance the lesson was available. She noticed that Ms. Palacios mentioned new tools in her weekly tech news e-mail. She described a student response system called *Socrative* that allows students to answer short quizzes, participate in polls, and complete

(continued on the next page)

Do Nows and exit tickets using various devices. Ms. Palacios explained that often these tools don't require students to create accounts, making the process easier for elementary students. The newsletter described how many of these systems allow you to see students' responses in real time and to track data over multiple lessons. Mrs. Pabst thought this sounded like an interesting tool and decided to include it as part of her lesson.

Ms. Palacios came to Mrs. Pabst's classroom a few minutes before the period began and set up iPads on a table in the room. She used her low-cost iPad holders (aka dish drying racks) to arrange them for easy student access.

At the beginning of class, Ms. Palacios demonstrated how to use *Socrative*, which the student pairs accessed on the tablets. She walked the students through joining Mrs. Pabst's "room" using a code generated by the site. Then they answered a practice question about their favorite breakfast foods. Mrs. Pabst asked the students to predict if they thought most goods were produced where the natural resources were found. She also asked questions about finding sources and how the products were manufactured. Students responded to the questions and Mrs. Pabst was able to track answers on her iPad and discuss the answers with the children. She also added an exit ticket to help her learn more about the students' understanding and plan where her next lesson should begin.

Other terms for this type of tool: student clickers, audience response systems

Related products: *Verso*, *Kahoot*, *Poll Everywhere*, *Geddit* and other products that connect with various brands of interactive whiteboards.

Note: Due to the constantly evolving nature of the Internet, it is a challenge to ensure that all of the links and Web services listed here are updated and functional when you read the technology sections. While specific tools or services may appear in the narrative, we have also included the general term for each tool. If a specific service does not work or is no longer available, search with the general term for the tool and you should be able to find a comparable Web site.

 Check Your Understanding
Click here to check your understanding of the concepts in Chapter 4, Comprehensible Input.

■ Summary

As you reflect on this chapter and consider the impact of comprehensible input on learning, consider the following main points:

- Although English learners learn in many of the same ways as fluent English-speaking students, they do require special supports or accommodations to make instruction understandable (August & Shanahan, 2006; Goldenberg, 2008).
- Effective SIOP teachers constantly modulate and adjust their speech to ensure that the content is comprehensible.
- Concepts are taught using a variety of techniques, including modeling, gestures, hands-on activities, and demonstrations, so that students understand and learn the content material.

- Effective SIOP teachers provide explanations of academic tasks in ways that make clear what students are expected to accomplish and that promote student success. They typically post or provide written instructions to complement what they tell students to do and work through an example or two of a task or show a model of a completed assignment.

■ Discussion Questions

1. In reflecting on the learning outcomes in the content and language objectives at the beginning of the chapter, are you able to:
   a. Identify techniques for presenting content information in ways that students comprehend?
   b. Review various ways to provide directions for completing academic tasks?
   c. Discuss modifications to teacher speech that can increase student comprehension?
   d. Write the steps needed for students to perform an academic task and have a partner perform each step?

2. Many times in classrooms, discipline problems can be attributed to students not knowing what they're supposed to be doing. If students don't know what to do, they find something else to do. What are some ways that you can avoid having students become confused about accomplishing academic tasks?

3. If you have traveled in another country, or if you are an English learner, reflect on difficulties you had in understanding others. What are some techniques people used to try to communicate with you? What are some techniques you can use in the classroom?

4. Using the SIOP lesson you have been developing, add to it so that the Comprehensible Input features in the lesson are enhanced.

5. For the lesson on natural resources, what are some comprehension checks that are quick, nonthreatening, and effective for determining if a student is ready to move on?

CHAPTER 5

Strategies

Learning Outcomes

After reading, discussing, and engaging in activities related to this chapter, you will be able to meet the following **content** and **language objectives**.

Content Objectives

Identify the learning strategies that your students are currently using, and suggest others that they need to learn and practice.

Identify techniques for verbal, procedural, and instructional scaffolding.

Language Objectives

Identify language learning strategies to include in a lesson.

Write a lesson plan that includes explicit instruction with learning strategies, and varied techniques for scaffolding student understandings.

Write a set of questions or tasks on a chosen topic with increasing levels of cognition.

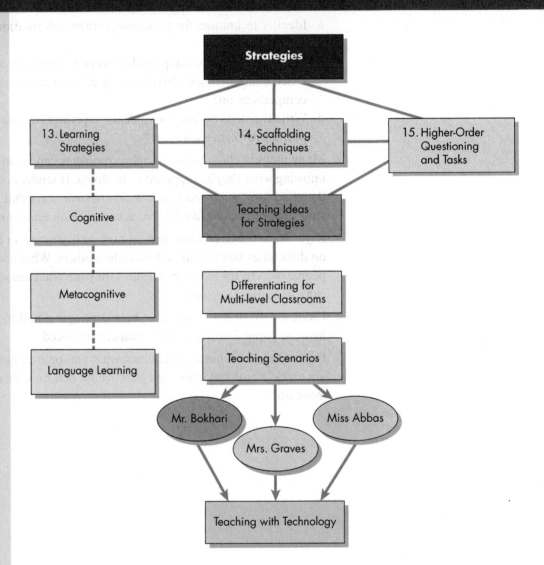

Think about a time

when you had to solve a really challenging problem. For example, you were trying to balance the family budget; or perhaps you were trying to find a particular location while driving, and your GPS was taking you in what seemed like the opposite direction; or maybe you were reading an important document that you didn't understand, and even though you read it twice, you still didn't get it.

If these were actual problems you were facing, what would you do to solve each one? More than likely, as an experienced learner, you would activate a plan for dealing with each problem, and you would do so by relying on a repertoire of strategies you have developed over the years, for balancing a budget, for finding your way from point A to point B, or for navigating difficult reading material. As you think about these strategies, which were taught to you by someone with more experience? Which did you learn by yourself through trial and error? ●

Peopleimages/E+/Getty Images

■ Background

As introduced in Chapter 3, researchers have found that information is retained and connected in the brain through "mental pathways" that are linked to an individual's existing schemata (Anderson, 1984; Barnhardt, 1997). If schemata for a particular topic are well developed and personally meaningful, it is easier to retain and recall new information; thus proficient learners are able to initiate and activate their associations between the new and old learning without difficulty. In cognitive theory, initiation and activation are described as the mental processes that enhance comprehension, learning, and retention of information.

Teachers of **English learners** sometimes have difficulty determining their students' proficiency with learning strategies, especially in the beginning stages of their acquisition of English. Teachers may observe English learners' lower *English* proficiency and mistake it as a symptom of poor or underdeveloped *learning* strategies. In this chapter, we discuss the importance of teaching and providing practice with a variety of learning strategies that facilitate knowledge acquisition. We also suggest that all students, including English learners, benefit from questions and tasks that involve higher levels of thinking. In order to accomplish these goals, teachers must carefully scaffold instruction for those who need additional support.

SIOP® FEATURE 13:

Ample Opportunities Provided for Students to Use Learning Strategies

> Watch this video in which Dr. MaryEllen Vogt describes learning strategies—what they are and how we can teach them meaningfully. Consider your own learning—under what conditions do you learn best, and which cognitive and metacognitive strategies do you regularly use? https://www.youtube.com/watch?v=rhYl3w5lOEA&index=4&list=PLT7cPjUGeZeY3eY2477U2PTE8-VRTTTcf

There is considerable evidence from research over the past four decades supporting the assertion that explicitly teaching a variety of self-regulating strategies improves student learning and reading (August & Shanahan, 2010; Dole, Duffy, Roehler, & Pearson, 1991; Pressley, 2000, Pressley, 2002; Snow, Griffin, & Burns, 2005; Vogt & Nagano, 2003). Many of these research studies focused on highly effective readers and learners who use a variety of strategies in an interactive and recursive manner. These readers use learning strategies that are flexible and appropriate to the task. They are also active and strategic thinkers who can readily transfer strategies to new tasks.

As English learners develop English proficiency, it is important that their language, literacy, and content instruction include a focus on learning and practicing a variety of strategies (Chamot, 2009; Dymock & Nicholson, 2010; National Institute of Child Health and Human Development, 2000; Vogt, Echevarría, & Short, 2010).

Among the strategies that can be taught and that generally transfer to new learning are:

1. **Cognitive Learning Strategies.** Cognitive strategies are used by learners when they mentally and/or physically manipulate information, or when they apply a specific technique to a learning task (McLaughlin, 2010; Vogt & Shearer, 2016). Examples of cognitive strategies include the following:
    - Previewing a story or chapter before reading
    - Establishing a purpose for learning
    - Consciously making connections with past learning
    - Using mnemonics
    - Highlighting, underlining, or using sticky notes to identify important information
    - Taking notes or outlining
    - Rereading to aid understanding
    - Mapping information or using a graphic organizer
    - Identifying key vocabulary
    - Identifying, analyzing, and using varied text structures

2. **Metacognitive Learning Strategies.** *Metacognition* is the process of purposefully monitoring our thinking (Baker & Brown, 1984). The use of metacognitive strategies implies awareness, reflection, and interaction, and effective learners use

these strategies in an integrated, interrelated, and recursive manner (Dole, Duffy, Roehler, & Pearson, 1991). Studies have found that when metacognitive strategies are taught explicitly and practiced frequently, reading comprehension is improved (Duffy, 2002; Snow, Griffin, & Burns, 2005; Shearer, Ruddell, & Ruddell, 2001; Vogt & Nagano, 2003). Examples of metacognitive learning strategies include:

- Predicting and inferring
- Generating questions and using the questions to guide comprehension
- Monitoring and clarifying ("Am I understanding? If not, what can I do to help myself?")
- Evaluating and determining importance
- Summarizing and synthesizing
- Making mental images (visualizing)

3. **Language Learning Strategies.** As they do with other aspects of learning, effective language learners consciously use a variety of strategies to increase their progress in speaking and comprehending the new language (Cohen & Macaro, 2008). Examples of language learning strategies include:

- Conscientiously applying reading strategies, such as previewing, skimming, scanning, and reviewing
- Analyzing and using forms and patterns in English, such as the *prefix + root + suffix* pattern
- Making logical guesses based on contextual and syntactic information
- Breaking words into component parts
- Purposefully grouping and labeling words
- Drawing pictures and/or using gestures to communicate when words do not come to mind
- Substituting a known word when unable to pronounce an unfamiliar word
- Self-monitoring and self-correcting while speaking English
- Paraphrasing
- Guessing and deducing
- Imitating behaviors of native English-speaking peers to successfully complete tasks
- Using verbal and nonverbal cues to know when to pay attention.

Other language learning strategies include those described as social-affective, such as seeking out conversational partners, taking risks with the new language, practicing English when alone, and combatting inhibition about using English by having a positive attitude. Another important social-affective strategy is asking for clarification, something that is often difficult for English learners.

Things to Consider When Teaching Learning Strategies

- The **Common Core State Standards** require that students adapt their communications for varied audiences, purposes, and tasks. While reading, writing, and speaking, students should be able to set and adjust their purposes as needed by the particular tasks (© Copyright 2010. National Governors Association Center for Best Practices and Council of Chief State School Officers. All rights reserved.) This is precisely what it means to be an effective user of reading and language strategies.

- Whichever sets of strategies are emphasized, learned, and used, it is generally agreed that they can be taught through explicit instruction, careful modeling, and scaffolding (Fisher & Frey, 2014; Harvey & Goudvis, 2013; Vogt & Shearer, 2016).

- Lipson and Wixson (Lipson, Wixson, 2012) suggest that just teaching a variety of strategies is not enough. Rather, learners need not only *declarative* knowledge (What is the strategy?), but also *procedural* knowledge (How do I use it?) and *conditional* knowledge (When and why do I use it?). Also, it is important that children practice and apply strategies with different tasks and genres.

- Many English learners who have been well schooled in their **home language** have developed a variety of learning strategies that they can talk about once they learn the English terms for them. Therefore, it's important to know your students' educational backgrounds and their native language literacy proficiency so you can be aware of the strategies they already know and can use in their home language.

  Strategies transfer to learning in the new language. For example, once you know how to find a main idea in a text written in your home language (L1), you can do it with a text in your target language (L2). Likewise, if you know how to make predictions in your L1, you can engage in making predictions in your L2.

- Remember that having students list, identify, and label strategies is not the end goal. Instead, the desired outcome is for children to engage in various learning strategies while they're reading, listening, writing, speaking, and working with other students (Marcell, DeCleene, & Juettner, 2010).

- To assist students in becoming effective strategy users, see the section Teaching Ideas for Strategies, later in this chapter. In particular, note the following instructional activities: Directed Reading-Thinking Activity (DR-TA), SQP2RS (Squeepers), Question-Answer Relationships (QAR), and Questioning the Author (QtA). Also, see Miss Abbas's lesson in the Teaching Scenarios section, and determine which cognitive, metacognitive, and language learning strategies this lesson incorporates.

SIOP® FEATURE 14:

Scaffolding Techniques Consistently Used, Assisting and Supporting Student Understanding

Scaffolding is a term coined by Jerome Bruner (Bruner, 1983) that is associated with Vygotsky's (Vygotsky, 1978) theory of the Zone of Proximal Development (ZPD). In essence, the ZPD is the difference between what a child can accomplish alone and what he or she can achieve with the assistance of a more experienced individual. The assistance that is provided by a teacher is called *scaffolding*.

Pearson and Gallagher (Pearson, Gallagher, 1983) described ZPD and scaffolding as the "gradual release of responsibility" (GRR) as it relates to classroom practices. Do a Web search for "gradual release of responsibility" and you will find several interesting graphics depicting the transition from teacher-regulated learning to student independence. The intent of the GRR model is to move from reliance on the teacher to independence of the students in applying key content concepts and vocabulary—but as we all know, a lesson may not move smoothly from one phase to the next.

What has been mostly absent in GRR explanations is the notion that teaching is a recursive, not linear, process. Therefore, we offer an alternative to GRR that has as its focus recursive teaching, which is essential for English learners and struggling students (see Figure 5.1). With gradual release of student independence (GISI), after the teacher has explicitly taught a concept (*I do. You watch and respond.*), children practice the concept with the teacher's assistance (*We do together. I help and respond.*). Children who are successful can then practice with other students, with minimal supervision (*You do together. I watch and respond.*). For some children it may be necessary to take a step back and reteach and re-model before moving again to supported practice. Of course, the goal for all students is independent application of key concepts and vocabulary (*You do independently. I watch and respond.*). This process is definitely not linear and it leads to differentiated teaching, enabling those who can move forward to do so. But for those who need additional modeling and support, opportunities are provided. Whether you are using the Common Core, the Next Generation Science, or other rigorous standards, it is essential for all students, including English learners, to have appropriate, scaffolded instruction that leads to eventual independence.

| FIGURE 5.1 | Scaffolding: Gradual Increase of Student Independence (GISI) |

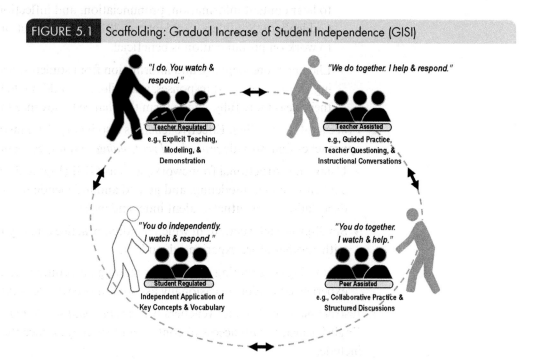

Reproduction of this material is restricted to use with Echevarría, J., Vogt, M.E., & Short, D. (2018). *Making Content Comprehensible for Elementary English Learners: The SIOP® Model* (3rd ed.) New York, NY: Pearson

Three Types of Scaffolding

Three types of scaffolding can be used effectively with English learners: Verbal, Procedural, and Instructional.

1. **Verbal Scaffolding.** Teachers who are aware of English learners' existing levels of language development use prompting, questioning, and elaboration to facilitate students' movement to higher **levels of language proficiency**, comprehension, and thinking. The following are examples of verbal scaffolding:

   ◆ Paraphrasing: Restating a student's response in another form or in other words to clarify and model correct English usage aids children's language development and comprehension.

   ◆ Using think-alouds: These structured models of how effective strategy users think and monitor their understandings usually are provided by the teacher, but they can also be modeled by other children. For example, ask a child to explain how he solved a particular problem in math, or figured out a challenging word in a story.

   ◆ Reinforcing contextual definitions: In the sentence, "Frogs, which have smooth skin that must stay wet, are amphibians," note that the words that follow *frogs* provide a partial definition of the word *amphibian* within the context of the sentence.

   ◆ Providing correct pronunciation by occasionally repeating children's responses: When teachers repeat English learners' correct responses, enunciating carefully and naturally, children have an additional opportunity to hear content information, pronunciation, and inflection. Saunders and Goldenberg (Saunders, Goldenberg, 2010) also suggest that dedicating time to work on pronunciation is beneficial.

   ◆ Eliciting more language and information from students: Rather than accepting one- or two-word responses, ask children to add on, tell more, or explain their ideas more fully, giving them the chance to advance their language skills.

2. **Procedural Scaffolding.** Effective teachers also incorporate instructional approaches that provide *procedural scaffolding*. Examples include:

   ◆ Using an instructional framework, such as GISI (Figure 5.1) that includes explicit teaching, modeling, and guided and independent practice, with an expectation of eventual student independence.

   ◆ Small-group instruction, in which children practice a newly learned strategy with another more experienced student.

   ◆ Partnering or grouping children for reading and content activities, with more experienced readers occasionally assisting those with less experience.

3. **Instructional Scaffolding.** Teachers use *instructional scaffolding* to provide English learners with access to content and language concepts. Examples include:

   ◆ Graphic organizers are used as a prereading tool to prepare students for the content of a textbook chapter. The organizer can also be used to illustrate a chapter's text structure, such as comparative or chronological order (Vogt & Echevarría, 2008).

♦ Models of completed assignments are instructional scaffolds, too. Teachers can show children products, such as posters, booklets, podcasts, and the like, to give them a clear picture of their goal.

As you begin to write SIOP lesson plans, keep this in mind: *A scaffold is a temporary structure for helping students complete a task that would otherwise be too difficult to do alone.* The release of verbal, procedural, and instructional scaffolds is gradual until student independence has been achieved. Resist the temptation to keep scaffolding in place beyond the point that children need it. Current assessments related to the Common Core State Standards require students to complete assessment tasks without teacher scaffolding, so stay alert to students' increasing independence with learning tasks.

SIOP® FEATURE 15:

A Variety of Questions or Tasks That Promote Higher-Order Thinking Skills

Another way that effective SIOP teachers can promote strategy use is by asking questions and providing tasks that promote critical thinking. Sixty years ago, Benjamin Bloom and colleagues (Bloom et al., 1956) introduced a now-familiar taxonomy of educational objectives that includes six levels, listed here from lowest to highest: *Knowledge, Comprehension, Application, Analysis, Synthesis,* and *Evaluation.* This taxonomy was formulated on the principle that learning proceeds from concrete knowledge to abstract values, or from the denotative to the connotative. For decades, educators adopted this taxonomy as a hierarchy of questioning that, when used effectively in the classroom, elicited varied levels of student thinking.

Subsequently, D. R. Krathwohl, who originally worked with Bloom and his colleagues, published a revised taxonomy (see Anderson & Krathwohl, 2001). In the revised taxonomy, the six levels are, again from lowest to highest: *Remember, Understand, Apply, Analyze, Evaluate,* and *Create.* Webb (Webb, 1997) developed a similar, but more complex system and criteria for aligning **standards**, teaching, and **assessment**, called Depth of Knowledge (DOK).

Whichever taxonomy teachers choose to use when designing lessons, it is important to carefully plan higher-order questions and tasks prior to lesson delivery. It is just too difficult to think of these questions on the spot when you're teaching. In fact, of the approximately 80,000 questions the average teacher asks annually, 80% of them are at the literal level (Gall, 1984; Watson & Young, 1986). This is especially problematic with English learners. When teaching children who are acquiring proficiency in English, it is tempting to rely on simple questions that result in yes/no or other one-word responses. It is possible, however, to reduce the linguistic demands of responses while still promoting higher levels of thinking. For example, in a study of plant reproduction, the following question requires little thought: "Are seeds sometimes carried by the wind?" A nod or one-word response is almost automatic if the question is understood. However, a higher-level question such as the following requires analysis, though not a significant language demand: "Which of these seeds would be more likely to be carried by the wind: the rough one or smooth one? Or this

Watch this video to hear Dr. Jana Echevarría talk about Right Away Questions, those that students work on as soon as they enter the classroom. In this example, students in a math class not only engage with math problems during the Right Away activity, but also respond to writing prompts about the problems. https://www.youtube .com/watch?v= 3ZUlXzy8Vyw one that has fuzzy hairs? Why do you think so?" Encouraging students to respond with higher levels of thinking requires teachers to consciously plan and incorporate questions and tasks at a variety of levels.

Teaching Ideas for Strategies

In the section that follows, you will find some teaching ideas to help you with preparing SIOP lessons that include higher level thinking questions and tasks.

- **Digital Storytelling** (Sylvester & Greenidge, 2009). A digital story combines old and new literacies as students speak, write, and create a multimedia text consisting of still images and a narrated soundtrack. Especially appealing to children who struggle with writing, including some English learners, digital stories provide an exciting, hands-on, and innovative way to create stories. In their stories, children focus on elements such as point of view, emotional content, pacing, and music to hold the viewer's interest (Sylvester & Greenidge, 2009). Note that creating and sharing digital stories requires students to engage with cognitive, metacognitive, and language learning strategies.

- **Directed Reading-Thinking Activity (DR-TA)** (Ruddell, 2007; Stauffer, 1969; Vogt & Echevarría, 2008). DR-TA is a very effective activity for encouraging strategic thinking while children are reading or listening to narrative (fiction) text. It's effective in all grades with the steps given below; only the difficulty level of the text changes for older students. Teachers of younger children (pre-K, grade 1) can encourage children to participate in a DR-TA with a picture book or Big Book. Whatever text is chosen, it should be rich, interesting, and, if possible, have a surprising or unanticipated ending. Throughout the reading of the story, stop periodically and have children contemplate predictions about what might follow logically in the next section of the text. Begin the DR-TA lesson with a question about what the class members think the story or book will be about, based on the title. As children respond, include a variety of probes, such as:

  - "With a title like . . . , what do you think this story will be about?"
  - "Let's read to find out."
  - "Did . . . happen? If not, why not?" (revisit predictions)
  - "What do you think is going to happen next? What makes you think so?"
  - "Where did you get that idea?"
  - "What made you think that?"
  - "Tell me more about that . . . "

  It is important that you revisit previously made predictions after chunks of text are read so that children come to understand how predictions (and their confirmation or disconfirmation) impact their comprehension. Students can "vote" on which predictions are most likely to be confirmed as they focus their thinking on character and author motivations, the problem a character is facing, reasons for a character's behavior, and/or how the plot unfolds. Note that a somewhat adapted DR-TA is also effective in the upper elementary grades for longer novels, with chapter-to-chapter discussions focusing on what children think will happen, what really happened, and why. (In Chapter 3, Mrs. Ornelas's lesson vignette includes a DR-TA activity.)

Watch this video to see and hear Dr. MaryEllen Vogt explain how to introduce and use Squeepers in your own classroom. After watching, consider how you might use this effective instructional technique with your students. https://www.youtube.com/watch?v=KOulq0IkRSk

- **SQP2RS ("Squeepers")** This popular and effective instructional framework for teaching content with expository texts includes the following steps (Vogt, 2000, Vogt, 2002; Vogt & Echevarría, 2008):

  1. **Survey:** Students preview and scan the assigned text for about one minute to determine key concepts that will be learned. For children in grades pre-K–2, preview an informational Big Book with your students.

  2. **Question:** In groups, students generate questions likely to be answered by reading the text. Post student questions, one by one on chart paper, and mark an asterisk by the question for each group that had the same or similar question. This is a great opportunity to model for beginning English speakers how questions are formed in English.

  3. **Predict:** As a whole class, students come up with three or four key concepts they think they will learn while reading; the predictions are based on the previously generated questions, especially those marked with asterisks. Model this step with younger children.

  4. **Read:** While reading (with partners or small groups, or with you in a small group), students search for answers to their generated questions and confirm or disconfirm their predictions. Use sticky notes or sticky strips to mark answers to questions and to indicate spots where predictions have been confirmed.

  5. **Respond:** Students answer questions (not necessarily in writing) with partners or group members and formulate new ones for the next section of text to be read; then, lead a discussion of key concepts, clarifying any misunderstandings.

  6. **Summarize:** Orally or in writing, alone or with a partner or group, students summarize the text's key concepts, using key vocabulary where appropriate.

Read Miss Abbas's lesson in the Teaching Scenarios section to see Squeepers in action. For math, see the adaptation of the Squeepers process in Figure 5.2.

- **GIST (Generating Interactions between Schemata and Texts)** This summarization procedure assists children in "getting the gist" from extended text (Cunningham, 1982; as cited in Muth & Alvermann, 1999). Together with students, read a section of text (150 to 300 words) displayed on a whiteboard, in a PowerPoint presentation, or in a handout. After reading, assist children in underlining 10 or more words or concepts that are deemed "most important" to understanding the text. List these words or phrases on the board. Without the text, together write a summary sentence or two using as many of the listed words as possible. Repeat the process through subsequent sections of the text. When finished, write a topic sentence to precede the summary sentences; the end result can be edited into a summary paragraph. This technique is also useful when viewing video clips. Students watch, record 10 key words or phrases, and then create summary sentences.

FIGURE 5.2 SQP2RS ("Squeepers") for Math

Note that this Squeepers adaptation works well for math lessons. The steps are the same, but how they work in the lesson is slightly different. The questions that follow are for the students to think about.

SURVEY Before you read, ask yourself: "What will this lesson be about?" Look at the types of problems you will solve.

QUESTION After your text survey, write 1–3 problems you may be able to solve by the end of this lesson.

PREDICT Predict 1–3 math skills you might use to solve the problems in this lesson. What prior knowledge or new knowledge is necessary?

READ Read the lesson.

RESPOND After you read, try to answer the sample questions and confirm your predictions about the necessary math skills.

SUMMARIZE After you read, write a 4-sentence summary:
   Sentence 1: The big idea of the lesson.
   Sentences 2–4: How would you explain how to solve the problems in this lesson to a classmate who was absent?

From "Downey Unified School District" by Karlin LaPorta & Melissa Canham. Reproduced with permission.

- **Graphic organizers** Graphic organizers provide scaffolding for children in the form of a visual representation of language (August & Shanahan, 2010). They are schematic diagrams of key concepts and other information, and students use them to organize the information they are learning. Examples include Venn diagrams, timelines, flow charts, semantic maps, and so forth. See Buehl (Buehl, 2013) and Vogt and Echevarría (Vogt, Echevarría, 2008) for many examples of effective graphic organizers. There is a caveat about using graphic organizers. Remember that the purpose of the tool is to help children organize content information. Therefore, graphic organizers shouldn't be used as "silent seat-work," but rather, to promote discussion and critical thinking about the topic at hand. You may also wish to have students occasionally map their understandings of a topic in their own structure, rather than one that is already created. Children's maps can provide a teacher with valuable assessment information about their understandings of content information.

- **Reciprocal Teaching** (Oczkus, 2010; Palinscar & Brown, 1984) Reciprocal Teaching incorporates four metacognitive strategies that teachers and children practice to improve comprehension of text:

  - Predicting

  - Questioning

  - Clarifying

  - Summarizing

  After children have learned each of these strategies, they meet in small groups to discuss which strategies they are using while reading. We have learned through teaching both techniques that when children learn to use the SQP2RS (Squeepers) steps first, they more readily engage in Reciprocal Teaching in small groups. (For detailed lesson plans, task cards, and other RT resources, see Oczkus, 2010).

- **Question-Answer Relationships (QAR)** (Raphael, 1984; Raphael, Highfield, & Au, 2006; Vogt & Echevarría, 2008). Children can become more strategic in their reading when they learn how to determine levels of questions. Some questions can be answered by looking "In the Book" (*Right There* or *Think and Search*). Other questions need to be answered with prior knowledge and experience, and they'll be found "In My Head" (*Author and Me* or *On My Own*). For children in grades K–2, you can start teaching the QAR process by introducing two levels of questions: *On the Page* and *In My Head*.

- **Pre-Questioning** Burke (2002) explains the importance of older elementary children writing their own research questions *before* they use the Internet to find information, so that they steer the inquiry, rather than just surf for answers. In science, students could also use this technique prior to making a hypothesis.

- **Questioning the Author (QtA)** (Beck & McKeown, 2006) Successful learners know how to use question-asking to help them construct meaning while they read (Taboada & Guthrie, 2006). They ask questions and challenge what the author says if something does not make sense to them. Because children's comprehension of textbook material sometimes can be disjointed and lacking in connections between ideas and key concepts, Beck and McKeown (2002, Beck, McKeown, 2006) recommend using the instructional approach known as Questioning the Author (QtA), which values the depth and quality of students' interactions with texts, and their responses to authors' intended meanings. QtA assists students in developing the ability to read text closely, as if the author were there to be questioned and challenged. For an overview of the process, see Read, Write, Think at *http://www.readwritethink.org/professional-development/strategy-guides/question-author-30761.html*. You'll also find a variety other effective teaching ideas at this very helpful Web site.

Differentiating Ideas for Multi-level Classes

Within the Strategies component, scaffolding is a focus, and by definition, scaffolding leads to **differentiated instruction**. One way to scaffold for English learners' varied language development needs while teaching learning strategies is through Strategic Sentence Starters (Olson, Land, Anselmi, & AuBuchon, 2011, p. 251). Giving students sentence starters or frames provides the support many need to be able to participate in literature and content area discussions. The following examples could be printed on small "cue cards" that children select and use as needed.

- *Planning and goal setting*
  - My purpose is . . .
  - My top priority (or most important job) is . . .
  - I will accomplish my goal by . . .
- *Tapping prior knowledge*
  - I already know . . .
  - This reminds me of . . .
  - This relates to . . .

- *Asking questions*
  - ◆ I wonder why . . .
  - ◆ What if . . . ?
  - ◆ How come . . . ?
- *Making predictions*
  - ◆ I'll bet that . . .
  - ◆ I think . . .
  - ◆ If _____, then . . .
- *Visualizing*
  - ◆ I can picture . . .
  - ◆ In my mind, I see . . .
  - ◆ If this were a movie, . . .
- *Making connections*
  - ◆ This reminds me of . . .
  - ◆ I experienced this once when . . .
  - ◆ I can relate to this because once . . .
- *Summarizing*
  - ◆ The basic gist is . . .
  - ◆ The key information is . . .
  - ◆ In a nutshell, this says that . . .
- *Monitoring*
  - ◆ I got lost here because . . .
  - ◆ I need to reread the part where . . .
  - ◆ I know I'm on the right track because . . .
- *Clarifying*
  - ◆ To understand better, I need to know about . . .
  - ◆ Something that is still not clear is . . .
  - ◆ I'm guessing that this means _____, but I need to know . . .
- *Reflecting and relating*
  - ◆ So, the big idea is . . .
  - ◆ A conclusion I'm drawing is . . .
  - ◆ This is relevant to my life because . . .
- *Evaluating*
  - ◆ I like/don't like _____ because . . .
  - ◆ My opinion is _____ because . . .
  - ◆ The most important message is _____ because . . .

(For more examples of SIOP lesson and unit plans in language arts, see Vogt, Echevarría, and Short, 2010.)

The Lesson

The lesson described in this chapter is taken from a fifth-grade reading/language arts theme titled Saving Our Planet.

Unit: Saving Our Planet (Fifth Grade)

The three classrooms described in the teaching scenarios in this chapter are heterogeneously mixed with native English speakers and English learners with varied levels of fluency. The elementary school is in a suburban community with Hispanic English learners constituting approximately 55% of the student population. There are also small numbers of English learners representing other language groups.

Mr. Bokhari, Miss Abbas, and Mrs. Graves are each teaching a reading/language arts unit on Saving Our Planet. The district-adopted reading series is used for most of the instruction for this unit, but teachers are encouraged to supplement the series with relevant trade books when appropriate. For the following two-period lesson, the fifth-grade teachers chose a beautiful informational trade book available in multiple copies from the school library. The book titled *Earth from Above for Young Readers* by Yann Arthus-Bertrand and Robert Burleigh (Harry N. Abrams, Inc., Publishers, 2001) includes stunning photographs taken from the air of interesting and beautiful countries around the world, some of which are in ecological danger. A brief and informative description accompanies each photograph.

The teachers' lessons are designed to address the following Common Core English Language Arts Standards for grade 5 (CCSS, 2010):

- Quote accurately from a text when explaining what the text says explicitly and when drawing inferences from the text.
- Determine the meaning of words and phrases as they are used in a text, including figurative language such as metaphors and similes.
- Describe how a narrator's or speaker's point of view influences how events are described.
- Analyze how visual and multimedia elements contribute to the meaning, tone, or beauty of a text.

Teaching Scenarios

To demonstrate how fifth-grade teachers Mr. Bokhari, Miss Abbas, and Mrs. Graves designed instruction for their students, including English learners, we look at how each prepared a two-day lesson using the trade book *Earth from Above for Young Readers*.

Mr. Bokhari

Mr. Bokhari began his lesson by distributing two copies of the trade book to the six table groups, which included either four or five students in each group. His 17 English learners were mixed heterogeneously in the class of 33 students. He asked the students, in pairs or triads, to thumb through the book and to use the photos and other textual features (e.g., titles, maps, and illustrations) to predict what they had to do with the unit theme, Saving Our Planet. One student in each group was to be the recorder who would jot down the group's thoughts, and the other group members were directed to be ready to explain how they came up with their predictions. Mr. Bokhari then asked the students to orally report their findings as he wrote them on the whiteboard. Next, he asked the table groups to select photographs of six countries depicted in the book that they would like to know more about, with each pair or triad reading about three of the countries. Once the children made their selections, they orally read the descriptions of their three countries by taking turns with their partners. Students were then directed to find the most important information in each of the three descriptions and, with their partner or triad, write a summary paragraph, including a quote from the text to use as evidence of a point that was made in their writing. Mr. Bokhari encouraged students to make connections between what they had been learning about the planet earth and what they were reading in the book. After students completed their paragraphs, the partners and triads shared them with their group members.

During the second day of the lesson, Mr. Bokhari reviewed each group's paragraphs, and then asked the groups to describe for the class their chosen photographs, including how the pictures and quotations provided information about the selected countries. Each group then voted on their favorite photograph in the book, and a spokesperson gave an oral rationale for the group's choice.

On the SIOP form in Figure 5.3, rate Mr. Bokhari's lesson on each of the Strategies features.

Miss Abbas

Miss Abbas began the lesson by introducing to her 31 students (of whom 22 were English learners at varied levels of English proficiency) the content and language objectives that she had written on sentence strips and placed in a pocket chart (see the following lesson plan—Figure 5.4—for the objectives). She distributed two copies of the book *Earth from Above for Young Readers* to each table group, and reviewed previously taught academic language (*environment, prediction, summarize*). She then reviewed the steps to SQP2RS ("Squeepers"), a process designed to engage students in critical and strategic thinking while reading challenging informational and expository texts (see pp. 133–134). Previously, Miss Abbas had taught, modeled, and provided practice with each of the six sequential steps in Squeepers, so students were able to begin the process with a quick review. Also in an earlier lesson in the reading series, the children had placed sticky notes on a world map designating places on earth where there are current and potential environmental problems. Miss Abbas referred to this map on the wall as she introduced the book for today's lesson, and she reminded students of some of the environmental issues they had previously discussed. She then directed students to think about the issues as they began to Survey

FIGURE 5.3	Strategies Component of the SIOP® Model: Mr. Bokhari's Lesson

4	3	2	1	0
13. Ample opportunities provided for students to use **learning strategies**		Inadequate opportunities provided for students to use **learning strategies**		No opportunity provided for students to use **learning strategies**

4	3	2	1	0
14. **Scaffolding techniques** consistently used, assisting and supporting student understanding (e.g., think-alouds)		**Scaffolding techniques** occasionally used		**Scaffolding techniques** not used

4	3	2	1	0
15. A variety of **questions or tasks that promote higher-order thinking skills** (e.g., literal, analytical, and interpretive questions)		Infrequent **questions or tasks that promote higher-order thinking skills**		No **questions or tasks that promote higher-order thinking skills**

? Reflect and Apply

Click here to explain your ratings for Mr. Bokhari's lesson on each of the Strategies features.

this new book to determine what they thought they would learn by reading it. Students were directed to carefully examine the large photographs and other illustrations during the two-minute survey.

Miss Abbas gave the signal to stop the surveying, and then directed her students to work with a partner to write two or three **Q**uestions they thought they might find answers to by reading some of the descriptions in the book that accompanied the photographs. After a few minutes, Miss Abbas then jotted the students' questions on chart paper, noting with asterisks which questions were asked by more than one group of students. From the questions, the class next predicted five important concepts or ideas they thought they would learn while reading this book (**P**redict).

Because this book is an informational text that can be challenging for some students, including English learners, Miss Abbas read aloud the first two brief descriptions about New Caledonia and Botswana. She modeled how to review the class list of posted questions to see if any had been answered at this point. She also modeled how to find specific quotes in the text that either answered one of the questions or confirmed or disconfirmed one of the predictions that had been made. She then reminded students to mark the quotes in the text with a sticky note. When students read a sentence about how hunters pose dangers for elephants in Botswana, several immediately remarked that this was similar to what they had read earlier in the week when they learned about other endangered species. All partner/triad groups also noted this sentence with a sticky note. Miss Abbas then directed the pairs and triads to **R**ead quietly together the brief descriptions of Mali, Indonesia, Argentina, Côte

FIGURE 5.4 SIOP® Lesson: Miss Abbas's Lesson Plan

Key: SW = Students will; TW = Teacher will; HOTS = higher-order thinking skills (questions and tasks)

Unit: Saving Our Planet   **Grade:** 5   **Teacher:** Miss Abbas
SIOP Lesson: Comparing environmental issues in seven countries outside the United States

Reading/Language Arts Content Standards (Comprehension):
  2.1 Understand how text features (e.g., format, graphics, sequence, diagrams, illustrations, charts, maps) make information accessible and usable.
  2.3 Discern main ideas and concepts presented in texts, identifying and assessing evidence that supports those ideas.
  2.7 Draw inferences, conclusions, or generalizations about text and support them with textual evidence and prior knowledge.
  2.8 Distinguish facts, supported inferences, and opinions in text.

Key Vocabulary: TW review *environment, prediction, summarize.* Teach meaning of *persuade;* In VSS, SW find key words and phrases in the descriptions. **HOTS:** Of the environmental problems described in the book we read today, which do you think are the most important for Saving our Planet? Why do you think so? a. Vegetation unable to grow in salt water because of human-made floods (New Caledonia). b. Animals like elephants becoming endangered by humans (Botswana). c. Agricultural land being used poorly and unwisely (Indonesia). d. Whales killed for the oil in their bodies (Argentina). e. Hydroelectric dams flooding needed agricultural land (Cote d'Ivoire). f. Climate changes resulting from logging in the Amazon forests (Brazil).	**Visuals/Resources:** Yann, Arthus-Bertrand & Burleigh Robert. (2001). *Earth From Above For Young Readers.* New York: Harry N. Abrams, Inc., Publishers. World map, sticky notes, chart paper, markers, binder paper, copies of questions for homework.

Connections to Prior Knowledge and Past Learning; Building Background:
  • Review steps to SQP2RS (Squeepers): Who remembers the steps?
  • Review unit theme by referring to world map and sticky notes placed there last week indicating places where serious environmental problems are currently occurring, including the United States.
  • Complete the Survey, Question, Predict steps of SQP2RS to narrow focus and build background.
  • Introduce book and share introductory information about the photographer, Yann Arthus-Bertrand.
  • Review the differences between a *fact* and an *opinion.*

Content Objectives:	Meaningful Activities: Lesson Sequence	Review and Assessment:
1. You will use photographs, maps, and illustrations to predict important information about environmental concerns in several different countries. 2. You will identify key information in written descriptions of five environmental problems. 3. You will select what you think is the most important environmental issue facing us today.	• TW post and orally explain content and language objectives. • TW briefly review meanings of words previously taught: *environment, prediction, summarize.* • TW review steps of SQP2RS • TW distribute copies of books, two/table group. • Introduce the photographer and author: Introduction (pp. 6–9). • TW review how to do a quick survey of informational text (2–3 min). • In partners or triads, SW write 2–3 questions generated from the survey. TW post questions on	Add 1–2 minutes to Survey if questions are lacking in substance. Review how to ask appropriate questions based on the text information (Practice and Application).

FIGURE 5.4 *Continued*

Language Objectives:

1. You will listen to two and will read five descriptions of environmental problems in the world.

2. You will write a brief summary about the environmental issues you read about.

3. You will try to *persuade* others about the environmental issue you think is most important by saying:

"I am going to *persuade* you that the environmental issue that is most important for saving our planet is:
_____ because _____."

My reason is a *(fact)* or *(opinion)*.

---

chart paper; mark with asterisks the questions generated by more than one group (i.e., 4 asterisks for a question asked by four groups).

- SW predict 3–4 most important concepts we will discuss and learn. TW post on chart paper.
- TW read first two descriptions of New Caledonia (pp. 10–11) and Botswana (pp. 12–13).
- SW read about Mali (pp. 16–17), Indonesia (pp. 28–29), Argentina (pp. 38–39), Cote d'Ivoire (pp. 44–45), Brazil (pp. 62–63), using sticky notes for noting key ("most important") information.
- VSS: SW find 2-3 vocabulary words or phrases in the seven descriptions that are related to Saving Our Planet Examples: p. 45: *"The vegetation was submerged."* What happened to the plants when the dam was built? Or p. 62: *"Here, as elsewhere, people must weigh the good results against the bad."* What is the meaning of *weigh* in this sentence? (Practice and Application)
- TW list words/phrases on white board. Explain/discuss as necessary.
- TW lead discussion on posted questions and spots in text with sticky notes. Check back on earlier predictions to see if they were confirmed or disconfirmed (Practice and Application).
- TW review how to use the key information from charts, maps, photographs; VSS words and phrases; and descriptions marked with sticky notes to write brief summaries (suggest at each table which partners or triads need to write paragraphs, which need to write good sentences).
- TW remind students to take summaries home along with homework questions.
- TW distribute and read aloud questions for homework discussion at home and in class tomorrow. Review the meanings of *fact, opinion.* Teach the meaning of *persuade.* Review sentence stem in language objectives. Chorally read the sentence starter several times for practice. Each student's job tomorrow is to try to *persuade* the others in his or her table group which is the most important environmental issue affecting the countries we read about. You can include your parents' or caregivers' opinions, too. Remember the differences between *facts* and *opinions* when you're trying to *persuade* others.

Check to see if predictions include most important information; if not, add another 1-min. survey.

Spot-check while students are quietly reading to each other to see what they're marking with sticky notes.

Spot-check to make sure all partners or triads are finding key vocabulary and/or phrases. Help with pronunciation and meanings, if necessary.

Are students able to answer their own questions? If not, why not?

Model with think-aloud how to take information from charts, map, and create 2–3 summary statements together with class. Circulate and spot-check while students are writing summaries, paragraphs, or sentences.

Check understanding of questions, and vocabulary *fact, opinion, persuade.*

Model pronunciation of sentence starter; listen during choral reading.

Ask for student examples of *facts* and *opinions* as review.

Wrap-up:

- Review the three key concepts about the environmental issues identified in the book descriptions: (1) humans flooding agricultural land, (2) animals being endangered by humans, (3) world climate changes because of humans.
- Review key vocabulary on VSS poster; review the meaning of *persuade.*
- Review content and language objectives by showing fingers: 1 = I met this objective, 2 = I'm getting close to meeting the objective, but need more practice; (3) I'm still confused and need some more help.

Lesson plan format created by Melissa Castillo & Nicole Teyechea. Used with permission.

d'Ivoire, and Brazil. She selected these particular photographs and descriptions because each picture and accompanying paragraph showed a vivid example of an environmental problem. As students read together, they noted with their sticky notes those sentences that answered their posted questions, as well as some that described an environmental concern. If students finished the reading task, they were encouraged to continue looking through the book, examining the photographs, and reading about places of interest.

When everyone was finished, Miss Abbas asked each set of partners or triads to return to the country descriptions, as well as the introductory descriptions that she had read aloud, and find descriptive words related to their unit on Saving Our Planet (VSS: Vocabulary Self-Collection Strategy, p. 87). These VSS words were shared with other table members and ultimately with the class, and as Miss Abbas and the students discussed the meanings, the words were posted on chart paper for future reference. In particular, Miss Abbas pointed out words students had identified in the text that were examples of figurative language.

Miss Abbas then directed students back to the questions they had earlier generated to see which had been answered and which remained unanswered. Also, during this **R**esponse time, the children reported on what they had discovered while reading and showed in their books where they had marked important quotations and other information with the sticky notes. They checked their predictions to see if they had been confirmed, and discussed why some were not, such as the author didn't include certain information in the descriptions.

Next, each set of pairs or triads was asked to **S**ummarize in writing (the length depending on levels of English proficiency) the key concepts that had been discussed and learned, using evidence from the texts, including quotations. Students were encouraged to use in their summaries the chart papers with the questions, predictions, and pages that had been noted with sticky notes, along with the key vocabulary that had been selected during VSS. Miss Abbas spot-checked throughout this final step in SQP2RS to make sure each individual was contributing to the group summary.

To prepare the students for the next day's activity, Miss Abbas reviewed the meaning of the word *persuade* by providing examples of how someone was trying to persuade another (e.g., persuading someone to buy a particular product, to go on a diet, or to vote for a candidate for office). She asked the students to take another look at a piece of text they had read in the trade book, and find a few examples of words used by the author to persuade readers to be concerned about an environmental problem. Miss Abbas then assigned the following questions for students to take home and discuss with their parents or caregivers during the evening. She indicated that the next day's discussion during their reading/language arts block would focus on the responses to the questions, and on words and phrases that can be used to persuade people. Each group would pool their responses and argue for the environmental issue they think is most important, using evidence and quotations from their reading and discussion to support their positions.

Of the environmental problems described in the book we read from today, which do you think are the most important for Saving Our Planet? Why do you think so?

a. Vegetation is unable to grow in salt water (New Caledonia).
b. Animals like elephants are becoming endangered because of humans (Botswana).

c. Agricultural land is being used poorly and unwisely (Indonesia).

d. Whales are being killed for the oil in their bodies (Argentina).

e. Hydroelectric dams are flooding needed agricultural land (Côte d'Ivoire).

f. Climate changes are the result of logging in the Amazon forests (Brazil).

On the SIOP form in Figure 5.5, rate Miss Abbas's lesson on each of the Strategies features.

Mrs. Graves

Mrs. Graves began her lesson by distributing two of the trade books to each table group (28 students; 16 of whom were English learners at varied levels of proficiency). She asked each student to complete a quick-write based on the cover photo of the book and the following prompts: Where do you think this photograph was taken? Where do you think the people on the walkway are going? (Note: The colorful photograph, taken from high in the sky, is of Yellowstone Park's hot springs with tourists walking by on a wooden walkway.) After students completed the quick-write, Mrs. Graves asked each child to read his or her writing to the others at their tables. Some students wrote paragraphs, while others wrote only a few words. A few students wrote nothing.

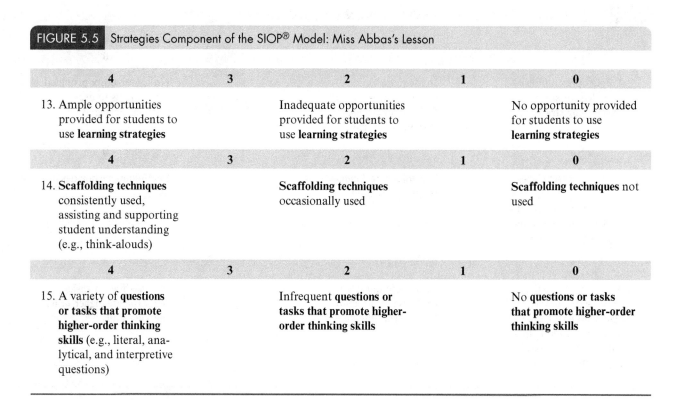

FIGURE 5.5 Strategies Component of the SIOP® Model: Miss Abbas's Lesson

4	3	2	1	0
13. Ample opportunities provided for students to use **learning strategies**		Inadequate opportunities provided for students to use **learning strategies**		No opportunity provided for students to use **learning strategies**

4	3	2	1	0
14. **Scaffolding techniques** consistently used, assisting and supporting student understanding (e.g., think-alouds)		**Scaffolding techniques** occasionally used		**Scaffolding techniques** not used

4	3	2	1	0
15. A variety of **questions or tasks that promote higher-order thinking skills** (e.g., literal, analytical, and interpretive questions)		Infrequent **questions or tasks that promote higher-order thinking skills**		No **questions or tasks that promote higher-order thinking skills**

Reflect and Apply

Click here to explain your ratings for Miss Abbas's lesson on each of the Strategies features.

Next, Mrs. Graves directed students to look through the book with other students in their group, find their favorite photographs, and try to figure out what the photos were all about. Because many of the students had reading problems and/or were limited English speakers, Mrs. Graves had students identify the page numbers of their favorite photos, and then she read aloud the descriptions for their favorites. This activity took the entire period on the first day, and most students enjoyed looking at the pictures.

At the beginning of the second day of the lesson, Mrs. Graves orally defined 10 vocabulary words from the trade book that she had listed on the whiteboard. The children were then directed to complete independently a Venn Diagram, comparing and contrasting any two photos and countries described in *Earth from Above*. She encouraged the class to look again at the trade book and find quotations that were interesting, and then write them down on the Venn Diagram. Students were also encouraged to use any of the listed vocabulary words on the graphic organizer. Students had completed Venn Diagrams frequently, so they began working when the organizers were distributed. Mrs. Graves said that the students could talk to each other quietly, but they were to work independently. She collected the graphic organizers at the end of the period so that she could generate a grade for the two-day lesson.

On the SIOP form in Figure 5.6, rate Mrs. Graves's lesson on each of the Strategies features.

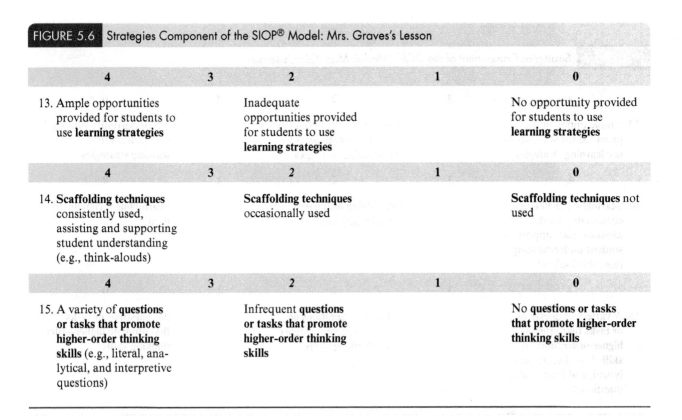

FIGURE 5.6 Strategies Component of the SIOP® Model: Mrs. Graves's Lesson

4	3	2	1	0
13. Ample opportunities provided for students to use **learning strategies**		Inadequate opportunities provided for students to use **learning strategies**		No opportunity provided for students to use **learning strategies**

4	3	2	1	0
14. **Scaffolding techniques** consistently used, assisting and supporting student understanding (e.g., think-alouds)		**Scaffolding techniques** occasionally used		**Scaffolding techniques** not used

4	3	2	1	0
15. A variety of **questions or tasks that promote higher-order thinking skills** (e.g., literal, analytical, and interpretive questions)		Infrequent **questions or tasks that promote higher-order thinking skills**		No **questions or tasks that promote higher-order thinking skills**

? **Reflect and Apply**
Click here to explain your ratings for Mrs. Graves's lesson on each of the Strategies features.

■ Discussion of Lessons

13. *Ample Opportunities Provided for Students to Use Learning Strategies*

Mr. Bokhari: 3

Miss Abbas: 4

Mrs. Graves: 1

- **Mr. Bokhari's** lesson received a "3" for the learning strategies feature. His students were required to make predictions about the content of the book they were going to read. After reading, the children evaluated the importance of the factual information in the descriptions of the three countries they had chosen while they were writing their paragraph. While Mr. Bokhari asked the students to make connections to earlier learning, he did not provide an example of what he meant nor did he discuss any students' connections, so it's impossible to know whether students really engaged in this important strategy. Students were asked to summarize in writing the information they had read and orally share it with their table group and ultimately with the class. Mr. Bokhari's lesson would have been stronger had he asked the students to return to their earlier predictions and confirm or disconfirm them after they had read the text selections.

- **Miss Abbas's** lesson received a "4" for the learning strategies feature because students engaged in using cognitive, metacognitve, and affective strategies throughout the period. During SQP2RS (Squeepers), students predicted, reexamined their predictions later in the lesson, generated questions about the reading materials, identified important information with sticky notes, read together and noted key points, selected key vocabulary, and wrote a partner or triad summary. Finally, everyone was asked to evaluate the relative importance of six environmental issues found throughout the world. Miss Abbas also encouraged her students to make connections with past learning.

- **Mrs. Graves's** lesson received a "1" for the learning strategies feature. While she attempted to engage the students in making predictions from the cover of the book, many of the English learners (and other students as well) knew little of Yellowstone Park's hot springs, and therefore they were disengaged because they couldn't relate to the photograph. Mrs. Graves also asked the students to evaluate their favorite photo of the 34, but because the students weren't expected to read or really learn much of anything from the accompanying descriptions for the photos, the task was more about looking at interesting pictures than engaging in strategic thinking.

14. *Scaffolding Techniques Consistently Used, Assisting and Supporting Students*

Mr. Bokhari: 2

Miss Abbas: 4

Mrs. Graves: 1

- **Mr. Bokhari** missed several opportunities to provide scaffolding for his English learners and struggling readers, and therefore his lesson received a "2" for the scaffolding feature. While he did have the students work in heterogeneous groups, which allowed them to work together and help each other, he did not remind the children how to use the textual features in the book to guide their predictions about the course content. He also could have scaffolded the group's selections of their countries by limiting the number so the task was more manageable, especially because some of the descriptions and photos aren't directly related to the unit theme. Instructional time was not used well by some groups because there were 34 descriptions with appealing photographs in the book, and several groups had a difficult time making their selections. The entire lesson would have been more effective if Mr. Bokhari had modeled exactly what the students were to do, including how to make their selections, how to forge connections with prior learning, and how to use their notes to create their oral summaries. These directions, as well as criteria for selecting the most important information in the descriptions, should have been written and posted for the students' use. This type of scaffolding is critical for English learners and other children who struggle, but it is also helpful for all students.

- **Miss Abbas's** lesson received a "4" for the scaffolding feature. Throughout her lesson, she provided the following scaffolds: (1) posting and orally explaining the lesson's content and language objectives; (2) reviewing essential academic language (prediction, summarize, environment), and teaching what could be new academic language to English learners (persuade); (3) reviewing the steps to SQP2RS (Squeepers); (4) grouping students heterogeneously in pairs or triads; (5) reviewing an earlier lesson by referring back to the world map; (6) introducing the photographer and author information from the book's introduction; (7) encouraging students to survey the text prior to reading; (8) listing the student-generated questions on chart paper and indicating with asterisks which questions had been asked by multiple groups, thereby narrowing the focus of the topic to important information; (9) limiting to five the number of descriptions that groups would read; (10) modeling by reading aloud the first two descriptions before the students read the others; (11) allowing students to find their VSS words, a process Miss Abbas frequently included in lessons after she initially taught the children how to find important words; (12) reviewing and discussing the questions the students had generated earlier; (13) adjusting the final written summary assignment according to the English learners' proficiency levels; (14) allowing all students to use their notes, charts, map, and Squeepers questions and predictions during the group summary writing; and (15) previewing the key question for the following day and allowing students to discuss this with family members at home. Because of the extensive scaffolding throughout the lesson, the children were able to complete the assigned tasks.

- **Mrs. Graves's** lesson received a "1" for the scaffolding feature because her attempts to assist the students actually may have hindered their learning. For example, she assigned a quick-write for everyone. While this activity is generally considered an effective way to activate students' prior knowledge about a topic, it was inappropriate for the selected book because the cover photo was taken from the air and is somewhat difficult to figure out even for those familiar with Yellowstone Park. The quick-write proved especially difficult for the English learners, not only because of their levels of English proficiency, but also because of their lack of prior knowledge about what they were viewing. A more effective activity would have been to allow the students to talk together about the cover photo and pool their ideas and predictions. In addition, many English learners have a very challenging time listening for an entire period while the teacher reads content material aloud. While Mrs. Graves believed she was supporting her English learners by reading the descriptions, in reality, the children were unable to follow what she was saying, even when they had the text in front of them. Remember that there were only two books for each table group, so many students had nothing to look at during the teacher's read-aloud. Finally, even though the students had prior practice with the Venn Diagram graphic organizer, it was unreasonable for Mrs. Graves to expect them to complete one based on the photos and her oral reading of the descriptions, especially when the students could not work together. It appears that the grade, not student mastery of clearly stated objectives, was Mrs. Graves's goal for the lesson.

15. *A Variety of Questions and Tasks That Promote Higher-Order Thinking Skills*

Mr. Bokhari: 3

Miss Abbas: 4

Mrs. Graves: 1

- **Mr. Bokhari's** lesson received a "3" for the tasks that required the students to engage in higher-order thinking. Students were engaged in predicting, summarizing, and evaluating during the lessons. However, some of the students, because of their limited English proficiency, had difficulty participating fully. Remember, as you plan SIOP lessons, that even when teachers include higher-order questions and tasks, if an adequate amount of scaffolding isn't included in the lesson, some students will not be able to engage in critical thinking, not because they lack the ability, but because they cannot carry out the tasks independently. Even the best lesson plan that promotes higher-order thinking will be ineffective in execution if students have difficulty completing the assigned tasks. This is precisely why the scaffolding feature is included in the Strategies component. See Chapter 8 for a complete discussion of this and other issues during lesson delivery.

Watch this video and observe Sarah Russell's class of English learners. Even though this is a secondary class, try to identify the learning strategies that Sarah is having her students practice and apply during this lesson. The techniques Sarah is using are appropriate for nearly any age group.

- **Miss Abbas's** lesson received a "4" for the higher-order thinking questions and tasks she included in the lesson. The steps of SQP2RS (Squeepers) promote critical thinking when students are engaged in predicting, questioning, monitoring their comprehension (when they are searching for answers to their questions and confirming/disconfirming predictions), determining what's really important, and summarizing. Keep in mind that the Squeepers technique can be used with students of all ages, including pre-K and K. The steps remain the same; the text is what changes according to age, English proficiency, and reading level. Also note that the final question of Miss Abbas's lesson that was to be discussed at home and the following day is written at the highest level of Bloom's Taxonomy (Evaluation).

- **Mrs. Graves's** lesson received a "1" for the final feature in the Strategies component. The initial questions in the lesson (Where do you think this photograph was taken? Where do you think the people on the walkway are going?) are thought provoking, but the manner in which they were asked (the quick-write) was inappropriate given the students' varied English proficiency levels. Having the students orally read their quick-writes in front of all classmates is also an ineffective (and frankly deleterious) practice, especially when children are acquiring a new language and/or are having difficulty with reading. Sharing a quick-write with a partner or triad is very different from reading in front of an "audience" of peers. Finally, while Venn Diagrams are intended to promote critical thinking (comparing and contrasting), when assigned as Mrs. Graves did without interaction and as a silent independent task, the graphic organizer became just another classroom worksheet.

Teaching with Technology

After talking with the teachers and discussing the lessons you read about in the Scenarios earlier in the chapter, our tech integrator, Ms. Palacios, offered some technology suggestions to enhance the teachers' lessons.

Student Selector and Question Stems. One afternoon, Ms. Palacios was at the elementary school working with Mr. Bokhari, to update his laptop computer. On Mr. Bokhari's desk, Ms. Palacios spotted a large can filled with sticks (such as tongue depressors) that were labeled with children's names. She asked the teacher if she could borrow the can for that week's after-school tech workshop.

Ms. Palacios, while a strong proponent of technology in the classroom, often reminds teachers when adopting a new technology tool to assess whether the tools are actually improving learning. To begin the workshop, Ms. Palacios put the can with the labeled sticks on the table in front of her, and asked the teachers in the room if they were using a similar technique with sticks, index cards, or another analog tool. She then challenged them to consider their current method of calling on students and to evaluate whether a tech tool might work even better. Ms. Palacios then showed them *StickPick*, an app available for iOS, Android, or laptops.

To demonstrate the benefits of *StickPick*, Ms. Palacios connected her iPad to the classroom projector, allowing all of the participating teachers to see her screen and observe the process of using the app. She asked Mr. Bokhari to tell her the names of a few of her students and then entered them into the app. Ms. Palacios then asked about their approximate academic language proficiency levels and which ones were English learners. Within a few moments they put together a class profile for the small group.

Ms. Palacios gently shook the iPad and the teachers noticed that one of the children was randomly picked. The student screen showed the pre-set questions with stems. After choosing a stem and hearing the student's response to that question, the app allowed the user to assess the student's response with a quick rubric that Ms. Palacios demonstrated. She repeated the process, inputting scores for hypothetical student answers. The teachers then saw that data from these responses were compiled as simple statistics in student reports. After seeing the app in action, the teachers were excited to try the new tool that could not only replace cans of sticks or stacks of index cards, but also enhance their classroom discussions.

Mr. Bokhari decided to test out *StickPick* during language arts. To launch a review of the the Saving Our Planet unit, he posted two questions on the board and asked the students to discuss them with a partner, informing them that there would be follow-up questions after turn-and-talk time. After allowing the partners to work for a few moments, Mr. Bokhari started using the app on his phone to help him call on students and prompt them with questions. Reflecting on the discussion portion of the lesson, Mr. Bokhari found the app to be helpful. He looked forward to seeing trends in students' responses, but also felt the tool would encourage him to maintain consistency when asking various types and levels of questions.

Other terms for this type of tool: random student generator, random name picker

Related products: *Pick Me!* app for iOS, *Make My Groups* iOS

Other tools worth exploring: *Group Picker*

Note: Due to the constantly evolving nature of the Internet, it is a challenge to ensure that all of the links and Web services listed here are updated and functional when you read the technology sections. While specific tools or services may appear in the narrative, we have also included the general term for each tool. If a specific service does not work or is no longer available, search with the general term for the tool and you should be able to find a comparable Web site.

Check Your Understanding

Click here to check your understanding of the concepts in Chapter 5, Strategies.

■ Summary

As you reflect on this chapter and the impact of learning strategies, scaffolding, and higher-order thinking questions and tasks, consider the following main points:

- In this chapter, we have described how to promote critical and strategic thinking for all students, but most especially for English learners. Learning is made more effective when teachers actively assist children in developing a variety of learning strategies, including those that are cognitive, metacognitive, and language based. Learning strategies promote self-monitoring, self-regulation, and problem solving.

- Children with developing English proficiency should be provided with effective, creative, and generative teaching while they are learning the language. Therefore, it is imperative that all teachers provide them with sufficient scaffolding, including verbal supports such as paraphrasing and frequent repetition; procedural supports, such as teacher modeling with think-alouds, one-on-one teaching, and opportunities to work with more experienced individuals in flexible groups; and instructional supports such as the appropriate use of graphic organizers and content and text adaptations. Through appropriate and effective scaffolding, English learners can participate in lessons that involve strategic and critical thinking.

- We frequently remind teachers, "Just because children don't read well doesn't mean they can't think!" A similar adage to this might be said of English learners: "Just because they don't speak English proficiently doesn't mean they can't think!" Therefore, SIOP teachers include in their lesson plans a variety of higher-order thinking questions and tasks.

■ Discussion Questions

1. In reflecting on the content and language objectives at the beginning of the chapter, are you able to:
   a. Select student learning strategies that are appropriate to a lesson's objectives?
   b. Incorporate explicit instruction and student practice with learning strategies when planning lessons?
   c. Identify techniques for verbal, procedural, and instructional scaffolding?
   d. Identify language learning strategies to include in lessons?
   e. Write lesson plans that include varied techniques for scaffolding student understandings?
   f. Write a set of questions or tasks on a chosen topic with increasing levels of cognition?

2. Reflect on a recent lesson in which you modeled a process, gave directions for students to follow, or provided steps for an experiment. What did you have to do to ensure that students could follow your instruction? What worked and what didn't? How could you have made things more clear?

3. If the concept of scaffolding is somewhat new for you, the definition in the Glossary may be helpful, as may be the following construction analogy. Picture a high-rise building as it is under construction. As new floors are added, scaffolding is built along the outside of the previously constructed floor (or level). This scaffolding allows access for the construction workers—they need to be able to get into the upper stories in order to continue the building process.

   Now, think of a content topic that you must teach that is challenging to students acquiring English as a second (or multiple) language. What types of scaffolds must you put in place for your students to successfully access the lesson's content and language objectives?

4. Here's a factual question a teacher might ask based on a social studies text: "Who was the first president of the United States?" Given the topic of the presidency, what are several additional questions you could ask that promote higher-order thinking? Why is it important to use a variety of questioning strategies with English learners? Use one of the taxonomies (Bloom's [1956] or Anderson & Krathwohl, 2001), or the Depth of Knowledge levels (Webb, 1997) to guide you.

5. The answers to higher-order thinking questions may involve language that is beyond a student's current level of English proficiency. Discuss the advantages and/or disadvantages of allowing English learners to use their **native language** for part of the lesson, if doing so enables them to participate at a higher cognitive level.

6. Using the SIOP lesson you have been developing, add meaningful activities that augment learning strategies. Determine how to scaffold English learners' access to your objectives. Write several higher-order thinking questions or tasks for your lesson.

CHAPTER 6

Interaction

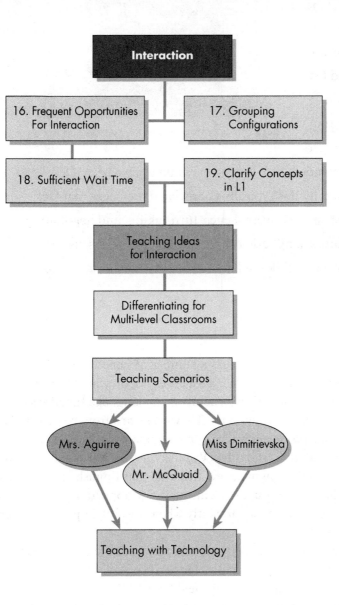

Learning Outcomes

After reading, discussing, and engaging in activities related to this chapter, you will be able to meet the following **content** and **language objectives**.

Content Objectives

Select a variety of activities that promote interaction and incorporate them into lesson plans.

Design grouping structures that support lesson content and language objectives.

Identify techniques to increase wait time.

List ways that collaborative conversations and discussions are aligned with the Interaction component.

Identify resources to support student clarification in the native language.

Language Objectives

Explain in writing the purpose of student–student interaction for language development.

Describe techniques to reduce the amount of teacher talk in a lesson.

Practice asking questions that promote student elaboration of responses.

Talking matters for learning. In fact, talking, listening, and thinking are a powerful combination of processes associated with learning, and each strengthens the others (City, 2014). It has never been more important to provide children with opportunities for talking, listening, and thinking in class about concepts, ideas, and information. At the same time that CCSS and other state standards have expectations that students will **engage** in substantive, collaborative discussions around text and concepts, outside of the classroom, students are increasingly communicating with electronic devices rather than face to face, and they aren't as exposed to extended discourse as they might have been a few years ago. The style of communication used is typically abbreviated messages that lack pragmatics (linguistic context clues such as nonverbal cues, turn-taking, and negotiating meaning) and are delivered while multitasking rather than focusing on the discussion (Rosen, 2012). The only opportunity many children have for quality talk around texts and topics is in the classroom. ●

Robert Daly/Caiaimage/Getty Images

Short and Echevarría (2016) discuss a number of benefits of collaborative academic discussions. As children talk about a topic, they have the opportunity to try out new words, grammatical structures, and language functions (see Chapter 2 for examples of language functions). They also learn from peers who have more advanced language proficiency, those "more capable others" who provide support for **English learners'** understanding (Vygotsky, 1978). Participation in discussions with peers provides the language practice time that English learners need. When working with the whole group, students have few opportunities for practice, but conversation time increases significantly when working in partners or groups of three to four children.

For English learners to understand and use academic English, they need to be provided with structured opportunities for practice in all subject areas throughout the school day, not just during a designated time. With the CCSS and other state standards' emphasis on high levels of language use, *all* teachers are teachers of English language development, even if students also have access to excellent **ESL** specialists. The integration of language development across the curriculum is vital and is recognized by some states as part of their instructional framework (see California Department of Education, 2014). As students are learning in and through a new language—English—teachers must create ample opportunities to practice using *academic* **language**, not just **social language**. It is recommended that English learners have daily opportunities to talk about content in pairs or small groups, practicing and extending material already taught (Baker et al., 2014). Unfortunately, this is typically not the case. In a classroom observation study, there was evidence of "academic dialog and discussion" in only .5% of the 1,500 classrooms observed (Schmoker, 2006).

For many teachers it may be challenging to move from presenting whole-class instruction to providing the kinds of small-group opportunities needed for students to have high-quality discussions. Sharing responsibility for learning with students working in small groups or with partners is an adjustment for many teachers, but it can make a significant impact on learning. Researchers have found that English learners were more engaged academically when working in small groups or with partners than they were in whole-class instruction or individual work (Brooks & Thurston, 2010). For students to connect with school and engage in learning at a level that will result in high achievement, we need to provide them with opportunities to interact with one another, to discuss and "puzzle over" genuine problems (Wiggins & McTighe, 2008). In this chapter, we present ways that teachers can use interaction to launch students to higher levels of English proficiency, improve academic outcomes, and meet standards including the **Common Core State Standards**.

Watch this video as Dr. MaryEllen Vogt discusses the importance of interaction. What does she say is the way to ensure that there is sufficient time for students to interact with one another? How might you provide more time for interaction with your students?

Background

"Use it or lose it" is a saying that conveys what we know from our own experience in learning a second language. If one doesn't practice using the language, it is difficult to maintain it. But what about learning a language in the first place—does speaking it help to develop the language? The answer is a resounding "Yes!" The role that conversation plays in the process of second language teaching and learning is clear. But discussion also offers important benefits for learning in general. As Gerald Graff puts it, "Talk—about books and subjects—is as important educationally as are the books and subjects themselves" (Graff, 2003, p. 9).

The issue is, why are there so few opportunities for students to interact in typical classrooms? Studies indicate that in most classrooms, teachers dominate the linguistic aspect of the lesson, leaving children severely limited in terms of opportunities to use language in a variety of ways (Cazden, 2001; Goodlad, 1984; Marshall, 2000). In a study with English learners (Porath, 2014), the teacher learned that by talking less and listening more, she was able to gain deeper insight into her students' learning needs and strengths. In our own work, we have observed teachers doing a significant amount of talking rather than providing the impetus for a discussion and then listening to what children have to say—either to the teacher or to one another.

There are many benefits to having students actively engaged in interaction around subject matter. Some include:

- **Deeper understanding of text, including vocabulary learning.** When teachers use thoughtful questioning to promote discussion, it encourages students to think critically about the passage. In doing so, children also think more deeply about the meaning of the words they encounter (Echevarría, 1995; Saunders & Goldenberg, 1999; Wasik & Iannone-Campbell, 2012). Also, new understandings are co-constructed through interactions (Fisher & Frey, 2013; McIntyre et al., 2010).

- **Oral language development.** Being exposed to and interacting with language that is just beyond their independent speaking levels move students to higher **levels of language proficiency**. However, these interactions must be carefully planned and carried out to yield gains in oral language (Saunders & Goldenberg, 2010).

- **Brain stimulation.** Interesting, engaging activities, including discussions, play an important role in learning. When children are engaged and their brains are activated, more of the pleasure structures in the brain fire than when students are simply asked to memorize information (Jensen, 2008; Poldrack et al., 2001).

- **Increased motivation.** Interaction with others is an important component of reading instruction that increases motivation and comprehension (Guthrie & Ozgungor, 2002).

- **Reduced risk.** The typical question-answer sessions in which teachers call on students may be threatening to some children, particularly those unprepared to respond. Some students have difficulty focusing on the content in this setting because it triggers the brain's "threat response" (Jensen, 2005, Jensen, 2008). Having young children talk in pairs or in small groups minimizes the risk and allows ideas to flow more easily.

- **More processing time.** Children need time to process after learning. Direct instruction should be limited to short increments followed by time for discussion.

- **Increased attention.** Use of pairs or teams can heighten attention levels. Students may be asked to work together to compare/contrast material learned, group and regroup the material, resequence it, or retell it from another point of view (Marzano, Pickering, & Pollock, 2001).

We find that it is both interesting and helpful to analyze actual transcripts from lessons to demonstrate the kind of teacher dominance that is so common in classrooms. The following transcripts are from a pilot SIOP study (Echevarría, Greene, & Goldenberg, 1996) in sixth-grade social studies classes. The teachers were videotaped teaching the same content about consumerism to English learners, with the first using a typical approach found in general education classes and the second using the SIOP Model. Both classes had approximately 25 students, and in this lesson children were learning how to read labels on clothing and on a bottle of antiseptic.

Typical Lesson

TEACHER: Look at the piece of clothing at the bottom. It says *(he reads)*, "This shirt is flame-resistant," which means what?

STUDENT: Could not burn.

STUDENT: Won't catch fire.

TEACHER: It will not burn, won't catch fire. Right *(continues reading)*. "To retain the flame-resistant properties"—what does "to retain" mean?

STUDENT: *(unintelligible)*

TEACHER: To keep it. All right. *(He reads)* "In order to keep this shirt flame-resistant wash with detergent only." All right *(he reads)*. "Do not use soap or bleach. Tumble dry. One hundred percent polyester." Now, why does it say, "Do not use soap or bleach"?

STUDENT: 'Cause it'll take off the . . .

TEACHER: It'll take off the what?

STUDENTS: *(fragmented responses)*

TEACHER: It'll take off the flame-resistant quality. If you wash it with soap or bleach, then the shirt's just gonna be like any old shirt, any regular shirt, so when you put a match to it, will it catch fire?

STUDENT: No.

TEACHER: Yes. 'Cause you've ruined it then. It's no longer flame-resistant. So the government says you gotta tell the consumer what kind of shirt it is, and how to take care of it. If you look at any piece of clothing: shirt, pants, your shirts, um, your skirts, anything. There's always going to be a tag on these that says what it is made of and how you're going to take care of it. Okay. And that's for your protection so that you won't buy something and then treat it wrong. So labeling is important. All right. Let's review. I'll go back to the antiseptic. What did we say indications meant? Indications? Raise your hands, raise your hands. Robert?

STUDENT: What's it for.

TEACHER: What is it for, when do you use this? Okay. What do directions, what is that for, Victor?

STUDENT: How to use . . .

TEACHER: How to use. Okay, so indications is when you use it *(holds one finger up)*, directions is how you use it *(holds another finger up)*, and warnings is what?

STUDENTS: *(various mumbled responses)*

TEACHER: How you don't use it. This is what you don't do.

The teacher in this case tended to finish sentences for the students and accept any form of student comment without encouraging extended expression. In examining the exchanges, what did the teacher do when students gave partial or incorrect answers? He answered the question himself. Children learn that they can disengage because the teacher will continue with the "discussion."

SIOP® Lesson

TEACHER: Most clothing must have labels that tell what kind of cloth was used in it, right? Look at the material in the picture down there *(points to picture in text)*.[1] What does it say, the tag right there?

STUDENT: The, the, the . . .

---

[1]The teacher explained then that they would be doing an activity in which they would read labels for information.

TEACHER: The tag right there.

STUDENT: *(Reading)* "Flame-resis . . ."

TEACHER: Resistant.

STUDENT: "Flame-resistant. To retain the flame-resistant properties, wash with detergent only. Do not use soap or bleach. Use warm water. Tumble dry."

TEACHER: "One hundred percent . . ."

STUDENT: "Polyester."

TEACHER: Now, most clothes carry labels, right? *(pointing to the neck of her sweater)*. They explain how to take care of it, like dry clean, machine wash, right? It tells you how to clean it. Why does this product have to be washed with a detergent and no soap or bleach?

STUDENT: Because clothes . . .

TEACHER: Why can't you use something else?

STUDENTS: *(several students mumble answers)*

STUDENT: *(says in Spanish)* Because it will make it small.

TEACHER: It may shrink, or *(gestures to a student)* it may not be . . . what does it say?

STUDENT: It's not going to be able to be resistant to fire.

TEACHER: Exactly. It's flame-resistant, right? So, if you use something else, it won't be flame-resistant anymore. How about the, uh, look at the *antiseptic (holds hands up to form a container)*—the picture above the shirt, the antiseptic?

STUDENT: Read it?

TEACHER: Antiseptic *(Teacher reads)* and other health products you buy without a prescription often have usage and warning labels. So what can you learn from this label? Read this label quietly please, and tell me what you can learn from the label. Read the label on that antiseptic. *(Students read silently.)*

TEACHER: What can you learn from this label?

STUDENT: It kills, oh I know.

TEACHER: Steve?

STUDENT: It kills germs.

STUDENT: Yeah, it kills germs.

TEACHER: It kills germs. You use it for wounds, right? What else?

STUDENTS: *(various enthusiastic responses)*

TEACHER: One person at a time. Okay, hold on. Veronica was saying something.

STUDENT: It tells you in the directions that, you could use it, that like that, 'cause if you use it in another thing, it could hurt you.

TEACHER: It could hurt you. Okay, what else? Ricardo?

STUDENT: If you put it in your mouth, don't put it in your mouth or your ears or your eyes.

TEACHER: Very good. Don't put it in your mouth, ears, and eyes. Okay, for how many days should you use it? No more than what?

STUDENT: No more than 10 days.

STUDENT: Ten days.

TEACHER: So don't use it—you have to follow what it says—so don't use it more than 10 days. Now, the next activity you're going to do . . .

The SIOP teacher allowed for a balance of teacher-to-student talk and encouraged student participation. She asked questions, waited for students' responses, and restated or elaborated on the responses. In this case, what did the teacher do to elicit answers to the question? She **scaffolded** the answer by encouraging the students to think about it, prompting them to give their responses.

The features of **SIOP** within the Interaction component are designed to provide teachers with concrete ways of increasing student participation and developing English **language proficiency**. When implemented consistently, these practices will facilitate students' ability to meet the Common Core State Standards and other state standards, especially in the areas of listening and speaking.

SIOP® FEATURE 16:

Frequent Opportunities for Interaction and Discussion Between Teacher/Student and Among Students, Which Encourage Elaborated Responses About Lesson Concepts

Oral Language Development

Watch this video about academic language. You will see and hear teachers discuss the importance of opportunities for discussion and interaction. How does teacher Megali Williams describe "intentional noise"?

This SIOP feature emphasizes the importance of balancing linguistic turn-taking between the teacher and students, and among students. It also highlights the practice of encouraging children to elaborate their responses rather than accepting yes/no and one-word answers, even from the youngest learners. As noted in the CCSS, "students must have ample opportunities to take part in a variety of rich, structured conversations" (National Governors Association Center for Best Practices and Council of Chief State School Officers, 2010a).

The findings of the National Literacy Panel on Language Minority Students and Youth (August & Shanahan, 2006) revealed the important relationship between oral proficiency in English and reading and writing proficiency. Specifically, reading comprehension skills and writing skills are positively correlated with oral language proficiency in English (Geva, 2006); these two areas are particularly challenging for English learners and are reflected in the Common Core State Standards. Solid reading comprehension is the foundation for achievement in nearly every subject area in school, and writing proficiency in English is an essential skill as well. Some other important findings include:

1. There has long been recognition that language, cognition, and reading are intimately related (Tharp & Gallimore, 1988). As one acquires new language, new concepts are developed. Think about your own language learning with respect to understanding computer functions. Each new vocabulary word and term you

learn and understand (e.g., *cloud*, *flash drive*, and *terabyte*) is attached to a concept that in turn expands your ability to think about how a computer works. As your own system of word-meaning grows in complexity, you are more capable of using the self-directed speech of verbal thinking ("Don't forget to save it on the Cloud."). Without an understanding of the words and the concepts they represent, you would not be capable of thinking about (self-directed speech) or discussing (talking with another) computer functions.

2. Language proficiency is a precursor to effective reading comprehension. Because an understanding of language makes acquiring knowledge possible, deriving meaning from texts in English will be challenging for English learners who may have difficulty reading unfamiliar words or comprehending their meaning.

3. Researchers who have investigated the relationship between language and learning suggest that interactive approaches—where there is more balance in student talk and teacher talk—are effective in promoting meaningful language learning opportunities for English learners (Cazden, 2001; Echevarría & Short, 2010; Fisher & Frey, 2013; McIntyre, et al, 2010; Saunders & Goldenberg, 2010; Tharp & Gallimore, 1988; Toth, 2013; Walqui, 2006). Called *collaborative conversations* (grades K–2) or *collaborative discussions* (grades 3–6) in the Common Core State Standards, teaching approaches that emphasize oral language development and promote meaningful discussions around academic topics and texts have also been called ***instructional conversations*** (ICs) (Goldenberg, 1992–93) and *academic conversations* (Zwiers & Crawford, 2009). This mode of instruction has some of the following characteristics:

- Emphasizes active student involvement and meaningful language-based teaching.
  - Uses extended expression around text and topics so that students develop content knowledge and language proficiency simultaneously.
- Differs from typical teaching because most instructional patterns in classrooms involve the teacher asking a question, the student responding, and the teacher evaluating the response and asking another question (Cazden, 2001). In contrast, in the typical format of an IC:
  a. The teacher begins by briefly introducing the group to a theme or idea related to the text, and then relating the theme to children's background experiences.
  b. Next, the teacher shows the text to be read and asks prediction questions.
  c. As the text is read, the teacher "chunks" the text into sections to provide maximum opportunity for discussion, constantly relating the theme and background experiences to a text-based discussion.
  d. Students are asked to support their comments with evidence from the text. Figure 6.1 illustrates the contrast in approaches.

A conversational approach is particularly well suited to English learners who frequently find themselves significantly behind their peers in most academic areas, usually due to low reading levels and underdeveloped language skills. ICs provide a context for learning in which language is expressed naturally through meaningful discussion. Further, the skills developed through ICs meet the Common Core State

FIGURE 6.1	Contrast Typical Instructions with Instructional Conversations

Typical Instruction	Instructional Conversation
Teacher-centered	Teacher facilitates
Exact, specific answers evaluated by the teacher	Many different ideas encouraged
No extensive discussion	Oral language practice opportunities using natural language
Skill-directed	Extensive discussion and student involvement
Easier to evaluate	Draw from prior background knowledge
Check for understanding	Student level of understanding transparent
Mostly literal level thinking and language use	Fewer black and white responses
	Mostly higher-level thinking and language use

Standards in the area of *Comprehension and Collaboration* in English Language Arts, *Speaking and Listening*. The following examples are taken from grade 4, but are similar across grade levels.

> *CCSS.ELA-Literacy.SL.4.1* Engage effectively in a range of collaborative discussions (one-on-one, in groups, and teacher-led) with diverse partners on grade 4 topics and texts, building on others' ideas and expressing their own clearly.
>
> ◆ Come to discussions prepared, having read or studied required material; explicitly draw on that preparation and other information known about the topic to explore ideas under discussion.
>
> ◆ Follow agreed-upon rules for discussions and carry out assigned roles.
>
> ◆ Pose and respond to specific questions to clarify or follow up on information, and make comments that contribute to the discussion and link to the remarks of others.
>
> ◆ Review the key ideas expressed and explain their own ideas and understanding in light of the discussion.
>
> © Copyright 2010. National Governors Association Center for Best Practices and Council of Chief State School Officers. All rights reserved.

A rich discussion, or conversational approach, has advantages for teachers as well and contributes to a culturally responsive classroom. Through discussion teachers can more naturally activate the class's background knowledge as they encourage children to share their knowledge of the world and ideas about how language works. When teachers and young students interact, it fosters a supportive environment and builds teacher–student rapport. Also, when working in small groups with each student participating in the discussion, teachers are better able to determine individual levels of understanding; weak areas are made transparent.

As mentioned previously, however, teachers typically do most of the talking in class. Of course, teachers have knowledge to share and discuss with students, but consistent teacher dominance reduces the opportunities children have to participate fully in lessons by discussing ideas and information, and practicing English as they express their ideas, opinions, and answers.

Effective SIOP teachers:

- Explicitly teach children rules and routines for engaging in high-quality discussions to ensure that they take turns, stay on topic, actively listen, build on one another's comments, and are respectful (Short & Echevarría, 2016).

- Structure their lessons in ways that promote student discussion. They also strive to provide a more balanced linguistic exchange between themselves and their students. It can be particularly tempting for teachers to do most of the talking when students are not completely proficient in their use of English, but these children are precisely the ones who need opportunities to practice using English the most.

- Encourage extended expression from students when discussing the lesson's concepts. The teacher elicits more elaboration from children by using a variety of techniques that will take students beyond simple yes or no answers and short phrases (Fisher & Frey, 2013; Saunders & Goldenberg, 2007; Toth, 2013). Some of these techniques include asking children to expand on their answers by saying "Tell me more about that" and by asking direct questions to prompt more language use such as "What do you mean by . . . ?" Another technique is to provide further information through questions such as "How do you know?" "What are the facts that support your ideas?" "Why is that important?"

- Use techniques such as offering restatements to scaffold replies: "In other words . . . is that accurate?" and frequently pausing to let students process the language and formulate their responses. If an English learner is obviously unsure about what to say, teachers call on other children to extend the response: "Vesna said . . . what can you add to that?"

It takes time and practice for these techniques to become a natural part of a teacher's repertoire. The teachers with whom we've worked report that they had to consciously work at overcoming the temptation to speak for children or to complete a child's short phrase. The preceding transcript shows how the first teacher spoke for students instead of encouraging students to complete their thoughts. The following segment from the transcript provides another example.

TEACHER: What do "directions" . . . what is that for, Victor?

STUDENT: How to use . . .

TEACHER: How to use. Okay, so "indications" is when you use it, "directions" is how you use it, and "warnings" is what?

STUDENTS: *(various mumbled responses)*

TEACHER: How you don't use it. This is what you don't do.

In this segment, the non-SIOP teacher could have encouraged a more balanced exchange between himself and the students. First, he did not encourage students to completely express their thoughts; he accepted partial and mumbled answers. Second, he answered for the students, dominating the discussion. It is easy to imagine how students could become uninterested, passive learners in a class in which the teacher accepts minimal participation and does the majority of the talking.

The SIOP teacher approached students–teacher interaction differently:

TEACHER: What can you learn from this label?

STUDENT: It kills, oh I know.

TEACHER: Steve?

STUDENT: It kills germs.

STUDENT: Yeah, it kills germs.

TEACHER: It kills germs. You use it for wounds, right? What else?

STUDENTS: *(various enthusiastic responses)*

TEACHER: One person at a time. Okay, hold on. Veronica was saying something.

STUDENT: It tells you in the directions that, you could use it, that like that, 'cause if you use it in another thing, it could hurt you.

TEACHER: It could hurt you. Okay, what else? Ricardo?

STUDENT: If you put it in your mouth, don't put it in your mouth or your ears or your eyes.

TEACHER: Very good. Don't put it in your mouth, ears, and eyes. Okay, for how many days should you use it? No more than what?

STUDENT: No more than 10 days.

STUDENT: Ten days.

TEACHER: So don't use it—you have to follow what it says, so don't use it more than 10 days. Now, the next activity you're going to do . . .

The SIOP teacher let the children have time to express their thoughts (e.g., a student says, "It kills . . . It kills germs."). The teacher could have completed the sentence for the student, but she waited for him to finish his thought. Also, the SIOP teacher encouraged and challenged the students more than the non-SIOP teacher did by asking twice, "What else?" Finally, the SIOP teacher nominated children who volunteered to talk and repeated what they said so that the class could hear a full response (e.g., Veronica).

Culturally responsive SIOP teachers plan instruction so that students have opportunities to work with one another on academic tasks, using English to communicate. Through meaningful interaction, children can practice speaking and making themselves understood. That implies asking and answering questions that probe for evidence, negotiating meaning, clarifying ideas, giving and justifying opinions, making well-reasoned statements, and more. Students may interact in pairs, triads, and small groups. Literature circles, think-pair-share, Jigsaw readings, debates, and science experiments are only a sample of the types of activities teachers can include in lessons to foster student–student interaction and discussion. An interactive approach has been shown to improve the achievement of young English learners with learning disabilities (Echevarría, 1995) as well as typically developing English learners (Dockrell, Stewart, & King, 2010; Saunders & Goldenberg, 2007; Van de Pol, Volman, & Beishuizen, 2010).

SIOP® FEATURE 17:

Grouping Configurations Support Language and Content Objectives of the Lesson

In order to meet the Common Core standards especially for Speaking and Listening, teachers provide a variety of grouping configurations including whole class, partners, and small group. The intent of CCSS and other state standards is to engage students more directly in learning by having a balance of teacher presentation and productive group work by children. The benefits of a balanced approach include the following:

- Varying grouping configurations—by moving from whole class to small group, whole class to partners, and small group to individual assignments—provides children with opportunities to learn new information, discuss it, and process it. Organizing students into smaller groups for instructional purposes provides a context that whole-class, teacher-dominated instruction doesn't offer.

- Allowing children to work together to critique or analyze material, create graphic representations of vocabulary terms or concepts, or summarize material makes information more meaningful and increases learning.

- Changing grouping structures and activities enhances learning. It is recommended that when working with younger learners, content, lectures, and cognitive activities should be limited to 5–10-minute periods each. With older students, content sessions should be limited to 10–15 minutes. These focused learning periods should be followed by interactive activities such as pair-shares or model building (Jensen, 2008).

In Chapter 5 of this book we present a process for teaching that slowly and purposefully shifts the workload from teacher to students and requires a variety of grouping configurations. As seen in Figure 5.1, "Scaffolding: Gradual Increase of Student Independence," the teacher uses a variety of groupings, such as presenting information to the whole class and explicitly teaching part of the lesson, followed by a different grouping configuration in which students are given an opportunity to collaborate and discuss ideas just learned, while practicing academic English. Then, when children have acquired sufficient background knowledge and language, they apply the information individually. Varying grouping structures provides more interaction, and students have more opportunities to participate actively in the lesson. In contrast, when children aren't learning, it is often because there has not been the critical scaffolding that Figure 5.1 represents. That is, teachers go directly from "I do it . . . you watch" to "You do it alone."

In small, guided instruction groups, the teacher naturally differentiates instruction as she works on focused skill instruction, language development, and/or **assessment** of student progress. Small-group instruction provides more opportunity to discuss text (Saunders & Goldenberg, 2007, Saunders, Goldenberg, 2010) and increases reading achievement (Vaughn et al., 2003). While the teacher is working with one group, the other children can work on familiar material in small groups,

Watch this video to see and hear third-grade teacher Deb Painter create opportunities for her students to interact with each other during a lesson on punctuation. What types of interactive activities might you use when teaching this topic?

with a partner, or individually, either at their desks or at workstations. Activities may include listening to recorded stories (at listening centers, on computers, or via electronic notebooks), reinforcing skills with computer games, creating graphic representations of vocabulary terms or concepts, summarizing material, practicing word sorts, or reading self-selected leveled readers. These activities are purposeful and meaningful, and they lead to increased learning. In our work, we have seen this type of grouping work successfully from kindergarten through high school.

Not surprisingly, the various kinds of grouping do not work equally well. It is important to acknowledge the following information about grouping and think about these points as you work with instructional groups.

- Grouping by ability, which divides students for instruction based on their perceived capabilities for learning (low group, average group, high group) has serious academic and social effects for students who are not in the top group (Callahan, 2005; Hiebert, 1983; Lucas, 1999). Futrell and Gomez (Futrell and Gomez 2008) make this point: "We cannot ignore the fact that for more than five decades, ability grouping has resulted in separation of students by race, ethnicity, and socioeconomic status. Many studies have confirmed that minority and low-income students of all ability levels are overrepresented in the lower tracks and underrepresented in the higher tracks" (p. 76).

- English learners, who learn from exposure to good language models, are often shut out of the groups with rich academic learning opportunities. In fact, in some schools, it has become common practice to group English learners with low-achieving children regardless of their academic ability and performance. This practice deprives English learners of the opportunity to learn grade-level academic skills and language.

- When working with low-achieving groups, teachers have been found to talk more, use more structure, ask lower-level questions, cover less material, spend more time on skills and drills, provide fewer opportunities for leadership and independent research, encourage more oral than silent reading, teach less vocabulary, and allow less wait time during questioning. In addition, they spent twice as much time on behavior and management issues (Oakes, 1985; Vogt & Shearer, 2016).

- All children, including English learners, benefit from instruction that frequently includes a variety of grouping configurations. Whole-class groups are beneficial for introducing new information and concepts, modeling processes, and review. Flexible small groups promote the development of multiple perspectives and encourage collaboration. Partnering encourages success because it provides practice opportunities, scaffolding, and assistance from classmates.

Effective SIOP classes are characterized by a variety of grouping structures, including individual work, partners, triads, small groups of four or five, cooperative learning groups, and whole class. Groups also vary because they may be homogeneous or heterogeneous by gender, language proficiency, language background, and/or ability. The decisions teachers make about how to group students should be purposeful, not arbitrary.

A case can be made for grouping students by how well they speak English during literacy instruction (Uribe & Nathenson-Mejía, 2008), but the teacher needs to be aware of each student's individual skill profile. For example, when working on fluency, English learners with strong decoding skills would not read the same text as an English learner who is still working on mastering phonics. Advantages of grouping English learners together are that teachers can target specific language instruction, and children are more apt to take risks in their second language. However, grouping students from very different grade levels (i.e., second through fifth grade) together based on language proficiency should be discouraged because these learners have very different social and academic needs (Uribe & Nathenson-Mejía, 2008).

There are other times that grouping by language proficiency level is useful. For example, if a teacher's goal is for children at beginning levels of English proficiency to practice using a particular language structure such as the present progressive (-*ing*) form within the context of a social studies lesson, then those students may be grouped together for that lesson. Likewise, when developing the skills of children with low levels of literacy, it makes sense to have those with similar ability grouped together for a particular lesson. Assigning all English learners to the same group regularly is *not* good practice, especially when total responsibility for teaching is turned over to a paraprofessional. In SIOP classes, English learners are given the same access to the curriculum and the teacher's expertise as native English-speaking students.

Using a variety of grouping configurations facilitates learning in a number of ways.

- It helps to maintain student interest because it is difficult for some children to stay focused when the teacher relies almost exclusively on whole-class instruction or having students work individually.
- Moving from whole class to small groups or partners adds variety to the learning situation and increases student involvement in the learning process.
- It provides much-needed movement for learners. When students are active, their brains are provided with the oxygen-rich blood needed for highest performance. Movement may be especially important for learners with special needs (Jensen, 2005).

It is recommended that at least two different grouping structures be used during a lesson, depending on the activity and objectives of the lesson.

In every case, peer discussions need to be structured so that children know their roles and responsibilities, and they need to be supervised appropriately. As more teachers move to implementing small group structures to address listening and speaking standards, we've noticed that in some classes, students are put into groups for collaborative work but little is accomplished. Groups are given a worksheet or other activity and are expected to complete it without much teacher input or oversight. Group work requires structure, with the teacher circulating, checking for understanding, prompting, questioning, and clarifying. Also, tasks should be assigned a specific amount of time so that children stay engaged and the pace of the class moves along.

SIOP® FEATURE 18:

Sufficient Wait Time for Student Responses Consistently Provided

Wait time is the length of time between utterances during an interaction. In classroom settings, it refers to the length of time a teacher pauses between asking a question and soliciting a response. A review of studies on wait time revealed that after a teacher asks a question, students must begin a response within an average time of one second. If they do not, the teacher repeats, rephrases, asks a different question, or calls on another student. Further, when a student makes a response, the teacher normally reacts or asks another question within an average time of 0.9 second (Rowe, 2003). Rather than filling the silence created by wait time, teachers should see the silence as an opportunity for students to process what is being asked of them. So teachers may need to practice using wait time to become comfortable allowing students the time they need (Wasik & Hindman, 2013/2014).

Wait time varies by **culture**. It is appropriate in some cultures to let seconds, even minutes, lag between utterances, while in other cultures utterances can overlap one another. In U.S. classrooms, the average length of wait time is clearly *not* sufficient. Imagine the impact of wait time on English learners who are processing ideas in a new language and need additional time to put their thoughts into words. Research supports the idea of wait time and has found it to increase student discourse and enhance student-to-student interaction (Honea, 1982; Rowe, 2003; Swift & Gooding, 1983; Tobin, 1987).

Effective SIOP teachers are culturally responsive and consciously allow children to express their thoughts fully, without interruption. Many teachers in U.S. schools are uncomfortable with the silence that follows their questions or comments, and they immediately fill the void by talking themselves. This situation may be especially pertinent in SIOP classes where English learners need extra time to process questions in English, think of an answer in their second language, and then formulate their responses in English. Although teachers may be tempted to fill the silence, English learners benefit from a patient approach to classroom participation, in which teachers wait for students to complete their verbal contributions.

While effective SIOP teachers provide sufficient wait time for English learners, they also work to find a balance between wait time and moving a lesson along. Some youngsters may become impatient if the pace of the class lags. One strategy for accommodating impatient students is to have them write down their responses while waiting, and then they can check their answers against the final answer.

SIOP® FEATURE 19:

Ample Opportunity for Students to Clarify Key Concepts in L1 as Needed with Aide, Peer, or L1 Text

Best practice indicates that English learners benefit from opportunities to clarify concepts in their first language (**L1**). In fact, the National Literacy Panel on Language Minority Students and Youth found that academic skills such as reading taught in the first language transfer to the second language (August & Shanahan, 2006). Although SIOP instruction involves teaching subject-matter material in English, children are given the opportunity to have a concept or assignment explained in their L1 as needed. Significant controversy surrounds the use of L1 for instructional purposes, but we believe that clarification of key concepts in students' L1 by a bilingual instructional aide or peer, or through the use of materials written in the students' L1, provides an important support for the academic learning of those children who are not yet fully proficient in English.

This feature on the SIOP protocol may have "N/A" circled as a score because not all SIOP classes need to use students' L1 to clarify concepts for them (especially for advanced English learners).

However, with Web sites and apps offering word translation capabilities and bilingual dictionaries available in book and computer program formats, all SIOP classrooms have access to resources in most of the students' **native languages**.

Teaching Ideas for Interaction

In the section that follows, you will find some teaching ideas to help you with preparing SIOP lessons.

- In math lessons, plan for targeted discussions in which children are taught a variety of discussion structures such as explaining their thinking, justifying the problem-solving strategy they used, and troubleshooting and revising their work (Kazemi & Hintz, 2014); these skills are reflected in the Common Core Standards for Mathematics.

- With appropriate supervision, children can interact with each other through a class electronic list, shared research files on a school network, or a planned pen pal e-mail or video camera exchange on the computer with another class elsewhere in the world.

- In a discussion of the importance of movement for learning at all ages, Jensen (2005) suggests a number of games such as rewriting lyrics to familiar songs in pairs or teams as a content review, and then performing the song; playing Simon Says using content such as "Point to the picture of a triangle, square, rectangle, etc."; or role-plays, charades, or pantomime to review main ideas or key points.

- Children may interact by sharing their expertise. In an Expert Stay & Stray activity, students work in small groups on an assignment, such as completing a chart summarizing the steps to solving math problems or listing key points from a unit of study. Students in the group number off. The teacher calls a number, e.g., #4, and student #4 takes his or her group's chart and goes to another table and shares the information with the new group. Then the student remains with the new group as the teacher calls another number, e.g., #1. Student #1 takes the chart of the student who shared (#4)—which encourages children to listen carefully—and goes to a new group and shares the information from the chart. This activity provides students with an opportunity to discuss the information while completing the chart, then to share the information orally while others listen attentively, and to paraphrase someone else's explanation of the chart. It can be adapted to any content area or grade level.

- Start the class each day with children in pairs and have them tell each other the day's content objective in a Partner Share. Then they move to find another partner and tell them the language objective.

- An activity appropriate for all elementary levels and most content areas is called Dinner Party (or Birthday Party for K–2). As an example, during reading instruction, children would respond to the prompt: "Suppose you could have a dinner party for authors or poets that we have studied. Who would you invite? Why would you select them? What would be the seating order of the guests at your table, and why would you place them in that order? What do you think the guests would talk about during dinner? Include specific references to the authors' lives and works in your response." The purpose is for children to act out the questions by assuming personas, such as characters in novels, scientists, historical figures, or artists. During each Dinner Party, specific content from texts must be included and the characters must respond to each other as realistically and accurately as possible (Vogt & Echevarría, 2008).

- The time-tested activity of using Dialogue Journals provides students with an opportunity to interact through writing about topics of interest or those related to lessons. In elementary classrooms, journaling is typically between teacher and child as they share ideas. Students learn from teachers as they model appropriate written text, and teachers learn about their children's ideas and ways of expressing themselves. The teacher participates in the dialogue every so often to monitor students' writing and to model correct writing.

- To support English learners, allow the techniques made popular by a television show: "50–50" and "phone a friend." Children who are unsure of an answer or are unable to articulate it well might ask to choose between two possible responses provided by the teacher (50–50) or ask a classmate for help (phone a friend). However, to ensure practice with the language, the original child must give "the final answer" to the teacher.

Watch this video to see and hear Dr. Jana Echevarría explain how developing students' oral language through SIOP can help them become college and career ready. As an elementary teacher, what kinds of activities can you do to increase your students' use of academic language in your classroom?

Differentiating Ideas for Multi-level Classes

We know that most classes with English learners are made up of students with multiple proficiency levels. Even those children designated as Emerging, for example, may have stronger listening skills than writing skills or stronger reading skills than speaking skills. Teachers have at their disposal a variety of ways to differentiate spoken English to make it comprehensible for our diverse English learners. The Interaction component lends itself well to meeting the variety of instructional needs and proficiency levels of students in your classrooms. Several considerations include the following:

- Use sentence frames for both oral and written answers. "It has often been said that teachers, rather than students, use academic language in the classroom. However, children won't learn academic vocabulary solely by listening to us; they need to practice using it themselves" (Donnelly & Roe, 2010, p. 135). Sentence frames have been mentioned several times in this book as effective ways to scaffold English learners while they are acquiring their new language. Donnelly and Roe (Donnelly, Roe, 2010, p. 132) suggest that teachers write sentence frames according to their students' English proficiency by:

1. Writing sentences that express a language function (e.g., compare/contrast), and replacing target language with blanks.
2. Replacing target words with blanks.
3. Creating a word bank or a list of words that were eliminated from the original sentences.

What is left are sentence frames with fill-in spaces that are **differentiated** for different language levels. Lower level frames are not as complex as those for more English-proficient students. For example: The expected outcome for children at levels 2, 3, and 4 working with comparison/contrast might be:

Level 2. Sentence frame with vocabulary underlined: *Carrots are <u>orange</u>. Peas are <u>green</u>.* (simple sentence)

Sentence frame with vocabulary removed: _____ are _____.

Level 3. Sentence frame with vocabulary underlined: *<u>Carrots</u> and <u>peas</u> are both <u>vegetables</u>, but <u>carrots</u> are <u>root vegetables</u> and <u>peas grow on vines</u>.* (comparative sentence)

Sentence frame with vocabulary removed: _____ and _____ are both _____, but _____ are _____ and _____.

Level 4. Sentence frame with vocabulary underlined: *The main difference between <u>carrots</u> and <u>peas</u> is that <u>carrots</u> are <u>root vegetables</u> while <u>peas grow on vines</u>.* (complex comparative sentence)

Sentence frame with vocabulary removed: The main difference between _____ and _____ is that _____ are _____, while _____.

Sentence frames can use familiar content such as illustrated above, or they can usespecific topics that are being studied. Other language functions, such as cause/effect, problem/solution, and so forth can serve as the basis of the differentiated sentence frames.

As you can see, less proficient students will use sentence frames to participate in discussions, Dialogue Journals, and written work. More proficient speakers have a model of correct syntax to assist their contributions.

- Allow older students to choose between two or more assignments to complete. When students have options, they are more engaged, feel more confident, and perform better (Sparks, 2010). Some students may opt for an oral presentation to demonstrate their knowledge rather than a written assignment. Lower proficiency students may be more comfortable with a different mode of assignment than more proficient students, and having some control over their learning may increase their achievement.

- Pair students with more proficient speakers to scaffold their participation. More proficient speakers have an opportunity to practice using academic English and negotiating meaning with peers while less proficient students have the support needed to complete academic tasks.

- Differentiate wait time by becoming accustomed to allowing more wait time for beginning English speakers and those students who require more time for processing information. More advanced speakers will require less wait time. However, don't forget that all children benefit from time to think about questions or new information.

- Partner together students who speak the same **primary language** so they have native language support as needed.

■ The Lesson

Addition and Subtraction (First Grade)

The first-grade teachers in this chapter, Mrs. Aguirre, Mr. McQuaid, and Miss Dimitrievska, work in a suburban school that has a 33% English learner population. Their classes have an even distribution of English learners, each with approximately 10% in their class. Although most of these children are at the intermediate to advanced levels of English proficiency, they still benefit from having teachers use SIOP techniques to increase their understanding of concepts and participate fully in lessons.

The teachers in this school plan math units around the Common Core State Standards. In the math lessons described, all classes are working on Standard 6, Operations and Algebraic Thinking: *Add and subtract within 20, demonstrating fluency for addition and subtraction within 10. Use strategies such as counting on; making ten (e.g., 8 + 6 = 8 + 2 + 4 = 10 + 4 = 14); decomposing a number leading to a ten (e.g., 13 − 4 = 13 − 3 − 1 = 10 − 1 = 9); using the relationship between addition and subtraction (e.g., knowing that 8 + 4 = 12 one knows 12 − 8 = 4); and creating equivalent but easier or known sums (e.g., adding 6 + 7 by creating the known equivalent 6 + 6 + 1 = 12 + 1 = 13).* (© Copyright 2010. National Governors Association Center for Best Practices and Council of Chief State School Officers. All rights reserved.)

The lessons described are part of a unit, and children have already learned and practiced the mechanics of addition and subtraction. In these lessons, the emphasis is on being aware of the most efficient strategy to use in solving word problems. The teachers co-plan lesson objectives each week so that they are teaching essentially the same content across the classes. In the scenarios that follow, the objectives are:

Content Objectives (CO): Students will solve addition and subtraction problems efficiently using strategies.

Language Objectives (LO): Students will orally express their reasoning when solving problems.

As you will see, although the objectives are the same, the teachers each have their own ways of teaching the lessons.

Teaching Scenarios

Mrs. Aguirre

As was her practice, Mrs. Aguirre began by reading to the children, the lesson's content and langauge objectives that were written on the board. She told the class that they would use counting strategies to solve addition and subtraction problems. She asked them to think about how objects can be used to find solutions.

Using an interactive whiteboard, Mrs. Aguirre put up 2 rows of circles. The circles were in groups of 5, each group a different color. She began by placing 5 red circles and 3 blue circles on the top line (8). Below she placed 5 red circles and 4 blue circles (9). She asked the students how many circles there were all together (17). A number of children raised their hands and she called on two to give their answer. After showing several more problems on the board (e.g., 7 + 7 and 9 + 6), she asked students how they were able to figure out the answers. She drew sticks with students' names on them from a can and called on those students to explain. If a student didn't respond right away, Mrs. Aguirre didn't want to put him or her on the spot so she drew another name. Most students were able to articulate a process such as adding the groups of 5 red circles first, then adding the blue circles (e.g., 5 + 5, then add 10 + 3 and 13 + 4 = 17). She asked the class repeatedly if anyone had a question.

Once Mrs. Aguirre thought that students knew how to complete addition problems, she repeated the procedure with subtraction problems; e.g., she showed 17 circles and asked what the amount would be left if she took away 5. She demonstrated taking away on the interactive whiteboard.

Next she called on individuals to play the role of "teacher." Four students were selected for this part of the lesson. Each took a turn putting up circles on the interactive whiteboard and adding to or taking away a certain number to create a problem. The class had to solve the problem.

For the final twenty minutes of the lesson, students took out their math texts and solved a variety of addition and subtraction problems found in the book. At the end of the lesson, they turned in their written work.

Check your understanding: On the SIOP form in Figure 6.2, rate Mrs. Aguirre's lesson on each of the Interaction features.

Mr. McQuaid

The lesson began with Mr. McQuaid having the class chorally read the content and language objectives. Mr. McQuaid asked students to turn to their partners and tell each other three counting strategies that they had learned. Then he asked several groups which ones they identified. Groups reported out the strategies using doubles (2 + 2), counting by 5s or 10s, and counting on.

After reviewing strategies, Mr. McQuaid showed a counting rack on the document viewer that had two parallel rods with 10 beads, 5 red and 5 white. There was space on each rod to move the beads back and forth. He moved the beads to form groups and said, "This is how many I have on my rack (8 on top and 9 below). Talk to your partner about how many are on the rack." Then he asked how they solved the problem. One group said that they used their double facts. He asked the class,

FIGURE 6.2 Interaction Component of the SIOP® Model: Mrs. Aguirre's Lesson

4	3	2	1	0
16. Frequent opportunities for **interaction** and discussion between teacher/ student and among students, which encourage elaborated responses about lesson concepts		**Interaction** mostly teacher-dominated with some opportunities for students to talk about or question lesson concepts		**Interaction** teacher-dominated with no opportunities for students to discuss lesson concepts

4	3	2	1	0
17. **Grouping configurations** support language and content objectives of the lesson		**Grouping configurations** unevenly support the language and content objectives		**Grouping configurations** do not support the language and content objectives

4	3	2	1	0
18. Sufficient **wait time for student responses** consistently provided		Sufficient **wait time for student responses** occasionally provided		Sufficient **wait time for student responses** not provided

4	3	2	1	0	N/A
19. Ample opportunities for students to **clarify key concepts in L1** as needed with aide, peer, or L1 text		Some opportunities for students to **clarify key concepts in L1**		No opportunities for students to **clarify key concepts in L1**	

Reflect and Apply

Click here to explain your ratings for Mrs. Aguirre's lesson on each of the Interaction features.

"What is this double fact?" and they replied together that 8 + 8 = 16. He pointed out that they would then add 1 to make 17.

Mr. McQuaid continued with several more problems on the screen, showing a variety of combinations of beads and asking the class to solve the problems efficiently in pairs and explain how they arrived at their solutions. With each problem he called on different pairs to report out how they arrived at their solution, which provided accountability for the pairs. If a group had difficulty articulating the strategy used, he asked, "Who can help your friends?" and another student would explain the strategy. Then Mr. McQuaid told the class that they would use the racks with a partner and solve word problems together. He called a student to the front of the room, and they modeled the procedure for working together. The student held the rack, and the teacher took a card out of a plastic bag and read the problem: "I have 9 people on the bus and 10 get on. How many are there?" The student put 9 beads on the top row and 10 on the bottom and said, "19." The teacher asked her how she solved it, and she said that 9 + 9 is a double fact so she had 18 and added 1 more. Then the teacher and student switched roles so that the teacher had the rack and the student selected a card. Mr. McQuaid reminded the children that this wasn't a winning game; it was a game for working together. They needed to share and help each other figure out the most efficient way to solve the problems.

For this activity, Mr. McQuaid paired English learners with native English speakers. While partners worked on the game, Mr. McQuaid circulated and assisted students as needed with prompts such as "How many are on the bus? How many got on? How many total? How did you figure it out?" He used a technique of counting to himself to be sure he allowed enough wait time for children to process the question or information. Some of the English learners spoke with their partner in their home language to express their ideas.

After all children had had a chance to solve about a dozen problems between them, they followed the same process with subtraction problems. Mr. McQuaid modeled the first problem: "There are 20 on the bus and 8 get off. How many are left? What is a good way to take 8 away?" When the partners had practiced subtraction problems for a while, Mr. McQuaid called them to whole-class formation. He asked for volunteers to come up and explain their reasoning. Various students said that they counted by 5, used double facts, and used counting on.

Finally, Mr. McQuaid gave the students a worksheet that had a number chart and addition and subtraction problems to solve. Students worked individually and finished at their own pace. At the conclusion of the lesson, Mr. McQuaid reviewed the content and language objectives and asked students to hold thumbs up if they met the objectives.

Check your understanding: On the SIOP form in Figure 6.3, rate Mr. McQuaid's lesson on each of the Interaction features.

Miss Dimitrievska

Miss Dimitrievska, known to her students as Miss D, began her lesson by saying, "Who can tell me a strategy we know that helps us add and subtract numbers efficiently?" A few children raised their hands, and she called on each one to elicit an answer. She wrote the strategies they named on an interactive whiteboard. Also written on the board were the content and language objectives for the lesson. Miss D read the objectives and, pointing to the strategies listed, said that they would be using those strategies in the lesson.

Miss D had each table captain distribute clicker responders. Then she put a line of 7 cars on the interactive whiteboard (5 yellow and 2 blue) and another line of 5 yellow cars below. She asked the class to figure out how many total cars were on the board. She reminded them to do it efficiently as she pointed to the list of strategies on the board. After a minute she told the children to enter their answers using the clickers. Each student responded and she could see who did and who did not have correct answers. She then told the students to explain to their partner how they arrived at the answer and asked for volunteers to share out. Several children named strategies such as counting on and using doubles. She repeated this process a number of times until nearly every clicked answer was correct.

Then Miss D introduced subtraction in the same way. She showed two lines of balls, took some away and asked the students to solve the problem and enter their answers. Again she had partners articulate their reasoning. She continued with this

FIGURE 6.3	Interaction Component of the SIOP® Model: Mr. McQuaid's Lesson

4	3	2	1	0
16. Frequent opportunities for **interaction** and discussion between teacher/ student and among students, which encourage elaborated responses about lesson concepts		**Interaction** mostly teacher-dominated with some opportunities for students to talk about or question lesson concepts		**Interaction** teacher-dominated with no opportunities for students to discuss lesson concepts

4	3	2	1	0
17. **Grouping configurations** support language and content objectives of the lesson		**Grouping configurations** unevenly support the language and content objectives		**Grouping configurations** do not support the language and content objectives

4	3	2	1	0
18. Sufficient **wait time for student responses** consistently provided		Sufficient **wait time for student responses** occasionally provided		Sufficient **wait time for student responses** not provided

4	3	2	1	0	N/A
19. Ample opportunities for students to **clarify key concepts in L1** as needed with aide, peer, or L1 text		Some opportunities for students to **clarify key concepts in L1**		No opportunities for students to **clarify key concepts in L1**	

? Reflect and Apply

Click here to explain your ratings for Mr. McQuaid's lesson on each of the Interaction features.

process until students were solving problems with a high degree of accuracy. Although the children enjoyed using the clickers, at times Miss D asked for the response before some of the English learners had processed the language associated with the problems, especially determining if it was an addition or subtraction problem. Also, they felt a bit rushed when explaining to their partner what strategy they used.

For the next part of the lesson, Miss D gave students plastic bags of beads and written addition and subtraction problems. Working with partners, each pair used the beads to represent the problems and solve them. Miss D circulated to make sure pairs were working cooperatively, solving the problems, and explaining which strategy they used. Some English learners spoke in their native language with their partner and Miss D gently asked students to speak in English.

Finally, students were given a worksheet with both addition and subtraction problems to solve independently. Miss D concluded the lesson by reviewing the content and language objectives and had students respond with their clickers if they had met each one.

Check your understanding: On the SIOP form in Figure 6.4, rate Miss Dimitrievska's lesson on each of the Interaction features.

FIGURE 6.4 Interaction Component of the SIOP® Model: Miss Dimitrievska's Lesson

4	3	2	1	0	
16. Frequent opportunities for **interaction** and discussion between teacher/ student and among students, which encourage elaborated responses about lesson concepts		**Interaction** mostly teacher-dominated with some opportunities for students to talk about or question lesson concepts		**Interaction** teacher-dominated with no opportunities for students to discuss lesson concepts	

4	3	2	1	0	
17. **Grouping configurations** support language and content objectives of the lesson		**Grouping configurations** unevenly support the language and content objectives		**Grouping configurations** do not support the language and content objectives	

4	3	2	1	0	
18. Sufficient **wait time for student responses** consistently provided		Sufficient **wait time for student responses** occasionally provided		Sufficient **wait time for student responses** not provided	

4	3	2	1	0	N/A
19. Ample opportunities for students to **clarify key concepts in L1** as needed with aide, peer, or L1 text		Some opportunities for students to **clarify key concepts in L1**		No opportunities for students to **clarify key concepts in L1**	

? Reflect and Apply

Click here to explain your ratings for Miss Dimitrievska's lesson on each of the Interaction features.

■ Discussion of Lessons

16. *Frequent Opportunities for Interaction and Discussion between Teacher/Student and Among Students Which Encourage Elaborated Responses About Lesson Concepts*

Mrs. Aguirre: 1

Mr. McQuaid: 4

Miss Dimitrievska: 4

There is growing awareness about the importance of students being actively engaged in learning and having opportunities to interact productively with peers and teachers. However, many teachers struggle to relinquish the "sage on the stage" type of teaching where most often the teacher talks and students listen. In their lessons, these teachers vary the opportunities they provide to their students.

- **Mrs. Aguirre's** lesson received a "1" because the format of her lesson was teacher controlled and did not provide sufficient interaction among the children. Student participation was individual responses to teacher prompts and was largely based on volunteering. This practice tends to mask struggling students and those who do not understand since they are unlikely to volunteer. Usually the children who least need practice using English or help with concepts are the ones who volunteer to participate in lessons. It is very difficult to determine the needs of students and gauge their understandings when relying almost solely on volunteer responses.

Although Mrs. Aguirre made use of technology, she used the interactive whiteboard just as she would a chalkboard. It was essentially a fancy way of writing problems on the board, calling on children individually to answer questions or to pose problems for classmates. She made the assumption that all students understood the lesson's objectives about using strategies to solve problems efficiently based on the participation of a few students.

- **Mr. McQuaid's and Miss D's** lessons received a "4" because they both encouraged lots of student-to-student and teacher-to-student interaction. By having the children explain to one another the process they used to solve problems, their thinking was made transparent and the teachers could readily ascertain who understood the strategies and was able to apply them and who needed more support.

- **Miss D** used clickers to make sure that each student was engaged and interacting with her in problem solving. It also gave her immediate feedback about how much practice was needed before moving to the next part of the lesson.

17. *Grouping Configurations Support Language and Content Objectives of the Lesson*

Mrs. Aguirre: 0

Mr. McQuaid: 4

Miss Dimitrievska: 4

Whole-class instruction has a role to play, but it should not be used extensively since it limits opportunities for students to ask questions, discuss ideas, and clarify information. The stated language objective for this lesson was that students would orally express their reasoning when solving problems.

- **Mrs. Aguirre's** lesson used whole-class instruction or individual work exclusively, which did not support the objectives, especially the language objective. Therefore, her lesson received a "0." Only once during the lesson did children have an opportunity to explain the strategies they used to solve problems, and the lack of grouping configurations limited opportunities for students to identify and discuss how they solved problems efficiently. English learners and those children who struggle academically may find whole-class instruction intimidating, as undoubtedly was the case with Mrs. Aguirre's lesson. Although she asked if students had questions, nobody was willing to speak up in the whole-class setting.

- **Mr. McQuaid** planned a lesson that used a balance of whole-class instruction for introducing the concepts and modeling expectations, and partner work that allowed students to create and solve problems and to articulate their reasoning. Varying grouping structures allowed for deeper understanding of the concept and also provided practice using academic English. Mr. McQuaid's lesson received a "4" for this feature.

- **Miss D's** lesson also provided optimal opportunity for interaction. She used whole-class instruction, individual response using clickers, and partner work. Miss D's lesson received a "4" on this feature.

18. *Sufficient Wait Time for Student Responses Consistently Provided*

Mrs. Aguirre: 0

Mr. McQuaid: 4

Miss Dimitrievska: 2

- The whole-class, teacher-dominated format of **Mrs. Aguirre's** lesson encouraged those students who were quick to respond (usually native speakers of English) to set the pace. Children who required more time to process information or to think of the words in English were essentially left out of the lesson, however unintentional this was on Mrs. Aguirre's part. When she called on students individually, she tried to spare them embarrassment when they didn't answer promptly by choosing someone else. It would have been more effective to scaffold the student's response with prompts and provide the wait time needed. Mrs. Aguirre's lesson received a "0" for this feature.

- **Mr. McQuaid** interacted with students in a way that allowed time for them to formulate their thoughts and express them in English. Also, working with partners and then sharing out gave additional time to students. Mr. McQuaid recognized that English learners need to have a little extra time when participating in class. His lesson received a "4" for this feature.

- Although English was **Miss D's** second language and she understands English learners' needs, she felt pressure to move the lesson along and didn't always provide sufficient wait time. Therefore, her lesson received a "2" for this feature.

19. *Ample Opportunity for Students to Clarify Key Concepts in L1 as Needed with Aide, Peer, or L1 Text*

Mrs. Aguirre: 0

Mr. McQuaid: 4

Miss Dimitrievska: 2

Watch this video to see Dr. Jana Echevarría discuss the importance of Interaction and the features in the Interaction component. What did the first-grade teacher say about the benefit of the SIOP Model for her students? What do you find most striking about the way the students in the first grade-class interact? What did teachers do to facilitate interaction?

- Again, the format of **Mrs. Aguirre's** instructional delivery did not allow children the opportunity to clarify concepts or information with others in their home language even if it would have improved their understanding. Therefore, her lesson received a "0" on this feature.

- **Mr. McQuaid's** lesson, on the other hand, provided lots of opportunity for student-to-student interaction, and students could use their native language when needed. Students were encouraged to discuss the math problems as well as their thinking about how they arrived at solutions. Participation in either language was accepted. Mrs. McQuaid's lesson received a "4" for this feature.

- **Miss D's** lesson also provided opportunities for children to work together and they naturally used their L1 when needed. Use of the native language wasn't forbidden; however, Miss D believed that she was helping students by encouraging English. Young learners, and beginning English speakers in particular, benefit from having opportunities to discuss and clarify concepts in the language they understand best. Miss D's lesson received a "2" because opportunities to use L1 were limited, even when it was clear that students needed that support.

(For more examples of lesson and unit plans in mathematics for grades K–12, see Echevarría, Vogt, & Short, 2010.)

Teaching with Technology

After talking with the teachers and discussing the lessons you read about in the Scenarios earlier in the chapter, our tech integrator, Ms. Palacios, offered some technology suggestions to enhance the teachers' lessons.

Book Creator: Before beginning the unit on addition and subtraction, Mrs. Aguirre sent an e-mail to Ms. Palacios on behalf of her first-grade team of Mr. McQuaid and Miss Dimitrievska. The elementary wing of the school recently received an iPad cart for shared use and they were curious about ideas for using the new tablets. In order to explore options, the three first-grade teachers and the tech integrator planned a workshop during an afternoon inservice. To start, the teachers explained the objectives of their current unit on addition and subtraction. Ms. Palacios listened carefully, gave each of the teachers an iPad, and then walked them through some options. They all agreed that they wanted a tool that would enhance their unit, yet also one that would be feasible for first graders to use. The team discussed screencasting as a possible option, but decided on *Book Creator*, an app for making e-books.

Ms. Palacios walked the teachers through the app, showing them how to create their own books by adding photos, making text boxes, editing the text, and adding voice recordings. Mrs. Aguirre brought some of the manipulatives from the unit to the table and the teachers explored ways to include the regular classroom materials in photos. Mr. McQuaid thought the students could take photos of their manipulatives and write captions for the photos to demonstrate their understanding of number sentences.

Before launch day, Ms. Palacios arranged the apps on the home screen of the iPad, placing unneeded apps into folders on another screen. Students only needed to use the *Book Creator* app and the camera. Because it was the first time that many of the students would be using an iPad, Ms. Palacios recommended letting them have some unstructured time with the device before the lesson. This gave the students a chance to explore the tablet.

During math time, each teacher set up a center where a small group of children would learn how to use the app. Then, working in pairs, the students used the app to take photos of different combinations of manipulatives. They used the *Book Creator* app to import photos and create captions for each photo, including an equation. The app facilitated discussion among the students. To avoid arguments, Ms. Palacios recommended that the teachers set up a timer at five-minute intervals. Each student took turns managing the iPad for five minutes and then would allow the partner to take over.

To extend the activity and challenge her students, Mrs. Aguirre also had some children create word problems for other students to solve. For additional oral language practice, Miss Dimitrievska showed students how

(*continued on the next page*)

to use the voice recording option to narrate the process of solving equations. After the lessons, Ms. Palacios came to check in on the teachers and assisted them with transferring the student-created e-books into the *iBooks* app, which allowed them to share the student work with parents during conferences.

Other terms for this type of tool: e-book creator, book creator app

Related products: *iBooks Author, My Story, Scribble Press*

Blogging for Students: A number of tools are available that allow educators to offer opportunities for student interaction beyond the classroom walls and after the school day. Blogging is one such tool. While blogs may prove challenging for the first graders described in this chapter's teaching scenarios, they are tools worth exploring for a number of reasons. Class blogs offer a safe playground for preparing our students to be responsible digital citizens while offering them chances to interact, read, write, and give meaningful feedback.

Platforms like *Kidblog* allow children to share their voices with a larger audience than just the teacher. Blogging platforms meant for children have multiple layers of built-in security features. The teacher can set controls to preview all posts and comments before they are published. Student information such as names and posts can be kept private behind a password. With regard to academic interaction, a blogging platform can be used to teach how to provide constructive feedback, and how to write for a specific audience. Often, publishing for peers—whether within the same school or to an international pen pal—adds extra motivation for children to improve their writing skills.

Other terms for this type of tool: student blogs, blogs for children, blogs for classroom

Related products: *Write About, Edublogs, Blogger* by Google.

Note: Due to the constantly evolving nature of the Internet, it is a challenge to ensure that all of the links and Web services listed here are updated and functional when you read the technology sections. While specific tools or services may appear in the narrative, we have also included the general term for each tool. If a specific service does not work or is no longer available, search with the general term for the tool and you should be able to find a comparable Web site.

Check Your Understanding
Click here to check your understanding of the concepts in Chapter 6, Interaction.

Summary

As you reflect on this chapter and the benefits of interaction for English learners, consider the following main points:

- You should create ample opportunities for English learners to practice using academic English among themselves and with you, the teacher. Children should elaborate and extend their comments and responses, not provide one- or two-word answers.

- The Common Core and other state standards require that students have ample opportunities to take part in a variety of rich, structured discussions—as part of a whole class, in small groups, and with a partner.

- Incorporating a number of grouping configurations into lessons facilitates using English in ways that support the lessons' objectives and develop children's English proficiency.

- Using a Gradual Increase of Student Independence approach ensures that a variety of groups are used in a lesson.

- For most teachers, it is challenging to balance the amount of teacher talk and student participation. Effective SIOP teachers plan for and incorporate structured opportunities for children to use English in a variety of ways.

- It may be beneficial for students to use their native language to clarify directions and express their ideas. However, the teacher may need to help them articulate their ideas in English, particularly as they advance in their proficiency levels.

■ Discussion Questions

1. In reflecting on the content and language objectives at the beginning of the chapter, are you able to:
   a. Select a variety of activities that promote interaction and incorporate them into lesson plans?
   b. Design grouping structures that support a lesson's content and language objectives?
   c. Identify techniques to increase wait time?
   d. List ways that CCSS collaborative conversations and discussions are aligned with the Interaction component?
   e. Identify resources to support student clarification in the native language?
   f. Explain in writing the purpose of student–student interaction for language development?
   g. Describe techniques to reduce the amount of teacher talk in a lesson?
   h. Practice asking questions that promote student elaboration of responses?

2. Think of a content concept that you might be teaching. Describe three different grouping configurations that could be used for teaching and learning this concept. How would you organize the children in each group? How would you monitor student learning? What would you want children to do while working in their groups? How would the grouping configurations facilitate learning for English learners?

3. Either film your own classroom while you're teaching a lesson or observe another teacher's classroom for a 15-minute segment. Estimate the proportion of teacher talk and student talk. Given the ratio of teacher–student talk, what are some possible ramifications for English learners in this class?

4. Productive discussions are usually the result of careful planning and preparation. What are some rules of discussion presented in this chapter that you would need to teach or reinforce with your students? What might be an appropriate language objective for a lesson on rules of discussion?

5. Using the SIOP lesson you have been developing, add activities and grouping configurations to enhance interaction.

CHAPTER 7

Practice & Application

Learning Outcomes

After reading, discussing, and engaging in activities related to this chapter, you will be able to meet the following **content** and **language objectives**.

Content Objectives

Identify a variety of ways for students to enhance their learning through hands-on practice.

Create application activities that extend the learning in new ways and relate to content or language objectives.

Language Objectives

Enhance typical lesson tasks so that different language skills are integrated.

Discuss the importance of linking practice and application activities to specific lesson objectives.

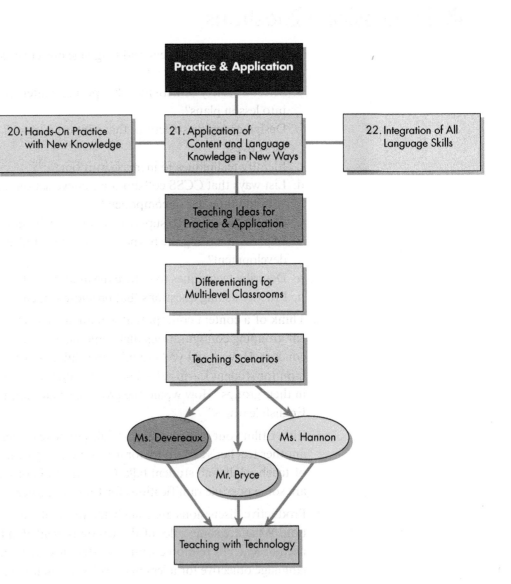

One common memory that most adults share is of learning to ride a full-sized bike. Even after riding smaller bicycles with training wheels, most of us were unprepared for the balancing act required for us not to fall down when riding a regular bike. If you had a parent or older brother or sister who talked you through the process, showed you how to balance, and perhaps even held on to the bike while you were steadying yourself, your independent practice time with the big bike was probably enhanced. Talking about the experience, listening to someone else describe it, observing other riders, and then practicing for yourself all worked together to turn you into a bicycle rider. That feeling of accomplishment, of mastering something new through practice and applying it to a bigger bike, or perhaps a motorcycle in later years, is a special feeling that most of us have experienced as learners. ●

© Creative Imaging Photography/Alamy Stock Photo

■ Background

Up to this point in a **SIOP** lesson, a teacher has introduced content and language objectives, built background or activated prior knowledge, introduced key vocabulary, identified a **learning strategy** and higher-order questions for students to focus on, developed a **scaffolding** approach for teaching the new information, and planned for student interaction. In the Practice & Application component, the teacher gives students a chance to practice with the new material, and, with careful teacher oversight, demonstrate how well they are learning it. In the same lesson or a subsequent one, the teacher plans a task so students can apply this new knowledge in various ways. It is well established that practice and application help one master a skill (Dean, Hubbell, Pilter, & Stone, 2012; Fisher & Frey, 2008; Marzano, 2007). For SIOP instruction, however, both the practice and application tasks should also aim for practice of all four language skills: reading, writing, listening, and speaking.

For **English learners**, this stage of a SIOP lesson is very important, especially for **academic language** development. As Saville-Troike (1984) pointed out, both language and academic learning occur through language use in the classroom. Second language acquisition research has shown repeatedly that for an individual to develop a high level of proficiency in a new language, he or she must have opportunities not only for comprehensible input (Krashen, 1985) but also for targeted output (Swain, 1985), namely oral and written practice. In a synthesis of 20 years of research on oral language development, Saunders and O'Brien (2006) conclude that English learners "are most likely to use the language used to deliver instruction in their interactions with peers and teachers" (p. 41). They further explain:

> [W]hile use and exposure are necessary conditions, they may not be sufficient conditions, especially when it comes to achieving higher levels of proficiency involving more academic uses of language. The content and quality of L2 exposure and use are probably of equal, if not greater, importance than L2 exposure and use per se (p. 41).

For SIOP teachers, this means that we need to carefully choose the activities we include in our lessons.

- Some activities may build foundational language knowledge, especially for young learners who enter school with few pre-academic experiences or newcomers to the United States who have had significant interruptions in their educational backgrounds and weak literacy skills in their native language.
- Some activities must strengthen the students' progress in meeting or mastering the content and language objectives. Suppose a language objective calls for a fifth grader to write a conclusion that supports the argument he or she made, and the language arts teacher instructs on ways to write a strong conclusion. Then a practice or application activity might have the students write a letter to the School Board on a topic related to the class reading, such as ways to promote more recycling of used goods like sports equipment and technology found at school.
- Some activities must advance student proficiency in using English. Zwiers and Crawford (2009) and Seidlitz (2008) recommend teaching sentence stems and language frames to help students articulate their thoughts and ideas. These frames link to language functions, and activities can be created to encourage more sophisticated use of these frames over time. For example, children may progress from expressing an opinion simply, as in "I believe that ____" to the more detailed "In my opinion, ____ is correct/incorrect because ____," and finally to the complex form "The scientist in this article claims ____, but I would argue that ____." Short and Echevarría (2016) present a range of stems organized by language function.

If the class includes students with multiple **language proficiency** levels, the Practice & Application component of the SIOP Model is the ideal place to differentiate instruction. For the language arts lesson mentioned above, the teacher facilitates a whole-class brainstorming of ways to promote more recycling at school. Students share ideas, some of which may come from their home or country backgrounds, and the teacher generates a list. Next, the class selects one action they might take as a test case and discusses reasons in favor of the idea as well as possible counter-arguments they might want to oppose. The teacher then reviews language frames and key words to use in a conclusion. Finally, some advanced-level students write individual letters, intermediate-level students write with one partner or two, and beginners work with the teacher to prepare a group letter.

Indeed, it is within this component that teachers can incorporate project-based learning (Seidlitz & Perryman, 2011) or other differentiated activities that explore learning styles, multiple intelligences, and cultural perspectives (Nieto & Bode, 2008) to meet the language needs of students (Tomlinson, 2014; Vogt & Echevarría, 2008; Vogt, Echevarría & Washam, 2015). As teachers plan these practice and application activities, they should consider the structure of the task and degree of difficulty for the resulting product, the grouping configurations, the type of feedback that will be provided so it is geared to proficiency level, and the expectations for student achievement (Vogt, 2012).

In this chapter, we discuss how sheltered language and content teachers provide English learners with the types of hands-on experiences, guidance, and practice that can lead to mastery of content knowledge and higher levels of language proficiency. The teaching vignettes demonstrate how three second-grade classroom teachers, all of whom have large numbers of English learners in their classes plus a few newcomers, delivered science lessons on weather precipitation.

SHELTERED INSTRUCTION
SIOP®
OBSERVATION PROTOCOL

SIOP® FEATURE 20:

Hands-On Materials and/or Manipulatives Provided for Students to Practice Using New Content Knowledge in the Classroom

As previously mentioned, riding a bike is usually preceded by practicing with training wheels and working with a more experienced bike rider. Obviously, the more practice one has on the bike, the more likely one is to become a good bike rider. Now let's apply this process to learning to play a musical instrument.

Some years ago, an entrepreneur decided to market a piano-teaching course that included a cardboard sheet printed with piano keys. Students were supposed to practice the piano on the paper keyboard by following the directions printed in the course manual. The black-and-white keys on the keyboard were printed, and dotted lines showed students where to place their fingers during practice sessions. It was little surprise that the paper keyboards didn't catch on even though the course manual clearly described in incremental steps how to play the piano, because even with hours of practice on the paper keyboard, students were still unable to play the piano well. In this case, it wasn't just the *practice* that was important. Without hearing the sounds during practice, learning to play the piano was an inauthentic and nearly impossible task.

When learning to ride a bicycle or play the piano, children have a greater chance of mastering skills when they are given multiple opportunities to practice in relevant, meaningful ways. The same holds true in class to master content concepts and skills, whether it is solving two-step math word problems or using technology that collects data during a science experiment and interpreting the results. When this practice incorporates "hands-on" experiences including manipulatives, practice sessions are enhanced.

Madeline Hunter (1982), a renowned expert in teaching methods, coined the term *guided practice* to describe the process of the teacher leading the student through practice sessions prior to independent application. In her lesson design, new material should be divided into meaningful parts. After students are introduced to each part, they should have short, intense practice periods with the content. Previously learned materials should be reviewed periodically with additional practice periods. Throughout, Hunter recommended, teachers should give students specific feedback so they know how well they are doing.

Although all children benefit from guided practice as they move to independent work, English learners make more rapid progress in mastering content objectives when they are provided with multiple opportunities to practice with hands-on materials and/or manipulatives. These may be created, counted, classified, stacked, experimented with, observed, rearranged, dismantled, and so forth. We would also include kinesthetic activities in a broad definition of this feature. Manipulating learning materials is important for English learners because it helps them connect abstract concepts with concrete experiences. Furthermore, manipulatives and other hands-on materials reduce the language load for students. Students with beginning proficiency in English, for instance, can still participate and demonstrate what they are learning.

Obviously, the type of manipulative employed for practice depends on the subject being taught. For example, in a math class in which students are learning how to draw congruent geometric shapes, content objectives might justify paper-and-pencil practice. However, if it is possible for you to incorporate hands-on practice with manipulatives (e.g., tangrams in this example), you will probably boost your students' learning.

Being told how to ride a bike or play the piano, reading about how to do so, or watching a video of someone else engaged in bike riding or piano playing is much different from riding down the bike path or listening to musical sounds you have produced yourself. Whenever it is possible and appropriate, use hands-on materials for practice.

Watch this video of a first-grade math lesson on graphing to see how children make bar graphs during a kinesthetic activity with hands-on materials. Why are these activities useful to help English learners practice the concept?

SIOP® FEATURE 21:

Activities Provided for Students to Apply Content and Language Knowledge

We all can recall our own learning experiences in elementary, middle, and high school, and the university. For many of us, the classes and courses we remember best are the ones in which we applied our new knowledge in meaningful ways. These may have included activities such as writing a diary entry from the perspective of a character in a novel, creating a semantic map illustrating the relationships among complex concepts, or completing comprehensive case studies on learners we taught and assessed. These concrete experiences forced us to relate new information and concepts in a personally relevant way. We remember the times when we "got it," and we remember the times when we gave it our all but somehow still missed the target.

Hunter (1982) recognized this: "The difference between knowing how something should be done and being able to do it is the quantum leap in learning . . . " (p. 71).

For children acquiring a new language, it is critically important that they have opportunities to apply the new information because discussing and "doing" make the abstract concepts more concrete. We must remember that we learn best by involving ourselves in relevant, meaningful application of what we are learning. Application can occur in a number of ways:

- Children can create a book jacket for a novel or story they have read.
- Students can be asked to generate solutions to real-life problems in their neighborhoods. These solutions may represent multicultural viewpoints.
- Students can play the role of broadcast news anchor and on-site reporters covering a current event.
- Students can debate a scientific controversy in class (e.g., "Life exists on a planet in another galaxy") and then write their opinion on the topic in a journal.

For English learners, application must also include opportunities for them to practice language knowledge in the classroom. For example, it is appropriate, depending on students' language proficiency, to ask them to explain a historical event to a peer using a newly learned sentence structure or to explain the steps in their solution to a math word problem using key terms. Activities such as retelling a story but with a different ending, acting out a science experiment, or creating an ad campaign for a nutritious diet all help English learners produce and practice new language and vocabulary, as long as they are in a supportive environment. These activities are also appropriate for struggling learners and other students.

In Chapter 5 we presented a model for scaffolding that shows how a teacher can gradually increase the students' responsibility for learning and doing, and we argued that collaborative practice and structured conversations along with recursive teaching are important bridging steps between guided practice and independent work. Through collaborative learning, children support one another in practicing or applying information while the teacher assists as needed. Some students may be able to move on to independent work, but others may need some targeted reteaching by the teacher.

SIOP® FEATURE 22:
Activities Integrate All Language Skills

Reading, writing, listening, and speaking are complex cognitive language processes that are interrelated and integrated. As we go about our daily lives, we move through the processes in a natural way, reading what we write, talking about what we've read, and listening to others talk about what they've read, written, and seen. Most young children become grammatically competent in their home language by age five, and their continuing language development relates primarily to vocabulary, more sophisticated grammar usage (e.g., using relative clauses and noun phrases), and functional as well as sociocultural applications of language (e.g., adjusting one's language to a particular audience, developing rhetorical styles) (Peregoy & Boyle, 2013). Proficiency in reading and writing is achieved much later, and differences exist among individuals in levels of competence. Children especially need to learn academic language for school settings where the use of the forms and functions of social language (e.g., simple sentence and question structures) diminish while academic forms and functions (e.g., sentences with embedded clauses and abstract concepts) escalate (see Chapter 1 for a detailed discussion).

Some English learners may achieve competence in the written domains of a second language earlier than in the oral language domains; others may become proficient speakers before they read and write well (August & Shanahan, 2006). But it is important to realize that the language processes—reading, writing, listening, and speaking—are mutually supportive. Although the relationships among the processes are complex, practice in any one promotes development in the others (Genesee, Lindholm-Leary, Saunders, & Christian, 2006; Hinkel, 2006). Research shows that oral and written language can be successfully developed in content area classrooms (Baker et al., 2014).

Effective SIOP teachers understand the need to create many opportunities for English learners to practice and use all four language processes in an integrated manner. Throughout the day, these teachers offer their students varied experiences such as:

- Linking oral discussions of essential questions to reading selections
- Structuring interaction with peers
- Guiding students to use sentence starters, signal words, and language frames
- Providing children with the chance to listen and react to peers' ideas
- Asking children to write about what is being learned
- Having students read peers' writing and give feedback aligned to a rubric

We do want to clarify two things about language development as part of the Practice & Application component:

1. Although all identified language objectives in a lesson need to be practiced and applied as the lesson advances, not all language skills that are practiced need to be tied to an objective. In other words, a language objective represents a key skill, language structure, or strategy the teacher plans to teach and intends for children to learn. In a SIOP lesson, the teacher teaches to this objective and assesses, formally or informally, how well students are meeting it. The objective may focus on one language domain, such as writing, but in the course of the lesson, students would likely have additional opportunities to read, speak, and listen. These should be carefully planned, but need not be assessed in the same way an objective would be.

2. Teachers are sometimes unsure about whether to correct English learners' language errors during practice time (Peregoy & Boyle, 2013). In general, consider students' levels of **English language development** when deciding whether to correct them. For young learners or beginning English speakers, errors may be developmental and reflect the children's native language use (e.g., not

Watch this video of Ms. Atristain's first-grade class to see how she builds multiple opportunities for language practice. Consider the activity planned. How do the children apply their knowledge? What language skills are practiced? How does the teacher accommodate English learners?

remembering to add past tense inflected endings to English verbs). Other errors may deal with placement of adjectives, sentence structure, plurals, word choice, and so forth. If errors impede oral communication, you can gently correct students by restating the sentence in proper form. Corrections usually can be modeled in a natural and nonthreatening way.

Otherwise, leave the errors alone. Research on error correction indicates that making impromptu corrections is less effective than setting aside a portion of a subsequent lesson to focus on the grammatical forms or usage issues that arise (Ellis, 2008). If you notice, therefore, that many children make the same error and it does not seem to be due to the language acquisition process, it is reasonable to plan a minilesson on the issue for a later class period. One exception is if errors are in a written product that is to be displayed. In that case, you may want to work with the child to edit it.

Teaching Ideas for Practice & Application

In the section that follows, you will find some teaching ideas to help you develop practice and application activities for SIOP lessons:

- **Manipulatives and Movement.** Have students manipulate objects or themselves instead of doing paper-and-pencil tasks for practice. For example, have students form a physical timeline about the Qin Dynasty of Ancient China with their bodies rather than complete a written timeline worksheet. Some students might have a card displaying a date; others would have one displaying an event or an achievement. The students would organize themselves, first pairing the dates and events, and then forming the human timeline.

- **Hands-on Games.** Educational, engaging, and fun games provide opportunities to practice or apply new content and language learning. For example, depending on the students' language levels, bingo could be played in the typical manner—the students hear a number or word said aloud and then mark its written form on the bingo card. Or definitions, synonyms, or antonyms could be read aloud, and students would find the corresponding term. In Piece O' Pizza, individual students or small groups create a pizza slice with information on it that differs from what is on their peers' slices. They put their slices together to address the main points of a key topic. See *99 Ideas and Activities for Teaching English Learners with the SIOP® Model* (Vogt & Echevarría, 2008) for more games.

- **Electronic Games.** Use PowerPoint slides or Web sites to build electronic game boards for *Jeopardy!, Who Wants to Be a Millionaire?*, or similar games. These games allow for differentiation as less proficient or less knowledgeable students can choose easier questions in the *Jeopardy* game or choose to "take the money" and stop advancing in the *Millionaire* game.

- **Foldables and Flip Charts.** Foldables and flip charts involve folding and/or cutting paper and offer a hands-on way for students to organize information. They can be made in various ways. With one type, a sheet of paper is held in a landscape orientation and then folded in half lengthwise (hot dog fold). The front

Watch this video to see bilingual second graders play the vocabulary game, "Hot Seat." Notice how the children apply their language skills and vocabulary knowledge.

half is then cut into a number of flaps (e.g., three), with the cut going up to the fold. On the outside front, a key word (e.g., *penny/nickel/dime*) may be written on each flap. When each is lifted, the numeric worth of the coin (e.g., 1¢) may be written on the top half and a picture or a math equivalent (e.g., 1 nickel = 5 pennies) may be placed on the bottom half. (For numerous examples, see Zike, 2000a, 2000b, 2004, 2007.)

- **Character Diaries.** Students take the role of a character from a novel, an historical figure, or an object, such as a plant seed. They create several entries in a diary, writing in the voice of that person/item, and including key events. Teachers may add other requirements to apply specific language objectives such as use of descriptive language, use of past tense or if-then clauses, or use of an academic language frame.

- **Reader's Theater, Role-Plays, and Simulations.** Students can build oral fluency, reinforce content knowledge, and practice language structures and academic vocabulary through Reader's Theater (Short, Vogt, & Echevarría, 2011a, pp. 58–60). Teachers create scripts on particular topics to be performed by small groups of students. The teacher may model the script before the students are assigned roles and perform. Role-plays are more informal, with students taking roles and deciding what they want to say while acting out a fictional, historical, or current event. Simulations may place students in real-life situations and have them work together to solve problems or attain a goal. Simulations are also available online and through computer programs.

- **Numbered Heads Together** (Kagan, 1994). Students form equal-size groups and then number off. The teacher poses a question and the members in each group work together to determine an answer. Each member should know the answer, but the teacher calls only one number and that individual responds. The benefit of this activity for English learners is that they collaborate with peers to generate the response and they can practice saying it aloud before being called on to speak to the whole class.

■ Differentiating Ideas for Multi-level Classes

The Practice & Application component offers teachers a relatively easy way to meet the needs of students with different abilities or proficiency levels in their classrooms. Consider the five options below when you want to adjust activities for your multi-level classes (Echevarría, Short, & Vogt, 2008; Tomlinson & Imbeau, 2010; Vogt, 2000).

1. **Group with a purpose.** Arrange students by language proficiency, learning style or multiple intelligences, demonstrated ability, perceived ability, or another reasoned way. Mix groups from time to time. Rotate roles so the more proficient students produce work or perform first and thus act as peer models for others.

2. **Differentiate the tasks.** Give each group a similar, yet specifically designed and equivalent task. Explain each group's assignment clearly, making sure it is as

demanding as the others. An "easy" task may be as cognitively demanding to lower proficiency students as a "hard" task is to native English speakers.

3. **Use motivational strategies.** Learn what will motivate your students to perform to their ability. The following may be considered:

   ◆ *Extrinsic:* Actual, physical rewards (points, homework passes, etc.) for accomplishing a task

   ◆ *Intrinsic:* The mental and emotional "reward" for accomplishing a task

   ◆ *Task engagement:* Positive feeling from being part of something that is stimulating, interesting, and do-able

   ◆ *Cooperative, competitive, individualistic:* The three most common classroom goal structures; each has a role, but cooperative goal structures tend to be the most motivational for students

   ◆ *Ego involvement:* Positive feeling about self when able to complete a task

4. **Use leveled questions to engage all learners.** As mentioned previously in Chapter 5, teachers tend to ask higher-level questions more frequently to high-performing students, and more literal-level questions to low-performing students. Instead, knowing your students' language levels (beginning, intermediate, etc.), prepare a hierarchy of questions so that students of all proficiency levels are able to participate—making sure you simplify word choice and structure in questions for newcomers and beginners. Allocate turns, monitor turn-taking, and make sure you allow enough wait time for less proficient students to respond. Be sure all students are given the chance to be involved.

5. **Select resources for differentiation.** Find leveled readers on the same or related topics. Bookmark Web sites and utilize **native language** Web sites or translations. Check the readability of texts you ask students to read. Use wordless books or photo journals with newcomers. Design activities at multiple levels of difficulty, such as the scaffolded cloze shown in Figure 7.1, a vocabulary worksheet with a word bank and a companion one without a word bank, or a writing assignment with different required lengths or research sources.

FIGURE 7.1 Scaffolded Listening Cloze Dictation Forms

More Proficient Students	**Less Proficient Students**
Fill in the blanks with the missing words while the teacher reads a passage aloud. You will hear the passage twice.	*Fill in the blanks with the missing words while the teacher reads a passage aloud. You will hear the passage twice.*
We _____ Earth into four _____ on a globe. The _____ hemisphere is above the _____ and the _____ hemisphere is _____ it. We also divide Earth into _____ and _____ hemispheres. The _____ is in the northern _____ and the western hemisphere. Tanzania is in the _____ hemisphere and the eastern _____.	We divide Earth into four _____ on a globe. The northern hemisphere is above the _____ and the southern hemisphere is below it. We also divide Earth into _____ and western hemispheres. The United States is in the northern hemisphere and the _____ hemisphere. Tanzania is in the _____ hemisphere and the eastern _____.

A few specific examples of activities follow:

- **Scaffolded Cloze Activities.** Consider a mixed class with **native English speakers** and English learners. For a listening cloze dictation, the native English speakers might record what the teacher says as a regular dictation. The English learners might have two different dictation forms with more or fewer words already written down (as in Figure 7.1 on the prior page). All the students listen to the paragraph the teacher reads on the second-grade geography topic, and all participate in the listening task, but the task format is differentiated to the students' English abilities. Cloze activities can be in writing, too, where students fill in words they generate or draw from a word bank.

- **Information Gap Activities.** These activities, which include Jigsaws, problem solving, and simulations, are set up so each student (generally in a group) has one or two pieces of information about a topic or event, or to help solve a puzzle, but not all the necessary information to get the full picture. Students must work together, sharing information while practicing their language, negotiating, and critical thinking skills. Teachers differentiate by assigning the amount and complexity of the specific pieces of information to students according to their language proficiency, background knowledge, and interests.

- **Read and Respond Paper Toss.** In this quick but engaging activity, students practice all four language skills (See Vogt, Echevarría & Washam, 2015, pp. 128–129). The teacher asks students in table groups to write down on a scrap of paper two quiz questions about the lesson's topic using key vocabulary, a grammar point, and/or written language function they have studied. When done the students scrunch the paper into little balls, stand up, and toss the paper balls in the center of their table. They then take turns picking up one ball (not their own), reading the questions aloud, and trying to answer it. The writer agrees or disagrees with the response. If the writer thinks the response is wrong, another student can answer, or the writer explains the answer. The teacher can differentiate by giving question frames to some students, asking some to write only one question, or giving students who will answer the option to confer with a table mate before responding.

■ The Lesson

Weather (Second Grade)

The three second-grade classrooms in these teaching vignettes are located in an urban elementary school in the Northeast. Approximately 40% of the 24 students are English learners from multiple-language backgrounds, including Spanish, Cape Verdean, and Haitian Creole. They range in proficiency from beginner to advanced. In each class, three of the children are recent arrivals with limited formal schooling. The other children in the class are native English speakers.

The state has developed science standards based on the **Next Generation Science Standards** and the district has a curriculum framework that the teachers follow. The state has English language proficiency standards for grades Pre-K–12.

(continued)

■ Teaching Scenarios

Ms. Devereaux

Ms. Devereaux entered class wearing a raincoat holding an open umbrella above her head. "What is the weather outside?" she asked. "Raining," shouted several second graders. She then took a piece of ice out of a container. "What weather does this remind you of?" "Winter" said one student. "Winter is a season," Ms. Devereaux replied. "I want to know the weather. Think about the forms of water we studied yesterday." One young girl said, "Ice." "Yes, it is ice," replied the teacher, "Can you also think of another kind of precipitation?" (She paused for several seconds.) "I'll give you a hint. It rhymes with *tail*." Sensing the students were still unsure, she told them to open their notebooks and find the weather words. One student finally said "hail" and Ms. Devereaux acknowledged he was right.

Ms. Devereaux pointed to the objectives on the board and told the students to copy them while she got supplies ready. The objectives were:

> **Content objective:** We will identify types of weather.
>
> **Language objective:** We will describe weather using adjectives.

Ms. Devereaux then showed the students the props they would use that day: a microphone, a map of their state, and a pointer. She asked the children to raise their hands if they had ever watched the news on television. Then she asked them to keep their hands up if they watched the weather broadcast. She called on one child with his hand still up to tell about a broadcast he saw. "The lady talked about the clouds and the rain." Ms. Devereaux replied, "Yes, she probably told you the temperature for the day and how cloudy it was and when the rain would come. Also she probably gave a prediction about the amount of rain and whether it would be windy or not. I bet she pointed to the weather map and showed you how a storm was moving across our state. Well, that's what I want you to do today in your groups."

She told them they could work with whomever they wanted in groups of three or four. They should prepare a two-minute broadcast about the weather, and they could decide what type of weather they would report on. She told them that when they performed their broadcast, they could use the props and she would record them with her digital camera.

Ms. Devereaux circulated among the groups and noticed that the English learners were mostly all together in three groups. All three groups planned to do a broadcast about rain. She tried to encourage them to do another form of weather, "What about snow? Or fog?" The students said they didn't know what to say about those. "I not see snow," said a newcomer student from Cape Verde who had only been in the United States for one week.

After 10 minutes of planning, the groups began to present their broadcasts. Ms. Devereaux noticed that the groups with the English learners had very little to say. One young broadcaster's statements were representative of all the English learner groups. "It is raining tomorrow. You get wet. Bring umbrella to school." She was disappointed that they weren't more descriptive about the upcoming weather and didn't seem excited about the activity, even though she was filming them.

Check your understanding: On the SIOP form in Figure 7.2, rate Ms. Devereaux's lesson on each of the Practice & Application features.

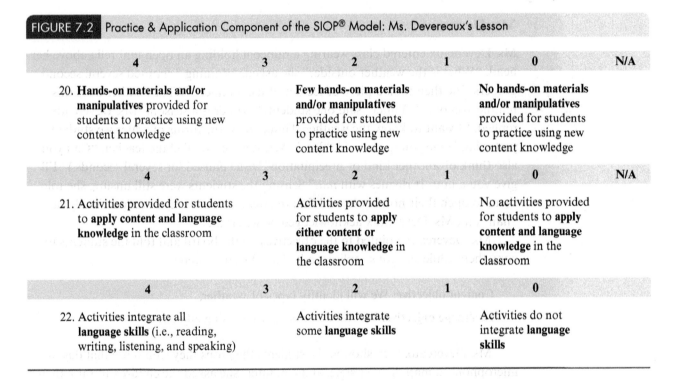

FIGURE 7.2 Practice & Application Component of the SIOP® Model: Ms. Devereaux's Lesson

4	3	2	1	0	N/A
20. **Hands-on materials and/or manipulatives** provided for students to practice using new content knowledge		Few hands-on materials and/or manipulatives provided for students to practice using new content knowledge		No hands-on materials and/or manipulatives provided for students to practice using new content knowledge	

4	3	2	1	0	N/A
21. Activities provided for students to **apply content and language knowledge** in the classroom		Activities provided for students to **apply either content or language knowledge** in the classroom		No activities provided for students to **apply content and language knowledge** in the classroom	

4	3	2	1	0
22. Activities integrate all **language skills** (i.e., reading, writing, listening, and speaking)		Activities integrate some **language skills**		Activities do not integrate **language skills**

? Reflect and Apply

Click here to explain your ratings for Ms. Devereaux's lesson on each of the Practice & Application features.

Mr. Bryce (see Figure 7.3 for a complete lesson plan)

Mr. Bryce reminded the second graders of the lesson they had started the day before. He showed some pictures of different types of weather and asked the children to identify the types of precipitation with a partner. He had previously paired his three newcomers with the most advanced English learners in the class. He continued by reading the objectives aloud from the board:

Content objective: We will distinguish among different forms of precipitation.

Language objective: We will write opinion sentences about the weather using the word "because."

| FIGURE 7.3 | SIOP® Lesson: Mr. Bryce's Lesson Plan for Grade 2 Science |

STANDARDS:
  SCIENCE: Students describe daily weather changes and seasonal weather patterns.
  WIDA ELD: English language learners communicate information, ideas, and concepts necessary for academic success in the content area of Science.

LESSON TOPIC: Weather

OBJECTIVES:
  Content objective: We will distinguish among different forms of precipitation.
  Language objective: We will write opinion sentences about the weather using the word "because."

LEARNING STRATEGIES: Visualize
[Note: Pair newcomers with advanced students]

KEY VOCABULARY: rain, hail, snow, ice, mist, fog, because

MATERIALS: pictures depicting types of precipitation, weather word cards, index cards, chart paper, markers, dot stickers, sample Wacky Weather! poster (e.g., People wearing bathing suits and standing in the snow with the caption, "The people are surprised because it is snowing at the beach.")

MOTIVATION: Review objectives with class in English and let students discuss what they mean. Review weather vocabulary with visuals. Have students quick draw.

PRESENTATION: Introduce the writing task and model how to extend "I like _____" with a *because* clause to add details. Model with wind. Have students practice with a partner asking questions and completing "I like wind because _____/I don't like wind because _____" statements.

PRACTICE: Distribute index cards and have students write a similar sentence using one of the six weather terms (rain, hail, snow, ice, mist, or fog). [Check on newcomer students.] Arrange students for the Conga Line activity, using their cards. Debrief Conga Line afterwards. If desired, students can edit their sentences.

APPLICATION: Have students create a Wacky Weather! poster. Show sample. Explain that groups will be assigned a form of precipitation to depict in a wacky or unusual way. They will write a caption for the picture, using a sentence with *because*. Have the class generate some terms and phrases for the six precipitation words and list on the board as a reference. [Try to put newcomers in groups with another student who speaks the same home language.]

REVIEW & ASSESSMENT: Monitor the posters and the captions. Review objectives. Have students self-assess 1, 2, 3 for each objective. (1 finger I know it well, 3 fingers I don't understand.)

EXTENSION: In the next lesson, have students complete the posters and do a Gallery Walk activity. Students will put a dot sticker on two posters that they think are the wackiest. Assess the posters for content and language.

He said, "Let's think, what do our objectives mean? Who can explain them? Look at the verbs in our objectives. What does *distinguish* mean? That's a high school word. Tell a partner." The students spoke softly in pairs and then several raised their hands.

"It means to tell them apart," said one young girl.
"Can anyone add on?" asked Mr. Bryce.
"To tell how rain and snow are different," responded a boy.
"Right" replied Mr. Bryce. "And what does our language objective tell us?"
"We are going to write today," said another boy.

Mr. Bryce extended this, "Yes. We will write sentences with the word *because*. Our sentences will give us more information, more details about our opinions. Who can remind me what an opinion is?" Several children replied.

Mr. Bryce began the first activity. He asked two students—one an English learner, the other a native English speaker—to find the word cards about precipitation on the word wall pocket chart that they had been studying. The children selected *rain, hail, snow, ice, mist,* and *fog* and brought the cards to him. He posted them across the board and checked that the students remembered the words by having six volunteers come up and quick-draw a picture of the water form next to the word.

Next, he explained the task. The students were to choose one of these words and write a sentence on an index card using the word. Using an electronic document reader, he displayed a sentence frame they could use: "I like _____ because _____." and reminded the students that they were going to write sentences with details—with more information.

He then revealed the first part of the sentence.

I like wind

He said, "This tells you one thing, but you want to know more. Why do I like wind?" He revealed the next word.

I like wind because ____.

He asked a few volunteers to suggest a reason. He acknowledged their ideas and then revealed the rest of the sentence.

I like wind because the leaves dance.

Mr. Bryce explained that using *because* gives more details. It can tell why something happened or why someone likes something. He asked the students to take turns asking their partners if they like wind and telling why or why not. As children conversed, he moved among the three pairs with the newcomer students and checked on their comprehension and ability to formulate the question and response.

Mr. Bryce next distributed index cards and gave the students a few minutes to write their own opinion sentences, again helping the newly arrived children. Then, he asked them to stand and form two rows (A and B), facing each other, to perform a Conga Line. At his signal, the students took turns reading their cards to their partner in the opposite row. At the next signal, the students in Row A took one step to their left and faced a new partner in Row B. Mr. Bryce repeated this process two more times and then had the students return to their seats. Because the students were familiar with the activity, the process took only eight minutes. He asked students to share one idea they heard. He also asked if any of the students had changed their sentences after reading it to a partner. Two students explained how they improved their idea based on feedback from a classmate. He gave the class two minutes to edit their sentence if they wanted.

Mr. Bryce introduced the next activity. In heterogeneous groups of four, the children would design a Wacky Weather! poster. They would choose a form of precipitation to depict in a wacky way. Then, they would write a caption for the picture, using a sentence with *because*. He showed a sample poster of people wearing bathing suits and standing in the snow. The caption read: "The people are surprised because it is snowing at the beach." He asked the students to generate some wacky weather ideas related to the six precipitation words that he listed on the board.

He then assigned a type of precipitation to each of the six groups, giving the less familiar types (*mist, fog*) to groups with more proficient students. He told them that they could choose one of those ideas or think of a new one in their groups. They should visualize the scene before sketching a draft. He informed the materials managers of each group that once they had finished a draft poster on scrap paper, they could come to him for chart paper and markers to create the final poster. He stated that he expected they would complete the posters the next day.

When time was up, the class went over the objectives and students indicated how well they had learned each one, rating them by showing 1, 2, or 3 fingers (1 = I know the concept well). Mr. Bryce explained that they would finish the posters the next day and display them in a Gallery Walk. The children would have a chance to choose the ones they liked best.

Check your understanding: On the SIOP form in Figure 7.4, rate Mr. Bryce's lesson on each of the Practice & Application features.

FIGURE 7.4 Practice & Application Component of the SIOP® Model: Mr. Bryce's Lesson

4	3	2	1	0	N/A
20. **Hands-on materials and/or manipulatives** provided for students to practice using new content knowledge		**Few hands-on materials and/or manipulatives** provided for students to practice using new content knowledge		**No hands-on materials and/or manipulatives** provided for students to practice using new content knowledge	

4	3	2	1	0	N/A
21. Activities provided for students to **apply content and language knowledge** in the classroom		Activities provided for students to **apply either content or language knowledge** in the classroom		No activities provided for students to **apply content and language knowledge** in the classroom	

4	3	2	1	0
22. Activities integrate all **language skills** (i.e., reading, writing, listening, and speaking)		Activities integrate some **language skills**		Activities do not integrate **language skills**

? Reflect and Apply

Click here to explain your ratings for Mr. Bryce's lesson on each of the Practice & Application features.

Ms. Hannon

Ms. Hannon greeted her second graders when they returned from lunch and reviewed the day's objectives on weather precipitation terms by asking the students questions about types of weather and weather words. The children copied the objectives in their notebooks:

> **Content objective:** We will identify types of precipitation: *rain, hail, snow, ice, mist,* and *fog.*
>
> **Language objective:** We will write words and phrases that describe weather.

Ms. Hannon divided the class into six groups, each with at least one native English speaker and one English learner. She pointed out the six concept maps posted on chart

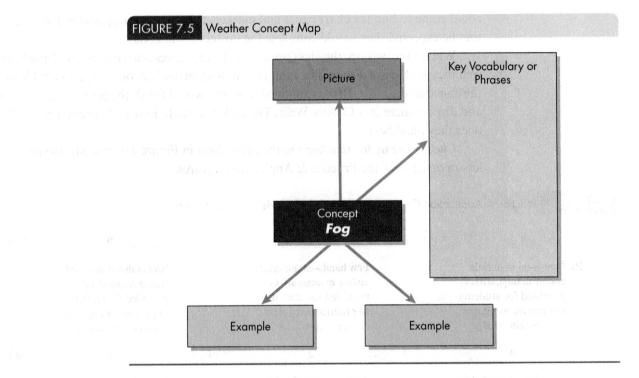

FIGURE 7.5 Weather Concept Map

paper around the room and explained the task. Each group would receive a concept map (see Figure 7.5). They would have five minutes to complete it and then they would place their maps back up on the walls. Next, they would move around the room in a Carousel fashion, with each group having two or three minutes at each map to add ideas before moving on to the next map at her signal. "Do you remember how we did the Carousel when we studied animals?" she asked, and most of the students responded "Yes."

Ms. Hannon distributed the concept maps to the student groups and they began work. As she circulated, she noticed that the children had many things to write down for some maps, like those for snow and rain, but less for others. She hoped that the Carousel activity would generate more ideas. After the allotted time, she had the groups post their maps and begin the Carousel. She reminded them that when a group reached a map, the students were to discuss their ideas, and then the recorder would add to the concept map. She noticed that her two newcomers stood back from their groups, however, not contributing anything.

After about 15 minutes, the groups returned to their original map, and she asked the reporter from each group to read what was written. This process started well, but after the first two maps, the students began to fidget. To maintain order, she ended this reading aloud after the third group finished and had everyone sit down.

She told the students that for the next activity they would write about their favorite type of weather. She told them to think of the six types of precipitation they studied and asked them to choose one. In a paragraph they were to write what they liked about that type of weather and why. They could use the words and ideas on the concept maps. The students worked on this task for about 10 minutes, although some of the English learners, including her two new students, struggled to write even one initial sentence. She talked to several of these students individually to get them started. When the time for science ended, she told the class to complete the paragraph for homework.

Check your understanding: On the SIOP form in Figure 7.6, rate Ms. Hannon's lesson on each of the Practice & Application features.

FIGURE 7.6	Practice & Application Component of the SIOP® Model: Ms. Hannon's Lesson

4	3	2	1	0	N/A
20. **Hands-on materials and/or manipulatives** provided for students to practice using new content knowledge		Few **hands-on materials and/ or manipulatives** provided for students to practice using new content knowledge		No **hands-on materials and/or manipulatives** provided for students to practice using new content knowledge	

4	3	2	1	0	N/A
21. Activities provided for students to **apply content and language knowledge** in the classroom		Activities provided for students to **apply either content or language knowledge** in the classroom		No activities provided for students to **apply content and language knowledge** in the classroom	

4	3	2	1	0
22. Activities integrate all **language skills** (i.e., reading, writing, listening, and speaking)		Activities integrate some **language skills**		Activities do not integrate **language skills**

? Reflect and Apply

Click here to explain your ratings for Ms. Hannon's lesson on each of the Practice & Application features.

Discussion of Lessons

20. *Hands-on Materials and/or Manipulatives Provided for Students to Practice Using New Content Knowledge*

Ms. Devereaux: 0

Mr. Bryce: 4

Ms. Hannon: 3

- **Ms. Devereaux's** lesson was primarily an application activity, but it was evident by the outcome that her students, in particular the English learners, needed some practice time first. This lesson received a score of "0" for practice using new content knowledge. The class didn't review the weather terms other than *rain* and *hail* with Ms. Devereaux's props. The fact that the students didn't recall *hail* without considerable prompting should have indicated to her that they were not ready to jump into a broadcasting activity. Further, there were no occasions for students to practice descriptive words that they might associate with different types of weather and there was no targeted support for her newcomer students.

- **Mr. Bryce's** lesson received a "4" for hands-on practice with new content knowledge. Knowing that his second graders didn't like to sit at their desks for long periods of time, he planned the Conga Line technique. He also carefully paired his newcomers with advanced learners to support their understanding of the weather concepts. First, he had students practice writing sentences using a *because* clause (which had been modeled) and a precipitation term. The students thought of a term they preferred and wrote the sentence independently. Then, they took turns reading their sentences to partners as they moved in the Conga Line.

- **Ms. Hannon's** lesson received a score of "3" for hands-on practice. Her concept map activity offered the students a chance to review and organize information they had learned about types of precipitation. It was hands-on and kinesthetic, which is beneficial with young children, especially after lunchtime. The students focused on one type initially and then had a chance to review other groups' work and add to their maps. The activity had to be cut short during the reporting stage, however, because the students lost concentration when the activity lasted too long. Also, the newly arrived students were not actively engaged.

21. *Activities Provided for Students to Apply Content and Language Knowledge*

Ms. Devereaux: 1

Mr. Bryce: 4

Ms. Hannon: 2

- **Ms. Devereaux's** lesson received a "1" for application of language and content knowledge. Although she had an interesting plan to have the students act as weather broadcasters, she did not prepare them well for the role. She asked a few students to talk about a weather report they'd seen on the television news, but she provided most of the details. Also, she did not make sure all the students were familiar with that type of broadcast. If she had shown a brief video clip, she would have modeled the activity for the students and thus given them a greater chance at being successful. Doing so might have helped her meet the language and content objectives. As it was, no attention was given to the language objective. No practice time was devoted to reviewing adjectives that could be used with weather terms.

- **Mr. Bryce's** lesson received a "4" for this application feature. After the Conga Line practice with the new sentence structure and the precipitation terms, he had students apply their language and content knowledge by creating a poster. The second graders enjoyed doing something amusing—in this case, designing a Wacky Weather! poster. It gave them a chance to consider characteristics of weather that are unexpected and also prompted them to write another sentence using a *because* clause. This activity used hands-on materials and had students working in small groups so that those with stronger academic language skills could support those with weaker ones. Mr. Bryce also checked in with the newcomer students to help them accomplish the assigned tasks.

- **Ms. Hannon's** lesson received a "2" for activities that apply language and content knowledge. She asked students to write a paragraph about their favorite type of precipitation, which would have been a good application task if it had been executed well. Unfortunately, Ms. Hannon did not scaffold the writing process. She provided no model paragraphs, nor did the students, as a class or in a group, brainstorm ideas or list information that could be included. The newly arrived students would have really benefitted from modeling. Her instructions were delivered only orally and the language objective was implicit, not explicit. The concept maps had information the students could draw from, but because they remained on the walls, the students did not make much use of them. When the English learners were unable to do the task well, she did not adjust her plan and pull them aside to work in a small writing group with her. This situation was an obvious opportunity for her to differentiate instruction for the English learners. Instead, she talked to them one by one. Finally, she moved the completion of the task to a homework assignment, which was unlikely to yield success for the children learning English as a new language if they were not sure how to complete the task in class.

22. *Activities Integrate All Language Skills*

Ms. Devereaux: 2

Mr. Bryce: 3

Ms. Hannon: 3

- **Ms. Devereaux's** lesson received a "2" for integrating all four language skills. The students focused only on listening and speaking as they prepared and then delivered their weather reports. No reading was required; even if some students wrote notes about what they intended to say, it was not part of the instructions to the children.

- **Mr. Bryce's** lesson received a "3" for integrating all four language skills in the lesson. The second graders had multiple opportunities to listen and speak (during the Conga Line, while at work in their groups, when the class was generating ideas for the poster) and to write (the *because* sentence and the poster caption). There was less reading in this particular lesson, although the children did read the precipitation word cards, the ideas listed on the board, and their sentences aloud. In the next lesson, they will do a Gallery Walk activity whereby each group posts its poster and the students circulate on their own to view them and read the captions. Students will put a dot sticker on two posters they think are the wackiest.

- **Ms. Hannon's** Concept Map/Carousel activity prompted students to practice all four language skills because they had to discuss ideas for the map and record those ideas, read what others had written on their maps and extend the ideas, and then listen while some students spoke during the reporting phase. The paragraph writing task was also intended to apply writing skills to the science topic. The lesson received a "3" on this feature of the SIOP component, however, because the reporting phase of the Carousel and the paragraph writing were not well accomplished.

Watch this video of a fourth-grade math lesson on equivalent fractions to see how manipulatives help the students learn the content concept. How do the manipulatives engage the students? In what way does the teacher's demonstration build knowledge?

(For more examples of lesson and unit plans in science for grades K–12, see Short, Vogt, and Echevarría, 2011b)

Teaching with Technology

After talking with the teachers and discussing the lessons you read about in the Scenarios earlier in the chapter, our tech integrator, Ms. Palacios, offered some technology suggestions to enhance the teachers' lessons.

Screencasting. Ms. Palacios suggested that Ms. Devereaux incorporate *screencasting* to enhance her lesson's broadcasting activity. Screencasting apps or programs, available on both computers and laptops, allow students to record their voices over images or other content on a screen. These programs also let the students annotate the images by drawing on them, which is very similar to how a television meteorologist might circle or highlight sections of a weather map. Ms. Palacios gave one caution—that the teacher consider using a larger room, the hallway, or the library for such an activity. The built-in microphones on many types of devices pick up a considerable amount of background noise that would include other students recording screencasts. Headsets with microphones were another option.

Ms. Devereaux adjusted her planned lesson for the next day to reteach and add the screencasting activity. She would do more review of the precipitation terms along with adjectives and then students would use the new technology tool to connect to the key concepts from the day before and also practice their oral presentations.

At the start of the next lesson, Ms. Devereaux introduced the screencasting app on the classroom iPads. She showed children how to screencast, using the state map she had marked to indicate a weather event and playing the audio that she had recorded the night before. She told the students they would prepare a map too and record their weather broadcasts using a screencasting app. She reviewed the weather terms and asked the class to generate some related adjectives, which she wrote on the board. She encouraged the children to use some of these adjectives in their broadcasts.

During this process of recording screencasts, Ms. Devereaux realized that the tool was valuable in numerous ways.

1. It offered students the opportunity for instant feedback. Immediately after recording, the children could listen to and evaluate their products. They could re-record. The students were motivated to improve not only their pronunciation and volume but also the quality of their broadcasts.

2. The tool was flexible. The students could take photos of their maps using the iPad's camera, save images from the Web, or create original illustrations using the built-in drawing tools.

3. Screencasting made assessment easier. Ms. Devereaux could periodically evaluate her students' oral language abilities. She recognized the value in listening to the students' speech multiple times. Screencasting allowed her to hear and assess the children with more than a single conversation.

4. The screencast could become part of an assessment portfolio where children could listen to various projects they had recorded throughout the year and discover how they improved over time.

5. Screencasting could also be leveraged to create instructional videos to be posted on a class Web site or shared with parents or other teachers.

Screencasting Products: *Explain Everything, DoodleCast Pro, ShowMe, ScreenChomp, Jing, Screencast-o-matic, Screencastify* (similar but worth mentioning: *Book Creator* app)

Note: Due to the constantly evolving nature of the Internet, it is a challenge to ensure that all of the links and Web services listed here are updated and functional when you read the technology sections. While specific tools or services may appear in the narrative, we have also included the general term for each tool. If a specific service does not work or is no longer available, search with the general term for the tool and you should be able to find a comparable Web site.

Check Your Understanding

Click here to check your understanding of the concepts in Chapter 7, Practice & Application.

Summary

As you reflect on this chapter and the impact that practice and application has on learning, consider the following main points:

- Students need practice and application of newly acquired skills to ensure mastery of content concepts. Be sure to offer multiple opportunities for them to do so with any new learning.

- You should plan a variety of hands-on activities and materials, including manipulatives and movement, to enable students to forge connections between abstract and concrete concepts in a less language-dependent way.

- When you create application activities to extend learning, be sure to relate the activities to both the language and the content objectives.

- Because students have different preferred learning styles, when teachers use different modalities for instruction and encourage students to practice and apply new knowledge through multiple language processes, they have a better chance of meeting students' needs and furthering both their language and content development.

Discussion Questions

1. In reflecting on the learning outcomes in the content and language objectives at the beginning of the chapter, are you able to:
   a. Identify a variety of ways for students to enhance their learning through hands-on practice?
   b. Create application activities that extend the learning in new ways and relate to language or content objectives?
   c. Design activities that integrate different language skills as students practice new content knowledge?
   d. Discuss the importance of linking practice and application activities to specific lesson objectives?

2. Compare and contrast the following two teachers' approaches to teaching a lesson on nutrition.
   a. One teacher's approach involves a lecture, a diagram of the USDA's Food Plate, and a list of appropriate foods for each group. Students are then tested about their knowledge of the percentages of each food type they should eat at a meal.
   b. The other teacher's approach begins with each student maintaining a food diary for a week. Copies of the Food Plate are distributed and explained, and all students must analyze their food consumption according to the national recommendations. With a partner, students must design a nutritionally sound weekly menu for each day of the following week, and they must be prepared to defend their food choices to peer group members.

   Which approach to teaching this content concept is most appropriate for English learners? How do you know? Be as specific as you can.

3. One way to ensure practice and application of new knowledge is through project-based learning. Develop a unit project that students can work on incrementally as the series of lessons progresses over several days or weeks. Identify the steps to completion that students will accomplish in each lesson of the unit. Try to collaborate with another teacher (e.g., classroom teacher and ESL/ELD teacher) to ensure targeted support for English learners. Plan a culminating presentation or performance that will enhance language practice.

4. English learners benefit from the integration of reading, writing, listening, and speaking during every lesson. What adjustments and techniques can a teacher use to provide successful experiences for students with limited English language proficiency while they read, write, listen, and speak about new information they are learning? Include specific activities and examples in your answer.

5. Elementary teachers are responsible for incorporating rigorous state **standards**, such as the **Common Core** and Next Generation Science, in their instruction. How is it possible to provide direct application and hands-on practice for lessons? What can teachers do to alleviate the conflict between "covering the content" and giving English learners time to practice the language along with the content?

6. Using the SIOP lesson you have been developing, write some activities for students to practice and then apply the key language and content concepts.

CHAPTER 8

Lesson Delivery

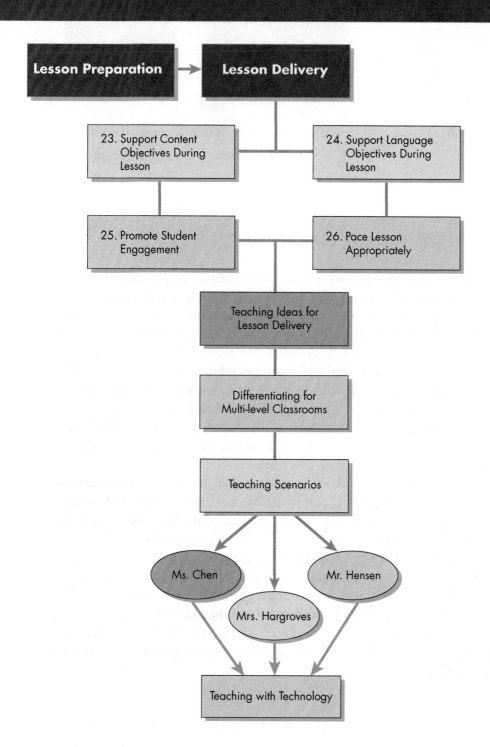

Learning Outcomes

After reading, discussing, and engaging in activities related to this chapter, you will be able to meet the following **content** and **language objectives**.

Content Objectives

Monitor lessons to determine if the delivery is supporting the objectives.

Determine how lesson preparation influences lesson delivery.

Generate activities to keep **English learners** engaged.

Language Objectives

Discuss characteristics of effective **SIOP** lesson delivery.

Explain how a focus on a lesson's objectives can aid in pacing.

Evaluate a situation in which a lesson plan is not enacted successfully and explain what might have gone wrong and what could be improved.

Stretch Photography/Blend Images/Alamy Stock Photo

■ Background

In Chapter 2, we explained the importance of carefully designing lessons with English learners in mind. Good preparation is the first step in delivering a lesson that leads to student learning, but those lessons need careful implementation as well. In the Lesson Delivery component, we monitor the success of a lesson in helping students meet objectives. Some lessons unfold as planned; however, some go awry, even if the plan is well written. Activities might be too easy or too difficult for the students. The lesson might be too long or too short. A student might ask an interesting but tangential question, and the ensuing class discussion consumes 10 unexpected minutes. The Lesson Delivery component of the SIOP Model reminds teachers to stay on track, and in this chapter we provide some guidance for doing so.

This chapter addresses the way a lesson is delivered, how well the content and language objectives are supported during the lesson, to what extent students are engaged in the lesson, and how appropriate the pace of the lesson is to students' ability levels. You will see that this chapter parallels Chapter 2, Lesson Preparation, because the two components are closely related. The effectiveness of a lesson's delivery—the level of student participation, how clearly information is communicated, students' level of understanding reflected in the quality of their work—often can be traced back to the preparation that took place before the students entered the classroom. We will meet the teachers from Chapter 2 again in the Teaching Scenarios and discuss how their level of preparation was executed in their lesson delivery.

> ▶ Watch this video of Kendra Moreno, a third-grade teacher and SIOP coach, as she discusses how the SIOP Model has improved her planning and delivery of lessons for English learners.

SIOP® FEATURE 23:
Content Objectives Clearly Supported by Lesson Delivery

As we discussed in Chapter 2, content objectives must be stated orally, and they must be written and displayed for students and teachers alike to see, preferably in kid-friendly language. The objectives serve to remind everyone of the focus of the lesson and to provide a structure to classroom procedures.

The **No Child Left Behind Act** raised the level of accountability in K–12 classrooms and the **Every Student Succeeds Act** continues the call for academic rigor. Teachers are expected to post objectives tied to state standards, and principals expect to see them. We caution against any inclination to list the standard in an abbreviated form, like CC.W.2.2 (for a Grade 2 writing standard), as an objective. It would be meaningless to the students. For young learners it may appear as gibberish; for older students, it is something to ignore. Further, a standard is conceptualized at the level of knowledge broader than that taught in an individual lesson plan.

Schmoker (2011) calls for more focus in classroom instruction. He proposes "simplicity, clarity and priority" regarding learning goals. He recommends "whole class lessons focused on a clear learning objective in short instructional 'chunks' or segments, punctuated by multiple cycles of guided practice and formative **assessment** ('checks for understanding')" (pp. 20–21). We know that written objectives guide learning and help students stay on task. SIOP teachers who attend to their lesson objectives make sure there are times during the lesson when some explicit instruction takes place that targets the objectives and other times when students have the opportunity to practice and make progress toward meeting those objectives. Throughout the lesson and at its conclusion, the teacher and learners can evaluate the extent to which the lesson delivery supported the content objectives.

SIOP® FEATURE 24:
Language Objectives Clearly Supported by Lesson Delivery

Language objectives are an important element of effective SIOP lessons. Teachers and students benefit from having a clear language objective that is written for them to see and that can be reviewed during the lesson. The objective may be related to a CCSS standard for language such as "Today we will find synonyms for closely related verbs" (*cf.* NGA Center and CCSSO, 2010, p. 27); or it may be related to teachers' scope and sequence of language skills that their own students need to develop, such as "Students will describe the three states of matter orally."

No matter which language objective is written for a lesson, this feature reminds teachers that they need to address it explicitly during instruction. For example, if first graders in a language arts lesson have to "retell a story" as their language objective after listening to *Lon Po Po* (Young, 1996), then we expect the teacher will spend some time teaching or reviewing *how to retell* with the children, perhaps using a different but familiar story, and also reviewing sequence terms. In sum, we will not promote students' **academic language** development without explicit instruction in elements of academic language and without students having multiple opportunities to practice and use the language in a variety of contexts.

SIOP® FEATURE 25:

Students Engaged Approximately 90% to 100% of the Period

This feature in the Lesson Delivery component calls on teachers to engage students 90% to 100% of the class period. By this we mean that the students are paying attention and on task. It does not mean they need to be highly active (writing, reading, moving) the entire time, but they are following the lesson, responding to teacher direction, and performing the activities as expected. When children are in groups, all are participating. Lessons where students are engaged less than 50% of the time are unacceptable. This situation tends to occur when teachers have not provided clear explanations of the assignment or have not **scaffolded** the process well. If students don't know what to do, they will find something else to do, and then misbehavior or inattention ensues.

Engagement, motivation, and **cultural responsiveness** are important factors in successful lessons—for both **native** and **non-native English-speakers** (Nieto & Bode, 2008; Turner, 2007). When learners are actively engaged, they are involved in tasks that challenge them and allow them to gain confidence. Younger learners prefer tasks with objects they can manipulate or movements they can perform, as well as puzzles and learning games. They will listen to or try to read texts above their level in subject matter that captures their imagination. Offering choices in tasks, texts, or partners, setting up learning centers, and differentiating instruction are key methods for accommodating classrooms with English learners of varying proficiency levels as well as those with both native English speakers and English learners. It is often through such modifications to a curriculum that student engagement can be enhanced (Buck, Carr, & Robertson, 2008).

English learners are the students who can least afford to have valuable time squandered through boredom, inattention, socializing, and other off-task behaviors. Time also is wasted when teachers are ill prepared, have poor classroom management skills, spend excessive amounts of time making announcements and passing out and collecting papers, and the like. The most effective teachers minimize these behaviors and maximize time spent actively engaged in instruction. English learners who are working to achieve grade-level competence benefit from efficient use of class time. If they have had uneven schooling experiences or a high degree of absenteeism, they are then further disadvantaged by inefficient use of class time.

There are three aspects to student engagement that should be considered during a lesson: (1) allocated time, (2) engaged time, and (3) academic learning time[1]

Watch this video of a kindergarten teacher who explains how she keeps her students engaged in class. In what ways are the challenges she faces similar to those found in classrooms of the upper grades? In what ways are they different?

---

[1]For a discussion of various researchers' understanding of engagement, use of time in the classroom, and relationship to student achievement, see McIlrath & Huitt (1995) and chapter 8 of the *Handbook on Effective Implementation of School Improvement Grants* (Perlman & Redding, 2011).

| FIGURE 8.1 | Amount of Academic Learning Time in Typical Instruction and SIOP® Instruction |

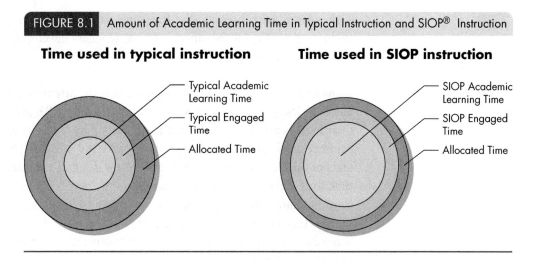

1. *Allocated time* reflects the amount of time spent studying a topic (e.g., math versus reading) and a given academic goal. As we have discussed throughout this book, effective SIOP teachers plan for and deliver lessons that are balanced between teacher presentation of information and opportunities for students to practice and apply the information in meaningful ways.

2. *Engaged time* refers to the time students are actively participating in instruction during the time allocated. The engaged time-on-task research has consistently concluded that the more actively students participate in the instructional process, the more they achieve. Instruction that is understandable to English learners, that creates opportunities for students to talk about the lesson's concepts, and that provides hands-on activities to reinforce learning captures students' attention and keeps them more actively involved.

3. *Academic learning time* focuses on students' time spent on a task that is related to the content and language objectives they will be tested on. Creative, fun activities are not effective if they are unrelated to the goals of the lesson. Equally, "skill and drill" exercises on discrete points (e.g., past tense verb endings) and endless multiple-choice practice tests are not engaging, and reduce academic learning time as students "tune out." SIOP teachers maximize the academic learning time for their students by being explicit in their expectations and making certain that their English learners understand which content and language objectives will be the focus of upcoming assessments. Figure 8.1 illustrates these points.

SIOP® FEATURE 26:

Pacing of the Lesson Appropriate to Students' Ability Levels

Pacing refers to the rate at which information is presented during a lesson. The pace of the lesson depends on the nature of the lesson's content, as well as the level of students' background knowledge. When working with English learners, it can be challenging to find a pace that doesn't present information too quickly yet is brisk enough to maintain students' interest, especially when a variety of English proficiency levels are represented in the same classroom. Finding an appropriate pace requires practice, but becomes easier as teachers develop familiarity with their students' language and academic skills.

- *Elementary teachers* know, for instance, that the attention span of a kindergartener or first grader is much shorter than that of a fifth grader, so they adjust their lessons accordingly. A practice activity may last only 5–7 minutes in the primary grades, whereas in the upper grades it could last 15–20. Elementary teachers also chunk important information in smaller conceptual units and allot time for processing the material taught in the new language between the chunks. Because many elementary schools have a less rigid bell schedule than secondary schools (i.e., children do not typically switch classes at a set time per period), on some days, teachers may extend certain lessons beyond the normal time frame to cover the material.

- *Content area teachers in some intermediate schools* may teach only certain subjects and at specific periods of time. However, teachers cannot move so quickly through the curriculum that they leave their English learners behind. They may need to carefully select the important concepts to focus on and adjust their planning accordingly.

> Watch this video of a teacher explaining how she paces her lessons to accommodate different learning needs and ability levels in a heterogeneous class of kindergarteners. How do you address pacing?

- *ESL teachers* can augment instructional time. When a grade-level or subject-area teacher collaborates with the ESL teacher, both language and content instruction benefit. The ESL teacher might introduce key vocabulary and build background on topics before they are covered in the content classroom, or provide additional practice and application activities afterward. This supports the student's content learning. It also supports the acquisition of academic English and motivates English learners because they address grade-level material in the ESL class and understand more in the content class. (See Lacina, Levine, and Sowa, 2006 for examples of ESL–elementary classroom teacher partnerships.)

In classes with both native English speakers and English learners, it can take some effort and experience to pace the lessons well. Investing in a slower pace in the first quarter of the year to teach instructional routines and task procedures, along with related language frames, reaps dividends later because students then know the classroom practices and have better academic language skills. Most children enjoy working with peers, so collaborative learning projects with tasks geared to proficiency level and interest are beneficial. On occasion, interdisciplinary projects could be planned, such as a project on Volcanoes Around the World that involves science (e.g., the steps in forming a volcano and leading to an eruption), math (calculating temperature of lava and rate of lava flow), geography (e.g., locations of active and dormant volcanoes), and reading (e.g., stories about volcanoes). Such projects not only spiral the content but also introduce and reinforce key language terms, functions, and sentence structures, allowing English learners time over the course of a unit and across several content areas to develop the academic English skills they need for success.

One important fact to remember is this: If a teacher wastes five minutes of a class period daily, perhaps by starting the lesson late or finishing early, over the course of 180 days, 15 hours of instructional time will be lost! Often, simple routines can help the pacing: a basket by the door where students deposit homework when they enter or class work when they leave, a materials manager for each group of desks who distributes books or worksheets to everyone in the group, routinized activities that do not need directions explained each time, and/or a classroom timer set to ring when an activity should end. If you finish a lesson early, don't let students chat or do homework; instead, play a game to review vocabulary or key concepts. We need to maximize the way we use time when we have English learners in the classroom.

Linking Lesson Preparation and Lesson Delivery

Now that you have read about the features of this component, you can see that strong, thoughtful lesson preparation is critical to effective lesson delivery. Without the planning necessary to make the content truly comprehensible for the diversity of learners in your class and without considering which aspects of academic English they need to learn or practice in a given lesson, your lesson may fly over their heads, and a day during which they could be learning may be wasted. Figure 8.2 shows how the features of Lesson Preparation influence the features of Lesson Delivery.

Supporting Content and Language Objectives.   The content and language objectives written on a lesson plan need to be presented and practiced in a way to support student learning. Not all students may master the objectives the first day they encounter them, but all students should make progress toward mastery. Just writing a content and a language objective on your lesson plan is not sufficient; you have to "deliver" on those learning goals in class.

When presenting a SIOP lesson, remember the objectives should be:

- **Observable**—an observer can see or hear students participating in activities related to the learning targets.
- **Measurable**—there is a way to determine whether students met the objectives, or made progress toward meeting them.
- **Assessable**—the objectives are reviewed at the end of the lesson, and the class determines if they were met.

FIGURE 8.2   The Relationship Between Lesson Preparation and Lesson Delivery

Lesson Preparation	*Lesson Delivery*
Plan for content objectives ⟶	Support learning of content objectives
Plan for language objectives ⟶	Support learning of language objectives
Address grade-level content	
Use supplementary materials	Promote student engagement
Use adapted content as needed	Pace the lesson appropriately
Plan meaningful activities with language practice	

Some teachers fail to write out and discuss the objectives with the students because the process is time consuming. We acknowledge that it takes time to determine good objectives for every lesson, but the investment in writing them and then teaching to them pays off in student achievement (Short, Fidelman, & Louguit, 2012).

Some teachers complain they can't write objectives in a manner that students will understand or are worried that they will not complete all of the objectives for the full lesson. Both of these arguments are easily addressed by practice and support. A SIOP coach or a fellow SIOP teacher can give guidance on writing student-friendly objectives. The students themselves will confirm if they understand the objective when it is presented in class. And as a teacher gets to know his or her students, writing for their age and proficiency level becomes easier.

If the problem is that the objectives are not being met by the end of the lesson, then the teacher and students can determine why as they review them. It may be that the activities took longer than planned or class discussions veered off track, but the presence of objectives can actually impose discipline on the pacing of each lesson. If a teacher consistently does not meet objectives, however, it may also be that too many objectives have been planned for the time frame of the lesson, or that time is lost during activity transitions or at the start or end of the period.

The following suggestions may help:

- Reread the objective chorally with the class during the lesson to re-focus the children.
- Ask students what they have done up to that point in the lesson that relates to the objective.
- Pause periodically and have students rate how well they are meeting the objective (e.g., Thumbs up ~ I got it. Thumbs down ~ I am lost. Thumbs sideways horizontally ~ I'm getting there).

Watch this video of a third-grade math lesson. How does the lesson help students meet the content and language goals that the teacher had prepared?

Promoting Student Engagement.   In Figure 8.2 on the prior page, you can see how student engagement depends in large part on what content you teach, how you adapt that content, what supplementary materials you include, and what activities you ask students to perform. English learners are motivated to learn what their English-speaking peers are learning. Sometimes, in order to provide that grade-level content in a comprehensible way, you will have to adapt it. You will decide whether the adaptation is through the texts they are reading (e.g., utilizing a book with a lower reading level) or the tasks they are being asked to do, but if the material is at or a little above their level of understanding, they can be engaged with it. And of course, the planned lesson tasks play a critical role in student engagement. "Skill and drill" exercises turn everyone off—English speakers and English learners alike. Creative activities related to the objectives that include plenty of language practice do not.

Pacing SIOP Lessons.   We can't discount how the choices we make when planning a lesson affect the pacing. If students use supplementary materials and the content has been adapted to their levels, they are better able to move through the materials with occasional support from the teacher. If, however, those materials are above their level, the class discussions and activities will get bogged down. More time will be spent explaining what something means than applying or extending the information. Likewise, if the activities are not meaningful or clearly explained, children may exhibit off-task behavior or dawdle while trying to complete the assigned work.

Teaching Ideas for Lesson Delivery

The following ideas can help a teacher check on student progress toward meeting objectives and promote student engagement:

- **Think-Pair-Share** (Lyman, 1981). This tried and true technique is an excellent means for teachers to monitor student understanding of the content or language objectives. Instead of asking questions to the whole class and calling on two or three students to respond, the teacher asks everyone to think of an answer or respond to a prompt, and tell it to a partner. Then, the teacher calls on some students to share their responses with the whole class. This relatively simple and quick technique gives *all* of the students a chance to think and speak about the topic, instead of just two or three. A variation called *Think-Pair-Square-Share* asks partners to pair up (square = four students) before the whole-class sharing out.

- **Chunk and Chew** (see Short, Vogt, & Echevarría, 2011, pp. 66–68 and Vogt & Echevarría, 2008, p. 164). To maintain the goal of chunking new information, this technique encourages teachers to pause after every 10 minutes of input to give students time to talk with a partner or in a small group about what they have just learned. In SIOP lessons, the student talk is carefully structured by the teacher in the lesson plan with specific prompts and/or sentence starters.

- **Roam and Review.** At the end of a lesson, the teacher may pose a reflection question (e.g., "What was the most important thing you learned today?" or "What surprised you in our studies today?") and have students think silently, then stand and roam the classroom, discussing their ideas with classmates. This is unstructured; students can roam and talk to whomever they choose.

- **Podcasts and Screencasts.** Students prepare a two- to three-minute oral summary on a topic that they have selected or that the teacher has assigned. They rehearse and then record it on a podcast or an audio file for use on the class computer. Screencasts are similar but allow students to record over images or other content on a screen.

- **TV Talk Show.** A wonderful project that addresses content and language objectives (particularly listening and speaking ones) and engages students is the TV talk show (Cloud, Healey, Paul, Short, & Winiarski, 2010; Herrell & Jordan, 2008). Small groups plan a talk show on a topic with multiple parameters that they have studied. One student is the host and interviewer; others are the guests. For example, after the class has studied extreme weather phenomena, one guest might be an expert on hurricanes, another on blizzards, a third on earthquakes, and a fourth on tornadoes. The talk shows could be videotaped for later viewing and analysis by the teacher or the students. The analysis might look at how well the students spoke, used key vocabulary, responded to host questions, and so forth.

- **Writing Headlines.** By writing a newspaper headline, students try to capture the essence of a day's lesson, section of a text read, video watched, or information presented orally. Teachers can encourage students to use descriptive language and focus on word choice to create compelling headlines.

- **E-Journals and Wiki Entries.** The teacher can have students write in an e-journal daily or once a week to reflect on what they have been learning. At the end of a unit, the teacher might ask students to write an online entry for a class wiki that presents key information on a topic being studied.

■ Differentiating Ideas for Multi-level Classes

As teachers deliver their lessons, they need to be cognizant of the learning process all of their students experience. The following ideas will help teachers differentiate activities among multi-level students as well as gauge which students are meeting the objectives and which need more assistance.

- **Pro-Rate the Task.** The product of a task need not be exactly the same across all students. The more advanced students are in their knowledge or language skills, the more they can be asked to do. In classes with both English learners and English speakers, a teacher might explain to English speakers that even if an assigned task for the English learners seemingly has less required output, it still is as cognitively challenging as the task for English speakers because the English learners are doing the work in a language they are still mastering.

- **Radio Advice Line.** The teacher can select two or three of the more advanced learners to be the radio show host. Other students can draft questions they have on a topic, perhaps as a review or as a way to seek clarification. They "call in" to pose the questions to the radio hosts, who take turns responding. The teacher can monitor what questions are being asked and which students seem to have a good or poor sense of the lesson's objectives.

- **Projects.** One of the best ways for students to work at their own ability level, language level, and interest level is through projects. Projects also offer a meaningful way to determine whether students can apply information they are learning, and they enable students to tap into their creativity, too.

- **Leveled Questions.** Teachers can modulate the questions they ask students according to their **levels of language proficiency**. If they plan them in advance, they can still ask questions that generate higher-order thinking but the language of the question can be simplified.

- **Homogeneous Small Group Rotations.** Teachers can cluster their students into homogeneous small groups based on their ability with the skill or topic (e.g., solving math problems, reading grade-level text) and set up three centers in the class: one for teacher-directed instruction, one for independent work, and one for small group or partner activities. The teacher always starts with the group of students who need the most support, and the instruction provides the foundation for their later small group and independent work. The other groups, when working with the teacher, might have their independent and small group work reviewed, might have some skill clarified, or might have an enrichment opportunity. In this set-up, the teacher can offer more assistance to those who are struggling while letting the others work on their own. (See Vogt, Echevarría & Washam, 2015, pp. 158–159, for a detailed description of how the rotation process can be designed.)

- **Scale of Student Mastery.** The teacher can keep track of how students are progressing in mastering the language and content objectives of a unit. At set moments of time (e.g., Day 1, Day 3, Day 7), the teacher records a score for the students' progress. The score might be on a continuum of 1–5, with 5 being mastery, or it might be a symbol like −, √, and +.

The Lesson

The Gold Rush (Fourth Grade)

We revisit the teaching vignettes described in Chapter 2 in this chapter. The fourth-grade classrooms of teachers Ms. Chen, Mrs. Hargroves, and Mr. Hensen, you may remember, are located in a suburban elementary school with heterogeneously mixed students. English learners represent approximately 30% of the student population, and the children speak a variety of languages. The majority of the English learners are at the intermediate stage of English proficiency.

As part of the fourth-grade social studies curriculum, Ms. Chen, Mrs. Hargroves, and Mr. Hensen planned a unit on the California Gold Rush. The school district requires the use of the adopted social studies series, although teachers are encouraged to supplement the text with primary source materials, literature, and **realia**. The content topics for the Gold Rush unit include westward expansion, routes and trails to the West, the people who sought their fortunes, hardships, settlements, the discovery of gold, the life of miners, methods for extracting gold, and the impact of the Gold Rush. The content of this lesson covers the Oregon Trail, the Overland Trail, and the Route around Cape Horn. To address the Common Core standards for literacy in history, the teachers plan various ways to help students access the textbook.

Teaching Scenarios

To refresh your memory about each lesson on westward expansion and the Gold Rush taught by Ms. Chen, Mrs. Hargroves, and Mr. Hensen, we summarize them in the sections that follow. (See Chapter 2, Teaching Scenarios, for a complete description of the three lessons.) As you read, consider the SIOP Model features for Lesson

Delivery: meeting content objectives, meeting language objectives, engaging students 90% to 100% of the time, and pacing the lesson appropriately for students' ability levels.

Ms. Chen

Ms. Chen began the lesson on westward expansion by reading aloud the content and language objectives for the day.

Content Objectives

1. Students will use map skills to find and label the three main routes to the West.
2. Students will identify one or two facts about each of the three trails.

Language Objectives

1. Students will take notes to distinguish among the trails.
2. Students will categorize vocabulary terms.

After a whole-class brainstorming and List-Group-Label activity about why people leave their homes and move to new locations, Ms. Chen assigned most of the class a quick-write on the Gold Rush. She then provided a "jump-start" for the English learners who had very limited proficiency by introducing key vocabulary, passing around iron pyrite ("fool's gold"), looking together at a map of the trails west, and viewing several pictures of pioneers and Gold Rush characters.

Following this, Ms. Chen introduced the key vocabulary to the entire class. She asked students to use the names of the trails to try to determine their location on maps of the United States and Western Hemisphere and then worked with the class to locate the three trails on interactive whiteboard maps. Student groups practiced map skills and marked the routes on their own copies.

Finally, Ms. Chen distributed a scaffolded outline for taking notes on the chapter and modeled how to fill it in after a shared reading on the Oregon Trail section. The outline's headings ("Locations," "Characteristics," "Challenges," and "Advantages") provided an organizer for the information, and in groups, students began working together to fill in the outline. The lesson concluded with a review of the content and language objectives. Then, several students volunteered to report on a number of facts about each of the trails.

Check your understanding: On the SIOP form in Figure 8.3, rate Ms. Chen's lesson for each of the features in Lesson Delivery.

Mrs. Hargroves

Mrs. Hargroves began her lesson on the trails west by stating, "Today you'll learn about the Oregon Trail, the Overland Trail, and the Route around Cape Horn. We'll also be working on maps, and I want you to color the Overland Trail a different color from the color you use for the Cape Horn route. When you learn about the Oregon Trail, you'll complete the map with a third color. By the time you're finished, you should have all three routes drawn on the map using different colors." She held up a completed map for the students to see as an example.

4	3	2	1	0
23. **Content objectives** clearly supported by lesson delivery		**Content objectives** somewhat supported by lesson delivery		**Content objectives** not supported by lesson delivery

4	3	2	1	0
24. **Language objectives** clearly supported by lesson delivery		**Language objectives** somewhat supported by lesson delivery		**Language objectives** not supported by lesson delivery

4	3	2	1	0
25. **Students engaged** approximately 90% to 100% of the period		**Students engaged** approximately 70% of the period		**Students engaged** less than 50% of the period

4	3	2	1	0
26. **Pacing** of the lesson appropriate to students' ability levels		**Pacing** inappropriate to students' ability levels		**Pacing** generally appropriate, but at times too fast or too slow

? **Reflect and Apply**

Click here to explain your ratings for Ms. Chen's lesson on each of the Lesson Delivery features.

Following a brief lecture on westward expansion, Mrs. Hargroves directed students to the respective chapter in the text and also displayed it using the electronic document reader. Students looked at the illustrations, and she responded to questions they had. She began reading the chapter, and after a few minutes, she directed students to complete the reading independently. She circulated through the room, answering questions, helping with difficult words, and getting some of the students back on task. After 20 minutes, Mrs. Hargroves stopped the reading, distributed colored pencils and maps, and asked students to complete the maps with partners. When the maps were completed, she collected them and assigned a brief essay on the topic "If you had been a pioneer, which trail would you have chosen? Why?"

Check your understanding: On the SIOP form in Figure 8.4 on the next page, rate Mrs. Hargroves's lesson for each of the Lesson Delivery features.

Mr. Hensen

Mr. Hensen began his lesson by asking how many of the students had traveled to California. They discussed the various modes of transportation used by students who had visited the state, and then Mr. Hensen linked their responses to the travel modes of the pioneers. Following a video on the westward expansion, he introduced the key vocabulary for the day's lesson (Oregon Trail, Overland Trail, Route around Cape Horn).

FIGURE 8.4	Lesson Delivery Component of the SIOP® Model: Mrs. Hargroves's Lesson

4	3	2	1	0
23. **Content objectives** clearly supported by lesson delivery		**Content objectives** somewhat supported by lesson delivery		**Content objectives** not supported by lesson delivery

4	3	2	1	0
24. **Language objectives** clearly supported by lesson delivery		**Language objectives** somewhat supported by lesson delivery		**Language objectives** not supported by lesson delivery

4	3	2	1	0
25. **Students engaged** approximately 90% to 100% of the period		**Students engaged** approximately 70% of the period		**Students engaged** less than 50% of the period

4	3	2	1	0
26. **Pacing** of the lesson appropriate to students' ability levels		**Pacing** generally appropriate, but at times too fast or too slow		**Pacing** inappropriate to students' ability levels

? **Reflect and Apply**

Click here to explain your ratings for Mrs. Hargroves's lesson on each of the Lesson Delivery features.

Next, Mr. Hensen read aloud two paragraphs from the textbook chapter. He numbered students off into six groups, assigned different sections of the text to the newly formed groups, and engaged them in a Jigsaw reading activity for the remainder of the chapter. English learners were partnered with more proficient English readers for the Jigsaw activity. After the Jigsaw groups completed their reading, they regrouped to share what they had learned from the assigned text. At least one student from each of the Jigsaw groups was placed in the new home groups so chapter sections were fully covered. English learners had support from students with greater English proficiency.

Mr. Hensen then directed the students in their home groups to divvy up the three trails. Some students were asked to draw the Oregon Trail on a map; others were to draw either the Overland or Cape Horn trails. Their next task was to show the other students in their group how to locate, draw, and label the trails on their maps, using the map in the text and their reading as a guide. Mr. Hensen circulated through the room, assisting as necessary, while the students completed the mapping activity. At the lesson's conclusion, students were directed to pass in their maps. Those who had not finished were assigned the map task as homework.

Check your understanding: On the SIOP form in Figure 8.5, rate Mr. Hensen's lesson for each of the Lesson Delivery features.

4	3	2	1	0
23. **Content objectives** clearly supported by lesson delivery		**Content objectives** somewhat supported by lesson delivery		**Content objectives** not supported by lesson delivery

4	3	2	1	0
24. **Language objectives** clearly supported by lesson delivery		**Language objectives** somewhat supported by lesson delivery		**Language objectives** not supported by lesson delivery

4	3	2	1	0
25. **Students engaged** approximately 90% to 100% of the period		**Students engaged** approximately 70% of the period		**Students engaged** less than 50% of the period

4	3	2	1	0
26. **Pacing** of the lesson appropriate to students' ability levels		**Pacing** generally appropriate, but at times too fast or too slow		**Pacing** inappropriate to students' ability levels

? **Reflect and Apply**

Click here to explain your ratings for Mr. Hensen's lesson on each of the Lesson Delivery features.

Discussion of Lessons

23. *Content Objectives Clearly Supported by Lesson Delivery*

Ms. Chen: 4

Mrs. Hargroves: 1

Mr. Hensen: 3

We advocate for teachers to include content and language objectives in every lesson, and our research supports their value, especially for the English learners who need to have a clear, explicit understanding of what the teacher's expectations are for a lesson (Short, Echevarría & Richards-Tutor, 2011; Short, Fidelman, & Louguit, 2012). Recall that only Ms. Chen wrote her content and language objectives on the board and read them aloud for her students. While Mrs. Hargroves had a content objective (but no language objective) written in her plan book, she stated her plans for the day orally to her students, without clearly defining their learning objectives. Mr. Hensen had neither content nor language objectives written in his plan book, yet he appeared to have a clear idea of where he was going with his lesson. However, at the outset of the lesson, his plans may not have been clear for some students.

In this component of the SIOP Model (Lesson Delivery), we consider more than having the content and lesson objectives written in plan books and on the board. Rather, the focus here is on whether the actual lesson delivery matches the stated (or implied, in Mr. Hensen's case) objectives.

- From the beginning of the lesson, **Ms. Chen** had a clearly defined content objective, and her lesson delivery supported it. Her focus on the three routes to the West was supported by (1) activating students' prior knowledge about why people leave their homes and move to a new location; (2) engaging some students in a quick-write about the Gold Rush; (3) practicing map skills with the interactive whiteboard; (4) doing a shared reading of the textbook chapter; and (5) having students share facts about the three trails. The lesson was rated a "4" for supporting content objectives.

- In contrast, **Mrs. Hargroves's** lesson received a "1" on this feature. As you may recall, she did not write an objective on the board, and she hurriedly stated what she wanted the students to do for the lesson. What is also problematic about her lesson is that the coloring of the maps seemed to be what was important to her, rather than her confirmation that each student understood the information about the trails west. Students were expected to finish reading the chapter independently, which was most likely impossible for struggling readers and the English learners.

  Further, her lecture may have been difficult for her English learners to follow. The writing assignment, while a worthwhile topic ("If you had been a pioneer, which trail would you have chosen? Why?"), was not scaffolded, so it may or may not have been appropriate for her students, depending on their English proficiency and their ability to access the information in the text. Therefore, her lesson delivery did not support her intended content objective very well.

- Although **Mr. Hensen** did not state the objectives, they were implied and supported by his lesson. For example, at the end of the period, he asked several students to report on some differences among the trails; this initial feedback provided information about whether the students had met the day's objective. His constant monitoring and the various grouping activities provided additional information about who was meeting the objective and who was having difficulty. He might have added a quick group-response activity (pencils up/pencils down) to determine if all students understood the differences among the trails. Had Mr. Hensen written his objectives on the board and reviewed them with his students, his lesson would have received a "4" for this feature. Because he did not, his lesson received a "3" for supporting content objectives.

24. *Language Objectives Clearly Supported by Lesson Delivery*

    Ms. Chen: 4

    Mrs. Hargroves: 0

    Mr. Hensen: 2

    - **Ms. Chen's** lesson was rated "4" on this feature. Language objectives were clearly written and stated, and students had several opportunities to meet them. They categorized related terms in a List-Group-Label activity.

Ms. Chen built vocabulary and text understanding for the least proficient English learners with the jump-start mini-lesson. She also modeled reading aloud and completing a section of the scaffolded outline so students could in turn take notes themselves.

- **Mrs. Hargroves** did not write or state any language objectives. Although she did assign a reading and writing activity, the text was inaccessible for many of the students and the writing activity was difficult, if not impossible, for them to complete. Moreover, as we pointed out in Chapter 2, a language activity is not the same as a language objective. Her lesson received a "0" for supporting language objectives.

- **Mr. Hensen** did not write or state his language objectives, but as with the content objectives, they were implied as something to do with reading comprehension. He engaged students in a Jigsaw activity for reading the text, and then they returned to their home groups and explained what they had learned from the reading. His lesson received a "2."

25. *Students Engaged Approximately 90% to 100% of the Period*

Ms. Chen: 4

Mrs. Hargroves: 1

Mr. Hensen: 4

- **Ms. Chen** is an enthusiastic teacher who plans lessons that use each minute of class time to its fullest. As illustrated in the lesson, Ms. Chen spent time presenting materials, and she allowed students to work together. They eagerly participated in whole-group and small-group discussions, and Ms. Chen made sure they were on task. In addition, the content of the lesson was directly related to the district's **content standards** on which the students will be assessed at the end of the unit.

  Her lesson received a "4" for this feature because it met all the criteria for active student engagement: She maximized the academic learning time in an effective way, basing the lesson on the text, teaching outlining and mapping skills, providing opportunities for interaction and application of concepts, and so forth. Students were active and on task throughout, and the material was relevant to the assignment.

- Recall that **Mrs. Hargroves** read part of the text chapter aloud, which cut its substantial length. She then allotted 20 minutes for students to read the remaining portion of the text chapter. Not all students stayed on task. Some began talking among themselves, while others were trying to finish the reading. Overall, students were engaged less than 50% of the period. During Mrs. Hargroves's lecture on westward expansion, some students were disengaged except when she used the electronic document reader and discussed the illustrations and the trails on the map in the text. This lesson received a "1" for engaging the students.

- **Mr. Hensen's** students were actively engaged throughout the lesson. From the opening question about trips to California through the video and the Jigsaw activity, all students were held accountable for learning the material. During the map activity, students not only located and labeled a trail, but also were responsible for assisting each other in finding, drawing, and labeling the additional trails. This lesson was rated a "4" for this feature.

26. *Pacing of Lesson Appropriate to Students' Ability Levels*

Ms. Chen: 4

Mrs. Hargroves: 1

Mr. Hensen: 3

- **Ms. Chen** understood that the English learners in her class might need a slower pace than the native English speakers. Therefore, she provided a jump-start mini-lesson that enabled them to keep up with the whole-class activities. She also moved the pace along by doing a shared reading of the text. In this way, she adapted instruction for the English learners, and all students were able to work at roughly the same pace. The groups for the map activity included four to five students with both native English speakers and English learners who assisted one another as needed. Her lesson received a "4" for pacing.

- The pacing of **Mrs. Hargroves's** lesson was slow and monotonous at times, especially when she lectured, yet she covered material too quickly at other times. Many students were off task because of the problematic pace of the lesson. Her lesson received a "1" for pacing because it was inappropriate for the students' ability level—too slow to maintain interest and too quick for English learners to understand the information presented orally.

- **Mr. Hensen** included discussions, videos, a Jigsaw reading activity, group work, and mapping; some students, especially the English learners, may have felt a bit rushed to accomplish all of these tasks. However, he also provided scaffolding and did allow some students to complete their maps at home. The students participated well and understood most concepts. This lesson was rated a "3."

Watch this video of Kendra Moreno's third-grade lesson on distinguishing fact from opinion. How would you rate the lesson on the four features for Lesson Delivery? In what ways did it target the content and language objectives? At what point do you think the students met the objectives?

(For more examples of lesson and unit plans in social studies and history for grades K–12, see Short, Vogt, and Echevarría, 2011.)

Teaching with Technology

After talking with the teachers and discussing the lessons you read about in the Scenarios earlier in the chapter, our tech integrator, Ms. Palacios, offered some technology suggestions to enhance the teachers' lessons.

Timers: While reflecting on a few recent lessons where the activities ran behind schedule and the class had to rush to get ready for lunch, Ms. Chen asked Ms. Palacios about options for using alarms to better manage the time in her classroom. Ms. Palacios suggested the classroom iPad could help. Upon exploring the clock app that comes standard on the tablet (also called a native app), Ms. Chen discovered that she could set multiple alarms within one school day.

Looking over her daily class schedule, she set alarms for each section of the day that required the students to make the transition from one activity to another. While viewing the selection of different alarm sounds,

Ms. Chen also determined that she could use songs as the alarm alerts instead of the preset tones. She could choose songs of a certain genre or length according to the type of task in the classroom.

Ms. Chen brought these ideas to her colleagues, and they brainstormed adaptations for each of their routines. Mrs. Hargroves decided to use calm jazz music to indicate the end of independent reading time when students would return their materials and gather their reflection journals. Ms. Chen helped Mr. Henson to set alarms to mark "5 minutes to go" at the end of a lesson. These alarms helped them manage the pacing of the lesson, ensuring appropriate time for review, exit tickets, and other end of the lesson tasks.

Other terms for this type of tool: timer app, stopwatch, clock app with multiple alarms, alarm clock

Related products: *Timely* (Android), *Alarm Clock* (iOS), *Alarmed* (iOS)

Virtual Corkboard: Later in the Gold Rush unit, students work in groups to research the most important geographic locations during that time period. When students are conducting this type of research with the help of laptops, Mr. Hensen typically stops them after a period of time and conducts quick check-ins. He has the groups share discoveries and next steps for research and records that information on the whiteboard. These check-ins only take a few minutes but offer Mr. Hensen a chance to hear about his students' progress and offer support as needed. Additionally, the children can see and hear what other groups have discovered and have a reminder of their next actions for the project.

Unfortunately, after each social studies period, Mr. Hensen has to erase the information he collected during the class in order to use the whiteboard for other instruction. He thought about using a digital camera to capture the board after each class, but wondered if there were another technology tool that could help. Based on a recommendation from Ms. Palacios, he decided to try *Padlet*, a digital version of a corkboard. Much like a traditional corkboard, *Padlet* users can add or pin different links, images, and text to a shared wall that other users can see. Intrigued by this tool, Mr. Hensen shared the Web site with the other teachers, and they planned to use it as the classes continued research on important locations for the Gold Rush.

In order to launch the new tool, the teachers each created new *Padlet* "walls" and changed the background image wall to a map of California. The teachers posted the unique Web addresses for the class walls on their Web sites and gave the students a quick tutorial on how to access and use the tool. Next, the teachers assigned each group a particular location where gold was discovered. The teams investigated the location and then wrote short descriptions of the area and described its significance. Alongside the power of having students work collaboratively and share knowledge, each teacher had a useful artifact for reference, further instruction, and review of key concepts.

Other terms for this type of tool: backchannel, online corkboards

Related Products: *TodaysMeet, Edmodo, Popplet*

Note: Due to the constantly evolving nature of the Internet, it is a challenge to ensure that all of the links and Web services listed here are updated and functional when you read the technology sections. While specific tools or services may appear in the narrative, we have also included the general search term for each tool. If a specific service does not work or is no longer available, search with the general term for the tool and you should be able to find a comparable Web site.

 Check Your Understanding
Click here to check your understanding of the concepts in Chapter 8, Lesson Delivery.

Summary

As you reflect on this chapter and the impact of effective lesson delivery, consider the following main points:

- The importance of setting and meeting objectives cannot be overemphasized. Many teachers may feel comfortable having a general objective in mind and moving along with a lesson's flow, but that approach is not helpful for English learners.
- If you plan objectives, you have to teach to them. Delivering a lesson geared to objectives allows the teacher to stay on track and lets the students know what is important to focus on and remember.
- By incorporating a variety of techniques that engage students throughout the lesson, teachers not only give students opportunities to learn, practice, and apply information and language skills, but also help to ensure the students meet the lesson's objectives.
- An appropriate pace for a lesson is critical for English learners. Information that is presented at a pace suitable for native English speakers may render that information meaningless, especially for beginning English speakers. Finding the right pace for a lesson depends in part on the content of the lesson, students' prior knowledge about the topic, and differentiation. Effective SIOP teachers use instructional time wisely.

Discussion Questions

1. In reflecting on the content and language objectives at the beginning of the chapter, are you able to:
   a. Monitor lessons to determine if the delivery is supporting the objectives?
   b. List strategies for improving student time-on-task throughout a lesson?
   c. Generate activities to keep English learners engaged?
   d. Discuss characteristics of effective SIOP lesson delivery?
   e. Explain how a focus on a lesson's objectives can aid in pacing?
   f. Evaluate a situation where a lesson plan has not been enacted successfully and explain what might have gone wrong and what could be improved?

2. Reflect on a lesson that you taught or observed that did not go well. What happened? When did it go awry? Can you identify a feature in Lesson Delivery that might have caused the lesson to be less successful? Or a feature from another SIOP component? In retrospect, how might your delivery of the lesson have been improved?

3. Suppose three new children, all with **limited English proficiency**, joined a fifth-grade class midyear. The other students in the class include a few former English learners and native English speakers. What are some language objectives the teacher could write for each of the following content concepts?

   a. Discoveries during the Lewis and Clark Expedition
   b. Constitutional amendments during the Reconstruction

How might the teacher pro-rate the tasks associated with the language objectives to meet the different academic development needs of the students?

4. How does a teacher or supervisor determine whether a majority of students, including English learners, are engaged during a lesson? What techniques could be used to sustain engagement throughout the period? What should the teacher do if he or she senses that students are off task? Why is sustained engagement so critical to English learners' academic progress?

5. Look over a SIOP lesson you have been working on. Write down the amount of time you expect each section (or activity) of the lesson to take. Teach the lesson and compare your expectations with reality. Do you have a good handle on pacing? If not, review your lesson for tightening or extending. What can you add or take away? List some routines you could implement in your classroom so you will do less talking, or less distributing and collecting. Share with a colleague your ideas for maximizing time-on-task and student engagement.

CHAPTER 9

Review & Assessment

Learning Outcomes

After reading, discussing, and engaging in activities related to this chapter, you will be able to meet the following **content** and **language objectives**.

Content Objectives

Identify the challenges in assessing content and language learning of students with limited English proficiency.

Create a plan for formative **assessment** for the linguistically diverse students in your classroom that will provide you with the information you need to make sound instructional decisions during lesson planning.

Determine opportunities for reviewing and assessing key vocabulary and key content concepts during and at the end of your lesson plan.

Language Objectives

Provide effective academic oral and written feedback to **English learners** during a lesson.

Compare and contrast characteristics of informal and formal assessments.

Explain the meaning of the following assessment terms: *form ative* and *summative assessment*; *authentic assessment*; *multidimensional indicators*; *multiple indicators*.

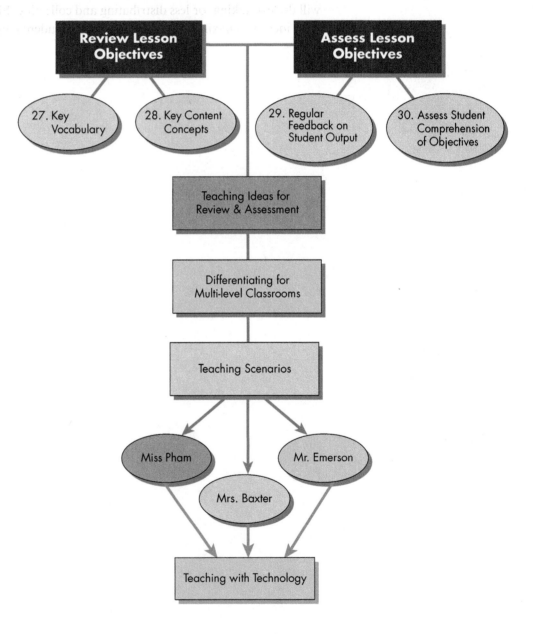

Over the years, teachers have asked us why Review & Assessment is the eighth component in the SIOP Model. Usually the question is preceded by a comment such as, "Shouldn't the assessment of students' strengths and needs come before any instruction?" Our response is always, "Of course!" Clearly, assessment and instruction are inextricably linked. Effective SIOP teachers use assessment findings to plan their lessons according to students' needs and strengths, review students' progress toward meeting content and language objectives throughout each lesson, and evaluate how effectively their lessons have been delivered. Therefore, in this chapter, we focus on a very important aspect of teaching: assessing your students' strengths, needs, experiential backgrounds, and language proficiencies. Please note that it is beyond the scope of this book to provide detailed information about specific language, literacy, and general academic assessments that are appropriate for English learners. ●

FatCamera/E+/Getty Images

■ Background

Watch this video to hear Dr. MaryEllen Vogt describe informal assessment. As you read, consider the types of assessments that are described. Which do you already use and which might you want to add? https://www.youtube.com/watch?v=8xpYxnPbat0

Throughout this book, we have discussed many aspects that impact the achievement and language development of English learners. Essentially, these are the instructional features of the SIOP Model. Each of these features, along with other factors (e.g., classroom management and teacher effectiveness), determines the classroom context for English learners and your other students.

Perhaps it is not surprising that effective SIOP teachers consider the context of the classroom when planning opportunities to review and assess children's comprehension of a lesson's language and content concepts. These teachers plan so that their students eventually will reach independence in application of these concepts (as depicted in Figure 5.1 in Chapter 5). It is likely that some children will need substantial vocabulary and concept review, along with additional practice before they reach the goal of independence. With ongoing assessment throughout a lesson, teachers are able to ascertain who is ready to move on and who needs further reteaching, review, and practice.

Classroom Context and the Review & Assessment Component

When considering classroom context as you plan for review and assessment throughout a lesson, think about each of your students, both those who perform satisfactorily and those who struggle with your lessons. For children who are having little or no difficulty, there probably is a close match between the classroom context and their needs. However, for those students who struggle, there could be a mismatch between the classroom context and their academic and language needs. In a classroom with data-driven, culturally responsive instruction that is guided by periodic review and assessment, students are more likely to achieve an instructional match.

The following questions may help you locate possible areas of match and mismatch between your students and your classroom context (Vogt & Shearer, 2016). Keep in mind that there may be other areas of instruction that you need to explore (e.g., classroom management and room organization), but the questions that follow can get you started. For those of you who are in schools with **Response to Intervention** (RTI), these questions can be part of the progress monitoring process (see Echevarría, Richards-Tutor, & Vogt, 2015, for more information).

1. *Is there a match between the student and the classroom context? If so, what needs to be continued?* Informal measures such as teacher observation and in-class assignments provide information, as well as more formal measures, such as unit exams and standardized test scores.

2. *Is there a mismatch between the student and the classroom context?* Again, observations and student work samples are a start; additional information, such as English proficiency level, information about L1 language and literacy acquisition, and the student's educational history may be needed.

3. *If there is a mismatch, what could create a better match for the student?* Check the student's reading skills in English and other academic abilities to determine areas of mismatch with instructional materials; ascertain if the student understands task directions and what might be preventing success with in-class and out-of-class assignments.

4. *How can you tell whether the changes you are making are achieving a closer match for the student in question?* Use formative assessments such as teacher observation, in-class and out-of-class assignments; and summative assessments, such as periodic measures of language and literacy proficiency, end-of-chapter or unit tests.

When review and assessment are linked to instruction that targets a lesson's content and language objectives, it is easier to answer these questions. Just as students need to know what the objectives are for a lesson, they also need to be informed about how they will be assessed on them. Both formative and summative assessments of children's progress provide information about whether it is appropriate to move on or whether it is necessary to reteach and review (Bean, 2014; Kapinus, 2014).

Formative and Summative Assessment

Historically, educators have blurred somewhat the line between assessment and evaluation, generally using the term *evaluation* for both formative and summative judgments. The teacher's role in evaluation was primarily as an "evaluator," one who conveyed a value on the completion of a given task. This value was frequently determined from the results of periodic quizzes, essays, reports, oral or written presentations, or tests that served as the basis for report card grades in elementary and secondary schools.

Today, however, educators distinguish between assessment and evaluation (Lipson & Wixson, 2013; Vogt & Shearer, 2016). *Assessment* is defined as the gathering and synthesizing of information concerning students' learning, while *evaluation* is defined as making judgments about students' learning. The processes of assessment and evaluation can be viewed as progressive: first, assessment; then, evaluation. Formative and summative assessments that are multifaceted and attentive to the various contexts of a student's life (e.g., home, school, **culture**, **native language**, and literacy development in both **L1** and **L2**) provide relevant and practical information to the teacher about how to design appropriate and culturally relevant content and language instruction for linguistically and culturally diverse students.

Informal Assessment

The assessment measures generally used by teachers to gather data about their students' academic and language performance in the classroom tend to be *informal*. Other qualities of effective classroom assessments include: they are *authentic*, *multidimensional*, with *multiple indicators* that reflect student learning, achievement, motivation, and attitudes (Lenski, Ehlers-Zavala, Daniel, & Sun-Irminger, 2006; Malloy, Marinak, Gambrell, & Mazzoni, 2013; McLaughlin, 2010; O'Malley & Pierce, 1996; Vogt & Shearer, 2016). These qualities are described as follows:

- **Informal assessment** involves on-the-spot, ongoing opportunities for determining the extent to which children are learning content. These opportunities may include teacher observations, anecdotal reports, teacher-to-student and student-to-student conversations, quick-writes and brainstorming, or any number of tasks that occur within regular instruction. They are not intended to be graded or evaluated according to set criteria.
- **Authentic assessment** is characterized by its application to real life, where children are engaged in meaningful tasks that take place in real-life contexts.
- **Multidimensional assessments** are usually part of authentic assessments because teachers use different ways of determining student performance. These may include written pieces, student and parent interviews, video clips, observations, creative work and art, discussion, performance, oral group responses, and so forth.
- **Multiple indicators** are specific pieces of evidence students complete that are related to a lesson's content and language objectives. They provide a teacher with several ways of looking at a student's **language proficiency** and content knowledge. For example, a student may demonstrate proficiency with a language

Watch this video to see and hear teachers talk about how they assess their students. Dr. MaryEllen Vogt also explains the relationship between assessment and instruction. What information about your students do you need to gather before you begin planning lessons for them?

Watch this video and see how Bianca Nache, a sixth-grade Dual Language teacher, encourages reflection about portfolio evidence collected over the years. In what ways do portfolios demonstrate the characteristics of informal assessments?

objective through a piece of writing, active participation in a group activity, or insightful questions asked during discussion. The teacher thus has more than one piece of evidence indicative of progress toward mastery of a particular objective.

This approach to informal assessment is congruent with RTI (progress monitoring), the **Common Core State Standards** and **Next Generation Science Standards** (high academic standards for all students), culturally responsive teaching, and, of course, the SIOP Model.

Formal Assessment

Formal assessments can be formative (to achieve a baseline or beginning point) or summative (to determine progress over time). One type is standardized and norm-referenced, and it ranks students' scores in comparison to a normed group of students. Another type of standardized measure is criterion-referenced. These tests measure students' performance as compared to a set of academic skills or objectives. Generally, formal assessments are used by schools and districts to look at academic trends over time and to identify subgroups of students who are performing extremely well or unsatisfactorily.

So, what does this have to do with the SIOP Model? English learners are at a particular disadvantage when they are taking a standardized test that presumes the test taker is proficient in English. One important thing that you, as a teacher of English learners and struggling students can do is to explicitly teach, model, and provide practice with the general academic words (cross-curricular/process/ function) that are described in Chapter 3. These are frequently the types of words that are used in standardized test questions, and they're the ones that English learners and struggling readers often find difficult.

SIOP®

SIOP® FEATURE 27:

Comprehensive Review of Key Vocabulary

During class, English learners receive 20 to 30 minutes or more of input in a new language. Unless the teacher takes the time to highlight and review key information and explicitly indicate what is important to learn, English learners and other students may not understand the lesson's focus. Children, especially those at the early stages of English acquisition, devote considerable energy to figuring out at a basic level what the teacher is saying or the text is telling them. These students are much less able to evaluate which pieces of information and which vocabulary terms are important to remember, given all the input they receive. That is why the teacher must take the time to review key vocabulary and key concepts throughout a lesson and as a wrap-up at the end.

We know that children with robust vocabularies are more successful in school. Therefore, it stands to reason that teachers would want to revisit and review key words each day and make sure students are adding to their vocabulary knowledge. Researchers differ on the number of exposures that children need to internalize words at a deep level, but all agree the number is high, over 40 and up to 160! Repetition isn't simply about having students write words repeatedly. Rather, it is important to use the words in a variety of ways during a lesson, referring to the words on the board, on charts, on word walls, and so forth. Encourage children to use the key words or terms in their discussions and hold them accountable for doing so: "I noticed that in your group each of you used our three key words in your conversation!"

There are varied techniques for effectively reviewing academic vocabulary with children during a lesson, including the following (see the Teaching Ideas section in this chapter for additional ways to provide vocabulary review):

- Use analogies, the process of relating newly learned words to other words with the same structure or pattern. For example, previously we gave the example of the root *photo* (meaning light) in a lesson on photosynthesis, and suggested referring students to other words with the same word root (e.g., *photography*, *photocopy*). Use the Common Word Roots chart in Chapter 3 (Figure 3.2) to assist you in teaching the process of analogy.

- Point out multiple meanings, such as those that have one meaning in conversational English (e.g., "The laundry *product* I'm looking for in the supermarket is one that includes both detergent and bleach"), and another that is discipline-specific (e.g., "The *product* of 25 × 4 is 100").

- Point out synonyms and antonyms for key vocabulary, when possible. Four-corner charts can be helpful for review when they include (1) the vocabulary word, (2) a synonym, (3) an antonym, and (4) "what the word is not." For example: (1) *democracy*, (2) *republic*, (3) *dictatorship*, (4) *totalitarian state*. A math example is: (1) *fraction*, (2) *portion*, (3) *whole*, (4) *a whole number*.

- Draw students' attention to how words are used in various contexts (pragmatics), because they may differ across cultures and languages. For example, a discussion of human reproduction is appropriate in an upper grade science lesson but may be very inappropriate at a family gathering. As we move throughout our day, whatever the context, we continually adjust our speech, facial expressions, and body language accordingly. It's important to talk to children about how language is used in different contexts and how something that might be appropriate in one context may be inappropriate in another.

- As mentioned previously, repetition of academic words and terms has benefits to students. Provide multiple exposures to new terminology to build familiarity, confidence, and English proficiency. Words and concepts may be reviewed through paraphrasing, such as "Remember to *share your ideas*; that is, if you have something you want to say, tell it to the others in your group." Another example of a paraphrase (and contextualized sentence) is *"The rabbit nested in the deep grass, by turning in small circles until there was a soft spot to rest."* Paraphrasing as review provides an effective scaffold for English learners, especially after words and phrases have been previously defined and discussed in context.

- A final vocabulary review is also beneficial at the conclusion of a lesson. Children might share understandings with a partner while you check their explanations; write a quick definition (in their own words) on individual whiteboards and hold them up to show you; do a quick match of words and definitions on an interactive whiteboard; write two or three sentences including the words on tickets-out cards that you collect as they leave the classroom (or before transitioning to a new subject); and so forth. What is important is that you plan for the final review just as you plan for the other activities in your lessons.

Please remember that effective review does not include the "dreaded word list" described in Chapter 3, or the equally ineffective assignment of having children write vocabulary or spelling words 10 (or more) times each. Research findings are very clear—isolated word lists and dictionary definitions alone do not promote vocabulary and language development. Rather, provide as many exposures as possible to new, important words through meaningful tasks that incorporate multiple modalities: reading, writing, illustrating, acting out, rhyming, and so forth.

SIOP® FEATURE 28:

Comprehensive Review of Key Content Concepts

Just as it is important to review key vocabulary periodically throughout a lesson and at its conclusion, it is also essential that English learners have key content concepts reviewed both during and at the end of the lesson. Understandings are scaffolded when you stop during a lesson and briefly summarize key content concepts covered up to that point. For example, in a lesson on cloud formations, you might say something like, *"Before we move on, let's remember how the Cumulus cloud looks. See, it is fluffy like cotton on the top, but it's flat on the bottom, as you can see in this photograph. Another type of cloud is the Stratus cloud. What do you think it might look like?"* This type of review is usually informal, but it must be stated carefully so children know exactly what to recollect. Ideally, the review leads into the next section of the text or to a discussion: *"Let's read this next section to learn about the Stratus cloud, which is very different from the fluffy Cumulus cloud."* Or, if predictions about an upcoming section of a text have been made or hypotheses about an experiment developed, teachers can refer to these afterward and confirm or disconfirm them when the time is right. This teaching-reviewing-assessment process should be ongoing throughout the lesson.

One of the great benefits of having posted content and language objectives is that you can, at any time, refer to them during a lesson. We all know how easy it is to "bird-walk," a term coined by teaching expert, Madeline Hunter (1982). An eager child's hand goes up, you call on him or her, and for the next several minutes you hear a story about something that is only marginally (or not at all) related to the topic at hand. Other students chime in with their experiences, and before you know it, the bell rings! By referring, as needed, to your objectives throughout the lesson, it's much easier to stay on track, and students begin to distinguish between contributions that may or may not be appropriate to the lesson's topic.

One favorite end-of-lesson review technique of SIOP teachers is Outcome Sentences. A teacher can post sentence starters on the whiteboard or chart paper, such as:

I wonder . . .

I discovered . . .

I still want to know . . .

I learned . . .

I still don't understand . . .

I still have a question about . . .

Something I will remember is . . .

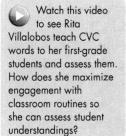 Watch this video to see Rita Villalobos teach CVC words to her first-grade students and assess them. How does she maximize engagement with classroom routines so she can assess student understandings?

Students take turns selecting and completing an outcome sentence orally or in writing on a tickets-out slip of paper. They can also confer with a partner before responding.

A more structured review might involve children summarizing with partners, writing in a journal, or listing key points on the interactive whiteboard. Toward the end of the lesson, a final review helps English learners assess their own understandings and clarify their misconceptions. Students' responses to a review can guide a teacher's decisions about what to do next, such as administering a summative assessment or, if needed, additional reteaching and assessing.

SIOP® FEATURE 29:

Regular Feedback Provided to Students on Their Output

Periodic review of language, vocabulary, and content enables teachers to provide specific oral and written academic feedback to students to clarify confusing points and to correct misconceptions and misunderstandings. Effective feedback for English learners:

- **Supports and validates.** In order for English learners to receive teacher feedback, they must be able to provide output. Quiet, shy, and unconfident children can go unnoticed, and sometimes their coping strategies mask weaknesses in language production. Throughout this book we have suggested ways to encourage student interaction and participation. Perhaps the most important way to do so is through being supportive and validating when students do interact, participate, and engage meaningfully.

- **Is specific and academically oriented.** While support and validation are certainly important, how we do both is critical. For some teachers, it's almost a habit to say, "Good job!" or "Nice work!" or "Well done!" While these comments feel good when children hear them, they don't provide much information about what was good about the job or nice about the work. English learners and students who struggle need very specific academic feedback, and for some, it is best if it is given in private. They need to know exactly what they did that's right so they can do it again and/or build upon it. For example, compare the praise phrase, *Good job!* to the following: *Enrique, I noticed that you had a question about one of*

Background

the items on the study guide. I saw you look back at the chapter for help, and then I noticed you turned to Felipe with a question. Those were good strategies to try! And, thanks, Felipe for helping Enrique with his question! Of course, not all comments need to be this detailed; just remember to be specific about what you have observed and communicate it directly to the student(s) involved. Also, remember that immigrant children who have attended school with a classroom context different from that of their current school benefit greatly from specific feedback as they are learning to negotiate their new educational environment.

- **Focuses on both content and language.** Many English learners plateau at the intermediate level, in part because they are exited prematurely from ESL programs, but also because when they are exited they don't have teachers who continue to develop academic language while teaching content. Therefore, encourage these students to use increasingly sophisticated words, phrases, and sentences by modeling their use in your teaching and during teacher-student conversations. Remember to continue to provide temporary scaffolds, as needed, as you did when these students had lower levels of English proficiency.

- **Includes modeling.** Teachers can model correct English usage when restating a student's response: *"Yes, you're correct that the Stratus, that rhymes with "flat-us," are clouds that are flat and dull and grey."* Overly correcting English learners' grammar and pronunciation tends to shut them down. Therefore, simply restating the sentence with correct form (or pronunciation, as illustrated in the example), while validating, provides feedback that is instructive and helpful. However, if you want children to start using the correct pronunciation or sentence structure, you need to dedicate some time to teaching and practicing pronunciation and sentence structure. An explicit focus on form makes more of a difference than a teacher-corrected restatement of a student's response (Saunders & Goldenberg, 2010).

- **Includes paraphrasing.** Paraphrasing also supports children's understandings and validates answers when we add, "Is this what you were thinking/or saying?" after a paraphrase. If you know that some children are only able to respond to questions in one or two words, you can extend their responses in complete sentences: *"Yes, Nimbus are rain clouds. They're also dark and grey, are full of water, and they are spread far and low in the sky."* Of course, always give students a chance to elaborate on their own first thoughts, with phrases such as, "Tell me (or us) more about that."

- **Includes facial expressions and body language.** A nod, smile of support, pat on the shoulder, or encouraging look can take away fear of speaking aloud, especially for young children or those English learners who are beginning to develop English proficiency. At the same time, a teacher's facial expressions and body language conveying frustration, impatience, or ambivalence speak volumes to a student who is trying to learn challenging content and a new language at the same time.

- **Can be provided by students for each other.** Partners or groups can discuss among themselves, giving feedback on both language production and content understanding to each other, and then report back to the whole class. The teacher can facilitate effective feedback by providing appropriate modeling of how it is done. Sentence frames also assist students in getting started: "What you said was really interesting, because ____"; "One word that you used that helped me understand your point was ____"; "One question I have about what you said is ____."

SIOP® FEATURE 30:

Assessment of Student Comprehension and Learning of All Lesson Objectives Throughout the Lesson

The purpose of this section is to offer suggestions for SIOP lessons and recommendations for how to assess the degree to which individual children meet or are making progress toward meeting a lesson's content and language objectives. In SIOP lessons, assessment takes place at any time during a lesson, and teachers are encouraged to assess students whenever they have an opportunity. Examples include:

1. The lesson begins with an activity that activates children's prior knowledge and experience, and provides an opportunity to build background for those who need it. This presents a great opportunity to assess those who may lack background information about the topic and/or have difficulty with the content and language concepts in the forthcoming lesson.

2. During the lesson, while children are practicing and applying the lesson's key vocabulary and concepts, there is another opportunity to see who may need more review or reteaching. Informal assessments, including teacher observation, spot-checking with individuals, using group response techniques (such as thumbs-up/-down, individual whiteboards), conversations with children about their progress, and so forth can be used.

3. At the end of the lesson, SIOP teachers assess which students have met the content and language objectives by reviewing them with individuals and with the class. This final review of all content and language objectives is critically important. It provides you with information to guide the planning of your subsequent SIOP lesson. See suggestions for soliciting student responses to this review in the Teaching Ideas and Teaching with Technology sections of this chapter.

Some teachers who are learning to implement the SIOP Model express concern about having varied assessments throughout a lesson, in part because of the perceived amount of work it takes to create them, and also because some believe it is unfair if children are not assessed equally. While acknowledging this concern, we also believe that for English learners, assessment adaptations must be made if teachers are to ascertain accurately the extent to which lesson objectives and standards are met. Often, English learners do know the information on which they are being assessed, but because of language proficiency issues, including vocabulary, reading, and writing, they are unable to demonstrate their knowledge fully.

Therefore, to the extent possible, students should be assessed individually to determine if learning has taken place. In sheltered classes in particular, where students may have different **levels of language proficiency**, the value of assessment becomes readily apparent (Vogt, 2014). If teachers gather baseline data on what their students know and can do with the content information before instruction occurs, and then assess what they know and can do during a lesson and after its conclusion, they can identify student growth more accurately.

Teaching Ideas for Review & Assessment

Review and assessment can be accomplished with individual, group, or whole-class activities. Group response techniques quickly inform a teacher about how well each student is progressing, and they are especially sensitive to the needs of English learners.

- **Handheld Devices.** There are a number of electronic resources available that can be used to provide informal review and assessment. Handheld devices, such as clickers and classroom performance tools, can be used in many ways, including recording student responses, learning about concepts in measurement, practicing multiplication tables, and taking notes, to name a few. Teachers can use clickers for a group review: children hold their clickers and respond to a prompt with multiple-choice options. The computer records and displays the class results, along with the correct answer. Teachers can pose yes/no, true/false, or multiple-choice questions, and children respond anonymously. The data are quickly collated and displayed so the teacher and students can see the number of correct responses and determine how many students might need reteaching.

- **Word Study Books.** Word Study books can include a student's own illustrations as mnemonics (pictures to remember word meanings and usage), and/or rebus pictures for definitions (difficult words are represented by simple drawings, usually provided by the teacher). As young children are learning to write, they can use their own Word Study books as references for spellings and meanings of the words to which they have had exposure. Usually, words are presented in alphabetical order, but some teachers prefer to have them organized by sounds (such as open/long sounds or closed/short sounds, initial consonants, blends, digraphs, etc.), content topics, and so forth.

- **Vocabulary Journals.** Somewhat similar to Word Study books, Vocabulary Journals are intended for particular subject areas (Rothenberg & Fisher, 2007). One section of the journal might focus on multiple-meaning words. For example, a math journal might have four columns labeled with "Word," "Common Definition," "Math Definition," and "Where I Found It." The student might fill in the columns as follows: Word: *prime*; Common Definition: *The best*; Math Definition: *A number that can only be divided by itself and 1*; Where I Found It: *In our textbook*. Students' Word Study books or Vocabulary Journals provide the opportunity to review words any time they wish.

- **Non-Print Review.** Children should be encouraged to review and practice words and idioms in non-print ways as well. Students may draw a picture to depict a concept or to remember a word. They may demonstrate the meaning through physical gestures or by acting out several words within the context of a role-play. The technique works especially well with children in grades pre-K–2, and can be used for phonemes (sounds) as well as words.

- **Games.** Playing *Pictionary, Bingo, Jeopardy,* and charade-like games at the end of a lesson can stimulate an engaging review of newly learned vocabulary and key concepts.

- **Rubrics.** Often, **rubrics** (such as the SIOP protocol) are used to ascertain a developmental level of performance for a particular goal, objective, or standard. For example, on a developmental rubric, student performance may be characterized as "emergent," "beginning," "developing," "competent," or "proficient." Other rubrics may communicate evaluative information, such as "inadequate," "adequate," "thorough," or "exceptional." Whichever rubric is used, the results of assessment and evaluation are often shared with other interested stakeholders, such as parents and administrators, as well as with the children themselves.

- **Group Response Techniques (GRT).** GRT enable you to immediately determine each individual student's understanding during an assessment activity with the whole class. Here are examples of some ways to generate group responses (see the Teaching with Technology section in this chapter for more ideas):

  ◆ *Thumbs Up/Thumbs Down (or Pencils Up/Down for older students).* Used to signal *agree/disagree*; *yes/no*; *true/false*; students indicate *I don't know* by making a fist or holding a pencil, in front of the chest, and wiggling it back and forth.

  ◆ *Number Wheels.* A low-tech alternative to handheld devices, Number Wheels provide the teacher with immediate information about students' comprehension of content concepts. A number wheel is made from tag board strips (5" × 1") held together on a metal ring fastener. Each strip has a number printed on it, with 0 to 5 or 0 to 10, or a–d, depending on your needs and children's ages. Students use their individual number wheels to indicate their answers to questions or statements that offer multiple-choice responses. Possible answers are displayed on the board, chart paper, or pocket chart, and the teacher asks the questions or gives the statements orally. For example, if you were teaching a lesson on possessives, you could write the following on the board:

    1. boys

    2. boy's

    3. boys'

    Each student holds a number wheel and you say, *"Show me the correct use of the word 'boys' in the following sentences. Remember that you can show me a '0' if you don't know the answer. 'The little boy's dog was hungry and was barking.' Think. Get set. Show me."* At the "Get set" cue, students find the strip with the number 2, and hold the number wheels in front of their chests. When you say, "Show me," they display their answers. They repeat the process as you give the next sentence. Be sure to give the cues (*Think; Get Set*) before giving the direction, *Show me!*

  ◆ *Response Boards.* Popular dry-erase boards and dry-erase pens are great to have on hand for group responses. Ask a question and students respond on their boards and then turn them to face you when you say, *"Show me!"*

Dry-erase boards (12" × 12") can be inexpensively cut from "bathroom tile board," available at home and building supply stores; laminated tag board or plastic insert sleeves also can be used in the same way.

◆ *Numbers 3, 2, 1 for Self-Assessment.* As an alternative to a simple yes/no response, this is a quick and easy way to have students self-assess the degree to which they think they have met a lesson's content and language objectives. Students simply indicate with one, two, or three fingers how well they think they met a lesson's objectives:

3 = I fully met (or can do) the objective.

2 = I'm making progress but I need more help (or practice) to meet the objective.

1 = I didn't (or can't) meet (or do) the objective.

Depending on how children indicate their understanding of a lesson's key concepts (the objectives), the teacher can reteach, provide additional modeling, group students for further instruction and practice, and so forth.

● **On-the-Spot Assessment.** This is another low-tech, but effective method of gathering on-the-spot information while observing children as they work independently or in groups. Put several pages of sticky address labels (3" × 5" or a size of your choice) on a clipboard. As you walk around the room and observe what a particular student is doing, jot brief notes on a sticky label, along with the student's name. At a later time, you can transfer the day's notes to students' assessment files by attaching them to pages used for this purpose. You will end up with a consecutive list of observation notes that can be used for parent, ESL, or IEP conferences, and/or for grading purposes. The great thing about this idea is that you don't have to transfer your notes by writing, or input anything into the computer (unless you want to).

● **Stock Market** (grades 3–6). Stock Market is great for an end-of-unit review prior to an exam because it provides the teacher with information about student misconceptions, factual errors, etc. It's also lots of fun!

1. Prepare *Monopoly* or other "play" money in denominations of 5, 10, 20, 50, 100. A variety of different play money templates are available on the Internet.

2. Generate content questions (some from an actual quiz or test you're going to give) so that you can assess your students' readiness to take the test. Mix challenging and easier questions so that you'll have at least 10–15 to choose from, depending on the grade you teach.

3. Also write some trivia questions of interest to the grade level of your students (such as the principal's first and last name; the U.S. President's first name, the street name where your school is located, the correct spelling of the school's name, etc.). Children also enjoy questions about popular culture, such as the names of musicians, actors, etc., but take care to ask questions on varied topics so that your immigrant English learners are not disadvantaged because they lack background knowledge about American popular culture.

4. On Stock Market day, group children heterogeneously (4–5 per group). This is very important so that all groups have a mix of kids, languages, abilities, etc.

5. Provide each table group with one worksheet with two columns:

a. for dollar "investments"

b. for students to write answers to the questions you will be asking

6. Each group receives $25 in play money. A recorder for the group must write an "investment" dollar amount on the Stock Market worksheet prior to the teacher's asking a question. Groups cannot risk more than 50% of what they have in their group's "bank." For example, if they have $120, the most they can invest is $60. You don't want to have any group "go broke" so they can't continue to play.

7. Ask the question (either content-related or trivia). After students have jotted their group answer on the worksheet, walk around to each group and assess whether the response is correct or incorrect. If a group's answer is correct, the "bank" pays; if not, the "bank" (you, the teacher) takes the investment.

8. Use both content and trivia questions, and alternate frequently, but don't let students know which type of question will be asked. If students miss several content questions in a row, you know you'll need to do some reteaching later. To keep everyone in the game, switch to some easier trivia questions that all groups are sure to answer correctly.

9. Reward groups that are behaving well and cooperating by secretly slipping them some extra play money. It's also fun to give bonuses ($25 or more) to groups for providing the correct spelling of answers to particular questions, either trivia or academic content. You don't need to "fine" groups for misbehavior or spelling; just reward or bonus them when they're on task, working well together, and conscientiously answering the questions.

10. If a group falls perilously behind, slip them some money so they won't go broke. If you do this discreetly, no one notices, and the group receiving the bank's assistance won't say a word.

11. Make the final question about content (not trivia), and tell groups they can invest all or some of their earnings—it's their choice. After the question is asked and answered, the group with the most money in the end is declared the winner for that day's Stock Market.

Differentiating Ideas for Multi-level Classes

The Center for Intercultural and Multilingual Advocacy (CIMA) at Kansas State University, based on recommendations made by Deschenes, Ebeling, and Sprague (1994), summarized types of assessment adaptations that permit teachers to more precisely determine students' knowledge and understanding. We have modified them to enable teachers to more accurately assess and give grades (when necessary) to English learners in a culturally responsive way.

- **Range.** Adapt the number of items the English learner is expected to complete, such as even or odd numbers only (see Leveled Study Guides in Chapter 2 as another example). Determine percentages of correct responses based on the number of items assessed.

- **Time.** Adapt the amount of time the English learner has for completing a task, such as providing more processing time and/or breaking tasks into manageable chunks. Unless there is a requirement to have a timed test, allowing additional time should not impact a student's score or grade.

- **Level of support.** Adapt the amount of **scaffolding** provided to an English learner during assessments by asking an aide, peer assistant, or parent volunteer to read and/or explain the task, or even read aloud (and translate, if necessary and possible) the items for the assessment. Remember the difference between assessing an English learner's ability to *read* and follow *written* directions and his or her ability to complete a task or answer questions about a content topic. If you are looking for a student's content knowledge (not his or her ability to read directions), it is fine to have someone else help with reading or clarifying the expectation for the task.

- **Difficulty.** Adapt the skill level, type of problem or task, and the process for how an English learner can approach the task, such as allowing a calculator, dictionary, or simplified instructions. Once again, you are not reducing the expectation that the English learner should know the material—you're just making it easier for him or her to demonstrate understanding.

- **Product.** Adapt the type of response the English learner is allowed to provide, such as permitting drawings, a hands-on demonstration, a verbal response, or, if necessary, a translated response. Whereas native speakers may be required to write a paragraph summary or essay, it may be reasonable for an English learner to submit an illustration, poster-board explanation, or other kind of product that doesn't rely so much on sophisticated English usage.

- **Participation.** Adapt the degree of active involvement of students in assessment, such as encouraging individual self-assessment, assistance in creating rubrics, and cooperative group self-assessment. As you have read often in this book, content learning is enhanced for all children, but especially for English learners, through interaction and group work. English learners can certainly be involved in their own assessment progress, particularly in the upper elementary grades.

- **Role.** When children are working in collaborative groups, they often assume roles, such as recorder, timekeeper, reader, discussant, and so forth. While it is important for English learners to be able to participate fully, some roles (such as timekeeper) require less language. Of course, when a student gains language proficiency, he or she should be encouraged to take on a role that requires reading, writing, and speaking.

■ The Lesson

Measurement and Data:
Describing and comparing measurable attributes (Kindergarten)

The classrooms described in the vignettes in this chapter are in a small rural elementary district in the midwestern United States. Until recently, there were very few children whose home language was not English. However, there has been a substantial increase in the number of children coming to kindergarten with little or no English, and now approximately 30% of the children in the district's four elementary schools speak Spanish as their primary language. Nearly all of these children are native born, and most of their parents are immigrants from Central America and Mexico.

Most of the children do not have any formal preschool experiences, although some attended the day care facility at the recently built meat-packing plant where their parents currently work. In addition to the children who live in town, a large number of children, both English speaking and Spanish speaking, are regularly bused to school from farms and neighboring small towns. The three kindergarten classes depicted here have an average of 25 students.

The three kindergarten teachers, Miss Pham, Mr. Emerson, and Mrs. Baxter, teach mathematics each day after the reading/language arts block. The lessons described in the vignettes were designed to meet the following Common Core Mathematics Standards for Kindergarten: Measurement and Data.

CCSS.Math.Content.K.MD.A.1

Describe measurable attributes of objects, such as length or weight. Describe several measurable attributes of a single object.

CCSS.Math.Content.K.MD.A.2

Directly compare two objects with a measurable attribute in common, to see which object has "more of" / "less of" the attribute, and describe the difference.

■ Teaching Scenarios

The following vignettes illustrate how Miss Pham, Mr. Emerson, and Mrs. Baxter review vocabulary and key concepts, and assess student learning in their kindergarten math lessons. Each of the lessons was planned to last approximately 20 to 30 minutes. The kindergarten classes are full day with substantial Title I funding, so instructional assistants are available, but not on a full-time basis. Because nearly all of the parents are employed, classroom volunteers are available infrequently.

Miss Pham

Miss Pham's lesson began with the children on the rug. She had a portable whiteboard and markers, and she had written the following words on the board: *taller*, *shorter*, *lighter*, *heavier*, *holds less*, *holds more*. She had placed several objects on a table near the whiteboard, including one large can of tomato juice, one small can of tomato juice, one large drinking glass, and one small drinking glass. She introduced the words on the board by asking the children if anyone recognized any of them. Several of the English-speaking children raised their hands, and Miss Pham called on them for their responses. The selected children read some of the words they recognized. Next, Miss Pham read all of the words and asked the children to chorally read them after her. Nearly all the children were able to echo-read each of the words as the teacher pointed to them.

Then, the teacher pointed to the tomato juice cans and asked the class which can was taller and which was shorter. Again, several hands were raised. Miss Pham called on these children, and one by one they came to the table. As before, all of the children who volunteered were native English speakers. The teacher asked, "Which can is taller?" and a student pointed to the large can of tomato juice. She then asked, "Which can is smaller?" and the next child pointed to the small can of tomato juice. Miss Pham smiled and said, "Very good." She then asked for two more volunteers who came to the table, and Miss Pham asked, "Which can is heavier?" and the first child pointed to the large can of tomato juice. The next child pointed to the small can when Miss Pham asked, "Which can is lighter?" The same routine was followed when the teacher asked the children, "Which of these glasses, the taller one or the shorter one, will hold more tomato juice?" Again, two volunteers (both of whom speak English fluently) came forward and each pointed to the respective glass. Miss Pham smiled warmly and said, "Good job, class!"

At this point, the children were directed to return to their desks. Miss Pham distributed a math worksheet with three lines of illustrations that were of familiar objects. The teacher orally presented the following directions while she pointed to the worksheet: "On the first line, cross out the picture of the *taller* item. On the second line, cross out the *heavier* item. On the third line, cross out the item that *holds more*. When you are finished, you may take out your crayons and color the pictures on the worksheet."

The children began working. Some made X's on the correct illustrations, while others looked around and followed the lead of the students who understood what to do. These students marked the same pictures as the other children. When some were finished and began coloring, others observed this and they also began coloring the pictures on their worksheets. When all children appeared to have marked their worksheets and were coloring, Miss Pham called the end of the period and the children turned in their work for the lesson.

Check your understanding: On the SIOP form in Figure 9.1, rate Miss Pham's lesson for each of the Review & Assessment features.

Mr. Emerson

Mr. Emerson also began his lesson on the rug. Referring to a pocket chart, Mr. Emerson pointed to, orally read, and explained the math lesson's content objective:

- We will *compare* people and objects to see which are *taller* and which are *shorter*.

He then read and explained the language objectives:

- We will learn the difference between the words *taller* and *shorter*.
- We will write a sentence using "_(blank)_ is *taller* than _(blank)_."
- We will write a sentence using "_(blank)_ is *shorter* than _(blank)_."

Mr. Emerson held up pictures of a watermelon and a tennis ball. He reminded the students that in their last math lesson, they had talked about the words *bigger* and *smaller*. He wrote the words on the whiteboard. He then asked each child to think-think-think (they all followed his lead and tapped their index fingers on their

FIGURE 9.1 Review & Assessment Component of the SIOP® Model: Miss Pham's Lesson

4	3	2	1	0
27. Comprehensive **review of key vocabulary**		Uneven **review of key vocabulary**		No **review of key vocabulary**

4	3	2	1	0
28. Comprehensive review **of key content concepts**		Uneven **review of key content concepts**		No **review of key content concepts**

4	3	2	1	0
29. Regular **feedback** provided to students on their output (e.g., language, content, work)		Inconsistent **feedback** provided to students on their output		No **feedback** provided to students on their output

4	3	2	1	0
30. **Assessment** of student **comprehension and learning of** all lesson objectives (e.g., spot checking, group response) throughout the lesson		**Assessment of student comprehension and learning** of some lesson objectives		No **assessment of student comprehension and learning** of lesson objectives

? Reflect and Apply

Click here to explain your ratings for Miss Pham's lesson on each of the Review & Assessment features.

temples) and decide which is bigger: a *watermelon* or a *tennis ball*. The unanimous decision was that the watermelon was bigger. He asked the students to think-think-think about which object was smaller; again there was a unanimous vote for the tennis ball. He reviewed with the children the word *compare* that they had used previously; they had just *compared* the watermelon and tennis ball to see which was *bigger* and which was *smaller*. "Today," he said, "we will *compare* people and objects, and use the words *taller* and *shorter*." He pointed once again to the words *taller* and *shorter* in the lesson's objectives.

Next, Mr. Emerson asked two of the boys (one taller than the other) to stand up. He asked the children, in pairs, to think and talk about different ways they could *compare* these two friends. He asked the partners to put their thumbs together (up high so he could see) when they were finished with the task. Mr. Emerson also asked the two boys who were standing to think and talk about the same question.

After about two minutes, Mr. Emerson asked the children what they talked about with their partners. One child said, "They're both boys." "Yes," Mr. Emerson confirmed, "they are both boys." Another student suggested, "They both have brown hair." Again, Mr. Emerson repeated the response, "Yes, they both have brown hair." One of the boys standing in front of the class said, "I'm shorter than Jed is." Mr. Emerson said, "Yes, Julio is shorter than Jed! And Jed is taller than Julio!" The children all giggled.

Mr. Emerson then asked all the children to stand with their partners. On chart paper, he had written the following: "____ is *taller* than ____." He introduced the sentence stem and said that it could be used to *compare* two people or other objects. Mr. Emerson then asked the students to read (nonreaders could echo-read) the words *is*, *taller*, and *than* several times. Further, he explained that in English we can talk about a person as being *short* and we also talk about a person as being *tall*. He motioned with his hands what *short* would look like and then he motioned what *tall* would look like. Mr. Emerson explained that when we compare the height of two people, we can use the words *taller* and *shorter* (and he pointed again to the words in the language objectives). He used the words again in the sentence: "Jed is taller than Julio. Julio is shorter than Jed."

Next, Mr. Emerson asked the children to sit back down on the rug. He then asked all the students to stand up if they thought they were *tall*. Several students stood. Mr. Emerson then asked all the "tall children" to sit down except for two, one of whom was considerably taller than the other. He then pointed to the word *taller* as he wrote it on the whiteboard and asked, "Who is *taller*? Raphael or Isabelle?" As he asked the question, Mr. Emerson held his hand over each child, emphasizing the difference in their heights. He asked the children to "vote" on who they thought was *taller*, Raphael or Isabelle. Mr. Emerson then asked the students on the rug to use the sentence starter, as he pointed with a pointing stick to the words on the chart paper, "I think ____ is taller than ____." He also asked Raphael and Isabelle to practice saying the same sentence, using their first names.

The children practiced with their partners saying the sentence starter several times, including Raphael and Isabelle's names. During this time, Mr. Emerson walked the perimeter of the rug and listened carefully to what the students were saying, intervening when necessary. He then asked each set of partners to chorally use the sentence starter, inserting the names of the respective children, until everyone had a chance to practice the sentence in front of the other class members.

Mr. Emerson then asked two other children to stand, one of whom was considerably shorter than the other. He asked the class to talk with their partners and *compare* Graciela and Blaine, to see who was *shorter*. The children chatted and put their thumbs together when they were finished. Mr. Emerson flipped the chart paper and a new sentence starter appeared: "____ is *shorter* than ____." The children repeated the earlier practice round with Mr. Emerson closely monitoring their responses, which was followed by each partner saying together the sentence using *shorter*.

Next, Mr. Emerson asked the children to return to their table groups. He provided each table group with several small trees and bushes (such as one would find in a crafts store). He asked each table group (three to four children) to sort the trees and bushes from tall to short (notice he was careful not to use *tallest* to *shortest* at this time). Once the children had finished this task, he asked them to again use the sentence starters to *compare* the trees, but this time they were to write the words into the blanks on the sentence starters. He modeled with a tree and a bush and used the sentence starters he had written on sentence strips on chart paper: "This tree is *taller* than this bush. This bush is *shorter* than this tree."

While the children were working, Mr. Emerson walked the room, monitoring and providing feedback, such as, "You two are working so well together. Can you show your sentences to your other table group members?" "Wonderful! I just heard you use the words *taller* and *shorter* correctly. You are doing a great job of *comparing* your tree and bush!" "Oops, let's check your spelling of the word *taller*. Can you find

FIGURE 9.2 Review & Assessment Component of the SIOP® Model: Mr. Emerson's Lesson

4	3	2	1	0
27. Comprehensive **review of key vocabulary**		Uneven **review of key vocabulary**		No **review of key vocabulary**

4	3	2	1	0
28. Comprehensive **review of key content concepts**		Uneven **review of key content concepts**		No **review of key content concepts**

4	3	2	1	0
29. Regular **feedback** provided to students on their output (e.g., language, content, work)		Inconsistent **feedback** provided to students on their output		No **feedback** provided to students on their output

4	3	2	1	0
30. **Assessment of student comprehension and learning of** all lesson objectives (e.g., spot checking, group response) throughout the lesson		**Assessment of student comprehension and learning** of some lesson objectives		No **assessment of student comprehension and learning** of lesson objectives

? Reflect and Apply

Click here to explain your ratings for Mr. Emerson's lesson on each of the Review & Assessment features.

the word on the chart? Show me . . . that's right! Now, do you see what needs fixing? Good, now it's correct!"

At the end of the lesson, Mr. Emerson brought the children back to the rug. He reviewed the meanings of the words *compare*, *taller*, and *shorter* with the class. Finally, he reviewed the lesson's objectives, asking the children to respond with a silent cheer for each objective if they thought they had met it. The classroom resounded with silent, kindergarten cheers. Mr. Baxter concluded the lesson with, "Yes, I agree. You all met the objectives by *comparing* the children and the trees and shrubs, by using our key words *taller* and *shorter* when you were saying the sentences. Later, you used the words in your sentences. You also worked very well with your partners and groups. Nice job, kindergartners!"

Check your understanding: On the SIOP form in Figure 9.2, rate Mr. Emerson's lesson for each of the Review & Assessment features.

Mrs. Baxter

Mrs. Baxter decided to teach the math lesson using Cuisenaire Rods to develop the math concept of comparison. First, she brought the children to the rug and explained that they were going to be learning about the words *longer* and *shorter*. She didn't write the words on the board because she believed that doing so would only confuse her kindergartners, especially the English learners; they didn't know how to read English words yet. She began by introducing how Cuisenaire Rods are used, and she held up several of the colorful rods as examples. She told the students, "Some of these rods are long and others are short. Some are fat and others are thin." The children nodded in agreement. "Today we are going to compare the sizes of these rods, using the words *longer* and *shorter*." She then asked the children to return to their desks. She distributed a worksheet with drawings that represented various sizes of the Cuisenaire Rods:

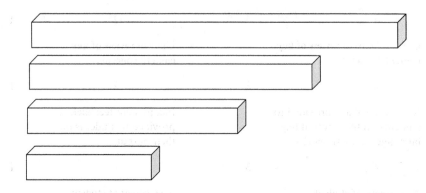

On each desk was a box with some Cuisenaire Rods, and the children began dumping them out. Mrs. Baxter directed them to find the sizes of the rods that fit into the diagrams on the worksheet. Most students did this with ease and began playing with the rods, using them to stack and sword fight. The teacher brought the kindergartners back to attention and she asked them to look at their papers with the rods. She then asked which of the rods was the *longer* one and which was the *shorter* one. One of the boys responded by pointing to the longest rod on the paper and saying, "Teacher, this one is *longerest* and this one is *smallerest*." Mrs. Baxter said, "Okay, let's use the words *longer* and *shorter*." She then held up two rods, one considerably longer than the other. She said, "See, this rod is taller so it is *longer* than the *shorter* one." The child persisted, "Yep, that's what I said. It's bigger." At this point, Mrs. Baxter realized the children were confused. "Okay," she said, "let's just use two rods. Pick any two off your paper and put them like this. She held two different-size rods up next to each other. "Which is *longer* and which is *shorter*?"

Some of the children placed their rods vertically with the top ends parallel. When Mrs. Baxter asked the children to move the second rod down so one looked "taller" than the other, the children became more confused. She decided at that point that kindergartners were not really ready for Cuisenaire Rods *or* comparatives in English, and they all took an early recess.

Check your understanding: On the SIOP form in Figure 9.3, rate Mrs. Baxter's lesson for each of the Review & Assessment features.

FIGURE 9.3 Review & Assessment Component of the SIOP® Model: Mrs. Baxter's Lesson

4	3	2	1	0
27. Comprehensive **review of key vocabulary**		Uneven **review of key vocabulary**		No **review of key vocabulary**

4	3	2	1	0
28. Comprehensive **review of key content concepts**		Uneven **review of key content concepts**		No **review of key content concept**

4	3	2	1	0
29. Regular **feedback** provided to students on their output (e.g., language, content, work)		Inconsistent **feedback** provided to students on their output		No **feedback** provided to students on their output

4	3	2	1	0
30. **Assessment of student comprehension and learning** of all lesson objectives (e.g., spot checking, group response) throughout the lesson		**Assessment of student comprehension and learning** of some lesson objectives		No **assessment of student comprehension and learning** of lesson objectives

? Reflect and Apply

Click here to explain your ratings for Mrs. Baxter's lesson on each of the Review & Assessment features.

■ Discussion of Lessons

27. *Comprehensive Review of Key Vocabulary*

Miss Pham: 2

Mr. Emerson: 4

Mrs. Baxter: 1

- In her lesson, **Miss Pham** introduced the challenging academic vocabulary by having those students who could already read the words do so for the other children. She also pronounced the words, followed by the children's echo-reading of the words. For the children who are native English speakers already familiar with the words and concepts Miss Pham was presenting, this quick review might have been adequate. However, for English learners and other children unfamiliar with English comparatives (e.g., *taller*, *heavier*), the very brief introduction was inadequate. Miss Pham did provide familiar, concrete examples with the tomato juice cans and drinking glasses to illustrate the challenging academic vocabulary, yet the only children who had an opportunity to demonstrate their understanding were the ones who clearly understood the concepts. By not providing many more opportunities for students to practice with the concrete examples, Miss Pham had little idea of which children comprehended the vocabulary and which did not. Therefore, the lesson received a "2" for this feature.

- **Mr. Emerson's** lesson received a "4" for the comprehensive review of vocabulary feature. At the beginning of the lesson, he reviewed the academic vocabulary by going over the language objectives. He reviewed the words *compare*, *bigger*, *smaller* from a previous lesson before teaching the new and related words. He provided multiple opportunities for the children to practice using the words, and while they were practicing, he was able to monitor and correct, if needed. Because all students were engaged with every part of the lesson, he had ample opportunities to observe informally which students were having difficulty with pronunciations and usage. Even though many of the kindergartners could not read the words in the objectives and sentence stems, Mr. Emerson provided practice in speech-to-print match, a very important prereading and vocabulary learning skill. At the end of the lesson, Mr. Emerson reviewed once again the academic vocabulary for the day when he reviewed the language objectives.

- **Mrs. Baxter's** lesson received a "1" for this feature. Unfortunately, she did not believe that kindergarten children were ready to begin using print because many were still nonreaders. Therefore, she did not have her objectives, vocabulary words, or directions for the day's activity on the board. She did say the words *longer* and *shorter* several times and she tried to explain their meanings. However, the children did not understand why they were "playing" with the Cuisenaire Rods or why it was important to use the words *longer* and *shorter*. Instead of realizing that the children didn't understand what they were supposed to do, stopping, and going back to introduce the lesson objectives and explicitly teach the math lesson's academic language, both the teacher and children eventually moved on to recess.

28. *Comprehensive Review of Key Concepts*

Miss Pham: 2

Mr. Emerson: 4

Mrs. Baxter: 1

- **Miss Pham's** lesson received a "2" for this feature. The worksheet activity, intended for use as an assessment of the children's understandings of the academic language and key concepts of the math lesson, was largely ineffective because, once again, the children who already understood the vocabulary and concepts zipped through it; those who did not understand were able to mimic what the others were doing. In the end, Miss Pham had little idea of whether her English learners and struggling students had made any progress toward mastering the standards that guided her lesson planning. This happens too often when teachers assess responses only from those who volunteer, and when their activities, such as the worksheet, do not really provide assessment information about who understood key concepts and who did not.

- **Mr. Emerson's** lesson received a "4" for this feature. As with vocabulary, Mr. Emerson reviewed the content concepts from the previous lesson before beginning the new lesson. It was essential that the children understand what it means to *compare* (especially in math), so his examples were concrete and meaningful. Now that they understood the fundamentals (*bigger, smaller, taller, shorter*), they could move to the next steps (*heavier, lighter, holds more, holds less*), all of which involved more comparisons. In his lesson, Mr. Emerson carefully developed each level of learning, and he did so by continuing to review prior to moving to the next step. The practice activities, with the whole class, partners, and small groups enabled him to assess on the spot and provide intervention as necessary. Because Mr. Emerson continued to develop these measurement concepts in a purposeful and sequential manner, all of the students, including his English learners and struggling learners, had the opportunity for success with the content concepts and with English language development.

- **Mrs. Baxter's** lesson received a "1" for this feature. She made two attempts with the Cuisenaire Rods to have the students place their rods in different positions, but because she did not have clear content objectives for the lessons, the students didn't understand the purpose for what they were doing. The Cuisenaire Rods were also new to the children; they represented a novelty and seemed like blocks to play with rather than learning tools. Mrs. Baxter might have modeled use of the rods on the classroom document camera to demonstrate precisely what the children were to do with them. She could have said, "Let's *compare* these rods. Notice how this rod is *longer* than this rod. Notice how this rod is *shorter* than this rod. No matter how I place the rods, this one will always be *longer* than this rod. Watch while I move them. Now, let's *compare* them again." If Mrs. Baxter had provided explicit instruction and modeling, the children would have been able to practice with the rods, and she would have had an opportunity to review and assess their understandings.

29. *Regular Feedback Provided to Students on Their Output*

Miss Pham: 2

Mr. Emerson: 4

Mrs. Baxter: 1

- **Miss Pham's** lesson received a "2" for this feature because she did attempt to provide feedback to those students who volunteered to come to the table and point to the respective items. However, "Very good!" and "Good job!" are comments that are ubiquitous in many classrooms, but they provide very little information to English learners about what the children did to deserve the warm smile and congratulations. Miss Pham could have followed the accolades with specific academic feedback such as, "You listened carefully for the word *taller* and then you compared the two cans. You saw that one can is definitely *taller* than the other. Good job!" Holding up the two cans of tomato juice so all students could clearly compare them would have also provided more effective and specific feedback.

- **Mr. Emerson's** lesson received a "4" for this feature because all of his feedback to his students was specific and academic. From the beginning of the lesson, he repeated his students' responses, extending each of them. He let his students know exactly what they had done correctly so they could repeat the behavior at another time. At the end of the lesson, after the children's attainment of the objectives, Mr. Emerson paraphrased the objectives one more time, repeating and reviewing the key vocabulary and content concepts that were the goals for the lesson.

- **Mrs. Baxter's** lesson received a "1" for this feature because she provided little academic feedback to her students. She repeated and corrected one child's incorrect English, but because the other students had little opportunity to demonstrate their understandings, other feedback was not provided.

30. *Assessment of Student Comprehension and Learning of All Lesson Objectives*

Miss Pham: 2

Mr. Emerson: 4

Mrs. Baxter: 0

- **Miss Pham's** lesson received a "2" for this feature because her objectives were not made clear to her students, and in reality, she may not have been clear about them herself. Had she clearly thought through what her *lesson objectives* were (not just the standards), she probably would have seen that it was unrealistic to expect her young students, especially the English learners, to be able to master the academic language and key concepts all in one lesson without considerable scaffolding. Each of the vocabulary words and math concepts should have been introduced, practiced, reviewed, and assessed before she moved on to the other vocabulary and concepts. Additionally, while part of this lesson could have been taught effectively with the whole class, many of the students would have benefitted from differentiated, small-group instruction and practice. "Backwards planning" (thinking ahead of time about what students really need to know and be able to do in order to accomplish this day's objectives) and then assessing and reteaching when students are not understanding are critical elements of effective SIOP lessons.

- **Mr. Emerson's** lesson received a "4" for this feature. Throughout the lesson, Mr. Emerson reviewed the progress his students were making toward meeting the objectives. He modeled what he wanted his students to do, he provided students with the opportunity to model for each other, he had his students work in pairs to practice further, and then he had the students practice their sentences orally with the entire class. Following the oral practice, the students then wrote sentences by using the sentence starter and filling in the appropriate words (*taller, shorter*), which were listed on the board. Note also that even though he was teaching math concepts, all of his students were expected to read, write, listen, and speak during this lesson, thus concurrently developing math content and English language proficiency.

- **Mrs. Baxter's** lesson received a "0" for this feature. Neither she nor her students had a clear idea of the language and learning goals of the lesson. Given the short attention spans of kindergartners and the ease with which they can move off task, along with the lack of an understandable purpose for the activity, the children created their own goals. By the end of the lesson, Mrs. Baxter had underestimated both the learning capacity of her children and the potential benefits of manipulatives like Cuisenaire Rods.

Watch this video to note how Ms. Phillips assesses student learning in the middle-school science lesson you viewed in Chapter 7 (see the Summary for the link to Part I of this video). Using the SIOP protocol, see how many SIOP features you recognize in the two video clips.

Teaching with Technology

After talking with the teachers and discussing the lessons you read about in the Scenarios earlier in the chapter, our tech integrator, Ms. Palacios, offered some technology suggestions to enhance the teachers' lessons.

Jeopardy Labs: Miss Pham, Mr. Emerson, and Mrs. Baxter were looking for an engaging way for their students to review the material at the end of the math lessons on describing and comparing measurable attributes. At lunch one day, Mr. Emerson explained how he likes to create a simple *Jeopardy* game on his whiteboard, drawing the boxes and categories by hand. Ms. Palacios asked if he had ever seen *Jeopardy Labs*, an easy-to-use Web site that enables teachers to quickly create game boards. In addition to creating original games, the site allows users to search for games created by other teachers and use them as a basis for a new one. Mr. Emerson shared the Web site with his team and they decided to give it a try for their final review of the math unit.

In order to involve the kindergarten children more in the process, Mr. Emerson reviewed with the children the words they had learned during the unit for comparing people and objects: *bigger, smaller, taller, shorter, heavier, lighter, holds more, holds less.* With questions and answers entered about objects and people that could be compared, he then had to determine how to make the activity work in a classroom with many kindergarten students, not just three contestants.

How would students be selected to answer questions? What about a bell? How should they keep track of points? In order to answer these questions, Ms. Palacios suggested a slight adaptation that mixed a bit of the analog world with the digital world. Instead of a system in which students had to "ring in" to answer a question, she suggested dividing the class into small groups of three or four children and providing each group with a small whiteboard. To meet the needs of his young students, Mr. Emerson decided that he would read an answer to a *Jeopardy* question and then show a picture of two objects (or people). For example, "Here are two trees. Which tree is bigger, number 1 or number 2?" "Here are two pots of water. Which pot holds more water, #1 or #2?" Each team then had a minute to discuss the answer and write the correct number on the whiteboard. When the time was up, the team leader held up the board so the teacher could award points for the correct answer. In order to provide some choice during the game, the teachers allowed the teams to choose the categories and points on a rotating basis. By slightly changing the dynamic of the game and using whiteboards, the children had more opportunities to hear and review the material, including key vocabulary and content concepts.

Other terms for this type of tool: online *Jeopardy* game

Related Products: *Jeopardy Rocks*, *Jeopardy* PowerPoint templates

Online Rubric Creator: Rubrics are an essential component in the SIOP teacher's toolkit, and the Internet has made it possible to easily find many samples of teacher-created rubrics for a variety of content areas or purposes. One afternoon, Ms. Palacios and the team visited a number of such Web sites. They noticed that as with the options explored with *Jeopardy Labs*, many rubric creator sites allow users to create original rubrics or find others that could be adapted. The teachers found the Web sites to be helpful for suggestions of descriptors and ideas regarding scoring.

Other terms for this type of tool: Rubric maker, online rubric creator

Note: Due to the constantly evolving nature of the Internet, it is a challenge to ensure that all of the links and Web services listed here are updated and functional when you read the technology sections. While specific tools or services may appear in the narrative, we have also included the general term for each tool. If a specific service does not work or is no longer available, search with the general term for the tool and you should be able to find a comparable Web site.

Check Your Understanding
Click here to check your understanding of the concepts in Chapter 9, Review & Assessment.

Summary

As you reflect on this chapter and the impact and role of review and assessment of vocabulary and content and language objectives, consider the following points:

- Review and assessment are integrated processes, essential for all students, but they are critical to the success of English learners.
- Informal assessment is attentive to the classroom context, is authentic and multi-dimensional, and includes multiple indicators of students' performance.
- Effective SIOP teachers carefully plan for review and informal assessment of key vocabulary throughout a lesson and at its conclusion.
- Formal assessments (e.g., standardized tests) require that children understand and apply content knowledge on tests that have high stakes. Therefore, it is important to teach, review, and assess English learners' understandings of the cross-curricular/process/function words and terms that are often found in test questions.
- At the conclusion of a SIOP lesson, teachers assess the degree to which students have met all content and language objectives.
- Most important, review and assessment guide teaching and reteaching, inform decision making, lead to supportive and academic feedback, and provide for fair and comprehensive judgments about student performance.

Discussion Questions

1. In reflecting on the content and language objectives at the beginning of the chapter, are you able to:
   a. Identify the challenges in assessing content and language learning of students with limited English proficiency?
   b. Create a plan for formative assessment for the linguistically diverse students in your classroom that will provide you with the information you need to make sound instructional decisions during lesson planning?
   c. Determine opportunities for reviewing and assessing key vocabulary and key content concepts in your lesson plan?
   d. Provide effective academic oral and written feedback to English learners during a lesson?
   e. Compare and contrast characteristics of informal and formal assessments?
   f. Explain the meaning of the following assessment terms: *formative* and *summative assessment*; *authentic assessment*; *multidimensional indicators*; *multiple indicators*?

2. Many teachers introduce key vocabulary at the beginning of the lesson, but often neglect to revisit the new terms systematically throughout the lesson and review them at its conclusion. How can you ensure that a SIOP lesson's key academic vocabulary is reviewed at the end of each lesson? Describe a variety of ways you would review the terms, as well as the techniques you could put in place to build a vocabulary review into each lesson. Which of the activities introduced in this chapter would you select? Why?

3. Research has shown that gratuitous compliments to students (e.g., "Good job" or "Keep up the good work") do little to motivate them or assist with their learning. Instead, teachers should give regular, substantive feedback to students on their verbal contributions and on their academic work. What are some ways to provide constructive, specific academic feedback to students? Consider class size and English proficiency levels as you answer this question.

4. Reflect on the ideas presented in this chapter, as well as all the other activities you have used to assess student learning of specific lesson objectives. How much time do you think you should allocate for review and assessment during each lesson? What if you discover (as is often the case) that some students are ready to move on, while others need more review and/or reteaching?

5. Using the SIOP lesson you have been creating, provide specific provisions for students at varying levels. Plan multiple indicators throughout the lesson that will enable you to assess on-the-spot progress toward meeting the lesson's content objectives. Then determine what you will do for (1) independent or partner work for students who are ready to move on and (2) a reteaching or review minilesson for those who need additional assistance from you. This is probably the most challenging aspect of providing differentiated instruction, not only for English learners, but for all students. How will you assess who is ready to move on? How will you assess the students in the reteaching/review group to determine if and when they're ready to move on? What will you do if a few students are still struggling? These are the *big* questions to ask (and answer) when planning for a lesson's review and assessment.

CHAPTER 10

Issues of Reading, RTI, and Special Education for English Learners

Learning Outcomes

After reading, discussing, and engaging in activities related to this chapter, you will be able to meet the following content and language objectives.

Content Objectives

Explain how linguistic differences in **home languages** and English can affect English learners' reading and writing development.

Describe in-class supports and/or modifications that content teachers can provide to English learners and struggling readers.

Delineate an effective RTI process to ensure appropriate services for English learners.

Language Objectives

Discuss with a group how to plan appropriate instruction for English learners who may have reading and learning difficulties.

Write a lesson plan that develops vocabulary and reading proficiency for English learners who struggle to read and learn.

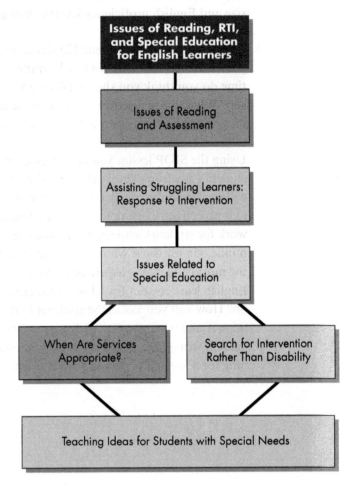

Issues of Reading, RTI, and Special Education for English Learners

Issues of Reading and Assessment

Assisting Struggling Learners: Response to Intervention

Issues Related to Special Education

When Are Services Appropriate?

Search for Intervention Rather Than Disability

Teaching Ideas for Students with Special Needs

In our work with teachers and administrators throughout the United States, a persistent question concerns appropriate instruction for **English learners** who exhibit difficulties with reading and learning. Teachers often feel ill prepared to provide content instruction for these children because they're not sure whether a student's difficulty is due to a reading problem, a learning disability, a lack of schooling, or limited English proficiency. **Response to Intervention** (RTI) was developed, in part, to more accurately identify

Syda Productions/Fotolia

learning disabilities. In this chapter, we provide a brief overview of RTI, and we discuss issues of assessment, identification, and instruction for children who may be experiencing reading and/or learning problems. With more rigorous English language arts and content standards in place, a process for supporting struggling students is even more essential.

Although it is not the intent of this book to provide a comprehensive treatment of the topic of struggling learners, we hope this chapter will stimulate your thinking about and discussion with colleagues regarding these issues, especially as they affect English learners. We begin with a discussion of reading development and assessment for English learners and examine how RTI provides assistance to teachers and learners alike. We then move on to issues related to special education. (For a full discussion of RTI, see *Response to Intervention (RTI) and English Learners: Using the SIOP® Model* [Echevarría, Richards-Tutor & Vogt, 2015]. For a discussion of special education and English learners, see Echevarría & Graves, 2015.) ●

Issues of Reading Development and Assessment

Teachers face many challenges related to the literacy development of English learners. The task of teaching English learners to read is made difficult in part due to the complexity of learning to read and write in a language the students do not understand completely. Also, it is not always possible for children to learn to read in their primary

Watch this video to see two grade 3 literacy teachers probe students' thinking about what makes a good reader, through paraphrasing, elaboration of student responses, and think-alouds. Why is this type of conversation with students so valuable for English learners and struggling readers?

language at school (which would enable them to carry over their knowledge of reading in the L1 to reading in English). These students may have difficulty with attending to the distinct sounds of English, letter identification, and comprehension because they lack familiarity with the purposes and mechanics of reading. As a result, some English learners are behind before the onset of school (Snow, Burns, & Griffin, 1998).

Not surprisingly, research suggests that English learners need systematic, high-quality literacy instruction from the start. According to the Report of the National Literacy Panel on Language-Minority Children and Youth (August & Shanahan, 2006), teachers of English learners must provide substantial instruction in the key components of reading as identified by the National Reading Panel (National Institute of Child Health and Human Development [NICHD], 2000). These include phonemic awareness, phonics, fluency, vocabulary, and comprehension. As important as these are, they are not sufficient for English learners. Oral language development, often overlooked during literacy instruction, is also critical.

To promote English learners' oral language development, the following suggestions are offered:

- Engage children in "picture walks" or text walks where English learners and native speakers take turns describing a book's illustrations (or graphic elements, such as tables and charts), which they use to predict the content of the story or chapter before reading.

- Provide repeated readings of highly predictable picture or pattern books for young children/or and beginning English speakers, so that children can internalize and then orally produce the patterns, rhyming words, and rhythm.

- Record the reading of stories, articles, or chapters so English learners can listen to them and then retell what they learn as they refer to pictures they have drawn about the text's content.

- Use the Language Experience Approach (LEA) to record on chart paper English learners' dictated short stories and/or experiences, such as what occurred during a recent field trip or their description of an event at school or at home. After the dictation, the text is used for repeated readings, discussion, and instruction. LEA is very effective for developing oral language and oral reading proficiency, vocabulary, and an understanding of English syntax, all essential for reading proficiency (Roskos & Neuman, 2014). It is recommended that children have their own copies of the dictated texts so they can underline words they recognize each time they orally and silently reread their stories (Rasinski & Padak, 2004; Stauffer, 1980).

A challenge that is particularly acute when teaching immigrant English learners to read in English is accurately determining their reading proficiency in their home languages. Children who have well-developed reading skills in their **native language** may have mastered many of the essentials of reading, such as:

- The knowledge that print carries meaning.
- The alphabetic principle: If childrens' home language (**L1**) is alphabetic, they have learned that phonemes (sounds) are represented by graphemes (letters and

letter combinations), and that when put together these graphemes create words and meaning (the alphabetic principle).

- Knowledge of syntax: Children have also learned the syntax (sentence structure) of their L1, and although learning English syntax may challenge them, they can use their knowledge of the L1 structure to make connections with English.
- Comprehension: Once children have learned what it means to strategically comprehend text in their native language, they are able to transfer cognitive, metacognitive, and language learning strategies from their L1 to English (Genesee, Linholm-Leary, Saunders, & Christian, 2006).
- Sound-symbol system of English: If children's L1 is non-alphabetic (such as Mandarin), they will need to learn the alphabetic sound-symbol system of English, but they can carry over to their new language their understandings of the reading and writing processes.

Students who read satisfactorily in their L1 do not have to relearn how to read or write. However, they do need to learn English. With comprehensible input and explicit instruction in English phonology, morphology, and syntax, they will have a better chance of transferring their existing reading skills to the reading of English. For example, for students whose L1 is Spanish, there are many cognates that link English vocabulary and spelling with Spanish (*estudiar* = study; *excepción* = exception). Using dictionaries in Spanish, English, French, and German as resources helps students make these connections as they explore similarities in these languages (Helman, Bear, Templeton, & Invernizzi, 2011).

It is also clear that English learners need to be immersed in print, with many opportunities to read books, stories, and informational texts that are at or a little above their level, ideally in their L1 as well as in English. English learners benefit when they learn to read and write in both their native language and in English.

In contrast to those English learners who have well-developed literacy skills in their L1, other students enter U.S. schools with little or no reading instruction in their primary language, or they find reading and writing very difficult. These students are often referred to special education programs without just cause, when other interventions may be more appropriate, such as longer exposure to high-quality, scaffolded instruction in English or their home language; more direct, small-group, or individual instruction; or referral to a reading specialist. It is important that teachers know whether their English learners can read in their primary language and that they are able to ascertain whether difficulty in content class work may be the result of a reading problem or a lack of English proficiency. If a particular student speaks a language that differs from other children in the school, it may be necessary for a community member who speaks the language to share reading material in the student's native language so that his or her literacy skills can be assessed.

Estimating Students' Reading Levels

Many teachers, rightly, want to determine the reading levels of their students. This information helps the teacher match texts to children's abilities. For example, if a fifth-grade student is reading at approximately the third-grade reading level, he is likely to have difficulty comprehending his fifth-grade social studies textbook without instructional modifications and **scaffolding**. Either the too-difficult text will need to be adapted or the student will require considerable assistance in accessing the content information from the text.

Classroom teachers and reading specialists use a variety of assessments to determine their students' reading proficiency. However, commonly used assessments that yield a particular reading level (such as fourth grade) may be inappropriate for English learners (Jiménez, 2004; Vogt, 2014). For example, a common diagnostic instrument for assessing students' fluency and comprehension is some sort of an informal reading inventory (IRI). During this assessment, a student reads a series of increasingly difficult, leveled passages silently or orally. The teacher or reading specialist marks reading errors, asks comprehension questions, and, based on the student's reading proficiency, determines approximate reading levels, labeled as: *independent* ("I can read this accurately without any help"); *instructional* ("I can read and understand this if someone helps me"); and *frustration* ("I can't read or understand this, even if someone tries to help me").

IRI-like assessments are also used to match books to a student's reading ability, using Lexile® bands, but too often, English learners and struggling readers are provided only with low-level books because their assessments indicate this is what they're able to read. Instead, we need to select texts that are written at the students' instructional level, if possible, and that account for students' different experiential backgrounds, and provide additional assistance so that the text becomes accessible. If this level and type of text isn't available, then we must adapt the grade-level text through rewriting, providing a detailed study guide, highlighting the key concepts, or providing detailed marginal notes (as discussed in Chapter 2). Without these modifications, the instructional- and frustration-level texts will be largely inaccessible, especially for English learners.

It's important to remember that successful reading of any text is also dependent on a number of other variables, including familiarity with the topic being read, vocabulary knowledge, the flexible use of a variety of reading skills and strategies, motivation, and purpose setting. For students who are reading in their native language, these variables are relatively easy to assess, and the selection of appropriate text materials can be made with a reasonable amount of confidence. However, many of our usual reading assessments may not yield reliable results for English learners, and therefore, selection of appropriate texts is considerably more difficult. A student who is assessed at grade level in his L1 may be assessed as reading at a much lower level in English. Thus, using results from an IRI or a standardized achievement test in English might suggest that the student has a serious reading problem. However, if he doesn't have difficulty reading in his native language, it's unlikely he'll have a serious reading problem in his new language. In contrast, if the child has a reading problem in his L1, he may very well have difficulty reading in English.

So how do we determine whether a child's academic difficulties are due to a reading problem or a lack of English proficiency? First, we need to recognize that English learners may need explicit instruction in the aspects of English that differ from their native languages, including the phonology (sounds), morphology (roots and affixes), and syntax of English (sentence structure). As an example, although you may teach phonics explicitly and effectively, some English learners may not hear or be able to reproduce the sounds of English because these sounds do not exist in their primary language. The consonant sounds may be considerably different, the number of vowels may vary, and such things as vowel combinations, commonly found in English (*ea, ie, oa*), may be nonexistent in the students' home languages (such as Spanish).

It's not just the sound system (the phonemes) that can cause difficulty for English learners. Because of English orthography (the spelling system), some English learners may have difficulty learning to read and write the language. Orthographies of various languages are described in terms of whether they are *transparent*, with highly regular words that are easy to decode (such as Spanish and Italian), or they are *deep* or *opaque*, with correspondences between letters and sounds that are much less direct (such as French and English). A language like German is considered to be *semitransparent* because its orthography lies somewhere between deep and transparent (Helman et al., 2011). The point is that some students who have a primary language that is transparent (such as Spanish) may have a difficult time learning a language that is deep (such as English). However, in some studies that compare orthographic knowledge, bilingual learners have been found to negotiate satisfactorily between their languages and literacies (Tolchinsky & Teberosky, 1998). Rather than being confused by orthographic differences, these students can apply what they know about the structure of their primary language to the language they are learning.

English Learners and the Common Core State Standards for Reading, Writing, Listening, and Speaking

For English learners and struggling readers, the **Common Core** English Language Arts Standards are especially challenging, but they also represent an opportunity for all students to reach high levels of literacy attainment. Many of the Common Core literacy skills English learners need to acquire are metalinguistic in nature. That is, they require students to be particularly aware of the features and uses of language (Jimenéz et al., 2015). An instructional example of how to help English learners employ metalinguistic strategies is to lead them through a brief content paragraph by examining each sentence, while pointing out that readers are likely to find one or more processes, such as *doing, sensing, being,* or *saying,* when reading expository text in science or another subject area text. This type of analysis and subsequent application of the metalinguistic strategy will assist English learners and others as they read increasingly complex texts.

With the Common Core State Standards now adopted by the majority of states, and with other states either adapting the Common Core or adopting similarly rigorous standards, it is imperative that all students, including English learners and struggling readers, be provided with appropriate reading instruction that focuses on, among other things, close reading of complex texts. Following are some ideas for providing opportunities for English learners and other students to meet these challenging literacy standards, especially with informational texts (Calkins, Ehrenworth, & Lehman, 2012; Vogt & Shearer, 2016).

1. *Implement the SIOP Model's 30 features to a high degree* and your students will be reading, writing, listening, and speaking throughout the day. As you've read throughout this book, developing English proficiency takes practice, practice, and more practice using the language.

2. ***Engage your students in reading more high-quality, high-interest, nonfiction texts.*** In many elementary language arts classrooms, the preponderance of text material is narrative fiction. Teachers and students alike love a good story, but with the focus of CCSS on close reading of expository texts, it's important to balance your instruction and students' practice with plenty of interesting and motivating nonfiction texts. It's not enough for children to thumb through a magazine or informational book—instead, it's about the volume of nonfiction texts that students are actually *reading*. This requires having available an ample number of independent or "just-right" books from which students can choose to read. In order to move toward the close reading of complex texts as required by CCSS, students need to practice reading independent-level texts and then work up to more challenging texts without having to complete a worksheet or other meaningless activity. Rather, engage students in talking about the big-picture ideas in the text, the language that is used, the author's purpose and motivation for writing it, and the ideas they find compelling during close readings. In part, close readings require students to critically analyze the author's message by reading beyond the information on the page or screen (McLaughlin, 2012). These kinds of conversations can take place during and after teacher read-alouds of nonfiction texts. Children can listen to and talk about texts that are too difficult for them to read independently, and when you engage them in critically thinking about something you've read aloud, you're preparing them to engage in the same kind of thinking when they read more challenging texts themselves.

   And, remember that close reading of texts isn't an every-period-every-day-every-text event. Use shorter texts that are complex and model what it means to read closely—how a reader approaches challenging text, how to analyze the language and textual features of what is being read, and how to find and cite evidence to support a position or argument (Serafini, 2014). Without this type of teaching, English learners and struggling readers will soon equate "complex text" with "frustration-level text" (See Calkins, Ehrenworth, and Lehman, 2012, for specific ideas about how to find appropriately leveled texts, and how to "nudge" children toward increasingly challenging reading material that requires close reading and structured discussion.)

3. ***Provide students with explicit and focused strategy comprehension instruction that is embedded in rich content and relevant texts.*** This can occur throughout the day in each subject area when you include primary sources and other interesting texts that provide the opportunity for children to work on the comprehension and learning strategies described in Chapter 5 (Strategies).

4. ***Engage your students in rich collaboration that promotes motivation and self-directed learning.*** Think about the **SIOP** component of Interaction and the Common Core Standards for listening and speaking. To meet the CCSS standards, children must learn to engage meaningfully with the teacher and with each other, and this involves both listening and speaking opportunities that are targeted and structured (Fisher & Frey, 2014). Teach children how to engage in discussions and instructional conversations about what they read (see Chapter 4), and model skills such as how to articulate positions, defend statements with specific evidence from the text, and analyze the author's perspective.

5. ***Provide scaffolding as needed.*** Some children benefit from relevant sentence frames during instruction and practice:

"From the text, I learned _____."

"I think _____ because in the text, I read that _____."

"I don't believe _____, because _____."

"The most important point the author made was _____ because _____."

"In the text I read that _____, but I question that because _____."

So what do we do about those who *are* confused, and despite appropriate instruction in English, reading, and language arts, are not making satisfactory progress? First, as discussed in Chapter 9, it's important to examine the students' present classroom context as it relates to literacy strengths and needs. The following questions might guide this inquiry:

1. What evidence do you have that a particular student is having difficulty with reading?

2. Do you have any evidence that this student has difficulty reading in his or her home language? If not, how might you gather some information? If you are not fluent in the student's language, is there another student who is? Is there a community liaison or family member who can provide information about the student's L1 literacy development?

3. If your evidence points to a reading problem, what instructional supports and/or modifications have you and other teachers tried to accommodate the student's needs?

   a. Are the student's teachers adapting content and texts to provide greater accessibility (see Chapter 2)?

   b. Are the teachers using instructional techniques that make the content and expectations understandable for English learners (see Chapter 4)?

   c. Are the student's teachers incorporating cognitive, metacognitive, and language learning strategy instruction in the ESL, language arts, and content subject areas (see Chapter 5)?

   d. Are the student's teachers scaffolding instruction through flexible grouping that promotes interaction both between the teacher and students and among students (see Chapters 5 and 6)?

   e. Are the student's teachers providing multiple opportunities for practice and application of key content and language concepts (see Chapter 7)?

   f. Are the student's teachers using effective assessment to determine what the student knows and can do related to content and language objectives, and to plan subsequent reteaching lessons (see Chapter 9)?

At this point, we hope you're getting the idea that appropriate instruction for this student involves all of the components of the SIOP Model—those listed above as well as appropriate pacing, meaningful activities, sufficient wait time, and so forth. Certainly, a student with reading problems will benefit from the effective practices advocated in the SIOP Model as he or she receives an appropriate intervention for the reading problems.

Reflect and Apply
Click here to describe potential problems for assessing English learners' reading development.

Will this type of instruction overcome a serious reading problem? Probably not, although research on effective literacy instruction for young children who are English learners is consistent with instruction based on the features of the SIOP Model. But here's the key: If you (and your colleagues) have done all you can to provide effective English language development and content instruction using SIOP and a student is still struggling with reading (or math), it may be appropriate for the student to receive intervention. This might be provided by the teacher in the classroom, a reading specialist, or another service provider. And that brings us to Response to Intervention.

■ Assisting Struggling Learners: Response to Intervention

Watch this video to see Dr. Jana Echevarría discuss creating an optimal learning environment for all students. In what ways do you think that RTI or MTSS can help to identify students with learning disabilities? How does it reduce inappropriate referrals for special education services?

Response to Intervention (RTI), also known as **Multi-tiered System of Supports (MTSS)**, is a service delivery model used to identify at-risk learners early and to provide appropriate supports including effective instruction in general education (typically called Tier 1), followed by targeted intervention as needed (Tier 2 and/or Tier 3). Although the terms RTI and MTSS are often used interchangeably, RTI differs from MTSS in that it focuses primarily on academic progress, whereas MTSS is more comprehensive, addressing behavioral, social, and emotional issues experienced by students.

Generally, RTI consists of skill screening for all children, close monitoring of student progress, and the use of interventions to bolster student achievement. RTI is founded on the principle that *all can learn* and is designed to catch learning problems early, thus reducing the number of students eligible for and in need of special education services (often Tier 3 or another level of intervention). Actually, early identification and intervention can help prevent reading difficulties altogether (Torgesen, 2012). With RTI, all children receive high-quality core instruction in general education, while some receive additional services for as long as there is evidence that they need those services. The focus is on finding ways to change variables such as teaching methods, materials, and/or student behaviors so the learner can be successful. RTI involves documenting a change in behavior or performance as a result of intervention and assessments, making it a recursive process with children moving in and out of interventions as needed. That is, children receive interventions for a specific amount of time and progress-monitoring data are analyzed to determine next steps. Does the child need the same level of intervention for a longer period of time and more intense intervention, or has the Tier 2 intervention been sufficient (and thus it is no longer needed)? Children aren't "stuck" in intervention indefinitely; their progress is closely monitored and decisions are made based on student need. In the IDEA 2004 reauthorization (Individuals with Disabilities Education Act), RTI was approved as an option for schools to use, and resources may be allocated from a number of sources such as Title I and special education funds (Klinger & Eppolito, 2014; Tilly, 2006).

Watch this video to see Drs. Jana Echevarría and MaryEllen Vogt discuss RTI and its relationship with SIOP. If a student is struggling academically, what should the RTI team first consider?
https://www.youtube.com/watch?v=dU9NFf_xA-E

As we begin a discussion of the specific components of a multi-tiered approach to instruction and intervention, keep in mind that effective instruction for English learners must be situated in a context that exudes high expectations for all children, respects their language and cultural backgrounds, considers families as valued partners in their children's education, and actively assists English learners with their language development (Echevarría, Frey, & Fisher, 2015). Instruction will not be effective if children are disengaged, distressed, or feel disrespected (Jensen, 2013).

Tier 1 represents general education. Beginning in the general education classroom, teachers use evidence-based practices that work for the individual student and monitor each student's progress. Since the SIOP Model has been found to be effective with all learners—and is essential for English learners—its features should be implemented consistently to provide high-quality instruction for all students. The importance of high-quality Tier 1 instruction cannot be overstated:

> Within RTI, the frontline of prevention is Tier 1, or the general education classroom, where every student regardless of ability is to receive *high-quality* instruction. Thus, the preventive possibilities of RTI are only as good as the Tier 1 supports classroom teachers provide students (Brozo, 2010, p. 147).

Students in Tier 1 who are not keeping up may need extra support, such as some of the supplemental supports listed below. For many students, the extra attention will be enough to catch them up.

- assignments that capitalize on student strengths and interests
- specialized materials including multimedia and computer programs
- small-group or individualized instruction
- family involvement/partnership
- primary language support
- explicit teaching of strategies for children with learning problems
- more intensive English language development
- modification of assignments
- counseling services
- Saturday school or after-school sessions

However, a subset of students (approximately 20% to 30%) who have received effective instruction may require more intensive interventions to meet their learning needs (Tier 2), and the interventions used should be scientifically validated through research. Some characteristics of Tier 2 (and Tier 3) intervention include:

- small-group, classroom-based reading intervention
- homogeneous grouping by area of need
- focused and targeted instruction delivered by the general education teacher, reading specialist, or other specialist
- explicit reading instruction that emphasizes key features important for English learners and other students, including developing and practicing oral language,

key vocabulary, interaction, phonemic awareness, phonics, fluency, comprehension strategies, and so forth.

The differences between Tier 1 and Tiers 2 and 3 are the individualized nature of the instruction, the level of intensity of the intervention, and the frequency of assessments. Based on progress monitoring, the RTI team may find some students (approximately 5% to 8%) who have had systematic, effective interventions, yet do not respond (Rinaldi & Samson, 2008). These children are eligible for Tier 3, which may include special education services. Few students would be placed in this category, and this consideration is based on a student's documented response to general education and Tier 2 interventions, along with the team's informed determination that an additional level of support is needed to increase achievement.

One of the main advantages of an RTI model is its emphasis on ensuring appropriate learning opportunities for all students, beginning in the general education classroom. All students receive instruction in the core curriculum, even those who receive additional services. In other words, Tiers 2 and 3 do not compensate for ineffective Tier 1 instruction. By focusing on interventions rather than learning problems, more students' needs will be met in the least restrictive environment, and decisions about student placement will be based on documented evidence over time.

■ Issues Related to Special Education

The discussion of reading at the beginning of the chapter is closely related to any discussion of special education because approximately 80% of referrals to special education are for reading problems. It is critically important that school personnel provide the support and assistance necessary when English learners exhibit learning difficulties, and that they exhaust every option through an RTI process before considering referral to special education. As mentioned, many reading difficulties can be ameliorated when they are identified early and when appropriate support is provided to the student. However, there are students with disabilities in our schools who have the right to an appropriate individualized education, and so it is equally important to identify those children for services. In some cases, a student's learning issues are significant enough to warrant more intensive services without spending valuable time going through each step of the school's RTI or MTSS process (Fuchs, Fuchs, & Compton, 2012).

In this section we touch on a variety of issues that teachers and administrators should think about when considering special education for English learners. Some issues include:

Watch this video and think about the difference between sequential and simultaneous bilingual development. What impact does this distinction have on testing? https://www.youtube.com/watch?v= 3irqd73SPe4

- **Overrepresentation.** The overrepresentation of culturally and linguistically diverse (CLD) students in high-incidence special education programs (e.g., intellectual disabilities, learning disabilities, and emotional disturbance) has been a serious concern for decades (Artiles, 1998; Dunn, 1968; Vasquez III et al., 2011). One of the issues related to overrepresentation is that "increasing diversity of student population, increasing number of primary languages spoken in many schools, and states raising the bar of the achievement expected of all students has placed additional demands on educators who are ill prepared to teach CLD learners or infuse appropriate practices to meet their needs" (Vasquez III et al., 2011, p. 85). Teachers may believe that special education is the only way to provide extra assistance to underachieving students. Further, teachers may have low expectations for CLD students or may misread their abilities due to their lack of understanding of cultural and linguistic differences.

- **Underrepresentation.** Recent research indicates that Black, Hispanic, and Asian children were less likely to receive special education services than otherwise similar White children, and that English learners are less likely to be identified as having learning disabilities or speech or language impairments (Morgan et al., 2015). In practice, English learners may be underreferred for special education services for some of the following reasons: (1) teachers may delay referral so that students have ample opportunity to learn English, which deprives them of valuable early intervention; (2) low expectations allow English learners to languish without services; or (3) district policies require an arbitrary amount of time (e.g., 12–18 months before starting the identification process) to pass before children can be referred for the services they need. Specifically, Hispanic students are underrepresented in some regions of the United States (Skiba et al., 2008) and Asian/Pacific Islanders are significantly underrepresented throughout the United States (Cortiella, 2011).

- **Cultural Differences.** Another factor may be that the classroom is not culturally responsive, leading to a mismatch between CLD learner characteristics and the materials and teaching methods presented in the school, which contributes to underachievement among this group of students (Powers, 2001; Vogt & Shearer, 2016). Much of what students understand and are able to do in school is based on their culture and background, and most academic tasks and curricula reflect middle-class values and experiences (see Chapter 3 for more discussion). Reliance on paper-and-pencil tasks, independent reading of dense text in upper elementary grades, and information presented orally are only some of the types of academic tasks that may create difficulties for English learners. Also, children who are culturally and linguistically diverse may not have the requisite background knowledge and experience to perform well academically.

- **Underachievement.** Poor performance that often leads to special education referral and placement may also be explained by factors such as the effects of low teacher expectations (Jensen, 2008), poor study habits and inefficient time management, cultural differences in students' and teachers' behavioral expectations (Vasquez III et al., 2011), language differences (Cummins, 1984; Echevarría & Graves, 2015), and poverty (Smith, 2009). In some states, almost twice as many students in low-SES schools are placed in classes for students with learning disabilities than those from high-SES districts (Cortiella & Horowitz, 2014). Obviously, all the complexities of underachievement cannot be ameliorated with good instruction alone; however, quality of instruction is a variable that makes a difference, and it is something that is under the control of school personnel.

- **Increased Inclusion.** Teachers may be tempted to refer English learners who struggle academically to special education services, thereby relegating responsibility for meeting these students' needs to special education teachers. They expect these specialists to "fix" the problem. In reality, special education services are part of a comprehensive education plan for students who are eligible for services. Most children with learning disabilities spend the majority of their school day in the general education classroom. In fact, over 60% of students with learning disabilities spend 80% or more of their in-school time in general education classrooms (Cortiella, 2011), so all teachers share responsibility for these students.

- **Better Training for School Personnel.** Professional preparation programs for all school personnel should address effective instruction for English learners—general education, special education, reading specialists, school psychologists, and administrators. Preparing general education and special education personnel to work together effectively with English learners begins at the preservice level. Teacher preparation programs (general and special education) that address issues of diversity, social equity, second language acquisition, culturally relevant instruction methods, and empirically supported interventions contribute to a teaching force that implements meaningful and appropriate instruction for students with differing abilities (Echevarría & Graves, 2015). Working effectively with diverse populations should be a priority for teacher preparation programs, especially given demographic trends. Further, RTI is becoming common practice in schools, and when intervention is necessary, it should be provided by a well-trained specialist who has a strong background in literacy and understands the needs of English learners (Vaughn & Ortiz, 2011).

- **Need for Improved Teaching.** When teachers feel unprepared to work with students who struggle academically or who exhibit inappropriate classroom behaviors, referral to special education is often the first option to which they turn. In many ways, a teacher is the key to a student's success or failure. Students' interactions with their teachers can be either disabling or empowering, and the quality of teacher–student interactions has a significant impact on academic performance and classroom behavior (Echevarría, Frey, & Fisher, 2015). In a study on teacher–student interaction (Yoon, 2008), it was found that when teachers treat English learners with respect and have positive interactions with them, English-speaking peers follow suit. In addition, in such settings, English learners participate in class to a greater extent and learning opportunities are enhanced.

Watch this video to hear a general education teacher and a special education teacher discuss how they meet the needs of special education students in a first-grade classroom. What are some ways you might collaborate with specialists at your school to improve learning for students?

Effective SIOP teachers are culturally responsive; they reflect on their practice and are mindful of the interaction between the learner and the instructional setting, materials, and teaching methods, and they make adjustments as needed to facilitate learning. The importance of context to learning cannot be overstated; characteristics of the classroom and school can increase the risk for academic and behavior problems (see Chapter 9 for more information about the role of classroom context). Teachers need training in understanding the interaction between learning and context, avoiding the deficit model that views academic and behavior problems as a within-student problem. We have empirical and anecdotal evidence that many academic and behavioral difficulties can be attributed to the impact of the instructional setting (teacher, materials, methods) on the student, rather than some inherent problem of the learner.

In fact, in our observation of classrooms, it seems that the best option for struggling students may be the type of program offered to our most capable students. In those classes, teachers tend to capitalize on students' strengths; validate cultural and linguistic differences as resources; provide positive behavior supports; allow students time to interact and discuss ideas; and teach in creative, stimulating ways. Too many classes for low-performing students are devoid of an excitement for learning, and teachers often have low expectations for students' potential.

Special Education Services: When Are They Appropriate?

Special education services are designed to provide children who have identified disabilities with the support they need to be successful in school. Forty-two percent of the 5.7 million school-age children with all kinds of disabilities who receive special education services, are served in the LD category (Cortiella, 2014). Although learning disabilities are real and last throughout one's life span, they comprise one of the disability categories in which identification is based on the judgment of school personnel rather than that of a medical professional—and the determination can be subjective. Some other "judgmental" categories include behavior disorders, language impairments, attention deficit hyperactivity disorder, and mild intellectual disability.

Actual learning disabilities are believed to be caused by differences in brain structure and function, and they affect the brain's ability to store, process, or communicate information. They may be passed from one generation of a family to the next, and may also be caused by prenatal and birth problems, childhood experiences of traumatic injuries, severe nutritional deprivation, and exposure to poisons, including lead. However, they are not primarily the result of low intelligence; intellectual disability; emotional disturbance; cultural, environmental, or economic disadvantages; or language acquisition. It's important to note that conditions such as ADHD, autism, and intellectual disabilities are frequently confused with learning disabilities (Cortiella, 2011).

Educators should be prepared to meet the needs of students with LD within the general education classroom because these students are no longer "referred out" of general education. In fact, in 2008, 62% of students with LD spent 80% or more of their in-school time in general education classrooms, double the amount of time spent in 2000. Increasingly, general education teachers are responsible for the progress of all their students, with the support of specialists (Cortiella, 2011).

It is easy to see the complexities involved in providing appropriate services to English learners who may have learning disabilities. Disproportionate representation of minority students in special education is most pronounced among the judgmental disability categories. For example, African American and Hispanic students are overrepresented in many states while Caucasian and Asian students are underrepresented in the LD category (Cortiella, 2014).

The characteristics of children in mild to moderate disability categories are not as easily identifiable as they are in children with more significant disabilities and therefore require subjective judgment. Research indicates that it is very difficult for school personnel to distinguish between the challenges associated with acquiring a second language and those related to a language-based learning disability (Klinger & Eppolito, 2014). The distinctions can be fairly subtle, as you can see in Figure 10.1. The subjectivity of identification is exacerbated because mild to moderate disabilities do not have a clear biological cause, prompting some to argue that the disabilities themselves are socially constructed (Barnes, Mercer, & Shakespeare, 1999). What is considered "normal" is influenced by a number of factors, including culture, age, community practice, point in history, and school expectations. The labels associated with mild disabilities may be assigned arbitrarily and are subject to extreme variability in identification rates The lowest rate of LD is reported among Asians. For example, in California just 3 percent of students with LD are Asian, while 11.2 percent of the total school enrollment is Asian (Cortiella, 2014).

FIGURE 10.1 Causes of Confusion in Assessing Students with Language Differences and/or Language Learning Disabilities

Language Differences	Language Learning Disabilities
Language performance is similar to that of other students who have had comparable cultural and linguistic experiences.	Language patterns are unique to the student and unlike others in the student's cultural community.
Limited vocabulary in the native language is due to lack of opportunity to use and hear the native language.	Student demonstrates limited vocabulary even when there are rich language opportunities in the native language.
Student shifts from one language to another within an utterance.	Word-finding problems are evident and student substitutes with another language.
Communication may be impeded by an accent or dialect.	Student exhibits deficits in expressive and receptive language, which impede communication.
Pragmatic skills such as ability to interpret facial expressions, appropriate physical proximity, and use and interpretation of gestures are age appropriate.	Student demonstrates difficulty using and interpreting nonverbal language, often leading to social problems.

In determining whether a student qualifies for special education services, we need to ensure that the student has been provided ample opportunity to respond to effective instruction and intervention and that an appropriate process of progress monitoring and intervention has been followed. The reality is that a number of variables affect what happens once a student experiences considerable difficulties in the general education program—academic, behavioral, or both. For English learners, low English **language proficiency**, gaps in educational experience, and cultural differences influence the referral process. Moreover, teachers have a tremendous impact on who is referred and who is not. Research indicates that two factors influence referral: (1) teacher tolerance and (2) the interaction of perceived student ability or behavior with the teacher's own expectations and approach to instruction and classroom management (Podell & Soodak, 1993). Subjectivity is part of the evaluation process—including whom to test, which test to use, when to use alternative **assessments**, and how to interpret the results (Klinger & Eppolito, 2014; Losen & Orfield, 2002). So if teachers have an understanding of cultural and linguistic differences and the modifications those differences require, effective instruction and intervention in the general education classroom is more likely.

Search for Intervention Rather than Disability

The principles of RTI have fostered increased awareness that learning difficulties are often the result of instructional issues, not an inherent problem in the learner. Since all students *can* learn, it is incumbent upon educators to find the best ways to reach and teach each struggling learner. Collaborative teams offer an effective means for supporting struggling students as well as providing support for teachers. Team members work together to explore options for instruction and intervention, monitor progress, and perform other related duties. Membership must include experts knowledgeable about English learners and second language acquisition, and parents should also be included since they offer valuable insight into their child's development and home life.

Collaborative site-based teams have been shown to decrease referral and special education placement and even to reduce disproportionate referrals of minority students to special education (Kampwirth & Powers, 2016; Klinger & Eppolito, 2015).

If a student does not improve after intensive intervention and progress monitoring have been tried and documented, he or she would be considered for special education services. All children eligible for special education services have gone through a referral, assessment, and placement process. In those states with an effective RTI process in place, failure to respond to intensive intervention would suffice for qualification. In others, a full battery of assessments is completed to determine eligibility for special education services.

Once it has been determined that a student qualifies for special education services, his or her individualized educational plan (IEP) will include instructional strategies and modifications that are tailored to demonstrated needs, including English language development (Echevarría, Powers, & Elliott, 2004). Further, instruction needs to be evidence based. Kretlow and Blatz (2011) identify the ABCs of evidence-based practice for special education teachers.

- **A**ccess evidence-based practice through journals and online resources such as the IRIS Center.

- **Be** careful with fidelity by implementing the practice in the way it was designed and tested through research. With the SIOP Model, we found that student achievement was directly linked to how well teachers implemented the model with fidelity (Echevarría, Richards-Tutor, Chinn, & Ratleff, 2011).
- Check student progress at regular intervals using progress monitoring and curriculum-based assessment.

Kretlow and Blatz (2011) conclude—and we concur—that "using evidence-based practices with fidelity and ongoing progress monitoring gives students with disabilities the best chance at achieving their goals" (p. 18).

Teaching Ideas for Students with Special Needs

In the section that follows, you will find some teaching ideas to help you prepare lessons that are designed for children who receive special education services.

- **Collaborative Strategic Reading (CSR).** This research-based intervention has been successfully implemented and studied in culturally and linguistically diverse, inclusive classrooms from fourth grade through middle school (Klingner, Vaughn, Argüelles, Hughes, & Ahwee, 2004). CSR includes strategies for summarizing information, asking and answering questions, monitoring comprehension and taking steps to improve understanding, and encouraging peer discussion. The structure of CSR is divided into before, during, and after reading activities.
- **Implement SIOP Components.** The SIOP Model is effective for children with learning differences. In studies that included students with learning disabilities, students made significant growth in writing when teachers used the SIOP Model (Echevarría, 1998; Richards & Funk, 2009).
- **Use Assistive Technology.** Children with severe reading disabilities may benefit from computer programs that can scan words and "read" them aloud via synthesized voices, some of which sound human. Also, voice recognition software can help children who have trouble writing their ideas down on paper by pen or typing. It allows them to talk into a microphone and immediately see their words on screen. Some programs use visual prompts and templates to help organize thoughts, improve writing skills, and keep track of tasks. The effectiveness of such programs has yet to be determined for individual students, especially for those who have difficulty with numerous visual cues. While there are myriad apps and programs to assist children with learning disabilities, only a small percentage—estimated at between 25% and 35%—of children with LD are being provided with assistive technology to support their instruction and learning (Cortiella, 2011).
- **Focus Students' Attention.** Limit the clutter and excessive visual stimuli in the classroom. While we advocate word walls and other visuals to assist students in information recall and vocabulary development, they must be used with discretion. Students with disabilities may have difficulty focusing on important posted information when they are distracted by artwork and projects hanging around the room.

- **Use Repetition.** Children will retain more information if it is repeated and reviewed frequently. Poor memory is often a characteristic of children with special needs, especially memory that is associated with symbols (e.g., letters and numbers).

- **Allow Extra Time for Students to Process Information.** Children with learning differences are often just processing a question by the time the answer is expected. Teachers may use strategies such as asking a question, letting the student know he or she will be asked for the answer, and then coming back to the student.

- **Scaffold Assessment to Measure Understanding.** Students' disabilities can interfere with their demonstration of knowledge and understanding. These children may have difficulty with learning vocabulary, expressing their ideas, or using language adequately. Rather than asking a student to write an explanation of a concept, have him or her list the features of the concept or label a graphic organizer that is provided; ask the child to complete an outline rather than generate a summary or essay; or have the student select examples from a list provided instead of asking him or her to produce examples.

- **Differentiate the Curriculum to Students' Needs.** Modify the number of items the child completes; increase the amount of personal assistance given; provide different materials to meet a child's individual needs; or allot a different amount of time for learning, task completion, or testing.

- **Be Sensitive to Frustration Levels.** Children with special needs often have a lower frustration threshold than typical learners, which may result in their having outbursts or giving up. A structured learning environment, scaffolded instruction, and opportunities to experience success help alleviate frustration.

All of these suggestions for assisting children with learning and behavior problems have commonalities: They must be used consistently; data must be used to monitor student learning; student well-being is the focus; and there is a commitment to enhancing learning for all students.

Reflect and Apply

Click here to reflect on your knowledge of multi-tiered systems of support.

Check Your Understanding

Click here to check your understanding of Chapter 10, Issues of Reading, RTI, and Special Education for English Learners.

◼ Summary

As you reflect on this chapter and the issues of reading, RTI, and special education for English learners, consider the following points:

- Traditional reading assessments, such as informal reading inventories and phonics tests, may be inappropriate for English learners. Teachers are cautioned to not overgeneralize the results of these assessments.

- Linguistic differences between students' home languages and English may cause English learners difficulty with literacy development. When classroom teachers implement the features of the SIOP Model, many children with reading and learning difficulties find success. Very often, students' academic difficulties have more to do with the curriculum, teaching methods, and classroom setting than with any disability the student may have.

- The Common Core and other rigorous state standards require sophisticated levels of reading, writing, listening, and speaking. Through the standards and with appropriate instruction, English learners and struggling readers are provided the opportunity to read and think deeply about complex texts they are taught to read. This requires that teachers know and use information about English learners' L1 language and literacy development.

- The SIOP Model provides teachers with a guide to lesson planning and delivery that offers an instructional program appropriate for *all* students in their classes: those with limited English proficiency, those who excel academically, those who are performing at grade level, those with low academic levels, those who find reading difficult, those who have experienced persistent failure, those who work hard but continue to struggle academically, and those with problematic behaviors.

- The result of an effective RTI process is that (a) fewer students from diverse backgrounds are inappropriately identified as having disabilities and (b) those who require special education services will have IEPs that include instructional strategies and modifications tailored to their demonstrated needs (Echevarría, Powers, & Elliott, 2004).

- Effective instruction and intervention offer supports to struggling students. Most importantly, we want to avoid labeling children with reading problems or disabilities and instead provide them with the most appropriate and effective instructional context possible.

■ Discussion Questions

1. In reflecting on the content and language objectives at the beginning of the chapter, are you able to:
   a. Explain how linguistic differences in home languages and English can affect English learners' reading and writing development?
   b. Describe in-class supports and/or modifications that content teachers can provide to English learners and struggling readers?
   c. Delineate a sequence of steps involved in an effective RTI process to ensure appropriate services for English learners?
   d. Discuss with a group how to plan appropriate instruction for English learners who may have reading and learning difficulties?
   e. Write a lesson plan that develops vocabulary and reading proficiency for English learners who struggle to read and learn?

2. Select an English learner in your class who is having difficulty with reading and/or content learning. Reread the questions in this chapter on pages p. 259. Begin with the first question:

   a. What evidence do you have that a particular student is having difficulty with reading? Try to provide answers to the other questions as they relate to your identified student.

   b. If questions 1a–e are answered negatively, what are the implications for your instruction of this student, and for the other teachers who work with him or her?

   c. Now examine Figure 10.1. From your work with this student, using your best guess as well as any assessment findings you have—including a measure of English language proficiency that you may need to obtain from your school's ESL specialist—see if any of the descriptions of Language Differences and/or Language Learning Disabilities match your student.

3. In this chapter, we have discussed some of the reasons why minority students, including many English learners, are over- and underrepresented in special education. How can RTI help ensure that English learners are receiving an appropriate education and that proper services are offered as needed?

4. How would you respond to a teacher who says, "Well, if I follow the SIOP Model and make sure my English learners are able to access content using these activities, techniques, and approaches, my on-level kids and **native English speakers** will be bored."

   a. Do you agree with this statement? Why or why not? What research presented in this book supports your position?

   b. How can teachers with only a few English learners in their classrooms organize instruction so that all children's needs are met?

   c. Which, if any, of the activities, methods, or SIOP features in this book are inappropriate for some students, such as accelerated learners?

   d. Recent research has shown that all students benefit from high-quality SIOP Model lessons. But from our experience, some teachers think otherwise. Prepare a response to these teachers' concerns.

CHAPTER 11

Effective Use of the SIOP® Protocol

Learning Outcomes

After reading, discussing, and engaging in activities related to this chapter, you will be able to meet the following **content** and **language objectives**.

Content Objectives

Examine how all **SIOP** features fit into one lesson plan.

Use the SIOP protocol to rate and assess a teacher's lesson.

Language Objectives

Discuss SIOP scores at a post-observation conference with the teacher whose lesson was rated.

Explain the value of observing and rating lessons over time using SIOP.

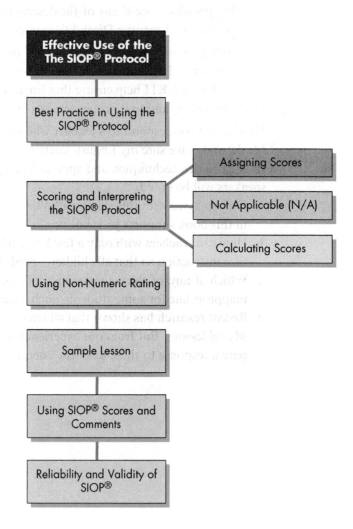

Effective Use of the The SIOP® Protocol

- Best Practice in Using the SIOP® Protocol
- Scoring and Interpreting the SIOP® Protocol
  - Assigning Scores
  - Not Applicable (N/A)
  - Calculating Scores
- Using Non-Numeric Rating
- Sample Lesson
- Using SIOP® Scores and Comments
- Reliability and Validity of SIOP®

Most of the previous chapters focused on the components of the SIOP Model and their implementation. We know that effective SIOP implementation is critical for improving student achievement (Echevarría, Richards-Tutor, Chinn & Ratleff, 2011), but how can it be measured? The SIOP protocol is an observation instrument that was designed to document the extent to which SIOP features are present in a lesson.

Fotostorm/E+/GettyImages

The SIOP Model and its protocol have been used in school districts and universities around the country since the 1990s with measurable success. We have interviewed many school personnel who have told us their stories of SIOP implementation (Echevarría, Short, & Vogt, 2008). From their stories and our experience with SIOP professional learning, we offer in this chapter suggestions and guidelines for using the protocol effectively. ●

■ Best Practice in Using the SIOP® Protocol

> Watch this video to see a SIOP coach discuss using the SIOP protocol. What are some ways the protocol was used with teachers? What are some ways you might use it?

Initially we developed the SIOP protocol because we found that school personnel and researchers wanted and needed an objective measure of high-quality **sheltered instruction** for English learners. Over time, uses of the SIOP protocol have expanded.

The SIOP protocol provides a tool for gauging the quality of a lesson. Qualitative and quantitative information written by an observer on the protocol form documents lesson effectiveness and shows areas that need improvement. The observation data recorded on the protocol may be used by teachers, coaches, administrators, university faculty, and researchers.

Teachers find the SIOP protocol useful for improving their own practice through self-reflection and/or peer coaching (Song, 2016). Some schools reported that their teachers regularly used the protocol to reflect on their lessons, completing the protocol after they taught a specific lesson. More effective is the practice of videotaping lessons and scoring the lessons on their various SIOP features. The objectivity the camera provides is valuable to teachers in helping them to recognize their strengths as well as areas that need attention.

Some schools used designated SIOP coaches or peer coaches to assist teachers in SIOP implementation. In one school district, a coach modeled a SIOP lesson for a group of three to five peers. Using the SIOP protocol without the rating numbers, the group debriefed the lesson and discussed the components of SIOP. The focus of the debriefing and discussion was on the comments written on the protocol. Participants wrote what they saw the coach do and described it on the protocol under each corresponding feature. At the conclusion of the session, one of the teachers in the group volunteered to model a lesson during the following two-month period. Because of the non-evaluative nature of the feedback, it wasn't difficult to get teachers to volunteer. The coach assisted the teacher volunteer in planning a lesson that was later modeled for the group. Feedback from the group was always limited to positive comments and a discussion of how the lesson matched SIOP features. After each teacher in the group had a turn at modeling a SIOP lesson for the group, the individuals then became coaches for another small group of teachers. In this way, a large number of teachers learned and practiced using the SIOP Model and had the opportunity to understand it deeply (Echevarría, Short, & Vogt, 2008).

A number of sources have reported that schoolwide use of the SIOP Model and protocol provides a common language and conceptual framework from which to work and develop a community of practice. School site administrators commented that the features of the SIOP bring together in one place many of the ideas and techniques staff have learned through district professional learning efforts. For example, a school's staff may have received inservice training in use of technology, Thinking Maps, productive group work, or differentiated instruction, but teachers may struggle with how to incorporate these varied ideas into their daily teaching practice. The SIOP provides a framework for systematically addressing and incorporating a variety of techniques and initiatives into one's teaching practice.

The SIOP protocol is useful for administrators because it provides them with a way of understanding instruction for English learners. Administrators typically do not have the same opportunities to learn about effective instruction for English learners that are available to the teachers on their staff (Short, Vogt, & Echevarría, 2017). Yet the administrator is responsible for observing and providing feedback to teaching personnel. The SIOP protocol gives administrators a means for providing clear, concrete feedback to the teachers they observe. The format allows for rating of lessons, but, more importantly, has space for writing comments that will be constructive for improving instruction for English learners.

University faculty have also found the SIOP Model and protocol to be useful in courses that specifically address the needs of English learners (Smolen et al., 2015). The individual components allow professors to focus on manageable chunks of information so that students learn and understand how to present effective instruction to English learners over time. Faculty who supervise field experience find that the SIOP protocol assists in providing concrete examples of techniques necessary for making instruction comprehensible for English learners and developing their English proficiency. Feedback on the rating and comments sections of the instrument assists student teachers in their professional development.

Finally, the SIOP protocol is a tool researchers can use to determine the extent to which SIOP instruction is implemented in a given classroom. It can also be used to measure consistency and fidelity of implementation. An increasing number of research studies have used the SIOP protocol to measure effective instruction for English learners (Bose, 2012; Rodriguez 2010; Torres, 2006; Vidot, 2011).

■ Scoring and Interpreting the SIOP® Protocol

The heading on the first page of the SIOP protocol is fairly self-explanatory (see Figure 11.1). It is intended to provide a context for the lesson being observed. There is space for the observer's name and the date of the observation. Other information, such as the teacher's name, school, grade of the class being observed, ESL level of the students, and the academic content area, is also included. We recognize that an observation at one point in time does not always accurately represent the teacher's implementation of SIOP strategies and techniques. Therefore, there is a place for the observer to indicate if the lesson is part of a multiday unit or is a single-day lesson.

In employing the SIOP protocol, we have found that it is most useful to videotape a lesson and analyze it later. Teachers, supervisors, and researchers alike have found this to be an effective way of recording and measuring teachers' growth over time. The recording number may be written on the heading to indicate its corresponding lesson.

Finally, there is a box for the total score the lesson received on the SIOP protocol. It is most useful to represent the score as a percentage because N/A (not applicable) affects a total score number (see the next section for an explanation of scoring).

When scoring a lesson is appropriate, an observer may assign scores in a number of ways: (1) during the observation itself, as individual features are recognized; (2) after the observation, as the observer reflects on the entire lesson, referring to observational field notes; or (3) after the observation while watching a videotape of the lesson. The third option is often useful so that the teacher and observer are able to share the same point of reference when discussing the lesson.

FIGURE 11.1 SIOP® Heading

The Sheltered Instruction Observation Protocol (SIOP®) (Echevarría, Vogt, & Short, 2000; 2004; 2008; 2013; 2017)

Observer(s): _____
Date: _____
Grade: _____
ESL Level: _____

Teacher: _____
School: _____
Class/Topic: _____
Lesson: Multiday Single-day
(circle one)

Total Points Possible: 120 (Subtract 4 points for each N/A given) _____

Total Points Earned: _____ Percentage Score: _____

Directions: Circle the number that best reflects what you observe in a SIOP lesson. You may give a score from 0–4 (or N/A on selected items). Cite under "Comments" specific examples of the behaviors observed.

It is important to stress that not all features on the SIOP will be present in every lesson. However, some features, such as items under Lesson Preparation, Comprehensible Input, Interaction, and Review & Assessment, are essential for each lesson. Over the course of time (several lessons, a unit, a week), all features should be represented.

Assigning Scores

We suggest that an observer determine the level of SIOP implementation by using the scenario descriptions in this book as a guide. Each chapter's scenarios were designed to show a clear example for each feature, with scores ranging from 0 to 4. The SIOP protocol provides a five-point scale as well as space for qualitative data. It is recommended that the observer use the "Comments" section to record examples of the presence or absence of each feature. That way, both the observer and the teacher have specific information, besides a score, to use in their post-lesson discussion. More information may be added to the Comments section during the post-lesson review of the SIOP protocol so that elements of the discussion are recorded for future reference. Also, these comments are useful when subsequent lessons are planned. In any case, sufficient notes with examples of how the feature was addressed should be included to provide concrete feedback with each score.

Naturally, there is an element of subjectivity to interpreting the features and assigning scores. Observers must be consistent in their scoring so establishing **inter-rater reliability** is important. (See *www.siop.pearson* for information on establishing inter-rater reliability.) For example, one person may think that for Feature #3 (Content concepts appropriate for age and educational background level of students) only grade-level materials are appropriate, while another observer may feel that the same content found in materials for lower grade levels can be used because of the students' low reading levels or because students have interrupted educational backgrounds. In either case, observers should establish a common understanding and interpretation of the features, and rate lessons accordingly across settings.

We suggest that to assist in more accurate scoring, the observer ask the teacher for a copy of the lesson plan in advance of observing the class. Ideally, the teacher and observer would meet for a pre-observation conference to discuss the lesson plan and provide the observer with background about the lesson. In this way, the observer is better able to rate the lesson, especially the Lesson Preparation section and N/A items.

Not Applicable (N/A) Category

The Not Applicable (N/A) rating is important because it distinguishes a feature that is "not applicable" to the observed lesson from a score of "0," which indicates that the feature should have been present but was not. For example, Mr. Leung taught a five-day unit on the solar system. During the first few lessons of the unit, Mr. Leung concentrated on making the rather dense information accessible to his students. He adapted the text to make it understandable for them and provided ample opportunities for students to use learning strategies. On the final day of the unit, an observer was present. Mr. Leung wrapped up the unit by having the students complete an enjoyable hands-on activity in which they applied the concepts they had learned. It was obvious that the students had learned the content and were able to use it in the activity. However, because of the nature of that particular lesson, there was no observed adaptation of content (Feature #5). The overall percentage score of Mr. Leung's lesson was not lowered by receiving a score of "0" on Feature #5 because the lesson did not lend itself to that item and he had covered it on another day. A rating of N/A would be correct in this case.

In contrast, consider the case of Mrs. Nash. She also taught a unit on the solar system. On the first day of the unit, she showed a video about the solar system and had a brief oral discussion with the class following the video. The next day an observer was present as she read from the text and then had students answer chapter questions. There was no evidence that any of the content had been adapted to the variety of student proficiency levels in her class. In fact, many students appeared to be confused as they tried to answer questions based on the grade-level textbook. So, in this case, it would be appropriate to rate Feature #5 as "0"; adaptation would have benefited the English learners.

The distinction between a "0" and "N/A" is an important one because a rating of "0" adversely affects the overall score for the lesson, while an "N/A" does not because a percentage is used to indicate a lesson's score.

Calculating Scores

There are 30 features on the SIOP protocol, each with a range of possible scores from 0 to 4, or N/A, for five features. After scoring each feature, the observer tallies all numeric scores. The tallied total is written over the total possible score, usually 120, so an example of a total score would be written 115/120. Because of the N/A, adding the individual scores for a grand total is meaningless. It is more informative to know the total score based on the total possible score.

Let's take a step-by-step look at how a lesson's total score is calculated.

Mr. Leung's lesson received a score of 4 on 20 features, a score of 3 on 5 features, a score of 2 on 4 features, and 1 N/A. The sum of those scores is 103.

$$20 \times 4 = 80$$

$$5 \times 3 = 15$$

$$4 \times 2 = \underline{8}$$

Total score = 103/116

The total possible score of 116 was derived in this way: If the lesson had received a 4 on each feature of the SIOP (a perfect score), it would have had a total score of 116.

$$29 \times 4 = 116$$

The number of features is 29 instead of 30 because one feature was not applicable (N/A); the lesson was rated on only 29 features.

Mr. Leung's lesson received a total score of 103/116. The total score can be converted to a percentage if that form is more useful. Simply divide the numerator by the denominator: $103 \div 116$. In this case, the SIOP was implemented at a level of 88%. You can see the importance of distinguishing between a score of 0 and N/A. For

Mr. Leung's lesson, a 0 score would have changed the total score from 88% to 85%. Let's see how.

$$20 \times 4 = 80$$
$$5 \times 3 = 15$$
$$4 \times 2 = 8$$
$$1 \times 0 = \underline{0}$$

Total score = 103/120

The highest possible score on the SIOP for all 30 features is 120 (30 items $\times$ a score of 4). If Mr. Leung's lesson were rated on all 30 features, the total score would be 103/120, or 85%.

The step-by-step process for tallying scores is shown in Figure 11.2.

In our research studies using the SIOP protocol for measuring level of implementation, we established the following guidelines:

High implementation—lessons that receive a score of 75% or higher

Medium implementation—lessons that receive a score between 50% and 75%

Low implementation—lessons that receive a score of 50% or lower

In determining the overall level of implementation, we typically conducted two or three observations from one teacher's class over the course of one year and averaged those scores.

FIGURE 11.2 The Step-by-Step Process for Tallying Scores

1. Add the lesson's scores from all features.
2. Count the number of N/As, multiply by 4, then subtract this number from 120.
3. Divide the number from step 2 into the number from step 1 (the adjusted possible score into the lesson's score).
4. The result is the percentage score.

■ Using Non-Numeric Rating

Our colleagues at the University of Houston–Clear Lake, Laurie Weaver and Judith Marquez, have used the SIOP Model extensively in teacher preparation. They also facilitate a SIOP professional development learning group at an elementary school where, in their fourth year, teachers observe one another. Through their experience, they found it useful to change the rating scale from 0–4 to Novice–Expert as seen in Figure 11.3. In this case, the observer would mark an X along the continuum to indicate if the feature was demonstrated at the expert level, novice level, or somewhere in between. Typically when they used the protocol with numbers, every teacher thought he/she would score a 4 in every category. Once Weaver and Marquez started talking about 4 being expert level, they began to see people thinking more realistically about their practice. The professors reported that conversations changed and teachers were more open to thinking deeply about how they might improve their practice. We have

FIGURE 11.3 Expert – Novice Rating

Expert		Novice
1. **Content objectives** clearly defined, displayed and reviewed with students	**Content objectives** for students implied	No clearly defined **content objectives** for students

Comments:

Expert		Novice
2. **Language objectives** clearly defined, displayed and reviewed with students	**Language objectives** for students implied	No clearly defined **language objectives** for students

Comments:

Expert		Novice
3. **Content concepts** appropriate for age and educational background level of students	**Content concepts** somewhat appropriate for age and educational background level of students	**Content concepts** inappropriate for age and educational background level of students

Comments:

also had situations where teachers interpreted the numbers as grades: A, B, C, D, and F and were sometimes defensive if they didn't receive what they perceived to be all A's. Removing the numbers diffuses those sorts of situations and allows observers and teachers to have more substantive and productive post-observation discussions.

Sample Lesson

In this section of the chapter, we will describe an entire science lesson conducted by a sixth-grade teacher and show how it was scored on the SIOP protocol. Ms. Clark received SIOP professional development and has been using the model for lesson planning and delivery for about 16 months. This observed lesson took place at the end of the first quarter of the school year. The class consisted of beginning ESL students from varying language backgrounds and countries of origin. The class has been studying a unit on minerals and visited a local natural history museum. The students have examined rocks in class as well. Ms. Clark provided us with a lesson plan before we conducted the observation.

In the classroom, the desks were arranged in three circular groups. Some students had to turn around to see the interactive whiteboard at the front of the room. The lesson objectives and agenda were written on a whiteboard at the side. Two bulletin boards in the back of the room displayed the students' work for a language arts project and a science project. A Spanish-speaking bilingual aide assisted the teacher and also helped newly arrived Spanish-speaking students. The class period was 45 minutes long.

The teacher began the class by complimenting the students for their performance on a test they had taken on minerals and singled out one student who received the highest A grade in the class. She then asked the students to read the objectives and activities for the day silently while she read them aloud:

Content Objective: Today we will:

- write facts about volcanoes using a semantic map.
- identify the sequence of events that leads to volcanic eruption.

Then she stated her plan for the day:

- First, I will demonstrate how rocks could move and what happens when they move.
- Second, you will use a semantic web worksheet to recall what you know about volcanoes.
- Third, I will use a model to show how a volcano erupts.
- Fourth, you will make predictions about the story *Pompeii . . . Buried Alive*, and then read pages 4 to 9 silently.
- Fifth, you will refer to information on page 6 in the book to write on a worksheet the steps that happen before a volcano erupts.
- Your homework is to draw a volcano and label the parts. The vocabulary words and terms for the day are: *melts, blast, mixture, rumbles, straw, pipe, shepherd, giant, peddler, crater, lava, magma, magma chamber.*

Ms. Clark then demonstrated for the class what happens when rocks move against each other, using two stacks of books. After placing the stacks side by side on a desk, she pushed against one stack so the other stack slid off the desk and books scattered onto the floor. She asked the students what happens when one set of rocks moves another set of rocks. The students responded that the rocks break.

The aide distributed semantic web worksheets to the students and asked them to write "Volcano" in the center circle. Then, in the other spaces, students were to write everything they already knew about volcanoes. While the students worked, the teacher and aide circulated to monitor the students' understanding of the task and to see how they were progressing.

After the students filled in their webs, the teacher led them in a discussion of what they had written and wrote some of their comments on the interactive whiteboard:

- Lava melts and explodes.
- When it erupts, all that force comes from the middle of the earth.
- Volcanoes are formed deep inside the earth.
- When a volcano is under water, the lava comes out and makes an island.

The teacher repeated that she was going to make a model volcano and asked the class what a "model" is. One student answered that it is an example, not a real volcano. All of the students watched as the teacher showed them a bottle and explained it would be like the magma chamber that is inside a volcano. She poured a cup of warm water inside the bottle. While it cooled slightly, she showed the class a diagram of the model for the experiment on the interactive whiteboard and highlighted the labels of the corresponding volcano parts as she explained. They discussed each part of the volcano and in doing so emphasized some of the key vocabulary terms: *crater, magma pipe, lava, magma, magma chamber, basin.*

The teacher returned to the model and placed a few drops of liquid dish detergent in the warm water. Next, she picked up an object and asked the students to identify it. One student said it was a measuring spoon. The teacher measured a teaspoon of baking soda and put it into the water and detergent mixture. She asked the students to identify where she was putting it. The students responded, "magma chamber." She put in a second teaspoon of baking soda and then held up the bottle for the students to observe, and then they reviewed the ingredients. To speed up the process, she added vinegar to the bottle. She asked them, "When was the last time we used vinegar?" The students said they had used it on the previous day. The "volcano" began to erupt, and the teacher displayed the bottle so that the students could see the foam overflowing.

The class reviewed the process and the ingredients for the model volcano. Individual students were called to the front to participate in a second volcano demonstration, each one completing one of the steps to produce another "eruption." The second "lava" flow was a bit larger than the first.

The teacher asked the whole class to consider this question: "What causes a volcano to erupt?" She added, "We used warm water. What will happen to heat in a chamber?" One student answered, "Heat rises." The teacher explained that it was not just the heat that caused the eruption and asked them to think of the other ingredients and what happened when they were mixed. The teacher went on to explain, "The mixture of gases produces carbon monoxide," and wrote "carbon monoxide" and its chemical symbol on the board. She also asked them what they knew about plants and said, "They breathe in carbon monoxide. We breathe out carbon monoxide; we breathe in oxygen." [This part was an error, but the teacher did not realize her mistake in calling carbon dioxide (for plants and humans), carbon monoxide.]

One student wanted to know why rocks come out of volcanoes and another student offered an explanation, "The volcano is inside of a mountain of rocks." The teacher commented that whatever is inside the chamber when it erupts will come out with the lava, and if they had put small bits of material inside their model, those bits also would have come out when it erupted.

The teacher and aide handed out the storybook *Pompeii . . . Buried Alive* to the students, and they began prereading activities. The teacher focused their attention on the title and asked them to predict what they thought the book would be about. One student said, "Volcanoes erupting." The teacher asked, "Where do you think it takes place?" Students guessed various places: Nicaragua, Rome, Greece, England. The teacher commented on the togas in the cover's picture. She then directed their attention to the back cover and read the summary aloud, stating the story took place

2,000 years ago in Italy. She asked, "Is it a true story?" Some students guessed yes; others no. "How do you know it's true?" They discussed that the term "took place" and the use of a specific time in history meant that it was true. The teacher then asked for a student volunteer to point out Italy on the wall map, and the class discussed the location of Italy in southern Europe.

The teacher asked how many of the students came from countries with volcanoes. Students from Ethiopia, El Salvador, and Guatemala said they knew about volcanoes in their countries. One student asked if it had to be a hot country to have a volcano. The teacher asked if they knew where a recent eruption had occurred. She told them it was Popocatépeti in Mexico and that volcanoes often occur in warm countries, but not all are in warm countries. She asked if they knew about a volcano in the United States and told them about Mount St. Helens in Washington, a state that is cold in winter. She showed them Washington on the map. One student commented on the way precipitation forms and tried to compare it with what happens in the formation of a volcano.

The teacher directed the students to read pages 4 to 9 silently for two minutes. While they were reading, she distributed worksheets with a sequencing exercise to describe what happens before a volcano erupts. The instructions told students to put the sentences in order according to what they read on page 6. They could refer back to the reading.

The teacher began to read the passage aloud slowly about three minutes later, although some students indicated that they had not yet finished reading it silently. As she read, she again displayed the model volcano diagram on the interactive whiteboard and referred to it and to the key vocabulary as she read. She also paused from time to time to ask comprehension questions. Students were able to answer questions orally, using the model and naming the parts of a volcano. They discussed unknown words in the reading, such as *peddler*, *rumbled*, and *shepherd*, as they went along.

As the period drew to a close, the teacher told the students they would complete the sequencing worksheet the next day. She reminded them of the homework—draw a volcano in their journal and label the parts. They were also told to place the webs they had completed in their journals. The teacher then led a brief wrap-up of the lesson, asking questions about a volcano, which students answered.

On the following pages (Figure 11.4), you will see how Ms. Clark's lesson was rated on the SIOP items and the Comments that provide evidence for the score.

■ Using SIOP® Scores and Comments

If lessons are rated, comments supporting the scores are essential. A completed protocol can be used as a starting point for a collaborative discussion between a teacher and a supervisor or coach, or among a group of teachers. We have found that videotaping a lesson, rating it (or writing comments without scores), and discussing it with the teacher provides an effective forum for professional growth. We also get valuable information from teachers explaining a student's behavior or why something may not have taken place despite it being included in the lesson plan, for example. The discussion may take place between the teacher and the observer, or a group of teachers

FIGURE 11.4 The Sheltered Instruction Observation Protocol (SIOP®)

The Sheltered Instruction Observation Protocol (SIOP®)
(Echevarría, Vogt, & Short, 2000; 2004; 2008; 2013; 2017)

Observer(s): J. Cruz
Date: 10/29
Grade: 6
ESL Level: Beginner

Teacher: Ms. Clark
School: Cloverleaf
Class/Topic: Science
Lesson: Multi-day (Single-day) (circle one)

Total Points Possible: 120 (Subtract 4 points for each N/A given) 120
Total Points Earned: 94   Percentage Score: 78%

Directions: Circle the number that best reflects what you observe in a sheltered lesson. You may give a score from 0–4 (or N/A on selected items). Cite under "Comments" specific examples of the behaviors observed.

Lesson Preparation

4	3	2	1	0
(4)		Content objectives for students implied		No clearly defined content objectives for students
1. Content objectives are clearly defined, displayed and reviewed with students				

Comments: Content objectives were written and stated at the beginning of the lesson.

4	3	(2)	1	0
		Language objectives for students implied		No clearly defined language objectives for students
2. Language objectives are clearly defined, displayed, and reviewed with students				

Comments: No specific language objective was written or stated. Key vocabulary was listed, but the language skills to be targeted were listed and stated as activities and not written as objectives. Implied reading and sequencing.

4	3	(2)	1	0
		Content concepts somewhat appropriate for age and educational background level of students		Content concepts inappropriate for age and educational background level of students
3. Content concepts appropriate for age and educational background level of students				

Comments: Students seemed to understand the concepts. However, several students mentioned that they studied volcanoes in earlier grades. It is unclear why volcanoes were taught when these concepts had been introduced previously.

4	3	2	1	0
(4)		Some use of supplementary materials		No use of supplementary materials
4. Supplementary materials used to a high degree, making the lesson clear and meaningful (e.g., computer programs, graphs, models, visuals)				

Comments: Good use of supplementary materials to enhance students' understanding of volcanoes such as copies of semantic maps, pull-down maps, a book, Pompeii ... Buried Alive, a projected image of the parts of a volcano, stacks of books to demonstrate rocks pushing against each other, household items to demonstrate a volcanic eruption.

(continued)

FIGURE 11.4 The Sheltered Instruction Observation Protocol (SIOP®) *(continued)*

Lesson Preparation (continued)

	4	3	2	1	0	N/A
5. **Adaptation of content** (e.g., text, assignment) to all levels of student proficiency	④		Some **adaption of content** to all levels of student proficiency		No significant **adaption of content** to all levels of student proficiency	

Comments: All students were given the same text with which to work. There were no specific adaptations made to the text itself to address the varying levels of language proficiency. However, the teacher had prepared a sequencing activity for students to complete where she identified sentences that explained the process of a volcanic eruption and students were required to put the steps in order. In addition, she began reading the text aloud to the students and paused frequently to ask questions and to check for clarification.

	4	3	2	1	0	N/A
6. **Meaningful activities** that integrate lesson concepts (e.g., surveys, letter writing, simulations, models) with language practice opportunities for reading, writing, listening, and/or speaking	④		**Meaningful activities** that integrate lesson concepts but provide little opportunity for language practice with opportunities for reading, writing, listening, and/or speaking		No **meaningful activities** that integrate lesson concepts with language practice	

Comments: There were a lot of meaningful and interesting activities that provided students with language practice (e.g., participation in building the model volcano, discussing information from their semantic maps about volcanoes, and reading authentic text).

Building Background

	4	3	2	1	0	N/A
7. **Concepts explicitly linked** to students' background experiences	④		**Concepts loosely linked** to students' background experiences		**Concepts not explicitly linked** to students' background experiences	

Comments: The teacher tapped into students' understanding of volcanoes by asking them to complete a semantic mapping exercise, writing everything they knew about volcanoes.

	4	3	2	1	0	N/A
8. **Links explicitly made** between past learning and new concepts			**Few links made** between past learning and new concepts ②		**No links made** between past learning and new concepts	

Comments: There were few links made between past learning and its connection to new concepts. The teacher initiated the class by reminding the students of the visit to the Museum of Natural History and also reminded them of the rocks they had brought in. However, she did not explain how the visit or the collection of rocks related to that day's lesson about volcanoes.

Building Background (continued)

4	3	2	1	0
9. **Key vocabulary** emphasized (e.g., introduced, written, repeated, and highlighted for students to see)		**Key vocabulary** introduced, but not emphasized		**Key vocabulary** not introduced or emphasized

Comments: The key vocabulary words used for this lesson were written on the board, stated to the students at the beginning of the lesson, and reiterated throughout the lesson, particularly when the teacher and students constructed the model volcano.

Comprehensible Input

4	3	2	1	0
10. **Speech** appropriate for students' proficiency level (e.g., slower rate, enunciation, and simple sentence structure for beginners)		**Speech** sometimes inappropriate for students' proficiency level		**Speech** inappropriate for students' proficiency level

Comments: The teacher used clear speech with vocabulary students were familiar with. The bilingual aide assisted the newly arrived students. Teacher read aloud slowly while students followed along.

4	3	2	1	0
11. **Clear explanation of** academic tasks		**Unclear explanation of** academic tasks		**No explanation of** academic tasks

Comments: The teacher explained tasks well and modeled the demonstrations first before the students participated.

4	3	2	1	0
12. **A variety of techniques** used to make content concepts clear (e.g., modeling, visuals, hands-on activities, demonstrations, gestures, body language)		Some **techniques** used to make content concepts clear		No **techniques** used to make content concepts clear

Comments: A variety of techniques were used in this lesson: the use of the projector with a diagram of a volcano and the labeled parts, brainstorming in the semantic mapping activity, demonstrating a model of a volcanic eruption, and reading about the topic after exploring it orally and visually. Used sequencing steps to check reading comprehension.

Strategies

4	3	2	1	0
13. **Ample** opportunities provided for students to use **learning strategies**	(3)	**Inadequate** opportunities provided for students to use **learning strategies**		**No** opportunity provided for students to use **learning strategies**

Comments: The teacher used various strategies with students such as accessing prior knowledge and having them make predictions. Students, however, used these strategies with the teacher, not with other students.

(*continued*)

FIGURE 11.4 The Sheltered Instruction Observation Protocol (SIOP®) (continued)

Strategies (continued)

4	3	2	1	0
14. **Scaffolding techniques** consistently used, assisting and supporting student understanding (e.g., think-alouds)		**Scaffolding techniques** occasionally used		**Scaffolding techniques** not used

Comments: The teacher used various scaffolding techniques throughout the lesson to promote and assess students' comprehension of content concepts by means of questions, visuals, models, graphic organizers, prereading predictions, and demonstrations.

4	③	2	1	0
15. A variety of **questions or tasks that promote higher-order thinking skills** (e.g., literal, analytical, and interpretive questions)		Infrequent **questions or tasks that promote higher-order thinking skills**		No **questions or tasks that promote higher-order thinking skills**

Comments: Most of the questions for this beginning level consisted of more factual/identification questions. In some cases, more elaborated responses were required of students; for example, "What happens when one set of rocks moves against another?" "Can you think of other places in the world where eruptions have occurred?" "Tell me about volcanoes in your country." "How do you know this is a true story?"

Interaction

4	③	2	1	0
16. Frequent opportunities for **interaction** and discussion between teacher/student and among students, which encourage elaborated responses about lesson concepts		**Interaction** mostly teacher-dominated with some opportunities for students to talk about or question lesson concepts		**Interaction** teacher-dominated with no opportunities for students to discuss lesson concepts

Comments: The teacher engaged the students in discussions about volcanoes throughout the class period. The semantic mapping exercise, the demonstration, and the prereading activity were all means that facilitated student interaction. The majority of interactions were teacher-student.

4	3	②	1	0
17. **Grouping configurations** support language and content objectives of the lesson		**Grouping configurations** unevenly support the language and content objectives		**Grouping configurations** do not support the language and content objectives

Comments: Although students were seated in groups, there was little opportunity for them to interact to practice their language skills. The whole-class setting supported the demonstration about volcanic eruption.

4	③	2	1	0
18. Sufficient **wait time for student responses** consistently provided		Sufficient **wait time for student responses** occasionally provided		Sufficient **wait time for student responses** not provided

Comments: At times there were students who wanted to respond but were overlooked, perhaps because the period was running out of time. For those students selected to respond, the teacher allowed them time to articulate their thoughts.

Interaction (continued)

4	3	2	1	0	N/A
19. Ample opportunities for students to **clarify key concepts in L1** as needed with aide, peer, or L1 text		Some opportunities for students to **clarify key concepts in L1**		No opportunities for students to **clarify key concepts in L1**	

Comments: *Only a few students could be identified as using their L1 during the lesson, and they were seated in the far left corner of the classroom where the bilingual aide assisted them. The other students in the classroom did not seem to need to use their L1 text.*

Practice & Application

4	③	2	1	0	N/A
20. **Hands-on materials and/or manipulatives** provided for students to practice using new content knowledge		**Few hands-on materials and/ or manipulatives** provided for students to practice using new content knowledge		**No hands-on materials and/or manipulatives** provided for students to practice using new content knowledge	

Comments: *The lesson involved manipulatives. During the experiment/demonstration for the volcanic eruption, for example, the teacher used materials such as a bottle, liquid detergent, warm water, measuring spoons, baking soda, and vinegar. Only a few students, though, used these materials themselves.*

4	③	2	1	0	N/A
21. Activities provided for students to **apply content and language knowledge** in the classroom		Activities provided for students to **apply** either **content or language knowledge** in the classroom		No activities provided for students to **apply content or language knowledge** in the classroom	

Comments: *For the most part, students applied content and language. More student-student interactions would have been beneficial and provided better opportunities for assessment.*

4	③	2	1	0
22. Activities **integrate all language skills** (i.e., reading, writing, listening, and speaking)		Activities **integrate some language skills**		Activities **do not integrate language skills**

Comments: *The lesson allowed students an opportunity to use all language skills (some more than others) such as listening, speaking, and reading. Writing was evident mostly in the semantic mapping activity. Some predicting and scanning for information were part of the reading skills practiced.*

Lesson Delivery

4	③	2	1	0
23. **Content objectives** clearly supported by lesson delivery		**Content objectives** supported somewhat by lesson delivery		**Content objectives** not supported by lesson delivery

Comments: **The demonstration and class discussion served to accomplish most of the content objectives for the lesson. While students seemed to indicate an understanding of what volcanoes are, it is not certain that they fully understand what causes them to erupt.**

4	3	②	1	0
24. **Language objectives** clearly supported by lesson delivery		**Language objectives** somewhat supported by lesson delivery		**Language objectives** not supported by lesson delivery

Comments: *Most of the implied language objectives were supported by the delivery. There was constant repetition of key vocabulary Students did not have a chance to complete the sequencing activity based on the reading in order to assess their reading comprehension.*

(continued)

FIGURE 11.4 The Sheltered Instruction Observation Protocol (SIOP®) (continued)

Lesson Delivery (continued)

4	3	2	1	0
25. **Students engaged** approximately 90% to 100% of the period		**Students engaged** approximately 70% of the period		**Students engaged** less than 50% of the period

Comments: Students were on task throughout the lesson activity.

4	3	2	1	0
26. **Pacing** of the lesson appropriate to students' ability levels		**Pacing** generally appropriate, but at times too fast or too slow		**Pacing** inappropriate to the students' ability levels

Comments: The pacing seemed fine, but was a little rushed at times, which prevented students from completing some activities such as the individual silent reading and sequencing activity.

Review & Assessment

4	3	2	1	0
27. **Comprehensive review of key vocabulary**		Uneven review of key vocabulary		No review of key vocabulary

Comments: Teacher reviewed key vocabulary at the beginning of the lesson and reinforced it throughout.

4	3	2	1	0
28. **Comprehensive review of key content concepts**		Uneven review of key content concepts		No review of key content concepts

Comments: The key content concepts were reviewed throughout the lesson, but there was no comprehensive review to wrap up the lesson, other than the final question posed to students at the end of the class, "What is a volcano?"

4	3	2	1	0
29. Regular **feedback** provided to students on their output (e.g., language, content, work)		Inconsistent **feedback** provided to students on their output		No **feedback** provided to students on their output

Comments: The teacher gave positive feedback to students' responses in most cases. In some instances, when time was short, she did not always respond to students whose hands were raised. She guided the brainstorming and prereading discussions.

4	3	2	1	0
30. **Assessment of student comprehension and learning** of all lesson objectives (e.g., spot checking, group response) throughout the lesson		**Assessment of student comprehension and learning** of some lesson objectives		No **assessment of student comprehension and learning** of lesson objectives

Comments: Throughout the lesson, the teacher checked students' understanding of some concepts and of the instructional tasks. She monitored the classroom to answer questions and to provide assistance. During the reading activity, however, students were not allotted sufficient time to read individually, and the sequencing activity was moved to the following day. Therefore, it is unclear how she was able to assess individual student comprehension before she began reading the text to students.

Watch the video and listen to Deborah Short discuss the use of the protocol over time.

may meet on a regular basis to provide feedback to one another and assist in refining their teaching.

Some schools and districts learn the SIOP over time and implement component by component. The appropriate portion(s) of the protocol can be used to support the implementation. For example, if teachers have studied lesson preparation and building background in the first quarter of the year, then observations may only rate those sections.

When they add comprehensible input and strategies to their professional learning in the next quarter, then the features of those components can also be rated in observed lessons.

Scores can also be documented on a SIOP Lesson Rating Form over time to show growth (see Figure 11.5). Using percentages, teachers can see how their implementation of the SIOP features improves. This type of documentation is also useful for research purposes (or if a school is conducting a formative evaluation of a SIOP initiative) to document systematic implementation of SIOP and fidelity of implementation.

FIGURE 11.5 SIOP® Lesson Rating Form

Teacher	Observation 1 Date/Score (%)	Observation 2 Date/Score (%)	Observation 3 Date/Score (%)

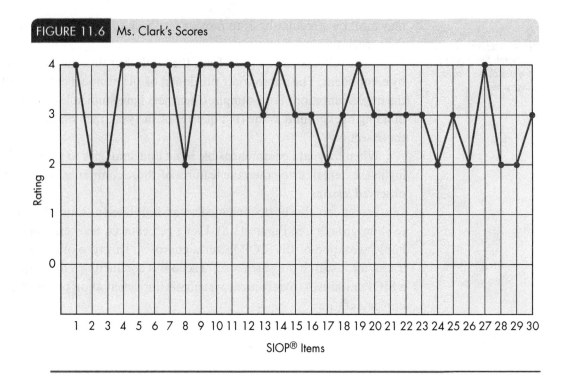

FIGURE 11.6 Ms. Clark's Scores

Further, plotting scores on a graph, as seen in Figure 11.6, is an effective way to illustrate areas of strength as well as areas that require attention, or areas teachers have highlighted as important for their own growth. If a lesson consistently shows low scores on certain features, this information provides the teacher with clear feedback for areas on which to focus. Staff developers and teacher educators may use the scores to determine areas for further discussion and practice in professional development and course sessions if several teachers are having difficulty with the same feature or component.

Finally, while the SIOP protocol is a useful tool for professional learning, scores should be used with caution. Many variables affect the success or failure of a given lesson, such as time of day, time of year, dynamics among students, and numerous other factors. Rather than just doing one observation and scoring of a lesson, an observer should rate several lessons over time for a more complete picture of the teacher's implementation of SIOP.

Reliability and Validity of SIOP®

After several years of field testing and refining the SIOP, a study was conducted (Guarino, Echevarría, Short, Schick, Forbes, & Rueda, 2001) to establish the **validity** and **reliability** of the instrument. The findings of the study indicated that SIOP is a highly reliable and valid measure of sheltered instruction (see Appendix C for a discussion of the study).

Summary

This book has been developed for teachers, supervisors, instructional coaches, administrators, teacher education faculty, professional developers, and researchers as a resource for increasing the effectiveness of instruction for English learners. We have

Watch the video clip and listen to Marcy Granillo, Issac School District School Improvement Coordinator, discuss SIOP professional development at her school.

presented a research-based, professional development model of sheltered instruction, the SIOP Model, whose protocol may be used as an observation instrument, as well as a lesson planning guide.

The SIOP Model and protocol provide concrete examples of the features of effective instruction for English learners, and this book has been written to illustrate and elucidate those features by describing how real teachers might actually teach SIOP lessons in elementary school. The use of vignettes allows readers to "see" what each feature might look like in a classroom setting. The features of the SIOP Model represent best practice for teaching English learners and have been shown to benefit English-speaking students as well.

Discussion Questions

1. The SIOP Model has a number of uses by different constituencies (e.g., teachers, supervisors, administrators, and researchers). How can you begin using SIOP? What additional uses might it have for you or other constituencies?

2. Reread the sample lesson on pages 279–282. Would you score this lesson differently from the sample SIOP scores? On which items would you differ? What was the basis of your disagreement?

3. Look at the sample SIOP protocol in Figure 11.4 and change any two scores to 1. What would be the total score and percentage score on the revised and recalculated SIOP?

4. Imagine that you and a supervisor or an instructional coach have just watched a videotape of your SIOP lesson. You are discussing the SIOP rating sheet that each of you scored independently. What would be the most collaborative way to approach the discussion of your lesson? What would yield the most useful information for improving your teaching?

CHAPTER 12

Frequently Asked Questions: Getting Started with the SIOP® Model

Learning Outcomes

After reading, discussing, and engaging in activities related to this chapter, you will be able to meet the following content and language objectives.

Content Objectives

Plan initial steps to get started with SIOP implementation in the classroom and school.

Identify a variety of uses for the SIOP protocol.

Language Objectives

Discuss with colleagues the most frequently asked questions and responses about the SIOP Model for those who are beginning "SIOPers."

Generate questions and possible answers of your own about the SIOP Model.

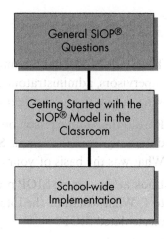

General SIOP®
Questions

Getting Started with the
SIOP® Model in the
Classroom

School-wide
Implementation

The purpose of this final chapter is to provide you with information and suggestions for beginning your work with the SIOP Model. Over the years, we have worked with thousands of teachers and administrators who are becoming "SIOPers." Frequently, we are asked about how to effectively implement SIOP in classrooms, schools, and districts. From many conversations, we have culled some of the most common questions and we provide answers to those questions in this chapter. ●

Ariel Skelley/Blend Images/Alamy

For a comprehensive guide to implementing SIOP, with profiles of 17 SIOP districts, information about funding sources, suggestions for creating a SIOP implementation plan, SIOP coaching, SIOP professional development, data collection, and more, see *Implementing the SIOP® Model through Effective Professional Development and Coaching* (Echevarría, Short, & Vogt, 2008).

■ General SIOP® Questions

1. Who can implement SIOP?
   - Keep in mind that SIOP is an instructional framework, not a program, not a lock-step way of teaching, or a curriculum. Therefore, as an instructional framework, it can be used in many educational contexts where students are diverse and learning is the goal. Pre-K, elementary, and secondary subject-area teachers, reading/language arts and English teachers, resource teachers, coaches, specialists, special educators, community college, and university professors implement the SIOP Model in a variety of educational program designs. Any teacher who has students learning content through a nonnative language can use SIOP effectively, as part of a general education program, an **ESL** program, a late-exit bilingual program, a dual language/two-way bilingual immersion program, a newcomer program, a **sheltered** program, or a foreign language immersion program. In order to implement the model well, we recommend teachers participate in professional development for at least one year.

Watch this video and hear the three SIOP authors talk about how SIOP benefits teachers and students. As you think of the teachers in your school, who might be likely candidates to begin SIOP training, and why do you think these individuals will be successful?

2. Is SIOP only for English learners?

- No. SIOP has been validated also with native-English speaking students, both general education and special education students, and former English learners. When teachers implement the 30 features consistently, all subgroups of students, including students receiving special education services, have been shown to demonstrate academic gains.

3. Isn't SIOP just good instruction?

- SIOP is excellent instruction with research-based features that have been proven effective with English learners and other students. What distinguishes it is the systematic, consistent, and simultaneous teaching of both content concepts and academic language through its 30 features.

- What also distinguishes SIOP is that, as of the time of this writing, it is the only empirically validated model of sheltered instruction for English learners that exists.

4. What is the relationship between SIOP and **Culturally Responsive Teaching**?

- Almost by definition, when teachers implement SIOP to a high degree, they're engaging in culturally responsive teaching. For example, SIOP respects children's home languages and cultures by incorporating their background knowledge and experiences into lessons.

- Effective SIOP teachers create groups where children work together on relevant activities, making sure that English learners are equal participants.

- With SIOP, teachers hold high expectations for all children, and adjust instruction and materials to provide access to the grade-level curriculum. Compare the tenets of culturally responsive teaching and the features of SIOP and you will see that they intersect naturally, and thus are not separate or competing instructional approaches.

5. What if there are only a few English learners in my classroom?

- We now have empirical evidence that all students benefit academically when teachers implement SIOP to a high degree. Therefore, all teachers who have English learners in their classrooms should become SIOP teachers, regardless of the number. SIOP isn't something that teachers "turn on" and "turn off," depending on the makeup of their classes. Rather, it becomes the way they teach from period to period, subject to subject, throughout the day.

6. What is the most important thing I should keep in mind (whether a teacher, coach, or administrator)?

- Recognize that learning to implement SIOP is a process. Not all features will be observed to a high degree in the beginning stages. Reflect on your lessons each day and use the SIOP protocol to assess your planning and delivery. Work through SIOP systematically to ensure it will become internalized and part of your regular classroom practice.

Questions About Getting Started with SIOP® in the Classroom

Watch this video to hear SIOP teacher Wanda Holbrook and principal Debbie Hutson talk about the need for administrative support when beginning SIOP implementation. Why do you think Ms. Hutson recommended starting with just "a few teachers?"

1. How do I get started using SIOP in my classroom?

   - Assess your areas of strength and your areas for needed improvement with the SIOP protocol.

   - Begin with one component at a time, gradually adding the others over time. We suggest that unless you'll be working alone to implement SIOP, you and your subject-area or grade-level colleagues should discuss and decide together which SIOP component will be your starting point.

   - As you attain proficiency in one component of SIOP, gradually add others to your teaching repertoire. Again, working with your colleagues on lesson planning, observing each other's lessons (in person or via video), and sharing techniques and ideas are all beneficial.

2. Do I have to implement the eight components in the order they're presented in the book?

   - No. There's no intended hierarchy or order of the components, with the exception, perhaps, of Lesson Preparation. However, teachers may choose to begin with another component first if that's more comfortable. We recommend that Lesson Preparation not be delayed beyond the second or third component because of the necessity of including content and language objectives in lessons.

3. Do I have to incorporate all 30 SIOP features in every lesson?

   - Eventually, yes. We recommend that elementary teachers begin implementing one component at a time in one subject area until all components are implemented in that subject area. The ultimate goal is to add other subjects until all are "SIOPized. However, there might be occasional lessons where not all features are present, such as in a review lesson at the end of a unit. If you're able to speed up this process (adding new components and subject areas or periods), so much the better!

   - Keep in mind that the definition of "a lesson" varies somewhat depending on the age of children you're teaching and the way the classroom day is organized. For example, pre-K, kindergarten, and first-grade teachers present many lessons in 15- to 20-minute (or less) blocks of time, while elementary teachers of older students may plan lessons ranging from 30–45 minutes. A rule of thumb is: What can you teach, provide practice and application for, and assess in a given period of time? That's what constitutes a "lesson" with SIOP.

4. What if I have students who can't speak any English? Will SIOP help?

   - SIOP will certainly help, but it's not enough. Beginning speakers, or newcomers, need intensive English instruction provided by an ESL or ELD teacher, in addition to effective SIOP instruction the rest of the day. If newcomer programs are not available, SIOP instruction provides students with the best opportunity to comprehend lessons, because SIOP teachers are teaching content and academic English concurrently.

5. How long will it take for me to become an effective SIOP teacher?

- It depends on the support you receive. Our research has shown teachers can become effective SIOP teachers in one year with coaching, observations, workshops, and planning time. Realistically, we generally say it takes two to three years with consistent focus on the eight components and 30 features to become a high implementer of the model. And, of course, follow-up professional development, observations, and coaching certainly help.

6. How should I use the **SIOP protocol**?

- Use it as a lesson plan checklist, self-assessment tool, and conversation starter with colleagues. You may wish to videotape yourself teaching and use the protocol to check the degree to which you are implementing particular features. SIOP teachers have found that sharing and discussing videotaped lessons is very beneficial for deepening their understandings of effective teaching. See Chapter 11 for additional information about uses of the SIOP protocol.

- Once you are familiar with the features in the individual components, use the protocol as a tool for post-teaching reflection. Two resources that may be helpful while planning lessons are books that offer a multitude of teaching ideas and activities for enhancing SIOP components and features in your lessons (see Vogt & Echevarría, 2008; Vogt, Echevarría, & Washam, 2015).

- Observe a peer's lesson and use the protocol to determine the degree to which SIOP features were present in the lesson you observed. You can then discuss together which SIOP features were highly evident, somewhat evident, or not evident in the lesson you observed.

7. Now that I've read the book and tried out some components, how do I deepen my SIOP knowledge?

- Collaborate with and observe other educators who are committed to excellent SIOP teaching.

- Observe other SIOP classrooms and frankly discuss what is working and what is problematic, and what a teacher can do to overcome any problems.

- Read the other SIOP books that are cited in this text. Also there are a number of research articles written about the SIOP Model. Form a cohort of "SIOPers" and have a study group with these resources.

- Connect with other SIOP schools and districts.

■ Questions About School-wide Implementation of the SIOP® Model

1. How should we get started in our school implementation?

- It's critically important that you have a plan in place, including who will receive professional development, who will provide it, where the funding will come from, and so forth. See Echevarría, Short, and Vogt (2008) for details about how to create a plan, and how other schools and districts have rolled out their plan once it was created.

- Get your school administrator on board with the SIOP Model as a school-wide initiative.

2. Who should receive SIOP professional development?

- Anyone who will be working with English learners, including teachers, support personnel, instructional assistants, and administrators, should participate in SIOP professional development.

- In addition, an overview of SIOP is beneficial for School Board members and district-level administrators so everyone is starting on the "same page," with the same ultimate goal.

3. What should SIOP professional development look like?

- Ideally, it should be a combination of workshops, coaching, observations and conferences, book study with this text and included video clips, and follow-up workshops focusing on individual SIOP components.

4. How should SIOP be used school-wide?

- As a source of conversation about best practices for teaching English learners

- As an informal observation instrument for peers, mentors, coaches, and administrators

- As a tool for observing growth in implementation of separate SIOP features, over time

- As a research observation tool for fidelity of model implementation.

  Please do not use the protocol for teacher evaluation, especially while the teachers are learning the model. In order to change their regular lesson planning style to the SIOP Model, teachers must take some risks. Because the process takes time and is challenging, lessons should not be rated early in the process of learning SIOP.

- The protocol is also an excellent tool for targeted and productive discussions among preservice student teachers, master teachers, and university supervisors, and between a teacher and a coach.

5. What should we do about resistant or reluctant teachers?

- Don't begin with them; instead, begin SIOP professional development with those who want to improve their instruction for English learners and other students.

- That said, if these teachers have English learners in their classrooms, eventually they will need to receive and be held accountable for SIOP professional development. From our experience, when resistant teachers hear their colleagues talk about SIOP successes, they come around and want to be part of the story, particularly if their English learners are not experiencing academic success, but the students of SIOP teachers are.

6. With whom should we collaborate during SIOP implementation?

- Collaborate with anyone who works with English learners, including the classroom teacher, ESL teacher, SIOP coaches, special educators, paraprofessionals, and administrators.

Watch this video to hear Principal Debbie Hutson talk about how her school in Phoenix started working with SIOP. Recall that in the second clip in this chapter she recommended starting with just a few teachers. How do you think she works with teachers who were a bit reluctant?

Watch this video to hear Dr. MaryEllen Vogt and Dr. Deborah Short talk about the Common Core State Standards and the SIOP Model. As you reflect on SIOP's instructional features, which ones provide a pathway for your students to meet the Common Core's rigorous standards? Why do you think so?

- Use a collaborative approach with teachers, including conferencing about observations, setting goals for implementing other features of the model, reflecting on progress in using SIOP, and so forth.

7. What does it mean to be a high-implementing SIOP teacher?

- The protocol, with the 0–4 **rubric**, can be used to measure levels of implementation of SIOP instructional features. From our research and that of others, we have learned that fidelity (level of implementation) to SIOP really makes a difference in student performance. High implementers are those teachers whose lessons consistently score 75% or higher on the SIOP protocol as measured during classroom observations. (See Chapter 11 for more information about uses of the SIOP protocol.)

8. Is SIOP compatible with the **Common Core State Standards**?

- Yes. The Common Core State Standards (or other rigorous state standards) can be used to guide the development of content and language objectives in English language arts and mathematics. The Common Core State Standards' Listening and Speaking Standards can also serve as a foundation for writing language objectives.

- The Common Core State Standards do not directly address *how* English learners (and struggling learners) are to attain the standards. For many teachers, SIOP provides a pathway for helping their students become successful in a Common Core classroom.

9. SIOP is a lesson planning and delivery system for teachers, but what about student outcomes?

- Our research has focused almost exclusively on the impact of SIOP on student achievement (see Appendices C and D). In the classroom, the features of the SIOP Model translate directly into student outcomes when implemented well. (See Figure 12.1 for ways that the features benefit students.) At the conclusion of an effective SIOP lesson, students should be able to demonstrate the outcomes as shown in Figure 12.1. This checklist may be used as a spot check to gauge the effectiveness of SIOP lessons.

10. As an administrator, where can I get some assistance?

- Additional information about school-level implementation of the SIOP Model from an administrator's perspective can be found in *The SIOP® Model for Administrators* (2nd ed.) (Short, Vogt, & Echevarría, 2017).

- Become familiar with the additional SIOP resources that support lesson planning and delivery. Books of lesson techniques, SIOP lessons and units for English-language arts, mathematics, history/social studies, and science, and of the Model's use in Response to Intervention programs are available. (See Appendix D for resources.)

- Other versions of this text, *Making Content Comprehensible for English Learners: The SIOP® Model*, have been written specifically for K–12, and secondary students (Echevarría, Vogt, & Short, 2017; 2018).

11. How can the SIOP protocol be used by researchers and program evaluators to measure teachers' level of SIOP implementation with the protocol?

FIGURE 12.1 Learner Outcomes

High Quality SIOP Lessons: Checking Learner Outcomes

Learners . . .

- demonstrated that they understood the purpose and objectives of the lesson.
- used the differentiated materials available and participated in meaningful activities.
- were actively encouraged to make links between their own background and the lesson's concepts and activities.
- had multiple opportunities to use new vocabulary in meaningful ways.
- responded to the teacher's modified speech and comprehensible input techniques.
- used learning strategies in completing tasks and assignments.
- were supported while completing tasks and assignments at their level of academic and language proficiency.
- were able to respond to a variety of questions including higher-order questions.
- demonstrated that they could work both independently and collaboratively, using academic English.
- participated in a variety of grouping configurations that facilitate interaction and discussion.
- used their home language as needed to clarify key concepts.
- contributed to the lesson by using hands-on materials and/or manipulatives to practice and apply content knowledge.
- were engaged and working at their potential throughout the lesson.
- followed the pace of the lesson.
- demonstrated understanding of the lesson's key vocabulary and content concepts.
- received appropriate and regular feedback on their output (e.g., language, content, work).
- were aware of their progress through assessment of the lesson's objectives.

- Because it is the only empirically validated, instructional approach for English learners at the time of this writing, the protocol can help determine if a school's or district's investment in SIOP staff development is returning dividends.
- Analyze student performance in conjunction with teachers' level of implementation.

As we conclude this third edition of *Making Content Comprehensible for Elementary English Learners*, we thank you for your interest in SIOP and hope that you find that the effort to become a high-implementing SIOP teacher (or effective coach or administrator) is well worth the journey. From our work, we have learned that the benefits of this effort include:

- teachers who are empowered to meet their students' needs
- improved academic achievement for English learners and other students
- gains in English language proficiency
- children who are active, engaged participants in their classrooms

The English learners in our schools deserve our best efforts because they and their native English-speaking peers are our future. Welcome aboard!

Observer(s): _____   Teacher: _____

Date: _____   School: _____

Grade: _____   Class/Topic: _____

ESL Level: _____   Lesson: Multi-day   Single-day   (*circle one*)

Total Points Possible: 120 (Subtract 4 points for each N/A given: _____)

Total Points Earned: _____   Percentage Score: _____

Directions: Circle the number that best reflects what you observe in a SIOP lesson. You may give a score from 0–4 (or N/A on selected items). Cite under "Comments" specific examples of the behaviors observed.

■ Lesson Preparation

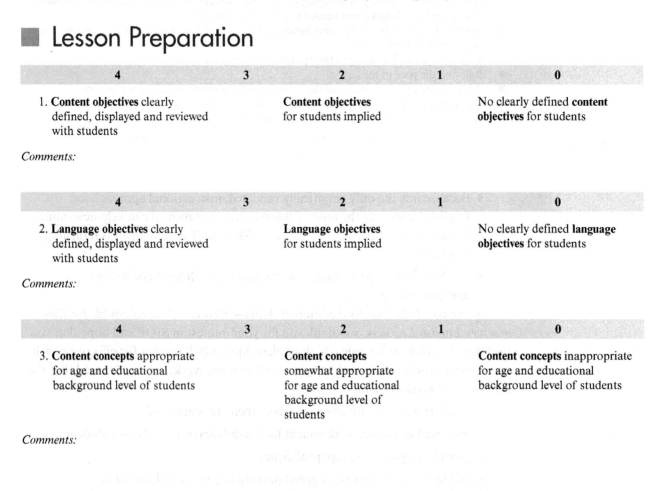

4	3	2	1	0
1. **Content objectives** clearly defined, displayed and reviewed with students		**Content objectives** for students implied		No clearly defined **content objectives** for students

Comments:

4	3	2	1	0
2. **Language objectives** clearly defined, displayed and reviewed with students		**Language objectives** for students implied		No clearly defined **language objectives** for students

Comments:

4	3	2	1	0
3. **Content concepts** appropriate for age and educational background level of students		**Content concepts** somewhat appropriate for age and educational background level of students		**Content concepts** inappropriate for age and educational background level of students

Comments:

(Echevarría, Vogt, & Short, 2000, 2004, 2008, 2013, 2017)

4	3	2	1	0
4. **Supplementary materials** used to a high degree, making the lesson clear and meaningful (e.g., computer programs, graphs, models, visuals)		Some use of **supplementary materials**		No use of **supplementary materials**

Comments:

4	3	2	1	0	N/A
5. **Adaptation of content** (e.g., text, assignment) to all levels of student proficiency		Some **adaptation of content** to all levels of student proficiency		No significant **adaptation of content** to all levels of student proficiency	

Comments:

4	3	2	1	0
6. **Meaningful activities** that integrate lesson concepts (e.g., interviews, letter writing, simulations, models) with language practice opportunities for reading, writing, listening, and/or speaking		**Meaningful activities** that integrate lesson concepts but provide few language practice opportunities for reading, writing, listening, and/or speaking		No **meaningful activities** that integrate lesson concepts with language practice

Comments:

■ Building Background

4	3	2	1	0	N/A
7. **Concepts explicitly linked** to students' background experiences		**Concepts loosely linked** to students' background experiences		**Concepts not explicitly linked** to students' background experiences	

Comments:

4	3	2	1	0

8. **Links explicitly made** between past learning and new concepts

Few links made between past learning and new concepts

No links made between past learning and new concepts

Comments:

4	3	2	1	0

9. **Key vocabulary** emphasized (e.g., introduced, written, repeated, and highlighted for students to see)

Key vocabulary introduced, but not emphasized

Key vocabulary not introduced or emphasized

Comments:

■ Comprehensible Input

4	3	2	1	0

10. **Speech** appropriate for students' proficiency levels (e.g., slower rate, enunciation, and simple sentence structure for beginners)

Speech sometimes inappropriate for students' proficiency levels

Speech inappropriate for students' proficiency levels

Comments:

4	3	2	1	0

11. **Clear explanation** of academic tasks

Unclear explanation of academic tasks

No explanation of academic tasks

Comments:

4	3	2	1	0

12. **A variety of techniques** used to make content concepts clear (e.g., modeling, visuals, hands-on activities, demonstrations, gestures, body language)

Some techniques used to make content concepts clear

No **techniques** used to make concepts clear

Comments:

Strategies

4	3	2	1	0
13. Ample opportunities provided for students to use **learning strategies**		Inadequate opportunities provided for students to use **learning strategies**		No opportunity provided for students to use **learning strategies**

Comments:

4	3	2	1	0
14. **Scaffolding techniques** consistently used, assisting and supporting student understanding (e.g., think-alouds)		**Scaffolding techniques** occasionally used		**Scaffolding techniques** not used

Comments:

4	3	2	1	0
15. A variety of **questions or tasks that promote higher-order thinking skills** (e.g., literal, analytical, and interpretive questions)		Infrequent **questions or tasks that promote higher-order thinking skills**		No **questions or tasks that promote higher-order thinking skills**

Comments:

Interaction

4	3	2	1	0
16. Frequent opportunities for **interaction** and discussion between teacher/student and among students, which encourage elaborated responses about lesson concepts		**Interaction** mostly teacher-dominated with some opportunities for students to talk about or question lesson concepts		**Interaction** teacher-dominated with no opportunities for students to discuss lesson concepts

Comments:

4	3	2	1	0
17. **Grouping configurations** support language and content objectives of the lesson		**Grouping configurations** unevenly support the language and content objectives		**Grouping configurations** do not support the language and content objectives

Comments:

4	3	2	1	0
18. Sufficient **wait time for student responses** consistently provided		Sufficient **wait time for student responses** occasionally provided		Sufficient **wait time for student responses** not provided

Comments:

4	3	2	1	0	N/A
19. Ample opportunities for students to **clarify key concepts in L1** as needed with aide, peer, or L1 text		Some opportunities for students to **clarify key concepts in L1**		No opportunities for students to **clarify key concepts in L1**	

Comments:

■ Practice & Application

4	3	2	1	0	N/A
20. **Hands-on materials and/or manipulatives** provided for students to practice using new content knowledge		Few **hands-on materials and/or manipulatives** provided for students to practice using new content knowledge		No **hands-on materials and/or manipulatives** provided for students to practice using new content knowledge	

Comments:

4	3	2	1	0	N/A
21. Activities provided for students to **apply content and language knowledge** in the classroom		Activities provided for students to **apply** either **content or language knowledge** in the classroom		No activities provided for students to **apply content and language knowledge** in the classroom	

Comments:

4	3	2	1	0

22. Activities integrate all **language skills** (i.e., reading, writing, listening, and speaking)

Activities integrate some **language skills**

Activities do not integrate **language skills**

Comments:

■ Lesson Delivery

4	3	2	1	0

23. **Content objectives** clearly supported by lesson delivery

Content objectives somewhat supported by lesson delivery

Content objectives not supported by lesson delivery

Comments:

4	3	2	1	0

24. **Language objectives** clearly supported by lesson delivery

Language objectives somewhat supported by lesson delivery

Language objectives not supported by lesson delivery

Comments:

4	3	2	1	0

25. **Students engaged** approximately 90% to 100% of the period

Students engaged approximately 70% of the period

Students engaged less than 50% of the period

Comments:

4	3	2	1	0

26. **Pacing** of the lesson appropriate to students' ability levels

Pacing generally appropriate, but at times too fast or too slow

Pacing inappropriate to students' ability levels

Comments:

■ Review & Assessment

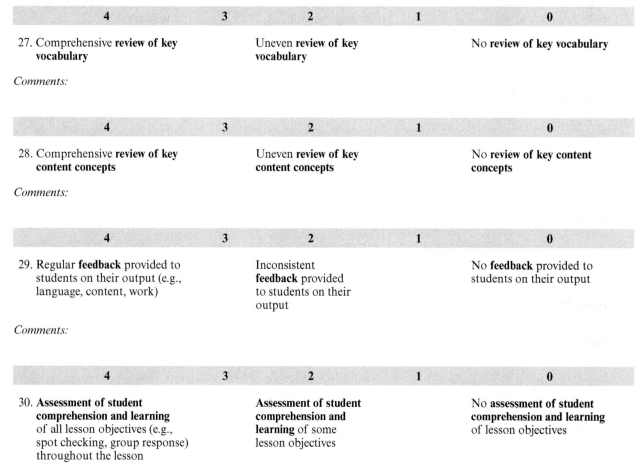

4	3	2	1	0
27. Comprehensive **review of key vocabulary**		Uneven **review of key vocabulary**		No **review of key vocabulary**

Comments:

4	3	2	1	0
28. Comprehensive **review of key content concepts**		Uneven **review of key content concepts**		No **review of key content concepts**

Comments:

4	3	2	1	0
29. Regular **feedback** provided to students on their output (e.g., language, content, work)		Inconsistent **feedback** provided to students on their output		No **feedback** provided to students on their output

Comments:

4	3	2	1	0
30. **Assessment of student comprehension and learning** of all lesson objectives (e.g., spot checking, group response) throughout the lesson		**Assessment of student comprehension and learning** of some lesson objectives		No **assessment of student comprehension and learning** of lesson objectives

Comments:

SIOP (Sheltered Instruction Observation Protocol)

(Echevarría, Vogt, & Short, 2000, 2004, 2008, 2013, 2017)

Observer(s): _____
Date: _____
Grade: _____
ESL Level: _____

School: _____
Teacher: _____
Class/Topic: _____
Lesson: Multi-day Single-day *(circle one)*

Total Points Possible: 120 (Subtract 4 points for each N/A given) _____
Total Points Earned: _____   Percentage Score: _____

Directions: Circle the number that best reflects what you observe in a SIOP lesson. You may give a score from 0–4 (or N/A on selected items). Cite under "Comments" specific examples of the behaviors observed.

	Highly Evident		Somewhat Evident		Not Evident	
Lesson Preparation	4	3	2	1	0	N/A
1. **Content objectives** clearly defined, displayed, and reviewed with students	❏	❏	❏	❏	❏	
2. **Language objectives** clearly defined, displayed, and reviewed with students	❏	❏	❏	❏	❏	
3. **Content concepts** appropriate for age and educational background level of students	❏	❏	❏	❏	❏	
4. **Supplementary materials** used to a high degree, making the lesson clear and meaningful (e.g., computer programs, graphs, models, visuals)	❏	❏	❏	❏	❏	
5. **Adaptation of content** (e.g., text, assignment) to all levels of student proficiency	❏	❏	❏	❏	❏	❏
6. **Meaningful activities** that integrate lesson concepts (e.g., surveys, letter writing, simulations, constructing models) with language practice opportunities for reading, writing, listening, and/or speaking	❏	❏	❏	❏	❏	

Comments:

	4	3	2	1	0	N/A
Building Background						
7. **Concepts explicitly linked** to students' background experiences	❏	❏	❏	❏	❏	❏
8. **Links explicitly made** between past learning and new concepts	❏	❏	❏	❏	❏	
9. **Key vocabulary** emphasized (e.g., introduced, written, repeated, and highlighted for students to see)	❏	❏	❏	❏	❏	

Comments:

	4	3	2	1	0
Comprehensible Input					
10. **Speech** appropriate for students' proficiency level (e.g., slower rate, enunciation, and simple sentence structure for beginners)	❏	❏	❏	❏	❏
11. **Clear explanation** of academic tasks	❏	❏	❏	❏	❏
12. **A variety of techniques** used to make content concepts clear (e.g., modeling, visuals, hands-on activities, demonstrations, gestures, body language)	❏	❏	❏	❏	❏

Comments:

Strategies	**4**	**3**	**2**	**1**	**0**	
13. Ample opportunities provided for students to use **learning strategies**	❑	❑	❑	❑	❑	
14. **Scaffolding techniques** consistently used assisting and supporting student understanding (e.g., think-alouds)	❑	❑	❑	❑	❑	
15. A variety of **questions or tasks that promote higher-order thinking skills** (e.g., literal, analytical, and interpretive questions)	❑	❑	❑	❑	❑	

Comments:

Interaction	**4**	**3**	**2**	**1**	**0**	**N/A**
16. Frequent opportunities for **interaction** and discussion between teacher/student and among students, which encourage elaborated responses about lesson concepts	❑	❑	❑	❑	❑	
17. **Grouping configurations** support language and content objectives of the lesson	❑	❑	❑	❑	❑	
18. Sufficient **wait time for student responses** consistently provided	❑	❑	❑	❑	❑	
19. Ample opportunities for students to **clarify key concepts in L1** as needed with aide, peer, or L1 text	❑	❑	❑	❑	❑	❑

Comments:

Practice & Application	**4**	**3**	**2**	**1**	**0**	**N/A**
20. **Hands-on materials and/or manipulatives** provided for students to practice using new content knowledge	❑	❑	❑	❑	❑	❑
21. Activities provided for students to **apply content and language knowledge** in the classroom	❑	❑	❑	❑	❑	❑
22. Activities integrate all **language skills** (i.e., reading, writing, listening, and speaking)	❑	❑	❑	❑	❑	

Comments:

Lesson Delivery	**4**	**3**	**2**	**1**	**0**
23. **Content objectives** clearly supported by lesson delivery	❑	❑	❑	❑	❑
24. **Language objectives** clearly supported by lesson delivery	❑	❑	❑	❑	❑
25. **Students engaged** approximately 90% to 100% of the period	❑	❑	❑	❑	❑
26. **Pacing** of the lesson appropriate to students' ability level	❑	❑	❑	❑	❑

Comments:

Review & Assessment	**4**	**3**	**2**	**1**	**0**
27. Comprehensive **review of key vocabulary**	❑	❑	❑	❑	❑
28. Comprehensive **review of key content concepts**	❑	❑	❑	❑	❑
29. Regular **feedback** provided to students on their output (e.g., language, content, work)	❑	❑	❑	❑	❑
30. **Assessment of student comprehension and learning** of all lesson objectives (e.g., spot checking, group response) throughout the lesson	❑	❑	❑	❑	❑

Comments:

SIOP® Lesson Plan Template 1

Date: _____   Grade/Class/Subject: _____

Unit/Theme: _____   Standards: _____

Content Objective(s): _____

_____

Language Objective(s): _____

_____

Key Vocabulary	Supplementary Materials

SIOP® Features

Lesson Preparation
- ___ Adaptation of Content
- ___ Links to Background
- ___ Links to Past Learning
- ___ Strategies incorporated

Scaffolding
- ___ Modeling
- ___ Guided practice
- ___ Independent practice
- ___ Comprehensible input

Grouping Options
- ___ Whole class
- ___ Small groups
- ___ Partners
- ___ Independent

Integration of Processes
- ___ Reading
- ___ Writing
- ___ Speaking
- ___ Listening

Application
- ___ Hands-on
- ___ Meaningful
- ___ Linked to objectives
- ___ Promotes engagement

Assessment
- ___ Individual
- ___ Group
- ___ Written
- ___ Oral

Lesson Sequence:

Reflections:

SIOP® Lesson Plan Template 2

STANDARDS:

LESSON TOPIC:

OBJECTIVES:
Content

Language

LEARNING STRATEGIES:

KEY VOCABULARY:

MATERIALS:

MOTIVATION:
(Building background)

PRESENTATION
(Content and language objectives, comprehensible input, modeling, strategies, interaction, feedback)

PRACTICE & APPLICATION:
(Meaningful activities, interaction, strategies, practice, application, feedback)

REVIEW & ASSESSMENT:
(Review objectives and vocabulary, assess learning)

EXTENSION:

SIOP® Lesson Plan Template 3

Topic:	Class:	Date:

Content Objectives:

Language Objectives:

Key Vocabulary:

Materials (including supplementary and adapted):

Higher-Order Questions:

Time:	Lesson Activities
	Building Background
	Links to Experience:
	Links to Learning:
	Key Vocabulary:

(Continued on next page)

Time:	**Student Activities** (Check all that apply for activities throughout lesson):
	Scaffolding: ❑ Modeling ❑ Guided Practice ❑ Independent Practice
	Grouping: ❑ Whole Class ❑ Small Group ❑ Partners ❑ Independent
	Processes: ❑ Reading ❑ Writing ❑ Listening ❑ Speaking
	Techniques: ❑ Hands-on ❑ Meaningful ❑ Links to Objectives
	Review & Assessment (Check all that apply):
	❑ Individual ❑ Group ❑ Written ❑ Oral
	Review Key Vocabulary:
	Review Key Content Concepts:
	Review Content and Language Objectives at end of lesson.

(Reproduction of this material is restricted to use with Echevarría, Vogt, and Short (2017),
Making Content Comprehensible for English Learners: The SIOP® Model.)

(Developed by John Seidlitz. Used with permission.)

SIOP® Lesson Plan Template 4

SIOP® Lesson Grade:	**Subject:**
Standards:	

Key Vocabulary:

Higher-Order Questions and Tasks:

Multimedia/Materials:

Building Background:

Objectives	Lesson Sequence	Review & Assessment
Content Objectives: **Language Objectives:**		

Wrap-up (including review of content and language objectives):

Lesson Reflection/Extension:

(Reproduction of this material is restricted to use with Echevarría, Vogt, and Short (2017),
Making Content Comprehensible for English Learners: The SIOP® Model.)

The SIOP Model has been developed and refined through 20 years of sustained research and development studies (Short, Echevarría, & Richards-Tutor, 2011, Short & Himmel, 2013). The following discussion highlights the investigations over time.

CREDE Research: Development of the SIOP® Model, Protocol, and Professional Development Program

- The first version of the SIOP began in the early 1990s as an observation tool to determine if observed teachers incorporated key sheltered techniques consistently in their lessons.

- The protocol evolved into a lesson planning and delivery approach, known as the SIOP Model (Echevarría, Vogt, & Short, 2000), through a 7-year, quasi-experimental research study, *The Effects of Sheltered Instruction on the Achievement of Limited English Proficient Students*, that was sponsored by the Center for Research on Education, Diversity & Excellence (CREDE) and funded by the U.S. Department of Education. It began in 1996.

  - The goals of the research project were to (1) develop an explicit model of sheltered instruction; (2) use that model to train teachers in effective sheltered strategies; and (3) conduct field experiments and collect data to evaluate teacher change and the effects of sheltered instruction on LEP students' English language development and content knowledge.

  - This original SIOP study involved collaborating middle school teachers in four large metropolitan school districts—two on the East Coast and two on the West Coast—who worked with researchers to identify key practices for sheltered instruction and develop a professional development model that would enable more teachers to use sheltered instruction effectively in their classrooms. Dr. Jana Echevarría of California State University, Long Beach, and Dr. Deborah Short of the Center for Applied Linguistics in Washington, DC, were co-project investigators.

  - Together, we reviewed the professional literature on best practices for English learners in the areas of ESL, bilingual education, reading, second language acquisition, discourse studies, special education, and classroom management and found many techniques that showed promise but hadn't been empirically investigated. We decided to test combinations of these techniques and thus built our initial model.

  - During four years of field testing, we analyzed teacher implementation and student effects as teachers tried out variations in their classrooms.

- In 2000, we finalized the format—30 features of instruction grouped into eight components essential for making content comprehensible for English learners—Lesson Preparation, Building Background, Comprehensible Input, Strategies, Interaction, Practice & Application, Lesson Delivery, and Review & Assessment (Echevarría, Vogt, & Short, 2000; Short & Echevarría, 1999). These components emphasize the instructional practices that are critical for second language learners as well as high-quality practices that benefit all students. The eight components are:

  - The six features under *Lesson Preparation* initiate the lesson planning process, so teachers include content and language objectives, use supplementary materials, create meaningful activities, and more.

  - *Building Background* focuses on making connections with students' background experiences and prior learning, and developing their academic vocabulary.

  - *Comprehensible Input* considers how teachers should adjust their speech, model academic tasks, and use multimodal techniques to enhance comprehension.

  - The *Strategies* component emphasizes teaching learning strategies to students, scaffolding instruction, and promoting higher-order thinking skills.

  - *Interaction* prompts teachers to encourage students to elaborate their speech and to group students appropriately for language and content development.

  - *Practice & Application* provides activities to practice and extend language and content learning.

  - *Lesson Delivery* ensures that teachers present a lesson that meets the planned objectives and promotes student engagement.

  - The *Review & Assessment* component reminds teachers to review the key language and content concepts, assess student learning, and provide specific academic feedback to students on their output.

- We created a 5-point scale for each feature on the observation protocol so we could measure the level of implementation in any lesson (4—closest to recommended practice, 0—no evidence of the use of the practice). A separate study confirmed the SIOP protocol as a valid and highly reliable measure of sheltered instruction (Guarino et al., 2001). Experienced observers of classroom instruction (e.g., teacher education faculty who supervise student teachers) who were *not* specifically trained in the SIOP Model were able to use the protocol to distinguish between high and low implementers of the model. A statistical analysis revealed an inter-rater correlation of 0.90 or higher.

- Because this CREDE study predated NCLB, most of the English learners in the research districts were exempted from the standardized testing process. To investigate whether the model yielded positive results in terms of student performance, we used pre- and post-measures of the Illinois Measurement of Annual Growth in English (IMAGE) writing test as an outcome measure of academic literacy. The IMAGE was the standardized assessment of reading and writing used by the state of Illinois to measure annual growth of these skills in their limited English proficient students in Grades 3–12. It was correlated to and a predictor of scores on the IGAP (the state standardized test of achievement) that was given to all students in Illinois, except those exempted for linguistic development reasons or learning disabilities. The IMAGE Writing Test provided separate scores for five features of writing: Language Production, Focus, Support/Elaboration, Organization, and Mechanics, as well as an overall score.

- Two distinct, but similar, cohorts of English learners in sheltered classes participated: students whose teachers were trained in implementing the SIOP Model (the treatment group), and students whose teachers had no exposure to the SIOP Model (the comparison group). The students in both groups were in Grades 6–8 in the same districts and represented mixed proficiency levels. We found that students who participated in classes taught by teachers trained in the SIOP Model improved their writing skills significantly more than students in classes with non–SIOP-trained teachers. They also made greater gains from the fall to spring administrations of the test. These findings were statistically significant (Echevarría, Short, & Powers, 2006).

- We found that this model can be applied in ESL classes as well as all content area classes because it offers a framework for instruction that incorporates best practices for teaching both language and content.

- From 1999 to 2002, we field-tested and refined the SIOP Model's professional development program that incorporates key features of effective teacher development as recommended then by Darling-Hammond (1998) and still recommended today (Darling-Hammond & Richardson, 2009). The program includes professional development institutes (see http://www.siop.pearson.com), videotapes of exemplary SIOP teachers (Hudec & Short, 2002a, 2002b), facilitator's guides (Short, Hudec, & Echevarría, 2002), and other training materials.

■ NJ SIOP® Research: Improvement in English Language Proficiency

- From 2004–2007 we replicated and scaled up the SIOP research in a quasi-experimental study. *Academic Literacy through Sheltered Instruction for Secondary English Language Learners* was conducted by researchers at the Center for Applied Linguistics in two districts in New Jersey and funded by the Carnegie Corporation of New York and the Rockefeller Foundation from 2004–2007. The treatment and comparison districts each had one high school and two middle schools with ESL programs and had multilingual student populations.

- In the treatment site, math, science, social studies, language arts, ESL, and technology teachers participated in ongoing SIOP Model training: approximately 35 teachers for two years (Cohort 1) and an additional 25 for one year (Cohort 2). The professional development program included summer institutes, follow-up workshops, and on-site coaching. The teachers in the comparison site did not receive any SIOP Model training.

◆ We collected teacher implementation data (two classroom observations each year, one in the fall, the other in the spring) using the SIOP protocol at both sites. We found that 56% of the treatment teachers in Cohort 1 became high implementers of the SIOP Model after one year and 71% were high implementers after two. Seventy-four percent of the Cohort 2 teachers who joined the Cohort 1 teachers at their schools reached the high implementation level in just one year. At the comparison site, fewer teachers implemented the SIOP features to a high level: 5% of the teachers in the first year; 17% by the second year (Short, Fidelman, & Louguit, 2012).

◆ We also collected student data from the state English language proficiency assessment at that time and the IPT (Idea Proficiency Tests) for all English learners in Grades 6–12. Students with SIOP-trained teachers made statistically significant gains in their average mean scores for oral language, writing, and total proficiency on the state assessment of English language proficiency, compared to the comparison group of English learners (Short, Fidelman, & Louguit, 2012).

CREATE Research: Fidelity Matters and All Students Benefit—English Learners and English Speakers Alike

● From 2005–2011, researchers from California State University, Long Beach, and the Center for Applied Linguistics participated in the program of studies at the National Center for Research on the Educational Achievement and Teaching of English Language Learners (CREATE), funded by the U.S. Department of Education. The study, *The Impact of the SIOP® Model on Middle School Science and Language Learning*, first examined the SIOP Model in middle school science classrooms (Himmel, Short, Richards, & Echevarría, 2009) and later applied the SIOP Model as the professional development framework for a school-wide intervention (Echevarría & Short, 2011). In this set of studies, we used an experimental design and English learners, former English learners, and native English speakers were part of the treatment and control student populations.

◆ A pilot study was conducted to develop SIOP science curriculum units, where local standards and curricula were enhanced with SIOP features, and to design and field-test science language assessments that would measure student scientific vocabulary, reading comprehension, and writing skills.

◆ In 2006–2007, an experimental study was conducted in eight middle schools for one semester. Five received the treatment, which was SIOP professional development, classroom-based coaching, and four SIOP science units developed by researchers and teacher consultants. Three schools were control sites where teachers taught in their regular fashion with their own lessons. Treatment and control teachers were observed and their lessons were rated using the SIOP protocol.

◆ Results showed that students in the treatment classes outperformed control students (Echevarría, Richards-Tutor, Canges, & Francis, 2011) and the higher the level of SIOP implementation, the better the students performed on assessments (Echevarría, Richards-Tutor, Chinn, & Ratleff, 2011). This result held true for English learners, former English learners, and native English speakers.

- ◆ During the 2009–2010 school year, another experimental study took place. A two-year intervention focused school-wide on Grade 7 and the SIOP Model was the overarching professional development framework (Echevarría & Short, 2011). Other content-specific curriculum interventions tested through earlier years of the CREATE program were implemented as well. Eight schools were randomly assigned to treatment or control. The four treatment schools had SIOP professional development and classroom-based coaching for SIOP implementation, and where applicable, for the content-specific curriculum intervention. The teachers in the four control schools delivered regular instruction without curriculum units or SIOP training. Their instruction was observed for research purposes, but they did not receive feedback.

- ◆ In the 2010–2011 school year, teachers in three of the prior year's control schools became treatment teachers and received the SIOP professional development and curriculum interventions as well. A new treatment school joined the study that year, bringing the number of schools to four.

- Researchers collected data in the treatment and control sites during both years. Teacher implementation levels were measured with the SIOP protocol and other tools. Student performance was measured with standardized tests and curriculum-based assessments. Analyses showed that this school-wide intervention improved outcomes in content knowledge and academic English for both English learners and native English speakers in the treatment classes. Specifically, students in SIOP curriculum groups outperformed control students to a significant degree on criterion-referenced vocabulary, science, and social studies measures (Short & Himmel, 2013).

Program Evaluation and Other Research

- School districts have conducted a number of program evaluations on their implementation of the SIOP Model that can be reviewed in *Implementing the SIOP® Model Through Effective Professional Development and Coaching* (Echevarría, Short, & Vogt, 2008). In addition, other researchers have studied SIOP Model professional development and classroom instruction (Batt, 2010; Friend, Most, & McCrary, 2009; Honigsfeld & Cohan, 2008; McIntyre et al., 2010; Smolen, et al., 2015; Song, 2016; Watkins & Lindahl, 2010; and Whittier & Robinson, 2007).

Uses of the SIOP® Model and Protocol

Since the SIOP Model was first published in 2000, the following uses for the observation tool and professional development program have been realized:

- Teacher lesson planning checklist and self-reflection guide
- Classroom observation tool for administrators and coaches
- Supervision tool for faculty to observe student teachers
- Research observation tool for fidelity of model implementation
- Program of professional development
- Framework for development of sheltered curricula

■ Conclusion: SIOP® Research to Date

By looking at these research studies as a whole, we can see that SIOP instruction is making a positive learning difference for English learners and other students who are in the classrooms. No one is disadvantaged by SIOP instruction; rather, the focus on academic literacy and scaffolded instruction help all students learn academic English and content curricula better.

Appendix D SIOP® Professional Development Resources

■ Books

Core SIOP Texts

Echevarría, J., Vogt, M.E., & Short, D. (2017). *Making content comprehensible for English learners: The SIOP® Model* (5th ed.). New York, NY: Pearson.

Echevarría, J., Short, D., & Peterson, C. (2012). *Using the SIOP® Model with pre-K and kindergarten English learners.* New York, NY: Pearson.

Echevarría, J., Vogt, M.E., & Short, D. (2018a). *Making content comprehensible for elementary English learners: The SIOP® Model* (3rd ed.). New York, NY: Pearson.

Echevarría, J., Vogt, M.E., & Short, D. (2018b). *Making content comprehensible for secondary English learners: The SIOP® Model* (3rd ed.). New York, NY: Pearson.

Additional SIOP Texts

Echevarría, J., Short, D., & Vogt, M.E. (2008). *Implementing the SIOP® Model through effective professional development and coaching.* New York, NY: Pearson.

Echevarría, J., Vogt, M.E., & Short, D. (2010). *The SIOP® Model for teaching mathematics to English learners.* New York, NY: Pearson.

Short, D., & Echevarría, J. (2016). *Developing academic language using the SIOP® Model.* New York, NY: Pearson.

Short, D., Echevarría, J., & Vogt, M.E. (2017). *The SIOP® Model for administrators* (2nd ed.). New York, NY: Pearson.

Short, D., Vogt, M.E., & Echevarría, J. (2011a). *The SIOP® Model for teaching history-social studies to English learners.* New York, NY: Pearson.

Short, D., Vogt, M.E., & Echevarría, J. (2011b). *The SIOP® Model for teaching science to English learners.* New York, NY: Pearson.

Vogt, M.E., & Echevarría, J. (2008). *99 ideas and activities for teaching English learners with the SIOP® Model.* New York, NY: Pearson.

Vogt, M.E., Echevarría, J., & Short, D. (2010). *The SIOP® Model for teaching English-language arts to English learners.* New York, NY: Pearson.

Vogt, M.E, Echevarría, J., & Washam, M. (2015). *99 more ideas and activities for teaching English learners with the SIOP® Model.* Boston, MA: Pearson.

Teaching English Learners with Learning Challenges

Echevarría, J., & Graves, A. (2015). *Sheltered content instruction: Teaching English learners with diverse abilities* (5th ed.). New York, NY: Pearson.

Echevarría, J., Richards-Tutor, C., & Vogt, M.E. (2015). *Response to intervention (RTI) and English learners: Using the SIOP® Model* (2nd ed.). New York, NY: Pearson.

Journal Articles and Book Chapters

Echevarría, J., & Colburn, A. (2006). Designing lessons: Inquiry approach to science using the SIOP® Model. In A. Fathman & D. Crowther, (Eds.), *Science for English language learners* (pp. 95–108). Arlington, VA: National Science Teachers Association Press.

Echevarría, J., Richards-Tutor, C., Canges, R., & Francis, D. (2011). Using the SIOP Model to promote the acquisition of language and science concepts with English learners. *Bilingual Research Journal, 34*(3), 334–351.

Echevarría, J., Richards-Tutor, C., Chinn, V., & Ratleff, P. (2011). Did they get it? The role of fidelity in teaching English learners. *Journal of Adolescent and Adult Literacy, 54*(6), 425–434.

Echevarría, J., & Short, D. (2004). Using multiple perspectives in observations of diverse classrooms: The Sheltered Instruction Observation Protocol (SIOP). In H. Waxman, R. Tharp, & S. Hilberg (Eds.), *Observational research in U.S. classrooms: New approaches for understanding cultural and linguistic diversity* (pp. 21–47). Boston, MA: Cambridge University Press.

Echevarría, J., & Short, D. (2010). Programs and practices for effective sheltered content instruction. In California Department of Education (Ed.), *Improving education for English learners: Research-based approaches* (pp. 250–321). Sacramento, CA: CDE Press.

Echevarría, J., Short, D., & Powers, K. (2006). School reform and standards-based education: An instructional model for English language learners. *Journal of Educational Research, 99*(4), 195–210.

Echevarría, J., & Vogt, M.E. (2010). Using the SIOP® Model to improve literacy for English learners. *New England Reading Association Journal (NERAJ), 46*(1), 8–15.

Guarino, A.J., Echevarría, J., Short, D., Schick, J.E., Forbes, S., & Rueda, R. (2001). The Sheltered Instruction Observation Protocol. *Journal of Research in Education, 11*(1), 138–140.

Kareva, V., & Echevarría, J. (2013). Using the SIOP Model for effective content teaching with second and foreign language learners. *Journal of Education and Training Studies, 1*(2), 239–248.

Short, D. (2013). Training and sustaining effective teachers of sheltered instruction. *Theory Into Practice, 52*(2), 118–127.

Short, D., Cloud, N., Morris, P., & Motta, J. (2012). Cross-district collaboration: Curriculum and professional development. *TESOL Journal, 3*(3), 402–424.

Short, D., & Echevarría, J. (2004/2005). Teacher skills to support English language learners. *Educational Leadership, 62*(4), 8–13.

Short, D., Echevarría, J., & Richards-Tutor, C. (2011). Research on academic literacy development in sheltered instruction classrooms. *Language Teaching Research, 15*(3), 363–380.

Short, D., Fidelman, C., & Louguit, M. (2012). Developing academic language in English language learners through sheltered instruction. *TESOL Quarterly. 46*(2), 333–360.

Vogt, M.E. (2012). English learners: Developing their literate lives. In R.M. Bean & A.S. Dagen (Eds.), *Best practice of literacy leaders: Keys to school improvement* (pp. 248–260). New York, NY: The Guilford Press.

Vogt, M.E., & Echevarría, J. (2015). Reaching English learners: Aligning the ELA/ELD Framework with SIOP. *The California Reader, 49*(1), 23–33.

Research Briefs (Downloadable)

Echevarría, J. (2012). *Effective practices for increasing the achievement of English learners.* Washington, DC: Center for Research on the Educational Achievement and Teaching of English Language Learners. Retrieved from http://cal.org/create/publications/briefs/effective-practices-for-increasing-the-achievement-of-english-learners.html

Echevarría, J., & Hasbrouck, J. (2009). *Response to intervention and English learners.* Washington, DC: Center for Research on the Educational Achievement and Teaching of English Language Learners. Retrieved from http://cal.org/create/publications/briefs/response-to-intervention-and-english-learners.html

Echevarría, J., & Short, D. (2011). *The SIOP® Model: A professional development framework for comprehensive school-wide intervention.* Washington, DC: Center for Research on the Educational Achievement and Teaching of English Language Learners. Retrieved from http://cal.org/create/publications/briefs/professional-development-framework.html

Himmel, J., Short, D.J., Richards, C., & Echevarría, J. (2009). *Using the SIOP® Model to improve middle school science instruction.* Washington, DC: Center for Research on the Educational Achievement and Teaching of English Language Learners. Retrieved from http://cal.org/create/publications/briefs/using-the-siop-model-to-improve-middle-school-science-instruction.html

Blogs

A number of current and archived blog posts about using the SIOP Model can be found at https://be.wordpress.com/tag/the-siop-model/

SIOP Website

Various resources are available, including video clips of SIOP classrooms, on our website at siop.pearson.com and at www.janaechevarria.com

Glossary

Academic language: Language used in formal contexts for academic subjects and purposes. The aspect of language connected with literacy and academic achievement. This includes technical and general academic terms (*see* Cognitive/Academic Language Proficiency– CALP) and reading, writing, listening, and speaking skills as used in school to acquire new knowledge and accomplish academic tasks.

Assessment: The orderly process of gathering, analyzing, interpreting, and reporting student performance, ideally from multiple sources over a period of time.

Basic Interpersonal Communicative Skills (BICS): Face-to-face conversational fluency, including mastery of pronunciation, vocabulary, and grammar. English learners typically acquire conversational language used in everyday activities before they develop more complex, conceptual, academic language proficiency. (*See* Social language.)

Bilingual education: School instruction using two languages, generally a native language of the student and a second language. The amount of time that each language is used depends on the type of bilingual program, its specific objectives, and students' level of language proficiency.

Cognitive/Academic Language Proficiency (CALP): Language proficiency associated with schooling, and the abstract language abilities required for academic work. A more complex, conceptual, linguistic ability that includes analysis, synthesis, and evaluation. (*See* Academic language.)

Common Core State Standards (CCSS): A set of Grades K–12 English language arts/literacy and mathematics standards, adopted by most states in the United States, the District of Columbia, and some U.S. territories.

Content-based ESL: An instructional approach in which content topics are used as the vehicle for second language learning. A system of instruction in which teachers use a variety of instructional techniques as a way of developing second language, content knowledge, and cognitive and study skills. It is often delivered through thematic units and tied to the subject area instruction that English learners receive. (*See* Designated ELD.)

Content objectives: Statements that identify what students should know and be able to do in a subject area for a given lesson. They support school district and state content standards and learning outcomes, and they guide teaching and learning in the classroom.

Content standards: Definitions of what students are expected to know and be capable of doing for a given content area; the knowledge and skills that need to be taught in order for students to reach competency; what students are expected to learn and what schools are expected to teach. May be national, state, or district standards.

Culturally responsive teaching/instruction: An approach to classroom instruction and communication that respects the different cultural characteristics of all students. The learning environment reflects high expectations for all. Class discussions are open to cultural viewpoints, student ways of knowing are elicited, collaboration is frequent, pedagogical materials are multicultural, and values are shared and affirmed. The goal is equitable access for all to high-quality instruction. Also known as *culturally relevant teaching.*

Culture: The customs, lifestyle, traditions, behavior, attitudes, and artifacts of a given people. Culture also encompasses the ways people organize and interpret the world, and the way events are perceived based on established social norms. A system of standards for understanding the world.

Designated ELD: A term used in the California ELA/ELD framework for classes dedicated to teaching English as a second language, focusing on the vocabulary, grammar, and discourse of academic language in the core curriculum. Similar to content-based ESL.

Differentiated instruction: In order to create a learning environment that addresses the diversity of abilities and language proficiency levels represented in many classrooms, teachers adjust the pace, amount, level, or kind of instruction to meet the individual needs and abilities of each learner. Teachers may differentiate the way new information is presented, the texts and materials being used, the tasks being required of students, or the grouping of the learners.

Dual language program: A type of bilingual education where the goal is bilingualism. English and a target language are used for instruction. It may follow a 90-10 model (where the earliest grades use the target language 90% of the instructional time and move to 50% by fifth grade) or a 50-50 model (where each language is used 50% of the instructional time in all grades). Some dual language programs have native speakers of English and native speakers of the target language (e.g., Spanish); others have speakers that come from the same language background. Sheltered instruction, like SIOP, is needed in classes when non-native speakers are present and learning through a language they are not proficient in.

Emergent bilinguals: A term used for learners of a new language that is in addition to their native language. Used in the U.S. primarily to refer to students in ESL/ELD programs or bilingual programs. (*See* English learners.)

Engagement: When students are fully taking part in a lesson, they are said to be engaged. This is a holistic term that encompasses active listening, reading, writing, responding, and discussing. The level of students' engagement during a lesson may be assessed to a greater or lesser degree. A low SIOP score for engagement would imply frequent chatting, daydreaming, non-attention, and other off-task behaviors.

English language development (ELD): Used in some regions to refer to programs and classes to teach students English as a second (or additional or new) language. May refer to the language teaching specialists and their teaching certifications or endorsements. (*See* ESL.) May refer to some state or district standards. (*See* ELP standards.)

English language proficiency (ELP) standards: Definitions of what students are expected to know and be capable of doing in English; the knowledge and skills that need to be taught in order for students to reach competency; what students are expected to learn and what schools are expected to teach. May be national, state, or district standards. Each state is required by the federal government to have ELP standards and related assessments. (*See* ELD).

English learners: Children and adults who are learning English as a second or additional or new language. This term may apply to learners across various levels of proficiency in English. English learners may also be referred to as English language learners (ELLs), non–English speaking (NES) students, limited English proficient (LEP), emergent bilinguals (EBs), and nonnative speakers (NNS).

English-only: Used in some regions, English-only refers to students whose native language is English.

ENL: English as a new language. Used in some regions to refer to programs and classes to teach students English as a new (or second or additional) language.

ESL: English as a second language. Used to refer to programs and classes to teach students English as a second (or additional or new) language. May refer to the language teaching specialists and their teaching certifications or endorsements.

ESOL: English speakers of other languages. Students whose first language is not English and who do not write, speak, and understand the language as well as their classmates. In some regions, this term also refers to the programs and classes for English learners.

Every Student Succeeds Act (ESSA): This federal education law replaced the No Child Left Behind Act (NCLB). It was signed in December 2015 with expected implementation in the 2017-2018 school year. The law changes some of the NCLB-era assessment and accountability practices for English learners. For example, English language proficiency assessments are to be included in each state's Title 1 accountability system.

Home language: The language, or languages, spoken in the student's home by people who live there. Also referred to as first language (L1), primary language, or native language.

Informal assessment: Appraisal of student performance during lessons; characterized as frequent, ongoing, continuous, and involving simple but important techniques such as verbal checks for understanding, teacher-created assessments, and other nonstandardized procedures. This type of assessment provides teachers with immediate feedback.

Instructional conversations (IC): An approach to teaching that is an interactive dialogue with an instructional intent. An IC approach encourages thoughtful discussion around a concept or idea with balanced participation between teacher and students.

Integrated ELD: A term used in the California ELA/ELD framework for subject area classes that develop both content knowledge and academic language, with scaffolding to support students. Similar to sheltered instruction.

Inter-rater reliability: Measure of the degree of agreement between two different raters on separate ratings of one assessment indicator using the same scale and criteria.

L1: First language. A widely used abbreviation for the first language learned. Also known as primary, home, or native language.

L2: Second language. A widely used abbreviation for the second (or additional or new) language learned.

Language minority: In the United States, a student whose native language is not English. The individual student's ability to speak English will vary.

Language objectives: Statements that identify what students should know and be able to do while learning English (or another language) in a given lesson. They support students' language development, often focusing on vocabulary, functional language, language skills in reading, writing, listening and speaking, grammatical knowledge, discourse structures, and language learning strategies.

Language proficiency: An individual's competence in using a language for basic communication and for academic purposes. May be categorized as stages of language acquisition. (*See* Levels of language proficiency.)

Learning strategies: Mental processes and plans that people use to help them comprehend, learn, and retain new information. There are several types of learning strategies, such as cognitive, metacognitive, and language-based, and these are consciously adapted and monitored during reading, writing, and learning.

Levels of language proficiency: Students learning language progress through stages. To date, the stages or levels have been labeled differently in a number of states. In seminal work in this area, Krashen and Terrell (1983) described the stages as the following: Preproduction, Early production, Speech emergence, Intermediate fluency, and Advanced fluency. At present, many states have five or six levels, such as the following:

Level 1: Lowest level, essentially no English proficiency. Students are often newcomers and need extensive pictorial and non-linguistic support. They need to learn basic oral language and literacy skills in English. Newcomer students who have had interruptions in their educational backgrounds of more than two years are often referred to as SIFE, students with interrupted formal education. Some are placed into newcomer programs.

Level 2: Students are beginners and can use and understand phrases, simple questions, and short sentences. They should be introduced to general content vocabulary and lesson tasks. They generally need targeted ESL/ELD classes along with sheltered instruction or bilingual classes.

Level 3: Students can use general and specific language related to the content areas; they can speak and write sentences and paragraphs although with some errors, and they can read with instructional supports. They too benefit from targeted ESL/ELD classes (although they may need less time per week than Level 1 and Level 2 students) along with sheltered or bilingual classes.

Level 4: Viewed as an intermediate level of proficiency. Students use general, academic, and specific language related to content areas. They have improved speaking and writing skills and stronger reading comprehension skills (compared to the Level 3). In some cases, they are no longer scheduled into ESL/ELD classes but are in sheltered classes where attention is paid to furthering their academic English, sometimes with an ESL teacher who acts as a co-teacher. If Level 4 students are in a bilingual program, they typically have some content classes taught in the native language and others taught in English.

Level 5: Viewed as an advanced intermediate or advanced level of proficiency. Students use general academic and technical language of the content areas. They can read and write with linguistic complexity. In some states, students at this level exit the ESL or ELD program but their language and academic performance is still monitored. They may be placed in general education or sheltered classes depending on their academic performance.

Level 6: At or close to grade-level proficiency. Students' oral and written communication skills are comparable to those of native English speakers at their grade level. Students at this level have exited the ESL or ELD program but their language and academic performance may still be monitored.

Limited English proficient (LEP): A term used to refer to a student with restricted understanding or use of written and spoken English; a learner who is still developing competence in using English. The federal government continues to use the term *LEP*, while *EL* or *ELL* is more commonly used in schools.

Long-term English learner: A term used for students who have been enrolled in U.S. schools and designated as English learners for six or more years. Definitions and classification criteria vary by state and district, with some stipulating fewer years as EL or specific levels of progress toward English proficiency and academic levels.

Multi-tiered System of Support (MTSS): Although the terms RTI and MTSS are often used interchangeably, MTSS differs from RTI in that it is more comprehensive, addressing behavioral, social and emotional issues experienced by students while RTI focuses primarily on academic progress. (*See* RTI.)

Native English speaker: An individual whose first language is English. (*See* English-only.)

Native language: An individual's primary, home, or first language (L1).

Newcomer program: Specially designed academic programs for students newly arrived in U.S. schools who are not proficient in English. Newcomers attend these programs for a limited period of time in order to develop academic English, acculturate to U.S. schools, and build subject area knowledge. The programs may be located within an existing school or at a separate site.

Next Generation Science Standards (NGSS): A set of Grades K–12 science standards, adopted by more than 15 states in the United States and the District of Columbia, as of the 2015–16 school year.

No Child Left Behind Act (NCLB): A major school reform initiative by the federal government, signed in 2001 and enacted in the 2002-03 school year. It held schools accountable for the success of all of their students, including English learners and other underserved populations, and required highly qualified teachers in core content areas. Each state had to have standards for mathematics, reading/ language arts, English language development, and science, and all implemented high-stakes tests based on these standards. It was replaced with the Every Student Succeeds Act (ESSA) which was signed in 2015.

Non-English speaking (NES): Individuals who are in an English-speaking environment (such as U.S. schools) but who have not acquired any English proficiency. May also be referred to as non-native English speaker.

Non-native English speaker: Individuals who do not speak English as a first language. May be at any level of proficiency in English.

Nonverbal communication: Paralinguistic messages such as intonation, stress, pauses, and rate of speech, and nonlinguistic messages such as gestures, facial expressions, and body language that can accompany speech or be conveyed without the aid of speech.

PARCC (Partnership for Assessment of Readiness for College and Careers): A set of K–12 computer-based assessments developed and used by states to measure student attainment of the Common Core standards in English language arts/literacy and mathematics.

Primary language: An individual's home, native, or first language (L1).

Pull-out instruction: Students are "pulled out" from their regular classes for separate classes of ESL or ELD instruction, remediation, or acceleration. These are more commonly found in elementary programs.

Realia: Real-life objects and artifacts used to supplement teaching; can provide effective visual scaffolds for English learners.

Reliability: Statistical consistency in measurements and tests, such as the extent to which one assessment will repeatedly produce the same results given the same conditions and student population.

Response to Intervention (RTI): The intent of RTI is to identify at-risk learners early and, using a tiered system, provide effective instruction in general education first (typically called Tier 1) followed by targeted intervention (Tiers 2 and 3) as needed. This process is designed to reduce the number of students eligible for and in need of special education services. The focus is on finding ways to change instruction (or student behaviors) so the learner can be successful. RTI involves documenting a change in behavior or performance as a result of intervention and assessments. SIOP instruction can be provided as Tier I instruction. (*See* MTSS.)

Rubrics: Statements that describe indicators of performance, which include scoring criteria, on a continuum; may be described as "developmental" (e.g., emergent, beginning, developing, proficient) or "evaluative" (e.g., exceptional, thorough, adequate, inadequate).

SBAC (Smarter Balanced Assessment Consortium): A set of K–12 computer-based assessments with adaptive technology that have been developed and used by states to measure student attainment of the Common Core standards in English language arts/literacy and mathematics.

Scaffolding: Support for student learning of new information and performance of the tasks. Often provided by the teacher through demonstration, modeling, verbal prompts (e.g., questioning), feedback, graphic organizers, language frames, and more, across successive engagements. These supports are gradually withdrawn, to transfer more autonomy to the learner, leading to independence.

Self-contained ESL class: A class consisting solely of English speakers of other languages for the purpose of learning English or a subject area. An effective alternative to pull-out instruction.

Sheltered instruction: A means for making content comprehensible for English learners while they are developing academic English proficiency. The SIOP Model is an empirically validated model of sheltered instruction. Sheltered classrooms may include a mix of native English speakers and English learners or only English learners. Sheltered lessons integrate language and content learning and may include culturally responsive instruction as well. (*See* SIOP®.)

SIOP®: The term for an empirically validated model of sheltered instruction designed to make grade-level academic content understandable for English learners while at the same time developing their academic English language proficiency. Formerly spelled out as the Sheltered Instruction Observation Protocol, the authors have stopped using the full acronym definition because the acronym SIOP is more commonly used in schools and in the professional literature. SIOP refers to the observation protocol and the lesson planning guide which ensure that teachers are consistently implementing practices known to be effective for English learners. It is often used as an adjective too, as in SIOP teachers, SIOP lessons, and SIOP classrooms.

Social language: Basic language proficiency associated with fluency in day-to-day situations, including the classroom. Also referred to as conversational language. (*See* Basic Interpersonal Communicative Skills [BICS].)

Sociocultural context: The environment or situation in which people live, work, or go to school that includes social and cultural elements. Student learning in a classroom may be influenced by social and cultural factors from outside the classroom, such as economic status, level of parental education, family structure, and discrimination.

Standards-based assessment: Assessment involving the planning, gathering, analyzing, and reporting of a student's performance according to the English language proficiency and/or content standards.

Two-way immersion program: A type of dual language program where the student population is generally half native speakers of English and half native speakers of the target language. All subjects are taught in one of the two languages. It may follow a 90-10 model (where the earliest grades use the target language 90% of the instructional time and move to 50% by fifth grade) or a 50-50 model (where each language is used 50% of the instructional time in all grades). Sheltered instruction is needed in all classes because non-native speakers are present. (*See* Dual language program.)

Unaccompanied minors: This term refers to students who have come to the United States without their parents. A large influx of such students in 2014 called attention to the struggles they experienced on their journey to the country as well as the educational challenges many of them face once they are enrolled in schools.

Validity: A statistical measure of an assessment's match between the information collected and its stated purpose; evidence that inferences from evaluation are trustworthy.

References

Chapter 1

Abedi, J. (2002). Standardized achievement tests and English language learners: Psychometric issues. *Educational Assessment, 8*(3), 234–257.

Abedi, J., & Lord, C. (2001). The language factor in mathematics tests. *Applied Measurement in Education, 14*(3), 219–234.

Alvermann, D.E., & Moore, D.W. (2011). Questioning the separation of in-school from out-of-school contexts for literacy learning: An interview with Donna E. Alvermann. *Journal of Adolescent & Adult Literacy, 55*(2), 156–158.

August, D., & Hakuta, K. (Eds.). (1997). *Improving schooling for language minority children: A research agenda.* Washington, DC: National Academy Press.

August, D., & Shanahan T. (Eds.). (2006). *Developing literacy in second-language learners: A report of the National Literacy Panel on Language-Minority Children and Youth.* Mahwah, NJ: Erlbaum.

Bailey, A., & Butler, F. (2007). A conceptual framework of academic English language for broad application to education. In A. Bailey (Ed.), *The language demands of school: Putting academic English to the test* (pp. 68–102). New Haven, CT: Yale University Press.

Baker, S., Lesaux, N., Jayanthi, M., Dimino, J., Proctor, C.P., Morris, J., Gersten, R., Haymond, K., Kieffer, M.J., Linan-Thompson, S., & Newman-Gonchar, R. (2014). *Teaching academic content and literacy to English learners in elementary and middle school* (NCEE 2014-4012). Washington, DC: National Center for Education Evaluation and Regional Assistance (NCEE), Institute of Education Sciences, U.S. Department of Education. Retrieved from http://ies.ed.gov/ncee/wwc/publications_reviews.aspx

Balfanz, R., & Byrnes, V. (2012). *Chronic absenteeism: Summarizing what we know from nationally available data.* Baltimore, MD: Johns Hopkins University Center for Social Organization of Schools.

Batt, E. (2010). Cognitive coaching: A critical phase in professional development to implement sheltered instruction. *Teaching and Teacher Education 26,* 997–1005.

Brown, B., & Ryoo, K. (2008). Teaching science as a language: A "content-first" approach to science teaching. *Journal of Research in Science Teaching, 45*(5), 529–553.

California Department of Education. (2010). *Improving education for English learners: Research-based approaches.* Sacramento, CA: CDE Press. (See http://www.cde.ca.gov/re/pn for more information.)

Cline, T., Crafter, S., O'Dell, L., & de Abreu, G. (2011). Young people's representations of language brokering. *Journal of Multilingual and Multicultural Development, 32*(3), 207–220.

Cloud, N., Genesee, F., & Hamayan, E. (2009). *Literacy instruction for English language learners.* Portsmouth, NH: Heinemann.

Collier, V.P. (1987). Age and rate of acquisition of language for academic purposes. *TESOL Quarterly, 21*(4), 677.

Cook, H.G., Boals, T., & Lundberg, T. (2011). Academic achievement for English language learners: What can we reasonably expect? *Phi Delta Kappan, 93*(2), 66–69.

Council of the Great City Schools. (2009). *Succeeding with English language learners: Lessons learned from the Great City Schools.* Retrieved from http://cgcs.schoolwires.net/cms/lib/DC00001581/Centricity/Domain/35/Publication%20Docs/ELL_Report09.pdf

Cummins, J. (2000). *Language, power and pedagogy*. Clevedon, England: Multilingual Matters.

Darling-Hammond, L., & Richardson, N. (2009). Teachers learning: What matters? *Educational Leadership, 66*(5), 46–53.

DeLeeuw, H. (2008). *English language learners in Washington State*. Executive Summary. Report to the Washington State Board of Education, Olympia, WA, January 10, 2008.

Dianda, M. (2008). *Preventing future high school dropouts: An advocacy and action guide for NEA state and local affiliates*. Washington, DC: National Education Association.

Echevarría, J., Richards-Tutor, C., Canges, R., & Francis, D. (2011). Using the SIOP Model to promote the acquisition of language and science concepts with English learners. *Bilingual Research Journal, 34*(3), 334–351.

Echevarría, J., Richards-Tutor, C., Chinn, V., & Ratleff, P. (2011). Did they get it? The role of fidelity in teaching English learners. *Journal of Adolescent and Adult Literacy, 54*(6), 425–434.

Echevarría, J., Richards-Tutor, C., & Vogt, M.E. (2015). *Response to intervention (RTI) and English learners: Using the SIOP Model* (2nd ed.). Boston, MA: Allyn & Bacon.

Echevarría, J., & Short, D. (2010). Programs and practices for effective sheltered content instruction. In California Department of Education (Ed.), *Improving education for English learners: Research-based approaches* (pp. 250–321). Sacramento, CA: CDE Press.

Echevarria, J., & Short, D. (2011). *The SIOP model: A professional development framework for a comprehensive school-wide intervention. CREATE Brief*. Washington, DC: Center for Applied Linguistics.

Echevarría, J., Short, D., & Powers, K. (2006). School reform and standards-based education: An instructional model for English language learners. *Journal of Educational Research, 99*(4), 195–211.

Echevarría, J., Short, D., & Vogt, M.E. (2008). *Implementing the SIOP Model through effective professional development and coaching*. Boston, MA: Pearson/Allyn & Bacon.

Echevarría, J., Vogt, M.E., & Short, D. (2000). *Making content comprehensible for English language learners: The SIOP Model*. Needham Heights, MA: Allyn & Bacon.

Echevarría, J., Vogt, M.E., & Short, D. (2017). *Making content comprehensible for English learners: The SIOP® Model* (5th ed.). Boston, MA: Pearson.

Flores, S.M., Batalova, J., & Fix, M. (2012). *The educational trajectories of English-language learners in Texas*. Washington, DC: Migration Policy Institute.

Freeman, Y., & Freeman, D. (2009). *Academic language for ELLs and struggling readers*. Portsmouth, NH: Heinemann.

Friend, J., Most, R., & McCrary, K. (2009). The impact of a professional development program to improve urban middle-level English language learner achievement. *Middle Grades Research Journal, 4*(1), 53–75.

Gay, G. (2010). *Culturally responsive teaching: Theory, research and practice*. New York, NY: Teachers College Press.

Genesee, F. (Ed.). (1999). *Program alternatives for linguistically diverse students*. Educational Practice Report No. 1. Santa Cruz and Washington, DC: Center for Research on Education, Diversity & Excellence.

Genesee, F., Lindholm-Leary, K., Saunders, W., & Christian, D. (2006). *Educating English language learners: A synthesis of research evidence*. New York, NY: Cambridge University Press.

Glick, J.E., & White, M.J. (2004). Post-secondary school participation of immigrant and native youth: The role of familial resources and educational expectations. *Social Science Research, 33*, 272–299.

Goldenberg, C. (1992–93). Instructional conversations: Promoting comprehension through discussion. *The Reading Teacher, 46*(4), 316–326.

Goldenberg, C. (2006, July 26). Improving achievement for English-learners: What the research tells us. *Education Week, 25*(43), 34–36.

Gonzalez, N., Moll, L., & Amanti, C. (Eds.). (2005). *Funds of knowledge: Theorizing practices in households, communities, and classrooms*. New York: Routledge.

Guarino, A.J., Echevarría, J., Short, D., Schick, J.E., Forbes, S., & Rueda, R. (2001). The Sheltered Instruction Observation Protocol. *Journal of Research in Education, 11*(1), 138–140.

Guglielmi, R. (2008). Native language proficiency, English literacy, academic achievement, and occupational attainment in limited-English-proficient students: A latent growth modeling perspective. *Journal of Educational Psychology, 100*(2), 322–342.

Hakuta, K., Butler, Y., & Witt, D. (2000). *How long does it take English learners to attain proficiency?* Policy Report 2000–1. Santa Barbara, CA: University of California, Linguistic Minority Research Institute.

Hart, R., Casserly, M., Uzzell, R., Palacios, M., Corcoran, A., & Spurgeon, L. (2015). *Student testing in America's great city schools.* Washington, DC: Council of the Great City Schools.

Himmel, J., Short, D.J., Richards, C., & Echevarría, J. (2009). *Using the SIOP Model to improve middle school science instruction* (CREATE Brief). Washington, DC: Center for Research on the Educational Achievement and Teaching of English Language Learners/CAL.

Honigsfeld, A., & Cohan, A. (2008). The power of two: Lesson study and SIOP help teachers instruct ELLs. *Journal of Staff Development, 29*(1), 24–28.

Hudec, J., & Short, D. (Prods.). (2002a). *Helping English learners succeed: An overview of the SIOP Model.* (Video). Washington, DC: Center for Applied Linguistics.

Hudec, J., & Short, D. (Prods.). (2002b). *The SIOP Model: Sheltered instruction for academic achievement.* (Video). Washington, DC: Center for Applied Linguistics.

Lacour, M., & Tissington, L. D. (2011). The effects of poverty on academic achievement. *Educational Research and Reviews, 6*(7), 522–527.

Lemke, C., & Coughlin, E. (2009). The change agents. *Educational Leadership, 67*(1), 54–59.

Lindholm-Leary, K., & Borsato, G. (2006). Academic achievement. In F. Genesee, K. Lindholm-Leary, W. Saunders, & D. Christian (Eds.), *Educating English language learners: A synthesis of research evidence* (pp. 176–221). New York, NY: Cambridge University Press.

McGraner, K., & Saenz, L. (2009). *Preparing teachers of English language learners.* Washington DC: National Comprehensive Center for Teacher Quality.

McIntyre, E., Kyle, D., Chen, C., Muñoz, M., & Beldon, S. (2010). Teacher learning and ELL reading achievement in sheltered instruction classrooms: Linking professional development to student development. *Literacy Research and Instruction, 49*(4), 334–351.

Menken, K., & Kleyn, T. (2010). The long-term impact of subtractive schooling in the educational experiences of secondary English language learners. *International Journal of Bilingual Education and Bilingualism, 13*(4), 399–417.

National Center for Educational Statistics [NCES]. (2016). English language learners in public schools. *The Condition of Education.* Retrieved from *http://nces.ed.gov/programs/coe/indicator_cgf.asp*

National Comprehensive Center for Teacher Quality. (2009). *Certification and licensure of teachers of English language learners.* Washington DC: Author. Retrieved from *www.tqsource.org/pdfs/ CertificationandLicensureforTeachersofELLs.pdf*

National Governors Association. Center for Best Practices and Council of Chief State School Officers. (2010a). *Common core state standards for English language arts and literacy in history/social studies, science, and technical subjects.* Washington, DC: Author.

National Governors Association. Center for Best Practices and Council of Chief State School Officers. (2010b). *Common core state standards for mathematics.* Washington, DC: Author.

National Institute of Child Health and Human Development (NICHD). (2000). *Report of the National Reading Panel. Teaching children to read: An evidence-based assessment of the scientific research literature on reading and its implications for reading instruction.* (NIH Publication No. 00–4769). Washington, DC: U.S. Department of Health and Human Services.

New York City Department of Education. (2011). *New York City Department of Education graduation results: 6-year outcome cohorts of 2001–2004 New York State calculation method by English language proficiency.* New York, NY: Author. Retrieved from *http://schools.nyc.gov/Accountability/data/GraduationDropoutReports/default.htm*

New York City Department of Education. (2015). *New York City Department of Education graduation results: 6-year outcome cohorts of 2001–2009 New York State calculation method by English language proficiency.* New York, NY: Author. Retrieved from http://schools.nyc.gov/Accountability/data/GraduationDropoutReports/default.htm

NGSS Lead States. (2013). *Next generation science standards: For states, by states.* Washington, DC: The National Academies Press. Retrieved from *http://www.nextgenscience.org/msls-ire-interdependent-relationships-ecosystems*

No Child Left Behind Act of 2001. 107th Congress of the United States of America. Retrieved from *www.ed.gov/legislation/ESEA02/107-110.pdf*

Olsen, L. (2010). *Reparable harm: Fulfilling the unkept promise of educational opportunity for California's long term English learners.* Long Beach, CA: Californians Together. Retrieved from *http://www.californianstogether.org/docs/download.aspx?fileId=12*

Palardy, G. J. (2008). Differential school effects among low, middle, and high social class composition schools: A multiple group, multilevel latent growth curve analysis. *School Effectiveness and School Improvement, 19,* 21-49.

Parish, T., Merikel, A., Perez, M., Linquanti, R., Socias, M., Spain, M., et al. (2006). *Effects of the implementation of Proposition 227 on the education of English learners, K–12: Findings from a five-year evaluation.* Palo Alto, CA: American Institutes for Research.

Reardon, S., & Galindo, C. (2009). The Hispanic-White achievement gap in math and reading in the elementary grades. *American Educational Research Journal, 46*(3), 853–891.

Rumberger, R. (2007). Lagging behind: Linguistic minorities' educational progress during elementary school. *University of California Linguistic Minority Research Institute Newsletter, 16*(2), 1–3.

Rumberger, R. (2011). *Dropping out: Why students drop out of high school and what can be done about it.* Cambridge, MA: Harvard University Press.

Saunders, W., & Goldenberg, C. (2010). Research to guide English language development instruction. In California Department of Education (Ed.), *Improving education for English learners: Research-based approaches* (pp. 21–81). Sacramento, CA: CDE Press.

Saunders, W., & Marcelletti, D. (2013). The gap that can't go away: The catch-22 of reclassification in monitoring the progress of English learners. *Educational Evaluation and Policy Analysis, 35*(2), 139–156

Short, D. (2013). Training and sustaining effective teachers of sheltered instruction. *Theory Into Practice, 52*(2), 118–127.

Short, D., & Boyson, B. (2012). *Helping newcomer students succeed in secondary schools and beyond.* Washington, DC: Center for Applied Linguistics.

Short, D., & Echevarría, J. (2016). *Developing academic language with the SIOP Model.* Boston, MA: Pearson/Allyn & Bacon.

Short, D., Echevarría, J., & Richards-Tutor, C. (2011). Research on academic literacy development in sheltered instruction classrooms. *Language Teaching Research, 15*(3), 363–380.

Short, D., Fidelman, C., & Louguit, M. (2012). Developing academic language in English language learners through sheltered instruction. *TESOL Quarterly, 46*(2), 333–360.

Short, D., & Fitzsimmons, S. (2007). *Double the work: Challenges and solutions to acquiring language and academic literacy for adolescent English language learners.* Report to Carnegie Corporation of New York. Washington, DC: Alliance for Excellent Education.

Short, D., & Himmel, J. (2013). *Moving research on sheltered instruction into curriculum and professional development practice.* Paper presented at American Educational Research Association (AERA) Annual Meeting, San Francisco, CA.

Skerrett, A., & Bomer, R. (2011). Borderzones in adolescents' literacy practices: Connecting out-of-school literacies to the reading curriculum. *Urban Education, 46*(6), 1256–1279.

Snow, C.E., Cancino, H., De Temple, J., & Schley, S. (1991). Giving formal definitions: A linguistic or metalinguistic skill? In E. Bialystok (Ed.), *Language processing and language awareness by bilingual children* (pp. 90–102). New York, NY: Cambridge University Press.

Solano-Flores, G., & Trumbull, E. (2003). Examining language in context: The need for new research and practice paradigms in the testing of English language learners. *Educational Researcher, 32*(2), 3–13.

Song, K. (2016). Applying an SIOP-Based instructional framework for professional development in Korea. *TESL-EJ, 20* (1).

State of New Jersey Department of Education. (2006). *Preliminary analysis of former limited English proficient students' scores on the New Jersey language arts and literacy exam, 2005–2006.* Trenton, NJ: State of New Jersey Department of Education, New Jersey State Assessment Office of Title I.

Sullivan, P., Yeager, M., O'Brien, E., Kober, N., Gayler, K., Chudowsky, N., Chudowsky, V., Wooden, J., Jennings, J., & Stark Rentner, D. (2005). *States try harder, but gaps persist: High school exit exams 2005.* Washington, DC: Center on Education Policy.

Teachers of English to Speakers of Other Languages, Inc. (TESOL). (2006). *Pre-K–12 English language proficiency standards.* Alexandria, VA: Author.

Thomas, W.P., & Collier, V.P. (2002). *A national study of school effectiveness for language minority students' long-term academic achievement.* Santa Cruz, CA, and Washington, DC: Center on Research, Diversity & Excellence.

Umansky, I.M., & Reardon, S.F. (2014). Reclassification patterns among Latino English learner students in bilingual, dual immersion, and English immersion classrooms. *American Educational Research Journal, 51*(5), 879–912.

U.S. Department of Education [USED]. (2015). *Fact sheet: Testing action plan.* Retrieved from http://www.ed.gov/news/press-releases/fact-sheet-testing-action-plan

U.S. Department of Education, Institute of Education Sciences, National Center for Education Statistics, National Assessment of Educational Progress (n.d.). *The nation's report card: 2015 mathematics and reading assessments.* Retrieved from http://www.nationsreportcard.gov/reading_math_2015/#?grade=4

U.S. Department of Education, National Center for Education Statistics, ED*Facts* file 141, Data Group 678, (2016), from the ED*Facts* Data Warehouse (internal U.S. Department of Education source); Common Core of Data (CCD), "State Nonfiscal Survey of Public Elementary and Secondary Education," 2008–09 through 2013–14. Retrieved from *https://nces.ed.gov/programs/digest/d15/tables/dt15_204.27.asp*

U.S. Department of Education, Office of English Language Acquisition. (2015). *English learner toolkit for state and local education agencies.* Retrieved from http://www2.ed.gov/about/offices/list/oela/english-learner-toolkit/index.html

U.S. Department of Justice, Civil Rights Division, & U.S. Department of Education, Office of Civil Rights. (2015). *Dear colleague letter: English learner students and limited English proficient parents.* Washington, DC: Authors. Available at *http://www2.ed.gov/about/offices/list/ocr/letters/colleague-el-201501.pdf*

Valentino, R.A., & Reardon, S.F. (2015). Effectiveness of four instructional programs designed to serve English learners. Variation by ethnicity and initial English proficiency. *Educational Evaluation and Policy Analysis.* Available online at *http://epa.sagepub.com/content/early/2015/04/01/0162373715573310.abstract*

Vogt, M.E., & Echevarria, J. (2015). Reaching English learners: Aligning the ELA/ELD framework with SIOP. *The California Reader, 49*(1), 23–33.

Vygotsky, L. (1978). *Mind and society: The development of higher psychological processes* (M. Cole, V. John-Steiner, S. Scribner, & E. Souberman, Eds. and trans.). Cambridge, MA: Harvard University Press.

WIDA. (2012). *2012 Amplification of the English language proficiency standards, kindergarten-grade 12.* Madison, WI: The Board of Regents of the University of Wisconsin System.

Zong, J., & Batalova, J. (2015). *The limited English proficient population in the United States.* Available online at *http://www.migrationpolicy.org/article/limited-english-proficient-population-united-states#LEP%20 Children*

Zong, J. & Batalova, J. (2016). *Frequently requested statistics on immigrants and immigration in the United States.* Online journal article. Retrieved from *http://www.migrationpolicy.org/article/frequently-requested-statistics-immigrants-and-immigration-united-states#Demographic,%20 Educational,%20Linguistic*

Chapter 2

Aronson, E., Blaney, N.T., Stephan, C., Rosenfield, R., & Sikes, J. (1977). Interdependence in the classroom: A field study. *Journal of Educational Psychology, 69,* 121–128.

August, D., & Shanahan T. (Eds.). (2006). *Developing literacy in second-language learners: A report of the National Literacy Panel on Language-Minority Children and Youth.* Mahwah, NJ: Erlbaum.

Buehl, D. (2009). *Classroom strategies for interactive learning* (3rd ed.). Newark, DE: International Reading Association.

Cloud, N., Genesee, F., & Hamayan, E. (2009). *Literacy instruction for English language learners.* Portsmouth, NH: Heinemann.

Dutro, S., & Kinsella, K. (2010). English language development: Issues and implementation at grades 6 through 12. In California Department of Education (Ed.), *Improving education for English learners: Research-based approaches* (pp. 151–207). Sacramento: CA Dept. of Education.

Echevarría, J., & Graves, A. (2010). *Sheltered content instruction: Teaching English learners with diverse abilities* (4th ed.). Boston, MA: Allyn & Bacon.

Echevarría, J., Short, D., & Vogt, M.E. (2008). *Implementing the SIOP Model through effective professional development and coaching.* Boston, MA: Pearson/Allyn & Bacon.

Echevarría, J., Vogt, M.E., & Short, D. (2010). *The SIOP Model for teaching mathematics to English learners.* Boston, MA: Pearson/Allyn & Bacon.

Ellis, R. (2006). Current issues in the teaching of grammar: An SLA perspective. *TESOL Quarterly, 40*(1), 83–107.

Ellis, R. (2008). *The study of second language acquisition.* 2nd ed. Oxford: Oxford University Press.

Fathman, A., & Crowther, D. (Eds.). (2006). *Science for English language learners: K–12 classroom strategies.* Arlington, VA: NSTA Press.

Gándara, P., & Rumberger, R. (2008). Immigration, language, and education: How does language policy structure opportunity? *Teachers College Record, 111*(3), 750–782.

Gass, S. (2013). *Second language acquisition.* New York: Routledge.

Gersten, R., Baker, S., Shanahan, T., Linan-Thompson, S., Collins, P., & Scarcella, R. (2007). *Effective literacy and English language instruction for English learners in the elementary grades: A practice guide* (NCEE 2007-4011). Washington, DC: National Center for Education Evaluation and Regional Assistance, Institute of Education Sciences, U.S. Department of Education. Retrieved from *http://ies.ed.gov/ncee*

Gibbons, P. (2015). *Scaffolding language, scaffolding learning: Teaching second language learners in the mainstream classroom* (2nd ed.). Portsmouth, NH: Heinemann.

Goldenberg, C. (2008). Teaching English language learners: What research does—and does not say. *American Educator, 32*(2), 8–23, 42–44.

Helman, M., & Buchanan, K. (1993, Fall). *Reforming mathematics instruction for ESL literacy students.* NCBE Program Information Guide Series, Number 15. Retrieved from *www.ncela.gwu.edu/ncbepubs/pigs/pig15.htm*

Hinkel, E. (2006). Current perspectives on teaching the four skills. *TESOL Quarterly, 40*(1), 109–131.

Lacina, J., Levine, L.N., & Sowa, P. (2006). *Helping English language learners succeed in pre-K–elementary schools.* Alexandria, VA: Teachers of English to Speakers of Other Languages, Inc.

McLaughlin, M., & Allen, M.B. (2009). *Guided comprehension: A teaching model* (2nd ed.). Newark, DE: International Reading Association.

National Governors Association [NGA]. Center for Best Practices and Council of Chief State School Officers. (2010a). *Common core state standards for English language arts and literacy in history/social studies, science, and technical subjects.* Washington, DC: Author.

National Governors Association [NGA]. Center for Best Practices and Council of Chief State School Officers. (2010b). *Common core state standards for mathematics.* Washington, DC: Author.

NGSS Lead States. (2013). *Next generation science standards: For states, by states.* Washington, DC: The National Academies Press. Retrieved from *http://www.nextgenscience.org/msls-ire-interdependent-relationships-ecosystems*

Nieto, S., & Bode, P. (2008). *Affirming diversity: The sociopolitical context of multicultural education* (5th ed.). Boston, MA: Allyn & Bacon.

Rance-Roney, J. (2010). Jump-starting language and schema for English-language learners: Teacher-composed digital jumpstarts for academic reading. *Journal of Adolescent and Adult Literacy, 53*(5), 386–395.

Readence, J.E., Bean, T.W., & Baldwin, R.S. (2012). *Content area literacy: An integrated approach* (10th ed.). Dubuque, IA: Kendall/Hunt.

Reeves, N., & Froman, N. (1992). *Into the Mummy's Tomb.* New York, NY: Scholastic/Madison Press.

Ruddell, M.R. (2007). *Teaching content reading and writing* (5th ed.). Hoboken, NJ: John Wiley & Sons, Inc.

Saunders, W., & Goldenberg, C. (2010). Research to guide English language development instruction. In California Department of Education (Ed.), *Improving education for English learners: Research-based approaches* (pp. 21–81). Sacramento, CA: CDE Press.

Schleppegrell, M. (2004). *The language of schooling: A functional linguistic perspective.* Mahwah, NJ: Erlbaum.

Schleppegrell, M., Achugar, M., & Orteíza, T. (2004). The grammar of history: Enhancing content-based instruction through a functional focus on language. *TESOL Quarterly, 38*(1), 67–93.

Short, D., & Boyson, B. (2012). *Helping newcomer students succeed in secondary schools and beyond.* Washington, DC: Center for Applied Linguistics.

Short, D., Cloud, N., Morris, P., & Motta, J. (2012). Cross-district collaboration: Curriculum and professional development. *TESOL Journal, 3*(3), 402–424.

Short, D., & Echevarría, J. (2016). *Developing academic language with the SIOP Model.* Boston, MA: Pearson/Allyn & Bacon.

Short, D., Vogt, M.E., & Echevarría, J. (2011a). *The SIOP Model for teaching history-social studies to English learners.* Boston, MA: Allyn & Bacon.

Short, D., Vogt, M.E., & Echevarría, J. (2011b). *The SIOP Model for teaching science to English learners.* Boston, MA: Allyn & Bacon.

Snow, M.A., & Katz, A. (2010). English language development: Issues and implementation at grades K through 5. In California Department of Education (Ed.), *Improving education for English learners: Research-based approaches* (pp. 83–148). Sacramento, CA: Department of Education.

TESOL International Association. (2013). *Implementing the Common Core State Standards for English learners: The changing role of the ESL teacher.* Alexandria, VA: Author.

Torgesen, J., Houston, D., Rissman, L., Decker, S., Roberts, G., Vaughn, S., Wexler, J., Francis, D., Rivera, M., & Lesaux, N. (2007). *Academic literacy instruction for adolescents.* Portsmouth, NH: RMC Research Corporation, Center on Instruction.

Turkan, S., de Oliveira, L., Lee, O., & Phelps, G. (2014). Proposing a knowledge base for teaching academic content to English language learners: Disciplinary linguistic knowledge. *Teachers College Record, 116*(1), 1–30.

Vacca, R., Vacca, J.A., & Mraz, M. (2010). *Content area reading: Literacy and learning across the curriculum* (10th ed.). New York, NY: Longman.

Vogt, M.E. (2000). Content learning for students needing modifications: An issue of access. In M. McLaughlin & M.E. Vogt (Eds.), *Creativity and innovation in content area teaching: A resource for intermediate, middle, and high school teachers*. Norwood, MA: Christopher Gordon Publishers.

Vogt, M.E., & Echevarría, J. (2008). *99 ideas and activities for teaching English learners with the SIOP Model*. Boston, MA: Allyn & Bacon.

Vogt, M.E., Echevarría, J., & Short, D. (2010). *Teaching English-language arts to English learners with the SIOP Model*. Boston, MA: Pearson.

Vogt, M.E., Echevarría, J., & Washam, M.A (2015). *99 more ideas and activities for teaching English learners with the SIOP model*. Boston, MA: Pearson Allyn & Bacon.

Chapter 3

Allen, J. (2007). *Inside words: Tools for teaching academic vocabulary, grades 4–12*. Portland, ME: Stenhouse Publishers.

Anderson, R.C. (1984). Role of the reader's schema in comprehension, learning, and memory. In R.C. Anderson, J. Osborn, & R.J. Tierney (Eds.), *Learning to read in American schools: Basal readers and content texts (pp. 243–258)*. Hillsdale, NJ: Erlbaum.

Anderson, R.C. (1994). Role of the reader's schema in comprehension, learning, and memory. In R. Ruddell, M. Ruddell, & H. Singer (Eds.), *Theoretical models and processes of reading* (4th ed., pp. 469–482). Newark, DE: International Reading Association.

August, D., & Shanahan T. (Eds.). (2006). *Developing literacy in second-language learners: A report of the National Literacy Panel on Language-Minority Children and Youth*. Mahwah, NJ: Erlbaum.

August, D., & Shanahan, T. (2010). Effective English literacy instruction for English learners. In California Department of Education (Ed.), *Improving education for English learners: Research-based approaches* (pp. 209–249). Sacramento, CA: CDE Press.

Baumann, J.F. (2005). Vocabulary-comprehension relationships. In B. Maloch, J.V. Hoffman, D.L. Schallert, C.M. Fairbanks, & J. Worthy (Eds.), *54th Yearbook of the National Reading Conference*. Oak Creek, WI: National Reading Conference, Inc.

Helman, L., Bear, D., Templeton, S., Invernizzi, F., & Johnston, F. (2012). *Words their way with English learners: Word study for spelling, phonics, and vocabulary instruction* (2nd ed.), Boston, MA: Pearson.

Bear, D.R., Invernizzi, M., Templeton, S., & Johnston, F. (2016). *Words their way: Word study for phonics, vocabulary, and spelling instruction* (6th ed.). Boston, MA: Pearson.

Beck, I.L, McKeown, M.G., & Kucan, L. (2002). *Bringing words to life: Robust vocabulary instruction*. New York, NY: Guilford Press.

Beck, I.L., Perfetti, C., & McKeown, M.G. (1982). Effects of long-term vocabulary instruction on lexical access and reading comprehension. *Journal of Educational Psychology, 74*, 506–521.

Biemiller, A. (2005). Vocabulary development and instruction: A prerequisite for school learning. In D. Dickinson & S. Neuman (Eds.), *Handbook of early literacy research*, Vol. 2. New York, NY: Guilford Press.

Blachowicz, L.Z., & Fisher, P. (2000). Vocabulary instruction. In R.L. Kamil, P.B. Mosenthal, P.D. Pearson, & R. Barr (Eds.), *Handbook of reading research* (Vol. 3, pp. 503–523). Mahwah, NJ: Erlbaum.

Buehl, D. (2014). *Classroom strategies for interactive learning* (3rd ed.). Newark, DE: International Reading Association.

Carrell, P. (1987). Content and formal schemata in ESL reading. *TESOL Quarterly, 21*(3), 461–481.

Chiesi, H., Spilich, G., & Voss, J. (1979). Acquisition of domain-related information in relation to high- and low-domain knowledge. *Journal of Verbal Learning and Verbal Behavior, 18,* 257–274.

Cunningham, P.M. (2004). *Phonics they use: Words for reading and writing* (4th ed.). New York, NY: Harper-Collins College Press.

Common Core State Standards. (2010). Retrieved from *www.doe.in.gov/commoncore*

Dalton, B., & Grisham, D. (2011). eVoc strategies: 10 ways to use technology to build vocabulary. *The Reading Teacher, 64*(5), 306–317.

Diamond, L., & Gutlohn, L. (2006). *Vocabulary handbook.* Berkeley, CA: Core Literacy Library.

Dole, J., Duffy, G., Roehler, L., & Pearson, P.D. (1991). Moving from the old to the new: Research in reading comprehension instruction. *Review of Educational Research, 61,* 239–264.

Donnelly, W.B., & Roe, C.J. (2010). Using sentence frames to develop academic vocabulary for English learners. *The Reading Teacher, 64*(2), 131–136.

Fisher, D., & Frey, N. (2008). *Wordwise & content rich: Five essential steps to teaching academic vocabulary.* Portsmouth, NH: Heinemann.

Fisher, D., & Frey, N. (2014). Content area vocabulary learning. *The Reading Teacher, 67*(8), 594–599.

Gillis, V. (2014). Talking the talk: Vocabulary across the disciplines (or what to do instead). *Journal of Adolescent & Adult Literacy, 58*(4), 281–287.

Graves, M.F. (2011). Ask the expert. *The Reading Teacher, 64*(7), 541.

Graves, M.F., & Fitzgerald, J. (2006). Effective vocabulary instruction for English-language learners. In C.C. Block & J.N. Mangieri (Eds.), *The vocabulary- enriched classroom: Practice for improving the reading performance of all students in grades 3 and up (pp. 118–137).* New York, NY: Scholastic.

Hart, B., & Risley, T.R. (2003). The early catastrophe: The 30 million word gap. *American Educator, 27,* 4–9.

Helman, L., Bear, D., Templeton, S., Invernizzi, F., & Johnston, F. (2012). Words their way with English learners: Word study for spelling, phonics, and vocabulary instruction (2nd ed.), Boston, MA: Pearson. Kucan, L. (2012). What is most important to know about vocabulary? *The Reading Teacher, 65*(6), 360–366.

Lesaux, N.K., Kieffer, M.J., Faller, S.E., & Kelley, J.G. (2010). The effectiveness and ease of implementation of an academic vocabulary intervention for linguistically diverse students in urban middle schools. *Reading Research Quarterly, 45*(2), 196–228.

Manyak, P.C. (2010). Vocabulary instruction for English learners: Lesson from MCVIP. *The Reading Teacher, 64*(2), 143–146.

Manyak, P.C., Von Gutten, H., Autenrieth, D., Gillis, C., Mastre-O'Farrell, J., Irvine-McDermott, E., Baumann, J., & Blachowicz, C. (2014). Four practical principles for enhancing vocabulary instruction. *The Reading Teacher, 68*(1), 13–23.

Nagy, W.M., & Townsend, D. (2012). Words as tools: "Learning academic vocabulary" as language acquisition. *Reading Research Quarterly, 47*(1), 91–108.

Neuman, S.B., Kaefer, T., & Pinkham, A. (2014). Building background knowledge. *The Reading Teacher, 68*(2), 145–148.

Ogle, D. (1986). K-W-L: A teaching model that develops active reading of expository text. *The Reading Teacher, 39,* 564–570.

Rance-Roney, J. (2010). Jump-starting language and schema for English-language learners: Teacher-composed digital jumpstarts for academic reading. *Journal of Adolescent and Adult Literacy, 53*(5), 386–395.

Rothenberg, C., & Fisher, D. (2007). *Teaching English learners: A differentiated approach.* Boston, MA: Pearson/Merrill/Prentice Hall.

Ruddell, M.R. (2007). *Teaching content reading and writing* (5th ed.). Hoboken, NJ: John Wiley & Sons, Inc.

Ruddell, M.R., & Shearer, B.A. (2002). "Extraordinary," "tremendous," "exhilarating," "magnificent": Middle school at-risk students become avid word learners with the Vocabulary Self-Collection Strategy (VSS). *Journal of Adolescent and Adult Literacy, 45*(4), 352–363.

Rumelhart, D.E. (1980). Schemata: The building blocks of cognition. In R.J. Spiro et al. (Eds.), *Theoretical issues in reading comprehension* (pp. 33–58). Hillsdale, NJ: Erlbaum.

Shearer, B.A., Ruddell, M.R., & Vogt, M.E. (2001). Successful middle school intervention: Negotiated strategies and individual choice. In T. Shanahan & F.V. Rodriguez (Eds.), *National Reading Conference Yearbook, 50* (pp. 558–571). National Reading Conference.

Short, D.J., & Echevarria, J. (2016). *Developing academic language with the SIOP Model.* Boston, MA: Pearson.

Stahl, S., & Nagy, W. (2006). *Teaching word meanings.* Mahwah, NJ: Erlbaum.

Townsend, D. (2015). Who's using the language? Supporting middle school students with content area academic language. *Journal of Adolescent Literacy, 58*(5), 376–387.

Vogt, M.E. (2014). Reaching linguistically diverse students. In S.B. Wepner, D.S. Strickland, & D. Quatroche (Eds.), *The administration and supervision of reading programs* (5th ed.), (pp. 180–189). New York, NY: Teachers College Press.

Vogt, M.E., & Echevarría, J. (2008). *99 ideas and activities for teaching English learners with the SIOP Model.* Boston, MA: Allyn & Bacon.

Vogt, M.E., Echevarría, J., & Short, D. (2010). *The SIOP Model for Teaching English-Language Arts to English Learners.* Boston, MA: Pearson.

Vogt, M.E., Echevarría, J., & Washam, M.A (2015). *99 more ideas and activities for teaching English learners with the SIOP model.* Boston, MA: Pearson Allyn & Bacon.

Vygotsky, L. (1978). *Mind and society: The development of higher psychological processes* (M. Cole, V. John-Steiner, S. Scribner, & E. Souberman, Eds. and trans.). Cambridge, MA: Harvard University Press.

Zwiers, J. (2008). *Building academic language: Essential practices for content classrooms.* San Francisco, CA: John Wiley & Sons, Inc.

Zwiers, J., O'Hara, S., & Pritchard, R. (2014). *Common Core Standards in diverse classrooms: Essential practices for developing academic language and disciplinary literacy.* Portland, ME: Stenhouse Publishers.

Chapter 4

August, D., & Shanahan T. (Eds.). (2006). *Developing literacy in second-language learners: A report of the National Literacy Panel on Language-Minority Children and Youth.* Mahwah, NJ: Erlbaum.

August, D., & Shanahan, T. (2010). Effective English literacy instruction for English learners. In California Department of Education (Ed.), *Improving education for English learners: Research-based approaches* (pp. 209–249). Sacramento, CA: CDE Press.

Baily, F., & Pransky, K. (2014). *Memory at work in the classroom.* Alexandria, VA: Association for Supervision and Curriculum Development.

Baker, S., Lesaux, N., Jayanthi, M., Dimino, J., Proctor, C.P., Morris, J., Gersten, R., Haymond, K., Kieffer, M.J., Linan-Thompson, S., & Newman-Gonchar, R. (2014). *Teaching academic content and literacy to English learners in elementary and middle school* (NCEE 2014-4012). Washington, DC: National Center for Education Evaluation and Regional Assistance (NCEE), Institute of Education Sciences, U.S. Department of Education. Retrieved from *http://ies.ed.gov/ncee/wwc/publications_reviews.aspx*

Crossley, S., McCarthy, P., Louwerse, M., & McNamara, D. (2007). A linguistic analysis of simplified and authentic texts. *The Modern Language Journal, 19*(2), 15–30.

Echevarría, J. (1998). *A model of sheltered instruction for English language learners.* Paper presented at the conference for the Division on Diversity of the Council for Exceptional Children, Washington, DC.

Echevarría, J., & Vogt, M.E. (2011). *RTI and English learners: Making it happen.* Boston, MA: Allyn & Bacon.

Goldenberg, C. (2008). Teaching English language learners: What research does—and does not say. *American Educator*, *32*(2), 8–23, 42–44.

Graham, S., Bollinger, A., Booth Olson, C., D'Aoust, C., MacArthur, C., McCutchen, D., & Olinghouse, N. (2012). *Teaching elementary school students to be effective writers: A practice guide* (NCEE 2012- 4058). Washington, DC: National Center for Education Evaluation and Regional Assistance, Institute of Education Sciences, U.S. Department of Education. Available from http://ies.ed.gov/ncee/wwc/pdf/practice_guides/writing_pg_062612.pdf.

Jensen, E. (2005). *Teaching with the brain in mind* (2nd ed.). Alexandria, VA: Association for Supervision and Curriculum Development.

Jensen, E. (2008). *Brain-based learning* (2nd ed.). Thousand Oaks, CA: Corwin Press.

Jensen, E. (2013). How poverty affects classroom engagement. *Educational Leadership*, *70*(8), 24–30.

Krashen, S. (1985). *The input hypothesis: Issues and implications*. New York, NY: Longman.

Marzano, R., Pickering, D., & Pollock, J. (2001). *Classroom instruction that works*. Alexandria, VA: Association for Supervision and Curriculum Development.

Reutebuch, C. (2010). *Effective social studies instruction to promote knowledge acquisition and vocabulary learning of English language learners in the middle grades*. Washington, DC: Center for Research on the Educational Achievement and Teaching of English Language Learners. Retrieved from *http://www.cal.org/create/resources/pubs/effective-social-studies-instruction.html*

Short, D., & Echevarria, J. (2016). *Developing academic language with the SIOP Model*. Boston., MA: Pearson.

Short, D., Vogt, M.E., & Echevarria, J. (2011). *The SIOP Model for teaching history/social studies to English learners*. Boston, MA: Allyn & Bacon.

Vogt, M.E., & Echevarría, J. (2008). *99 ideas and activities for teaching English learners with the SIOP Model*. Boston, MA: Allyn & Bacon.

Chapter 5

Anderson, R.C. (1984). Role of the reader's schema in comprehension, learning, and memory. In R.C. Anderson, J. Osborn, & R.J. Tierney (Eds.), *Learning to read in American schools: Basal readers and content texts (pp. 243–258)*. Hillsdale, NJ: Erlbaum.

Anderson, L.W., & Krathwohl, D.R. (Eds.). (2001). *Taxonomy for learning, teaching, and assessing: A revision of Bloom's Taxonomy of Educational Objectives*. Boston, MA: Longman.

August, D., & Shanahan, T. (2010). Effective English literacy instruction for English learners. In California Department of Education (Ed.), *Improving education for English learners: Research-based approaches* (pp. 209–249). Sacramento, CA: CDE Press.

Baker, L., & Brown, A.L. (1984). Metacognitive skills and reading. In P.D. Pearson (Ed.), *Handbook of reading research (pp. 353–394)*. New York, NY: Longman.

Barnhardt, S. (1997). Effective memory strategies. *NCLRC Language Resource*, *1*(6).

Beck, I.L., & McKeown, M.G. (2002). Questioning the author: Making sense of social studies. *Educational Leadership*, *60*(3), 44–47.

Beck, I.L., & McKeown, M.G. (2006). *Improving comprehension with Questioning the Author: A fresh and expanded view of a powerful approach*. New York, NY: Scholastic.

Bloom, B., Engelhart, M., Furst, E., Hill, W., & Krathworl, D. (Eds.). (1956). *Taxonomy of educational objectives: The classification of educational goals. Handbook I: Cognitive domain*. New York, NY: David McKay Co.

Bruner, J. (1983). *Child's talk: Learning to use language*. New York, NY: W.W. Norton.

Buehl, D. (2013). *Classroom strategies for interactive learning* (4th ed.). Newark, DE: International Reading Association.

Burke, J. (2002). The Internet reader. *Educational Leadership*, *60*(3), 38–42.

Chamot, A.U. (2009). *The CALLA handbook* (2nd ed.). Boston, MA: Pearson Education, Inc.

Cohen, A.D., & Macaro, E. (Eds.). (2008). *Language learner strategies: 30 years of research and practice*. Oxford, UK: Oxford University Press.

Common Core State Standards. (2010). Retrieved from www.doe.in.gov/commoncore

Dole, J., Duffy, G., Roehler, L., & Pearson, P.D. (1991). Moving from the old to the new: Research in reading comprehension instruction. *Review of Educational Research, 61,* 239–264.

Duffy, G.G. (2002). The case for direct explanation of strategies. In C.C. Block & M. Pressley (Eds.), *Comprehension instruction: Research-based best practices (pp. 28–41)*. New York, NY: Guilford Press.

Dymock, S., & Nicholson, R. (2010). High 5! Strategies to enhance comprehension of expository text. *The Reading Teacher, 64*(3), 166–178.

Fisher, D., & Frey, N. (2014). Content area vocabulary learning. *The Reading Teacher, 67*(8), 594–599.

Gall, M. (1984). Synthesis of research on teachers' questioning. *Educational Leadership, 42*(3), 40–47.

Harvey, S., & Goudvis, A. (2013). Comprehension at the Core. *The Reading Teacher, 66*(6), 432–439.

Lipson, M., & Wixson, K. (2012). *Assessment of reading and writing difficulties: An interactive approach* (5th ed.). New York, NY: Longman.

Marcell, B., DeCleene, J., & Juettner, M.R. (2010). Caution! Hard Hat Area! Comprehension under construction: Cementing a foundation of comprehension strategy usage that carries over to independent practice. *The Reading Teacher, 63*(8), 687–691.

McLaughlin, M. (2010). *Content area reading: Teaching and learning in an age of multiple literacies*. Boston, MA: Pearson.

Muth, K.D., & Alvermann, D.E. (1999). *Teaching and learning in the middle grades* (2nd ed.). Needham Heights, MA: Allyn & Bacon.

National Institute of Child Health and Human Development (NICHD). (2000). *Report of the National Reading Panel. Teaching children to read: An evidence-based assessment of the scientific research literature on reading and its implications for reading instruction*. (NIH Publication No. 00–4769). Washington, DC: U.S. Department of Health and Human Services.

NGSS Lead States. (2013). *Next generation science standards: For states, by states*. Washington, DC: The National Academies Press. Retrieved from *http://www.nextgenscience.org/msls-ire-interdependent-relationships-ecosystems*

Oczkus, L.D. (2010). *Reciprocal teaching at work: Strategies for improving reading comprehension* (2nd ed.). Newark, DE: International Reading Association.

Olson, C.B., Land, R., Anselmi, T., & AuBuchon, C. (2011). Teaching secondary English learners to understand, analyze, and write interpretive essays about theme. *Journal of Adolescent and Adult Literacy, 54*(4), 245–256.

Palinscar, A.C., & Brown, A.L. (1984). Reciprocal teaching of comprehension-fostering and comprehension-monitoring activities. *Cognition and Instruction, 1,* 117–175.

Pearson, P.D., & Gallagher, M. (1983). The instruction of reading comprehension. *Contemporary Educational Psychology, 8*(3), 317–344.

Pressley, M. (2000). What should comprehension instruction be instruction of? In M.L. Kamil, P.B. Mosenthal, P.D. Pearson, & R. Barr (Eds.), *Handbook of reading research* (Vol. III, pp. 545–561). Mahwah, NJ: Erlbaum.

Pressley, M. (2002). Comprehension strategies instruction: A turn-of-the-century status report. In C.C. Block & M. Pressley (Eds.), *Comprehension instruction: Research-based best practices* (pp. 11–27). New York, NY: Guilford.

Raphael, T.E. (1984). Teaching learners about sources of information for answering comprehension questions. *Journal of Reading, 27,* 303–311.

Raphael, T.E., Highfield, K., & Au, K.H. (2006). *QAR now: A powerful and practical framework that develops comprehension and higher-level thinking skills*. New York, NY: Scholastic.

Ruddell, M.R. (2007). *Teaching content reading and writing* (5th ed.). Hoboken, NJ: John Wiley & Sons, Inc.

Saunders, W., & Goldenberg, C. (2010). Research to guide English language development instruction. In California Department of Education (Ed.), *Improving education for English learners: Research-based approaches* (pp. 21–81). Sacramento, CA: CDE Press.

Shearer, B.A., Ruddell, M.R., & Vogt, M.E. (2001). Successful middle school intervention: Negotiated strategies and individual choice. In T. Shanahan & F.V. Rodriguez (Eds.), *National Reading Conference Yearbook, 50* (pp. 558–571). National Reading Conference (Now Literacy Research Association).

Snow, C.E., Griffin, P., & Burns, M.S. (Eds.). (2005). *Knowledge to support the teaching of reading: Preparing teachers for a changing world.* San Francisco, CA: Jossey-Bass.

Stauffer, R. (1969). *Teaching reading as a thinking process.* New York, NY: Harper & Row.

Sylvester, R., & Greenidge, W. (2009). Digital storytelling: Extending the potential for struggling writers. *The Reading Teacher, 64*(4), 284–295.

Taboada, A., & Guthrie, J.T. (2006). Contributions of student questioning and prior knowledge to construction of knowledge from reading information text. *Journal of Literacy Research, 38*(1), 1–35.

Vogt, M.E. (2000). Content learning for students needing modifications: An issue of access. In M. McLaughlin & M.E. Vogt (Eds.), *Creativity and innovation in content area teaching: A resource for intermediate, middle, and high school teachers.* Norwood, MA: Christopher Gordon Publishers.

Vogt, M.E. (2002). *SQP2RS: Increasing students' understandings of expository text through cognitive and metacognitive strategy application.* Paper presented at the 52nd Annual Meeting of the National Reading Conference.

Vogt, M.E., & Echevarría, J. (2008). *99 ideas and activities for teaching English learners with the SIOP Model.* Boston, MA: Allyn & Bacon.

Vogt, M.E., Echevarría, J., & Short, D. (2010). *Teaching English-language arts to English learners with the SIOP Model.* Boston, MA: Pearson.

Vogt, M.E., & Nagano, P. (2003). *Turn it on with Light Bulb Reading! Sound-switching strategies for struggling readers, The Reading Teacher, 57*(3), 214–221.

Vogt, M.E., & Shearer, B.A. (2016). *Reading specialists and literacy coaches in the real world* (3rd ed.). Boston, MA: Allyn & Bacon.

Vogt, M.E., Echevarría, J., & Short, D. (2010). *Teaching English-language arts to English learners with the SIOP Model.* Boston, MA: Pearson.

Vygotsky, L. (1978). *Mind and society: The development of higher psychological processes* (M. Cole, V. John-Steiner, S. Scribner, & E. Souberman, Eds. and trans.). Cambridge, MA: Harvard University Press.

Watson, K., & Young, B. (1986). Discourse for learning in the classroom. *Language Arts, 63*(2), 126–133.

Webb, N.L. (1997). Determining alignment of expectations and assessment in math and science education. *NISE Brief, 1*(1), 1–8. National Institute for Science Education, University of Wisconsin, Madison.

Chapter 6

August, D., & Shanahan T. (Eds.). (2006). *Developing literacy in second-language learners: A report of the National Literacy Panel on Language-Minority Children and Youth.* Mahwah, NJ: Erlbaum.

Baker, S., Lesaux, N., Jayanthi, M., Dimino, J., Proctor, C.P., Morris, J., Gersten, R., Haymond, K., Kieffer, M.J., Linan-Thompson, S., & Newman-Gonchar, R. (2014). *Teaching academic content and literacy to English learners in elementary and middle school* (NCEE 2014-4012). Washington, DC: National Center for Education Evaluation and Regional Assistance (NCEE), Institute of Education Sciences, U.S. Department of Education. Retrieved from *http://ies.ed.gov/ncee/wwc/publications_reviews.aspx*.

Brooks, K., & Thurston, L. (2010). English language learner academic engagement and instructional grouping configurations. *American Secondary Education*, *39*(1), 45–60.

California Department of Education. (2014). *ELA/ELD Framework*. Sacramento, CA: Author. Retrieved from *http://www.cde.ca.gov/ci/rl/cf/elaeldfrmwrksbeadopted.asp*

Callahan, R.M. (2005). Tracking and high school English language learners: Limiting opportunity to learn. *American Educational Research Journal*, *42*(2), 305–328.

Cazden, C. (2001). *Classroom discourse: The language of teaching and learning*. New York, NY: Heinemann.

City, E. (2014). Talking to learn. *Educational Leadership*, *72*(3), 10–16.

Dockrell, J., Stewart, M., & King, D. (2010). Supporting early oral language skills for English language learners in inner city preschool provision. *British Journal of Educational Psychology*, *80*, 497–515.

Donnelly, W.B., & Roe, C.J. (2010). Using sentence frames to develop academic vocabulary for English learners. *The Reading Teacher*, *64*(2), 131–136.

Echevarría, J. (1995). Interactive reading instruction: A comparison of proximal and distal effects of instructional conversations. *Exceptional Children*, *61*(6), 536–552.

Echevarría, J., & Short, D. (2010). Programs and practices for effective sheltered content instruction. In California Department of Education (Ed.), *Improving education for English learners: Research-based approaches* (pp. 250–321). Sacramento, CA: CDE Press.

Echevarría, J., Greene, G., & Goldenberg, C. (1996). *A comparison of sheltered instruction and effective non-sheltered instruction on the achievement of LEP students*. Pilot study.

Echevarría, J., Vogt, M.E., & Short, D. (2010). *The SIOP Model for teaching mathematics to English learners*. Boston, MA: Pearson/Allyn & Bacon.

Fisher, D., & Frey, N. (2013). Collaborative conversations. *Principal Leadership*, *13*(8), 57–61.

Futrell, M., & Gomez, J. (2008). How tracking creates a poverty of learning. *Educational Leadership*, *65*(8), 74–78.

Geva, E. (2006). Second-language oral proficiency and second-language literacy. In D. August & T. Shanahan (Eds.), *Developing literacy in second-language learners: Report of the National Literacy Panel on Language Minority Children and Youth*. Mahwah, NJ: Erlbaum.

Goldenberg, C. (1992–93). Instructional conversations: Promoting comprehension through discussion. *The Reading Teacher*, *46*(4), 316–326.

Goodlad, J. (1984). *A place called school: Prospects for the future*. New York, NY: McGraw-Hill.

Graff, G. (2003). *Clueless in academe*. New Haven, CT: Yale University Press.

Guthrie, J.T., & Ozgungor, S. (2002). Instructional contexts for reading engagement. In C.C. Block & M. Pressley (Eds.), *Comprehension instruction: Research-based best practices* (pp. 275–288). New York, NY: Guilford Press.

Hiebert, E.H. (1983). An examination of ability grouping for reading instruction. *Reading Research Quarterly*, *18*, 231–255.

Honea, J.M. (1982, December). Wait-time as an instructional variable: An influence on teacher and student. *Clearinghouse*, *56*(4), 167–170.

Jensen, E. (2005). *Teaching with the brain in mind* (2nd ed.). Alexandria, VA: Association for Supervision and Curriculum Development.

Jensen, E. (2008). *Brain-based learning* (2nd ed.). Thousand Oaks, CA: Corwin Press.

Kazemi, E., & Hintz, A. (2014). *Intentional talk: How to structure and lead productive mathematical discussions*. Portland, ME: Stenhouse Publishers.

Lucas, S.R. (1999). *Tracking inequality: Stratification and mobility in American high schools*. New York, NY: Teachers College Press.

Marshall, J. (2000). Research on response to literature. In R.L. Kamil, P.B. Mosenthal, P.D. Son, &

R. Barr (Eds.), *Handbook of reading research* (Vol. 3, pp. 381–402). Mahwah, NJ: Erlbaum.

Marzano, R., Pickering, D., & Pollock, J. (2001). *Classroom instruction that works*. Alexandria, VA: Association for Supervision and Curriculum Development.

McIntyre, E., Kyle, D., Chen, C., Muñoz, M., & Beldon, S. (2010). Teacher learning and ELL reading achievement in sheltered instruction classrooms: Linking professional development to student development. *Literacy Research and Instruction, 49*(4), 334–351.

National Governors Association. Center for Best Practices and Council of Chief State School Officers. (2010a). *Common core state standards for English language arts and literacy in history/social studies, science, and technical subjects*. Washington, DC: Author.

Oakes, J. (1985). *Keeping track: How schools structure inequality*. New Haven, CT: Yale University Press.

Poldrack, R., Clark, J., Pare-Blagoev, E., Shohamy, D., Creso Moyano, J., Myers, C., & Gluck, M. (2001). Interactive memory systems in the human brain. *Nature, 414*, 546–550.

Porath, S. (2014) Talk less, listen more. *The Reading Teacher, 67*(8), 627–635.

Rosen, L.D. (2012). *iDisorder*. New York, NY: St. Martin's Press.

Rowe, M. (2003). Wait-time and rewards as instructional variables, their influence on language, logic and fate control: Part one—wait-time. *Journal of Research in Science Teaching*, Vol. 40, Supplement S19–S32.

Saunders, W., & Goldenberg, C. (1999). The effects of instructional conversations and literature logs on limited and fluent English proficient students' story comprehension and thematic understanding. *The Elementary School Journal, 99*, 277–301.

Saunders, W., & Goldenberg, C. (2007). Talking texts: How speech and writing interact in school learning. In R. Horowitz (Ed.), *The effects of an instructional conversation on English language*

learners' concepts of friendship and story comprehension* (pp. 221–252). Mahwah, NJ: Erlbaum.

Saunders, W., & Goldenberg, C. (2010). Research to guide English language development instruction. In California Department of Education (Ed.), *Improving education for English learners: Research-based approaches* (pp. 21–81). Sacramento, CA: CDE Press.

Schmoker, M. (2006). *Results now*. Alexandria, VA: Association for Supervision and Curriculum Development.

Short, D., & Echevarría, J. (2016). *Developing academic language with the SIOP Model*. Boston, MA: Pearson/Allyn & Bacon.

Sparks, S. (2010). *Giving students a say may spur engagement and achievement*. Retrieved from *http://blogs.edweek.org/edweek/inide school-research/2010*

Swift, J.N., & Gooding, C.T. (1983). Interaction of wait time feedback and questioning instruction on middle school science teaching. *Journal of Research in Science Teaching, 20,* 721–730.

Tharp, R., & Gallimore, R. (1988). *Rousing minds to life*. Cambridge, MA: Cambridge University Press.

Tobin, K. (1987). The role of wait time in higher cognitive level learning. *Review of Educational Research, 57,* 69–95.

Toth, A. (2013) Not just after lunch. *The Reading Teacher, 67*(3), 203–207.

Uribe, M., & Nathenson-Mejía, S. (2008). *Literacy essentials for English language learners: Successful transitions*. New York, NY: Teacher's College Press.

Van de Pol, J., Volman, M., & Beishuizen, J. (2010). Scaffolding in teacher–student interaction: A decade of research. *Educational Psychology Review, 22*, 271–296.

Vaughn, S., Linan-Thompson, S., Kouzekanani, K., Bryant, D.P., Dickson, S., & Blozis, S.A. (2003). Reading instruction grouping for students with reading difficulties. *Remedial and Special Education, 24*(5), 301–315.

Vogt, M.E., & Echevarría, J. (2008). *99 ideas and activities for teaching English learners with the SIOP Model*. Boston, MA: Allyn & Bacon.

Vogt, M.E., & Shearer, B.A. (2016). *Reading specialists and literacy coaches in the real world*. (3rd ed.) Long Grove, IL: Waveland Press.

Vygotsky, L. (1978). *Mind and society: The development of higher psychological processes* (M. Cole, V. John-Steiner, S. Scribner, & E. Souberman, Eds. and trans.). Cambridge, MA: Harvard University Press.

Walqui, A. (2006). Scaffolding instruction for English language learners: A conceptual framework. *The International Journal of Bilingual Education and Bilingualism, 9*(2), 159–180.

Wasik, B., & Hindman, A. (Dec. 2013/Jan 2014). Realizing the promise of open-ended questions. *The Reading Teacher, 67*(4), 302–311.

Wasik, B., & Iannone-Campbell, C. (2012). Developing vocabulary through purposeful, strategic conversations. *The Reading Teacher, 66*(2), 321–332.

Wiggins, G., & McTighe, J. (2008). *Understanding by design*. Upper Saddle River, NJ: Prentice Hall.

Zwiers, J., & Crawford, M. (2009). How to start academic conversations. *Educational Leadership, 66*(7), 70–73.

Chapter 7

August, D., & Shanahan T. (Eds.). (2006). *Developing literacy in second-language learners: A report of the National Literacy Panel on Language-Minority Children and Youth*. Mahwah, NJ: Erlbaum.

Baker, S., Lesaux, N., Jayanthi, M., Dimino, J., Proctor, C.P., Morris, J., Gersten, R., Haymond, K., Kieffer, M.J., Linan-Thompson, S., & Newman-Gonchar, R. (2014). *Teaching academic content and literacy to English learners in elementary and middle school* (NCEE 2014-4012). Washington, DC: National Center for Education Evaluation and Regional Assistance (NCEE), Institute of Education Sciences, U.S. Department of Education.

Retrieved from *http://ies.ed.gov/ncee/wwc/publications_reviews.aspx*.

Dean, C.B., Hubbell, E.R., Pilter, H., & Stone, B.J. (2012). *Classroom instruction that works* (2nd ed.). Alexandria, VA: Association for Supervision and Curriculum Development.

Echevarría, J., Short, D., & Vogt, M.E. (2008). *Implementing the SIOP Model through effective professional development and coaching*. Boston, MA: Pearson/Allyn & Bacon.

Ellis, R. (2008). *Principles of instructed second language acquisition*. CAL Digest. Washington, DC: Center for Applied Linguistics.

Fisher, D., & Frey, N. (2008). *Better learning through structured teaching*. Alexandria, VA: Association for Supervision and Curriculum Development.

Genesee, F., Lindholm-Leary, K., Saunders, W., & Christian, D. (2006). *Educating English language learners: A synthesis of research evidence*. New York, NY: Cambridge University Press.

Hinkel, E. (2006). Current perspectives on teaching the four skills. *TESOL Quarterly 40*(1), 109–131.

Hunter, M. (1982). *Mastery teaching: Increasing instructional effectiveness in secondary schools, college, and universities*. El Segundo, CA: TIP Publications.

Kagan, S. (1994). *Cooperative learning*. San Clemente, CA: Kagan Publishing.

Krashen, S. (1985). *The input hypothesis: Issues and implications*. New York, NY: Longman.

Marzano, R. (2007). *The art and science of teaching: A comprehensive framework for effective instruction*. Alexandria, VA: Association for Supervision and Curriculum Development.

Nieto, S., & Bode, P. (2008). *Affirming diversity: The sociopolitical context of multicultural education* (5th ed.). Boston, MA: Allyn & Bacon.

Peregoy, S.F., & Boyle, O.F. (2013). *Reading, writing, and learning in ESL: A resource book for K–12 teachers* (6th ed.). New York, NY: Pearson.

Saunders, W., & O'Brien, G. (2006). Oral language. In F. Genesee, K. Lindholm-Leary, W. Saunders, & D. Christian (Eds.), *Educating English language learners: A synthesis of research evidence* (pp. 14–63). New York, NY: Cambridge University Press.

Saville-Troike, M. (1984). What really matters in second language learning for academic achievement? *TESOL Quarterly, 18,* 117–131.

Seidlitz, J. (2008) *Navigating the ELPS: Using the new standards to improve instruction for English language learners.* San Antonio, TX: Canter Press.

Seidlitz, J., & Perryman, B. (2011). *7 steps to a language-rich interactive classroom.* San Antonio, TX: Canter Press.

Short, D., & Echevarría, J. (2016). *Developing academic language with the SIOP Model.* Boston, MA: Pearson/Allyn & Bacon.

Short, D., Vogt, M.E., & Echevarría, J. (2011a). *The SIOP Model for teaching history-social studies to English learners.* Boston, MA: Allyn & Bacon.

Short, D., Vogt, M.E., & Echevarría, J. (2011b). *The SIOP Model for teaching science to English learners.* Boston, MA: Allyn & Bacon.

Swain, M. (1985). Communicative competence: Some roles of comprehensible input and output in its development. In S. Gass & C. Madden (Eds.), *Input in second language acquisition* (pp. 235–256). Rowley, MA: Newbury House.

Tomlinson, C. (2014). *The differentiated classroom: Responding to the needs of all learners* (2nd ed.). Alexandria, VA: Association for Supervision and Curriculum Development.

Tomlinson, C., & Imbeau, M. (2010). *Leading and managing a differentiated classroom.* Alexandria, VA: Association of Supervision and Curriculum Development.

Vogt, M.E. (2000). Content learning for students needing modifications: An issue of access. In M. McLaughlin & M.E. Vogt (Eds.), *Creativity and innovation in content area teaching: A resource for intermediate, middle, and high school teachers.* Norwood, MA: Christopher Gordon Publishers.

Vogt, M.E. (2012). English learners: Developing their literate lives. In R.M. Bean & A.S. Dagen (Eds.), *Best practice of literacy leaders: Keys to school improvement* (pp. 248–260). New York, NY: Guilford Press.

Vogt, M.E., & Echevarría, J. (2008). *99 ideas and activities for teaching English learners with the SIOP Model.* Boston, MA: Allyn & Bacon.

Vogt, M.E., Echevarría, J., & Washam, M.A (2015). *99 more ideas and activities for teaching English learners with the SIOP model.* Boston, MA: Pearson Allyn & Bacon.

Zike, D. (2000a). *The big book of math—Elementary K–6.* San Antonio, TX: Dinah-Might Adventures.

Zike, D. (2000b). *The big book of social studies—Elementary K–6.* San Antonio, TX: Dinah-Might Adventures.

Zike, D. (2004). *The big book of science—Elementary K–6.* San Antonio, TX: Dinah-Might Adventures.

Zike, D. (2007). *Foldables and VKVs® for phonics, spelling, and vocabulary PreK–3rd.* San Antonio, TX: Dinah-Might Adventures.

Zwiers, J., & Crawford, M. (2009). How to start academic conversations. *Educational Leadership, 66*(7), 70–73.

Chapter 8

Buck, B., Carr, S., & Robertson, J. (2008). Positive psychology and student engagement. *Journal of Cross-Disciplinary Perspectives in Education, 1*(1), 28–35.

Cloud, N., Healey, K., Paul, M., Short, D., & Winiarski, P. (2010). *Preparing adolescents for the academic listening demands of secondary school classrooms.* In N. Ashcraft & A. Tran (Eds.), *Listening: TESOL classroom practice series* (pp. 151–167). Alexandria, VA: Teachers of English to Speakers of Other Languages.

Herrell, A., & Jordan, M. (2008). *Fifty strategies for teaching English language learners* (3rd ed.). Upper Saddle River, NJ: Pearson/Merrill Prentice Hall.

Lacina, J., Levine, L.N., & Sowa, P. (2006). *Helping English language learners succeed in pre-K–elementary schools*. Alexandria, VA: Teachers of English to Speakers of Other Languages, Inc.

Lyman, F. (1981). The responsive classroom discussion. In A.S. Anderson (Ed.), *Mainstreaming digest*. College Park, MD: University of Maryland College of Education.

McIlrath, D., & Huitt, W. (1995, December). The teaching-learning process: A discussion of models. *Educational Psychology Interactive*. Valdosta, GA: Valdosta State University. Available from *http://www.edpsycinteractive.org/papers/modeltch.html*

National Governors Association Center for Best Practices [NGA Center] and Council of Chief State School Officers [CCSSO]. (2010). *Common core state standards for English language arts and literacy in history/social studies, science, and technical subjects*. Washington, DC: Author.

Nieto, S., & Bode, P. (2008). *Affirming diversity: The sociopolitical context of multicultural education* (5th ed.). Boston, MA: Allyn & Bacon.

Perlman, C., & Redding, S. (Eds.) (2011). *Handbook on effective implementation of school improvement grants*. Lincoln, IL: Center on Innovation and Improvement. (See Chapter 8, available from *http://www.centerii.org/handbook/*).

Schmoker, M. (2011). *Focus: Elevating the essential to radically improve student learning*. Alexandria, VA: Association of Supervision and Curriculum Development.

Short, D., Echevarría, J., & Richards-Tutor, C. (2011). Research on academic literacy development in sheltered instruction classrooms. *Language Teaching Research*, *15*(3), 363–380.

Short, D., Fidelman, C., & Louguit, M. (2012). Developing academic language in English language learners through sheltered instruction. *TESOL Quarterly*, *46*(2), 333–360.

Short, D., Vogt, M.E., & Echevarría, J. (2011). *The SIOP Model for teaching history-social studies to English learners*. Boston, MA: Allyn & Bacon.

Turner, J. (2007). Beyond cultural awareness: Prospective teachers' visions of culturally responsive teaching. *Action in Teacher Education*, *29(3)*, 12–24.

Vogt, M.E., & Echevarría, J. (2008). *99 ideas and activities for teaching English learners with the SIOP Model*. Boston, MA: Allyn & Bacon.

Vogt, ME., Echevarría, J., & Washam, M.A (2015). *99 more ideas and activities for teaching English learners with the SIOP model*. Boston, MA: Pearson Allyn & Bacon.

Young, E. (1996). *Lon po po*. New York, NY: Penguin Books.

Chapter 9

Bean, R. (2014). Developing a comprehensive reading plan (pre-K-Grade 12). In S.B. Wepner, D.S. Strickland, & D.J. Quatroche (Eds.), *The administration and supervision of reading programs* (5th ed., pp. 11–29). Columbia University. New York: Teachers College Press.

Common Core State Standards. (2010). Retrieved from www.doe.in.gov/commoncore

Deschenes, C., Ebeling, D., & Sprague, J. (1994). *Adapting curriculum and instruction in inclusive classrooms: A teacher's desk reference*. Bloomington, IN: Institute for the Study of Developmental Disabilities, Indiana University.

Echevarria, J., Richards-Tutor, C., & Vogt, M.E. (2015). *Response to intervention (RTI) and English learners: Using the SIOP Model* (2nd ed.). Boston, MA: Allyn & Bacon.

Hunter, M. (1982). *Mastery teaching: Increasing instructional effectiveness in secondary schools, college, and universities*. El Segundo, CA: TIP Publications.

Kapinus, B. (2014). Assessing students' reading achievement. In S.B. Wepner, D.S. Strickland, & D.J. Quatroche (Eds.), *The administration and supervision of reading programs* (5th ed., pp. 135–144). Columbia University, New York, NY: Teachers College Press.

Lenski, S.D., Ehlers-Zavala, F., Daniel, M.C., & Sun-Irminger, X. (2006). Assessing English-language learners in mainstream classrooms. *The Reading Teacher*, *60*(1), 24–34.

Lipson, M., & Wixson, K. (2012). *Assessment of reading and writing difficulties: An interactive approach* (5th ed.). New York, NY: Longman.

Malloy, J.A., Marinak, B.A., Gambrell, L.B., & Mazzoni, S.A. (2013). Assessing motivation to read: The Motivation to Reading Profile—Revisited. *The Reading Teacher, 65*(4), 273–292.

McLaughlin, M. (2010). *Content area reading: Teaching and learning in an age of multiple literacies.* Boston, MA: Pearson.

O'Malley, J.M., & Pierce, L.V. (1996). *Authentic assessment for English language learners: Practical approaches for teachers.* Reading, MA: Addison-Wesley.

Rothenberg, C., & Fisher, D. (2007). *Teaching English learners: A differentiated approach.* Boston, MA: Pearson/Merrill/Prentice Hall.

Saunders, W., & Goldenberg, C. (2010). Research to guide English language development instruction. In California Department of Education (Ed.), *Improving education for English learners: Research-based approaches* (pp. 21–81). Sacramento, CA: CDE Press.

Vogt, M.E. (2014). Reaching linguistically diverse students. In S.B. Wepner, D.S. Strickland, & D. Quatroche (Eds.), *The administration and supervision of reading programs* (5th ed.), (pp. 180–189) New York, NY: Teachers College Press.

Vogt, M.E., & Shearer, B.A. (2011). *Reading specialists and literacy coaches in the real world* (3rd ed.). Boston, MA: Allyn & Bacon.

Chapter 10

Artiles, A. (1998). Overrepresentation of minority students: The case for greater specificity or reconsideration of the variables examined. *The Journal of Special Education, 32*(1), 32–36.

August, D., & Shanahan T. (Eds.). (2006). *Developing literacy in second-language learners: A report of the National Literacy Panel on Language-Minority Children and Youth.* Mahwah, NJ: Erlbaum.

Barnes, C., Mercer, G., & Shakespeare, T. (1999). *Exploring disability: A sociological introduction.* Cambridge, MA: Polity Press.

Brozo, W. (2010). The role of content literacy in an effective RTI program. *The Reading Teacher, 64*(2), 147–150.

Calkins, L., Ehrenworth, M., & Lehman, C. (2012). *Pathways to the Common Core: Accelerating achievement.* Portsmouth, NH: Heinemann.

Cortiella, C. (2011). *The state of learning disabilities.* New York, NY: National.

Cortiella, Candace and Horowitz, Sheldon H. (2014) *The state of learning disabilities: Facts, trends and emerging issues.* New York: National Center for Learning Disabilities.

Cummins, J. (1984). *Bilingualism and special education: Issues in assessment and pedagogy.* Clevedon, England: Multilingual Matters.

Dunn, L. (1968). Special education for the mildly retarded: Is much of it *justifiable? Exceptional Children, 34*, 5–22.

Echevarría, J. (1998). *A model of sheltered instruction for English language learners.* Paper presented at the conference for the Division on Diversity of the Council for Exceptional Children, Washington, DC.

Echevarría, J., & Graves, A. (2015). *Sheltered content instruction: Teaching English learners with diverse abilities* (5th ed.). Boston, MA: Allyn & Bacon.

Echevarria, J., Frey, N., & Fisher, D. (2015). What it takes for English learners to succeed. *Educational Leadership, 72*(6), 22–27.

Echevarría, J., Powers, K., & Elliott, J. (2004). Promising practices for curbing disproportionate representation of minority students in special education. *Issues in Teacher Education: Themed Issues on Special Needs Education, 13*(1), 19–34.

Echevarria, J., Richards-Tutor, C., & Vogt, M.E. (2015). *Response to intervention (RTI) and English learners: Using the SIOP Model* (2nd ed.). Boston, MA: Allyn & Bacon.

Echevarría, J., Richards-Tutor, C., Chinn, V., & Ratleff, P. (2011). Did they get it? The role of fidelity in teaching English learners. *Journal of Adolescent and Adult Literacy, 54*(6), 425–434.

Fisher, D., & Frey, N. (2014). Content area vocabulary learning. *The Reading Teacher, 67*(8), 594–599.

Fuchs, D., Fuchs, L., Compton, D. (2012). Smart RTI: A next-generation approach to multilevel prevention. *Exceptional Children, 78*(3), 263–279.

Genesee, F., Lindholm-Leary, K., Saunders, W., & Christian, D. (2006). *Educating English language learners: A synthesis of research evidence.* New York, NY: Cambridge University Press.

Helman, L., Bear, D., Templeton, S., & Invernizzi, M. (2011). *Words their way with English learners: Words study for phonics, vocabulary, and spelling* (2nd ed.). Boston, MA: Pearson.

Jensen, E. (2008). *Brain-based learning* (2nd ed.). Thousand Oaks, CA: Corwin Press.

Jensen, E. (2013). How poverty affects classroom engagement. *Educational Leadership, 70*(8), 24–30.

Jiménez, R.T. (2004). More equitable literacy assessments for Latino students. *The Reading Teacher, 57*(6), 576–578.

Jiménez, R.T., David, S., Pacheco, M., Risko, V.J., Pray, L., Fagan, K., & Gonzales, M. (2015). Supporting teachers of English learners by leveraging students' linguistic strengths. *The Reading Teacher, 66*(6), 406–412.

Kampwirth, T., & Powers, K. (2016). *Collaborative consultation in the schools* (5th ed.). Columbus, OH: Pearson Press.

Klinger, J., & Eppolito, A. (2014). *English language earners: Differentiating between language acquisition and learning Disabilities.* Arlington, VA: Council for Exceptional Children.

Klingner, J.K., Vaughn, S., Argüelles, M.E., Hughes, M.T., & Ahwee, S. (2004). Collaborative strategic reading: "Real world" lessons from classroom teachers. *Remedial and Special Education, 25,* 291–302.

Kretlow, A., & Blatz, S. (2011) The ABC's of evidence-based practice for teachers. *Teaching Exceptional Children, 43*(5), 8–19.

Losen, D., & Orfield, G. (2002). *Racial inequity in special education.* Cambridge, MA: Harvard Education Publishing Company.

Lynch, S. (2000). *Equity and science education reform.* Mahwah, NJ: Erlbaum.

McLaughlin, M. (2012). Reading comprehension: What every teacher needs to know. *The Reading Teacher, 65*(7), 432–440.

Morgan, P., Farkas, G., Hillemeier, M., Mattison, R., Maczuga, S., Li, H., & Cook, M. (2015). Minorities are disproportionately underrepresented in special education: Longitudinal evidence across five disability conditions. *Educational Researcher, June/July 2015 44,* 278–292, DOI: 10.3102/0013189X15591157.

National Institute of Child Health and Human Development (NICHD). (2000). *Report of the National Reading Panel. Teaching children to read: An evidence-based assessment of the scientific research literature on reading and its implications for reading instruction.* (NIH Publication No. 00–4769). Washington, DC: U.S. Department of Health and Human Services.

Podell, D.M., & Soodak, L.C. (1993). Teacher efficacy and bias in special education referrals. *Journal of Educational Research, 86*(4), 247–253.

Powers, K., (2001). Problem solving student support teams. *The California School Psychologist, 6,* 19–30.

Rasinski, T., & Padak, N. (2004). *Effective reading strategies: Teaching children who find reading difficult.* Upper Saddle River, NJ: Pearson Merrill Prentice Hall.

Richards, C., & Funk, L. (2009). *Writing of students with LD who are also English learners.* Paper presented at the Council for Exceptional Children Convention, Seattle, WA.

Rinaldi, C., & Sampson, J. (2008). English language learners and response to intervention: Referral considerations. *Teaching Exceptional Children, 40*(5), 6–14.

Roskos, K., & Neuman, S.B. (2014). Best practices in reading: A 21st century skill update. *The Reading Teacher, 65*(7), 507–511.

Serafini, F. (2014). Close readings and children's literature. *The Reading Teacher, 67*(4), 299–301.

Skiba, R., Simmons, A.B., Ritter, S., Gibb, A.C., Rausch, M., Cuadrado, J., & Chung, C-G. (2008). Achieving equity in special education: History, status and current challenges. *Exceptional Children, 72*, 264–288.

Smith, D. (2009). *Introduction to special-education: Making a difference* (9th ed.). Boston, MA: Allyn & Bacon.

Snow, C.E., Burns, S., Griffin, P. (Eds.). (1998). *Preventing reading difficulties in young children.* Washington, DC: National Academy Press.

Stauffer, R. (1980). *The language-experience approach to the teaching of reading* (2nd ed.). New York, NY: Harper & Row.

Tilly, D. (2006). Response to Intervention: An overview. *The Special Edge, 19*(2), 1–5.

Tolchinsky, L., & Teberosky, A. (1998). The development of word segmentation and writing in two scripts. *Cognitive Development, 13,* 1–24.

Torgesen, J. (2012). Catch them before they fall: Identification and assessment to prevent reading failure in young children. *Reading Rockets.* Retrieved from *http://www.readingrockets.org/artivel/225/*

Vasquez III, E., Lopez, A., Straub, C., Powell, S., McKinney, T., Walker, Z., Gonzalez, T., Slocum, T., Mason, L., Okeeffe, B., & Bedesem, P. (2011). Empirical research on ethnic minority students: 1995–2009. *Learning Disabilities Research & Practice, 26*(2), 84–93.

Vaughn, S., & Ortiz, A. (2011). *Response to Intervention in Reading for English language learners.* Retrieved from *http://www.rtinetwork.org/learn/diversity/englishlanguagelearners*

Vogt, M.E. (2014). Reaching linguistically diverse students. In S.B. Wepner, D.S. Strickland, & D. Quatroche (Eds.), *The administration and supervision of reading programs* (5th ed., pp. 180–189) New York, NY: Teachers College Press.

Vogt, M.E., & Shearer, B.A. (2016). *Reading specialists and literacy coaches in the real world* (3rd ed.). Long Grove, IL: Waveland Press.

Yoon, B. (2008). Uninvited guests: The influence of teachers' roles and pedagogies on the positioning of English language learners in the regular classroom. *American Educational Research Journal, 45*(2), 495–522.

Chapter 11

Bose, D. (2012). *Effects of Just-in-Time online training on knowledge and application of the Sheltered Instruction Observation Protocol (SIOP) Model among in-service teachers.* Ph.D. thesis, Idaho State University.

Echevarría, J., Richards-Tutor, C., Chinn, V., & Ratleff, P. (2011). Did they get it? The role of fidelity in teaching English learners. *Journal of Adolescent and Adult Literacy, 54*(6), 425–434.

Echevarría, J., Short, D., & Vogt, M.E. (2008). *Implementing the SIOP Model through effective professional development and coaching.* Boston, MA: Pearson/Allyn & Bacon.

Echevarría, J., Vogt, M.E., & Short, D. (2000). *Making content comprehensible for English language learners: The SIOP® Model.* Boston, MA: Pearson/Allyn & Bacon.

Echevarría, J., Vogt, M.E., & Short, D. (2004). *Making content comprehensible for English learners: The SIOP® Model* (2nd ed.). Boston, MA: Pearson/Allyn & Bacon.

Echevarría, J., Vogt, M.E., & Short, D. (2008). *Making content comprehensible for English learners: The SIOP® Model* (3rd ed.). Boston, MA: Pearson/Allyn & Bacon.

Echevarría, J., Vogt, M.E., & Short, D. (2013). *Making content comprehensible for English learners: The SIOP® Model* (4th ed.). Boston, MA: Pearson/Allyn & Bacon.

Echevarría, J., Vogt, M.E., & Short, D. (2017). *Making content comprehensible for English learners: The SIOP® Model* (5th ed.). Boston, MA: Pearson.

Guarino, A.J., Echevarría, J., Short, D., Schick, J.E., Forbes, S., & Rueda, R. (2001). The Sheltered Instruction Observation Protocol. *Journal of Research in Education, 11*(1), 138–140.

Rodriguez Moux, S. (2010). *Teacher's perceptions of Sheltered Instruction Observation Protocol for teaching young English language learners: A qualitative case study.* Retrieved from ProQuest Dissertations and Theses. (ED 517156)

Short, D., Vogt, M.E., & Echevarria, J. (2017). *The SIOP Model for administrators* (2nd ed.). New York, NY: Pearson.

Smolen, L., Zhang, W, Vakil, S., Temsey, L., & Mann, N. (2015). Meeting the needs of English learners. In L. Minaya-Rowe (Ed.), *Effective educational programs, practices, and policies for English learners* (pp. 115–180). Charlotte, NC: Information Age Publishing, Inc.

Song, K. (2016,). Applying a SIOP-based instructional framework for professional development in Korea. *TESL-EJ, 20*(1).

Torres, N.L. (2006). Administrative support for English language learners: How the SIOP model empowers teachers, administrators, and English language learners. *Doctoral Dissertations.* Paper AAI3231250. Available from *http://digitalcommons.uconn.edu/dissertations/AAI3231250*

Vidot, J. L. (2011). *The efficacy of sheltered instruction observation protocol (SIOP) in mathematics instruction on English language learners.* (Doctoral dissertation) Available from http://scholarworks.waldenu.edu/dissertations/943/

Chapter 12

Echevarría, J., Short, D., & Vogt, M.E. (2008). *Implementing the SIOP Model through effective professional development and coaching.* Boston, MA: Pearson/Allyn & Bacon.

Echevarria, J., Vogt, M.E., & Short, D. (2018). *Making content comprehensible for secondary English learners: The SIO (3*rd *ed.)P Model.* Boston, MA: Pearson.

Short, D., Vogt, M.E., & Echevarria, J. (2017). *The SIOP Model for administrators (2*nd *ed.).* New York: Pearson.

Vogt, M.E., & Echevarría, J. (2008). *99 ideas and activities for teaching English learners with the SIOP Model.* Boston, MA: Allyn & Bacon.

Vogt, ME., Echevarría, J., & Washam, M.A (2015). *99 more ideas and activities for teaching English learners with the SIOP Model.* Boston, MA: Pearson Allyn & Bacon.

Appendix C

Batt, E. (2010). Cognitive coaching: A critical phase in professional development to implement sheltered instruction. *Teaching and Teacher Education 26,* 997–1005.

Darling-Hammond, L. (1998). Teacher learning that supports student learning. *Educational Leadership, 55*(5), 6–11.

Darling-Hammond, L., & Richardson, N. (2009). Teachers learning: What matters? *Educational Leadership, 66*(5), 46–53.

Echevarría, J., Richards-Tutor, C., Canges, R., & Francis, D. (2011). Using the SIOP Model to promote the acquisition of language and science concepts with English learners. *Bilingual Research Journal, 34*(3), 334–351.

Echevarría, J., Richards-Tutor, C., Chinn, V., & Ratleff, P. (2011). Did they get it? The role of fidelity in teaching English learners. *Journal of Adolescent and Adult Literacy, 54*(6), 425–434.

Echevarría, J., & Short, D. (2011). *The SIOP model: A professional development framework for a comprehensive school-wide intervention. CREATE Brief.* Washington, DC: Center for Applied Linguistics.

Echevarría, J., Short, D., & Powers, K. (2006). School reform and standards-based education: An instructional model for English language learners. *Journal of Educational Research, 99*(4), 195–211.

Echevarría, J., Short, D., & Vogt, M.E. (2008). *Implementing the SIOP Model through effective professional development and coaching.* Boston, MA: Pearson/Allyn & Bacon.

Echevarría, J., Vogt, M.E., & Short, D. (2000). *Making content comprehensible for English language learners: The SIOP Model.* Needham Heights, MA: Allyn & Bacon.

Friend, J., Most, R., & McCrary, K. (2009). The impact of a professional development program to improve urban middle-level English language learner achievement. *Middle Grades Research Journal, 4*(1), 53–75.

Guarino, A.J., Echevarría, J., Short, D., Schick, J.E., Forbes, S., & Rueda, R. (2001). The Sheltered Instruction Observation Protocol. *Journal of Research in Education, 11*(1), 138–140.

Himmel, J., Short, D.J., Richards, C., & Echevarría, J. (2009). *Using the SIOP Model to improve middle school science instruction* (CREATE Brief). Washington, DC: Center for Research on the Educational Achievement and Teaching of English Language Learners/CAL.

Honigsfeld, A., & Cohan, A. (2008). The power of two: Lesson study and SIOP help teachers instruct ELLs. *Journal of Staff Development, 29*(1), 24–28.

Hudec, J., & Short, D. (Prods.). (2002a). *Helping English learners succeed: An overview of the SIOP Model.* (Video). Washington, DC: Center for Applied Linguistics.

Hudec, J., & Short, D. (Prods.). (2002b). *The SIOP Model: Sheltered instruction for academic achievement.* (Video). Washington, DC: Center for Applied Linguistics.

McIntyre, E., Kyle, D., Chen, C., Muñoz, M., & Beldon, S. (2010). Teacher learning and ELL reading achievement in sheltered instruction classrooms: Linking professional development to student development. *Literacy Research and Instruction, 49*(4), 334–351.

Short, D., & Echevarría, J. (1999). The sheltered instruction observation protocol: Teacher-researcher collaboration and professional development. *Educational Practice Report No. 3.* Santa Cruz, CA, and Washington, DC: Center for Research on Education, Diversity & Excellence.

Short, D., Echevarría, J., & Richards-Tutor, C. (2011). Research on academic literacy development in sheltered instruction classrooms. *Language Teaching Research, 15*(3), 363–380.

Short, D., Fidelman, C., & Louguit, M. (2012). Developing academic language in English language learners through sheltered instruction. *TESOL Quarterly, 46*(2), 333–360.

Short, D., & Himmel, J. (2013). *Moving research on sheltered instruction into curriculum and professional development practice.* Paper presented at American Educational Research Association (AERA) Annual Meeting, San Francisco, CA.

Short, D., Hudec, J., & Echevarría, J. (2002). *Using the SIOP Model: Professional development manual for sheltered instruction.* Washington, DC: Center for Applied Linguistics.

Smolen, L., Zhang, W, Vakil, S., Temsey, L., & Mann, N. (2015). Meeting the needs of English learners. In L. Minaya-Rowe (Ed.), *Effective educational programs, practices, and policies for English learners* (pp. 115–180). Charlotte, NC: Information Age Publishing, Inc.

Song, K. H. (2016). Systematic professional development training and its impact on teachers' attitudes toward ELLs: SIOP and guided coaching. *TESOL Journal.* doi:10.1002/tesj.240

Watkins, N. M., & Lindahl, K. M. (2010). Targeting content area literacy instruction to meet the needs of adolescent English language learners. *Middle School Journal, 41*(3), 23–32.

Whittier, L. E., & Robinson, M. (2007). Teaching evolution to non-English proficient students by using Lego Robotics. *American Secondary Education, 35*(3), 19–28.

Index